The Holt Workbook

Nancy C. Martinez
Joseph G. R. Martinez
University of New Mexico/Valencia

Holt, Rinehart and Winston
New York   Chicago   San Francisco   Philadelphia
Montreal   Toronto   London   Sydney   Tokyo
Mexico City   Rio de Janeiro   Madrid

Publisher Susan Katz
Acquisitions Editor Charlyce Jones Owen
Development Editor Kate Morgan
Senior Project Editor Françoise Bartlett
Senior Production Manager Nancy Myers
Art Director Gloria Gentile
Design Caliber Design Planning

Library of Congress Cataloging-in-Publication Data

Martinez, Nancy C. (Nancy Conrad)
  The Holt workbook.

  Includes index.
  1. English language—Rhetoric—Problems, exercises,
etc. I. Martinez, Joseph G. R.
PE1413.M37   1986   808'.042   85-24700

ISBN 0-03-002967-8

Copyright © 1986 by CBS College Publishing

Address correspondence to:
383 Madison Avenue
New York, NY 10017

All rights reserved
Printed in the United States of America
Published simultaneously in Canada
6 7 8 9   090   9 8 7 6 5 4 3 2

CBS COLLEGE PUBLISHING

Holt, Rinehart and Winston
The Dryden Press
Saunders College Publishing

Acknowledgments are on page 560.

To the Instructor

The Holt Workbook is several books in one. As a companion to *The Holt Handbook*, it provides additional explanations and examples of key concepts as well as additional exercises for practicing skills. As an independent composition text, it approaches writing as a process and from the first unit asks students to apply concepts to the writing of sentences, paragraphs, and essays. And as a reference work for self-help and review, *The Holt Workbook* features preview and review exercises to enable students to assess their skills and measure their progress.

Like most workbooks, this one emphasizes active rather than passive learning—that is, *doing* instead of *reading about*. Unlike most workbooks, this text emphasizes writing, writing, and more writing.

As much as possible, the exercises call for students to write rather than simply underline or identify their responses. Each chapter includes a Writer's Casebook with writing applications that focus upon various topics—such as audience and purpose, business writing, writing-across-the-curriculum assignments, and rhetorical patterns. Each Casebook concludes with several case-style subjects, which may serve as writing topics or as models for the students to follow in selecting and providing a context for their own topics.

To develop and maintain student interest, the chapter exercises and writing assignments focus upon high-interest themes. For example, the theme of Chapter 11, "Sentence Fragments," is the environment. First, students do exercises that not only provide practice in finding and revising sentence fragments but also start them thinking about environmental issues. Then students write an essay that allows them to explore their own experiences and opinions about nature, pollution, or land use.

The text will function effectively in both individualized and group learning situations. The following study plans suggest some of the different sequences in which the chapters may be studied, depending upon the students' needs and the instructor's purpose.

Review of Basics   1: "Planning"; 11: "Fragments"; 20: "Parts of Speech"; 2: "Shaping"; 6: "Simple Sentences"; 12: "Comma Splices/Fused Sentences"; 3: "Writing/Revising"; 17: "The Dictionary," with 16, a–b: "Choosing Words"; 21: "Nouns/Pronouns"; 28: "The Apostrophe"; 4, a–b: "Paragraphs"; 7: "Compound and Complex Sentences"; 27: "The Semicolon"; 22: "Verbs"; 4, e–f: "Paragraphs"; 23: "Agreement"; 29: "Quotation Marks," and 32: "Italics"; 5: "Constructing a Logical Argument"; 13: "Misplaced/Dangling Modifiers"; 26: "The Comma"; 14: "Faulty Parallelism"; 9: "Concise Sentences"; 16, c–d: "Choosing Words"

Development of Basic Writing Skills 1: "Planning"; 6: "Simple Sentences"; 18: "Vocabulary," with 19: "Spelling"; 2: "Shaping"; 7: "Compound/Complex Sentences"; 17: "The Dictionary"; 11: "Fragments"; 25: "The Period, the Question Mark, and the Exclamation Point"; 3: "Writing and Revising"; 16, a–b: "Choosing Words"; 12: "Comma Splices/Fused Sentences"; 27, a–c: "The Semicolon"; 22: "Verbs"; 4, a–b: "Paragraphs"; 23: "Agreement"; 28: "The Apostrophe"; 4, c: "Paragraphs"; 14: "Faulty Parallelism"; 21: "Nouns/Pronouns"; 27, d–e: "The Semicolon"; 31: "Capitalization"; 4, d: "Paragraphs"

Development of Advanced Writing Skills 1: "Planning"; 6: "Simple Sentences"; 2: "Shaping"; 7: "Compound/Complex Sentences"; 3: "Writing/Revising"; 8: "Emphatic Sentences"; 5: "Constructing a Logical Argument"; 16: "Choosing Words"; 4, a–d: "Paragraphs"; 13: "Misplaced/Dangling Modifiers"; 10: "Varied Sentences"; 22, f–l: "Verbs"; 4, e–f: "Paragraphs"; 9: "Concise Sentences"; 14: "Faulty Parallelism"; 26: "The Comma," with 27: "The Semicolon"; 15: "Shifts/Mixed Constructions"; 30: "Other Punctuation Marks"

Acknowledgments

We wish to thank the following colleagues for their comments and sound advice: Eleanor Garner, George Washington University; Mary Ellen Grasso, Broward Community College; Jeffrey Richards, Lakeland College; Deborah Rosen, formerly of Broward Community College; Annette Schneider, Rockland Community College; and Marie T. Wolf, Bergen Community College. We are grateful to our students for testing the manuscript of the text in its various stages and for permitting us to use their work in our exercises and examples. We thank our editors, Charlyce Jones Owen and Kate Morgan, for their guidance and encouragement; Françoise Bartlett, senior project editor; Gloria Gentile, art director; and Nancy Myers, senior production manager.

Albuquerque, New Mexico N.C.M.
December 1985 J.G.R.M.

To the Student

Becoming a better writer begins with improving your writing process. Do you spend more time on writing the first draft of your paper than you do on planning your paper? Do you agonize over each word in your draft, looking up words in your dictionary and consulting your handbook for punctuation marks? Do you concentrate on correcting errors when you revise, avoiding changes in structure or content for fear you will add to your mistakes? If your answer to any of these questions is "yes," your development as a writer may be hampered by a fragmentary approach to writing.

In this text you will study a fuller approach. You will learn to spend more time planning and revising than you do writing the first draft. You will learn to draft quickly, writing to revise and reworking a paper thoroughly for organization and content before you edit it for mistakes. And you will learn to evaluate your own work and that of others, developing in the process the expertise and confidence necessary to make informed, productive decisions about your writing.

If you are working in this text on your own, use the preview and review exercises in each chapter as guides to problem areas. If your score is 80 percent or higher on the preview exercise, you may skip the chapter; if your score is less than 80 percent, you will want to study the explanations and practice the concepts by doing exercises until you are able to score 80 percent on the review exercise.

If you are studying *The Holt Workbook* as a class assignment, do not limit yourself to doing the work to be handed in and scored by your instructor. Complete as many exercises as necessary to master the concepts and develop your writing skills.

You will know that your skills have improved when you find yourself writing more—more freely, more fluently, more confidently; when you can read a draft, assess its weaknesses, and make a plan for correcting those weaknesses; and when you find yourself paying attention to the balances and rhythms of your writing style and to the depth of your content. Then you are on your way to mastering the complex skills of writing expository prose.

Contents

To the Instructor iii
To the Student iv

SECTION I Composing an Essay 1

1 Planning an Essay *1*
PREVIEW 1   *1*
1a Thinking About Writing   *1*
1b Getting Started   *2*
  Exercise 1-1   *7* • Exercise 1-2   *10* • Exercise 1-3   *12* • Exercise 1-4   *13*
REVIEW 1   *15*
The Writer's Casebook #1   *15*

2 Shaping Your Material *17*
PREVIEW 2   *17*
2a Grouping Ideas   *18*
2b Developing a Thesis   *18*
2c Preparing a Working Plan   *19*
2d Preparing an Outline   *20*
  Exercise 2-1   *23* • Exercise 2-2   *25* • Exercise 2-3   *27*
REVIEW 2   *29*
The Writer's Casebook #2   *29*

3 Writing and Revising *31*
PREVIEW 3   *31*
3a Using Thesis and Support   *31*
3b Writing a Rough Draft   *32*
3c Understanding Revision   *33*
3d Revising Your Drafts   *35*
  Exercise 3-1   *39* • Exercise 3-2   *40* • Exercise 3-3   *43* • Exercise 3-4   *45* • Exercise 3-5   *46*
REVIEW 3   *49*
The Writer's Casebook #3   *49*

4 Writing Paragraphs *51*
PREVIEW 4   *51*
4a Charting Paragraph Structure   *52*

4b Writing Unified Paragraphs   *52*
4c Writing Coherent Paragraphs   *53*
4d Writing Well-Developed Paragraphs   *57*
4e Using Patterns of Development   *58*
4f Writing Special Kinds of Paragraphs   *63*
  Exercise 4-1   *67* • Exercise 4-2   *69* • Exercise 4-3   *71* • Exercise 4-4   *73* • Exercise 4-5   *75* • Exercise 4-6   *76* • Exercise 4-7   *78* • Exercise 4-8   *80* • Exercise 4-9   *82* • Exercise 4-10   *83* • Exercise 4-11   *84* • Exercise 4-12   *85*
REVIEW 4   *87*
The Writer's Casebook #4   *87*

5 Constructing a Logical Argument *89*
PREVIEW 5   *89*
5a Planning Your Argument   *90*
5b Shaping Your Argument   *91*
5c Writing and Revising Your Argument   *92*
  Exercise 5-1   *95* • Exercise 5-2   *96* • Exercise 5-3   *98*
REVIEW 5   *101*
The Writer's Casebook #5   *102*

SECTION II Composing Sentences 104

6 Building Simple Sentences *104*
PREVIEW 6   *104*
6a Identifying the Basic Sentence Elements   *105*
6b Constructing Basic Sentence Patterns   *105*

vi

Contents

6c Forming Questions and Commands *107*
6d Identifying Phrases and Clauses *108*
6e Building Simple Sentences with Individual Words *109*
6f Building Simple Sentences with Phrases *110*
  Exercise 6-1 *113* • Exercise 6-2 *114* • Exercise 6-3 *115* • Exercise 6-4 *116* • Exercise 6-5 *117* • Exercise 6-6 *118* • Exercise 6-7 *119* • Exercise 6-8 *120* • Exercise 6-9 *121* • Exercise 6-10 *122* • Exercise 6-11 *124* • Exercise 6-12 *125*
REVIEW 6 *127*
The Writer's Casebook #6 *128*

7 Building Compound and Complex Sentences *130*
PREVIEW 7 *130*
7a Building Compound Sentences *131*
7b Building Complex Sentences *133*
  Exercise 7-1 *137* • Exercise 7-2 *139* • Exercise 7-3 *140* • Exercise 7-4 *142*
REVIEW 7 *143*
The Writer's Casebook #7 *144*

8 Writing Emphatic Sentences *147*
PREVIEW 8 *147*
8a Achieving Emphasis Through Word Order *148*
8b Achieving Emphasis Through Sentence Structure *149*
8c Achieving Emphasis Through Parallelism and Balance *150*
8d Achieving Emphasis Through Repetition *150*
8e Achieving Emphasis Through Active Voice *150*
  Exercise 8-1 *153* • Exercise 8-2 *155* • Exercise 8-3 *157*

REVIEW 8 *159*
The Writer's Casebook #8 *160*

9 Writing Concise Sentences *162*
PREVIEW 9 *162*
9a Eliminating Nonessential Words *163*
9b Eliminating Needless Repetition *164*
9c Tightening Rambling Sentences *165*
  Exercise 9-1 *167* • Exercise 9-2 *169* • Exercise 9-3 *170* • Exercise 9-4 *172*
REVIEW 9 *175*
The Writer's Casebook #9 *175*

10 Writing Varied Sentences *177*
PREVIEW 10 *177*
10a Varying Sentence Length *178*
10b Combining Choppy Simple Sentences *178*
10c Breaking Up Strings of Compounds *178*
10d Varying Sentence Types *179*
10e Varying Sentence Openings *179*
10f Varying Standard Word Order *179*
  Exercise 10-1 *181* • Exercise 10-2 *182* • Exercise 10-3 *183* • Exercise 10-4 *185*
REVIEW 10 *187*
The Writer's Casebook #10 *188*

SECTION III Solving Common Sentence Problems *190*

11 Sentence Fragments *190*
PREVIEW 11 *190*
11a Subordinate Clauses *191*
11b Prepositional Phrases *192*
11c Verbal Phrases *193*

11d	Absolute Phrases *192*		13f	Prepositional Phrases *229*
11e	Appositives *193*		13g	Elliptical Clauses *229*
11f	Compounds *193*			Exercise 13-1 *231* • Exercise 13-2 *233*
11g	Incomplete Clauses *193*			

Exercise 11-1 *195* • Exercise 11-2 *197* • Exercise 11-3 *198* • Exercise 11-4 *199* • Exercise 11-5 *200* • Exercise 11-6 *201* • Exercise 11-7 *203*

REVIEW 11 *205*
The Writer's Casebook #11 *206*

REVIEW 13 *235*
The Writer's Casebook #13 *235*

12 Comma Splices and Fused Sentences *209*

PREVIEW 12 *209*
The Comma Splice *210*
- 12a Period *211*
- 12b Semicolon *211*
- 12c Coordinating Conjunction *212*
- 12d Subordinating Conjunction or a Relative Pronoun *212*
- 12e Using Comma Splices Effectively *212*

The Fused Sentence *213*
- 12f Period *213*
- 12g Semicolon *213*
- 12h Comma/Coordinating Conjunction *214*
- 12i Using Subordination *214*

Exercise 12-1 *215* • Exercise 12-2 *217* • Exercise 12-3 *218* • Exercise 12-4 *220* • Exercise 12-5 *222*

REVIEW 12 *223*
The Writer's Casebook #12 *223*

13 Misplaced and Dangling Modifiers *226*

PREVIEW 13 *226*
Misplaced Modifiers *227*
- 13a Words *227*
- 13b Phrases *227*
- 13c Subordinate Clauses *228*
- 13d Intrusive Modifiers *228*

Dangling Modifiers *228*
- 13e Verbal Phrases *229*

14 Faulty Parallelism *238*

PREVIEW 14 *238*
- 14a Parallelism *239*
- 14b Revising Faulty Parallelism *240*

Exercise 14-1 *243* • Exercise 14-2 *245* • Exercise 14-3 *247*

REVIEW 14 *249*
The Writer's Casebook #14 *250*

15 Shifts and Mixed Constructions *253*

PREVIEW 15 *253*
- 15a Shifts *253*
- 15b Mixed Constructions *256*

Exercise 15-1 *259* • Exercise 15-2 *260* • Exercise 15-3 *261*

REVIEW 15 *263*
The Writer's Casebook #15 *263*

SECTION IV Using Words Effectively *266*

16 Choosing Words *266*

PREVIEW 16 *266*
- 16a Appropriate Words *267*
- 16b Accurate Words *270*
- 16c Fresh Language *272*
- 16d Figurative Language *273*
- 16e Ineffective Figures of Speech *275*

Exercise 16-1 *277* • Exercise 16-2 *278* • Exercise 16-3 *279* • Exercise 16-4 *280* • Exercise 16-5 *282* • Exercise 16-6 *283* • Exercise 16-7 *284*

REVIEW 16 *287*
The Writer's Casebook #16 *288*

17 Using the Dictionary 290
PREVIEW 17 290
17a Contents 291
17b Choosing 291
17c Abridged 291
17d Using 292
    Exercise 17-1 293
REVIEW 17 301
The Writer's Casebook #17 301

18 Building a Vocabulary 304
PREVIEW 18 304
18a Analyzing 305
18b Building 305
18c Avoiding Ineffective Vocabulary Building 306
    Exercise 18-1 307 • Exercise 18-2 310
REVIEW 18 313
The Writer's Casebook #18 314

19 Improving Spelling 315
PREVIEW 19 315
19a Spelling/Pronouncing Words 316
19b Spelling Rules 316
19c Spelling Skills 316
    Exercise 19-1 317 • Exercise 19-2 318 • Exercise 19-3 320
REVIEW 19 321
The Writer's Casebook #19 321

SECTION V Understanding Grammar 323

20 Identifying the Parts of Speech 323
PREVIEW 20 323
20a Nouns 324
20b Pronouns 324
20c Verbs 325
20d Adjectives 326
20e Adverbs 327
20f Prepositions 327
20g Conjunctions 328
20h Interjections 328
    Exercise 20-1 331 • Exercise 20-2 333 • Exercise 20-3 334
REVIEW 20 335
The Writer's Casebook #20 335

21 Nouns and Pronouns 338
PREVIEW 21 338
Case 339
21a Using the Subjective Case 339
21b Using the Objective Case 339
21c Using the Possessive Case 340
21d Correcting Common Errors: Case 340
Pronoun Reference 342
21e Making Pronoun References Clear 342
21f Revising Ambiguous or Vague Pronoun References 342
    Exercise 21-1 345 • Exercise 21-2 347 • Exercise 21-3 349 • Exercise 21-4 351 • Exercise 21-5 352 • Exercise 21-6 355
REVIEW 21 357
The Writer's Casebook #21 358

22 Verbs 360
PREVIEW 22 360
Verb Forms 361
22a Identifying the Principal Parts of Irregular Verbs 362
22b Using Correct Verb Forms 362
Tense 362
22c Using the Simple Tenses 363
22d Using the Perfect Tenses 363
22e Using the Progressive Tense Forms 364
22f Using the Correct Sequence of Tenses 365
Mood 366
22g Using the Indicative Mood 366
22h Using the Imperative Mood 367

22i Using the Subjunctive Mood 367
Voice *368*
22j Using the Passive Voice 368
22k Changing from Passive to Active Voice 368
22l Changing from Active to Passive Voice 369
Exercise 22-1 *371* • Exercise 22-2 *373* • Exercise 22-3 *374* • Exercise 22-4 *375* • Exercise 22-5 *376* • Exercise 22-6 *377* • Exercise 22-7 *378* • Exercise 22-8 *380* • Exercise 22-9 *382*
REVIEW 22 *385*
The Writer's Casebook #22 *386*

23 Agreement *388*
PREVIEW 23 *388*
23a Making Subjects and Verbs Agree 389
23b Making Pronouns and Antecedents Agree 394
Exercise 23-1 *397* • Exercise 23-2 *398* • Exercise 23-3 *400* • Exercise 23-4 *401* • Exercise 23-5 *403* • Exercise 23-6 *404*
REVIEW 23 *407*
The Writer's Casebook #23 *408*

24 Adjectives and Adverbs *409*
PREVIEW 24 *409*
24a Using Adjectives 411
24b Using Adverbs 411
24c Distinguishing Between Comparative and Superlative Forms 412
24d Using Nouns as Adjectives 414
Exercise 24-1 *415* • Exercise 24-2 *416* • Exercise 24-3 *418* • Exercise 24-4 *419*
REVIEW 24 *421*
The Writer's Casebook #24 *422*

SECTION VI Understanding Punctuation and Mechanics *424*

25 The Period, the Question Mark, and the Exclamation Point *424*
PREVIEW 25 *424*
25a Using Periods 425
25b Using Question Marks 426
25c Using Exclamation Points 427
Exercise 25-1 *429* • Exercise 25-2 *430*
REVIEW 25 *431*
The Writer's Casebook #25 *431*

26 The Comma *434*
PREVIEW 26 *434*
26a Setting Off Independent Clauses 435
26b Setting Off Items in a Series 436
26c Setting Off Introductory Elements 437
26d Setting Off Nonessential Elements from the Rest of the Sentence 438
26e Using Commas in Other Conventional Contexts 440
26f Using Commas to Prevent Misreading 442
26g Editing to Eliminate Misuse or Overuse of Commas 442
Exercise 26-1 *443* • Exercise 26-2 *444* • Exercise 26-3 *445* • Exercise 26-4 *446*
REVIEW 26 *449*
The Writer's Casebook #26 *449*

27 The Semicolon *453*
PREVIEW 27 *453*
27a Separating Independent Clauses 454
27b Separating Complex, Internally Punctuated Clauses 454
27c Separating Clauses Containing Conjunctive Adverbs 454

27d Separating Items in a Series *455*
27e Editing to Eliminate Misuse of Semicolons *455*
Exercise 27-1 *457* • Exercise 27-2 *458* • Exercise 27-3 *459*
REVIEW 27 *461*
The Writer's Casebook #27 *461*

28 The Apostrophe *464*
PREVIEW 28 *464*
28a Forming the Possessive Case *465*
28b Omitting the Apostrophe *466*
28c Indicating Omissions in Contractions *467*
28d Forming Plurals *468*
Exercise 28-1 *469* • Exercise 28-2 *471* • Exercise 28-3 *472*
REVIEW 28 *475*
The Writer's Casebook #28 *476*

29 Quotation Marks *478*
PREVIEW 29 *478*
29a Setting Off Direct Quotations *478*
29b Setting Off Titles *479*
29c Setting Off Words Used in a Special Sense *479*
29d Editing to Eliminate Misuse or Overuse of Quotation Marks *480*
29e Setting Off Dialogue, Long Prose Passages, and Poetry *480*
29f Using Quotation Marks with Other Punctuation *482*
Exercise 29-1 *485* • Exercise 29-2 *487*
REVIEW 29 *489*
The Writer's Casebook #29 *489*

30 Other Punctuation Marks *492*
PREVIEW 30 *492*
The Colon *493*
30a Using a Colon to Introduce Material *493*
30b Using a Colon Where Convention Requires It *493*
30c Editing to Eliminate Misuse or Overuse of the Colon *493*
The Dash *494*
30d Setting Off Parenthetical Material *494*
30e Introducing a Summary *494*
30f Indicating an Interruption *494*
30g Editing to Eliminate Misuse and Overuse of the Dash *495*
Parentheses *495*
30h Setting Off Nonessential Material *495*
30i In Other Conventional Situations *496*
Brackets *496*
30j Setting Off Comments Within Quotations *496*
30k In Place of Parentheses Within Parentheses *496*
The Slash *497*
30l Separating One Option from Another *497*
30m Separating Lines of Poetry Run into the Text *497*
30n Separating the Numerator from the Denominator in Fractions *497*
The Ellipsis Mark *497*
30o Indicating an Omission in a Quotation *497*
30p Indicating an Omission Within Verse *498*
30q Indicating Unfinished Statements *498*
Exercise 30-1 *499* • Exercise 30-2 *501*
REVIEW 30 *503*
The Writer's Casebook #30 *503*

31 Capitalization *506*
PREVIEW 31 *506*

- **31a** Capitalizing the First Word of a Sentence or of a Line of Poetry 507
- **31b** Capitalizing Proper Nouns, Titles Accompanying Them, and Adjectives Formed from Them 507
- **31c** Capitalizing Important Words in Titles 509
- **31d** Capitalizing the Pronoun *I* and the Interjection *O* 509
- **31e** Capitalizing Salutations and Closings of Letters 510
- **31f** Editing to Eliminate Misuse and Overuse of Capitals 510
  - Exercise 31-1 511 • Exercise 31-2 512

REVIEW 31 515
The Writer's Casebook #31 516

32 Italics 518
PREVIEW 32 518
- **32a** Setting Off Titles and Names 519
- **32b** Setting Off Foreign Words or Phrases 519
- **32c** Setting Off Elements Spoken of as Themselves and Terms Being Defined 520
- **32d** Using Italics for Emphasis 520
- **32e** Using Italics for Clarity 520
  - Exercise 32-1 521 • Exercise 32-2 522

REVIEW 32 523
The Writer's Casebook #32 523

33 Hyphens 526
PREVIEW 33 526
- **33a** Breaking Words at the End of a Line 527
- **33b** Dividing Compound Words 528
  - Exercise 33-1 529

REVIEW 33 531
The Writer's Casebook #33 532

34 Abbreviations 534
PREVIEW 34 534
- **34a** Abbreviating Titles 535
- **34b** Abbreviating Technical Terms and Agency Names 535
- **34c** Abbreviating Designations of Specific Dates, Times of Day, Temperatures, and Numbers 535
- **34d** Editing to Eliminate Misuse or Overuse of Abbreviations 535
  - Exercise 34-1 537

REVIEW 34 539
The Writer's Casebook #34 540

35 Numbers 542
PREVIEW 35 542
- **35a** Spelling Out Numbers That Begin Sentences 543
- **35b** Spelling Out Numbers That Can Be Expressed in One or Two Words 543
- **35c** Using Numerals for Numbers That Cannot Be Expressed in One or Two Words 543
- **35d** Using Numbers Where Convention Requires Their Use 544
- **35e** Using Numerals with Spelled-out Numbers 544
  - Exercise 35-1 545

REVIEW 35 547
The Writer's Casebook #35 547

Answers to Previews and Reviews 550
Credits 560
Index 562

SECTION I
Composing an Essay

1
Planning an Essay

Preview 1

Read the following statements carefully. If the statement is true, circle T; if it is false, circle F.

1. The tone of your writing is determined solely by your attitude.   T   F
2. Successful writing is product oriented.   T   F
3. The essay form is long and loosely organized.   T   F
4. An essay topic should be broad and general, enabling the writer to find plenty to say about it.   T   F
5. Freewriting is a means of organizing your essay.   T   F
6. Writer's block refers to the square pages used for writing.   T   F
7. The writing process consists of outlining, writing, and checking your writing for errors.   T   F
8. Journalistic questions provide a convenient topic outline for your final paper.   T   F
9. During the planning stage of writing, you prepare a rough draft.   T   F
10. Research can be equated with library work.   T   F

Score _____

Check your answers against those in the back of the book. Deduct 10 points for each error.

1a   Thinking About Writing

Writing is a *process with a purpose*—a series of actions undertaken with a specific objective in mind. In literature or imaginative writing the purpose may be to entertain, criticize, or draw a clearer picture of our realities; and the product may be a poem, a story, or a play. In academic writing the purpose is usually to explain, analyze, or inform; and the product may be a report, a summary, a critique, a term paper, or an essay. But in each case, the writing process involves many related and even overlapping actions, as the writers decide what to write about and how to write about it, that is, how to change, add, delete, reshape, and polish their materials.

For convenience, we divide the writing process into three stages: *planning*, when you discover and explore a subject; *shaping*, when you shape your materials to fit a specific format and compose a first draft; and *writing and revising*, when you rewrite and rework the draft to improve its structure, content, and style and edit for errors. However, these stages describe only the predominant pattern of your actions as you proceed toward a finished paper; at any point in the process, you may also be discovering more to say about your subject, rearranging your materials, and revising sentences or entire paragraphs.

This workbook focuses upon the *essay*—a short, tightly organized form that combines information or analysis with a first-person perspective. However, the techniques that you learn and practice while writing essays will carry over to other kinds of academic writing. Additional guidelines for writing instructions, reviews, summaries, or critiques will appear throughout the book.

1b Getting Started

As a process, writing not only consists of a variety of simultaneous and continuous actions, but it also takes place in a context. Why you are writing—your *purpose*—and who you are writing for—your *audience*—will help determine the materials you use and also the *tone* or attitude of your paper. For example, if you were writing about your career goals to a company that may offer you a job, you would emphasize your qualifications and motivation to succeed; your tone would be serious and fairly formal. However, if you were writing about the same subject to a friend, you might focus on the salary or benefits you hope to receive and the attractive co-worker you hope to date; your tone would be informal and, perhaps, humorous.

The audience for academic writing is usually your instructor and/or the generally educated reader, and the purpose is to show how much you know about a subject, how well you can think, and how well you can express what you know. An academic audience expects correct information; logical and effective organization; acceptable grammar, punctuation, and spelling; and a clear style. Usually the tone of academic writing is formal or semiformal.
NOTE: Do not make the mistake of thinking that only your composition instructor cares about the quality of your writing. Instructors in every discipline not only assign written work but also evaluate it according to the standards of academic writing.

(1) Choosing a topic

Choosing and narrowing a topic calls for considering your audience and purpose in the light of everything you know about an assignment. Sometimes you will be given free choice: write a paper and hand it in on Thursday. But most of the time your instructor sets some limits: write a 300-word essay on the eating habits of working college students or, using cause and effect, a 500-word essay on the need for improved public transportation in your city. If the audience is your classmates or your instructor, keep in mind that most will not mind being the object of good-natured humor, but none will tolerate slander.

Usually you will need to narrow an assigned topic further to make it manageable in the short space of 300 to 500 words. Wherever possible, limit the subject to one variety, kind, or quality. For example, you might limit the topic for the 300-word theme given above to the fast-food dinner before class. If a subject can be subdivided, limit your treatment to one subdivision, such as your city's need for a monorail or bus system. If the subject is a complex process or an event with multiple causes, limit your paper to one segment of the process or one cause of the event.

(2) Finding something to say

The content of a good paper rarely flows easily from your pen. New ideas or fresh perspectives result from vigorously examining your subject to discover what you or others know, think, or feel about it. One or more of the following strategies can help you to explore essay topics.

Brainstorming means literally creating a storm of ideas. Start with a large sheet of paper, and write down ideas as quickly as they come to you. You might draw circles and arrows or lines to indicate the directions your thoughts are taking—the current of your thoughts—but for the most part leave sorting and connecting ideas for later. For example, when brainstorming for a paper on your special problems as a working student, you might begin with something like the brainstorming sheet illustrated in Figure 1 on page 4 and then branch out to cover the entire paper.

Freewriting is a good way to break through writer's block—the inability to put words on the page. The "freest" freewriting has no subject but instead allows you to explore the "stream" of your thinking at a particular moment. However, when used as a strategy for generating ideas, freewriting helps you focus your thoughts and discover what you know about a particular subject. To begin, set an alarm clock for five or ten minutes, and make sure you have plenty of paper and pens. Then fix your mind on your subject and write nonstop, never letting your pen leave the page until the alarm goes off. Don't worry about logic, grammar, or details. If your mind wanders, write about whatever it wanders to—the weather, another assignment, friends, a fly on the wall. A freewriting session on a working student's problems might begin like this.

Problems? I've got problems--plenty of them. Everything around me is a problem--my house needs cleaning but I can't do it because I have to write a paper for English/Garbage to take out/Grass to mow/Leaking roof/Dishes to do/I have--can't think, can think--It's sunny out and I would like to play tennis but I'm stuck in here spilling my brains on paper. A kite is flying outside my window, purple tail and orange body/back to my problems . . . (Continue until time is up.)

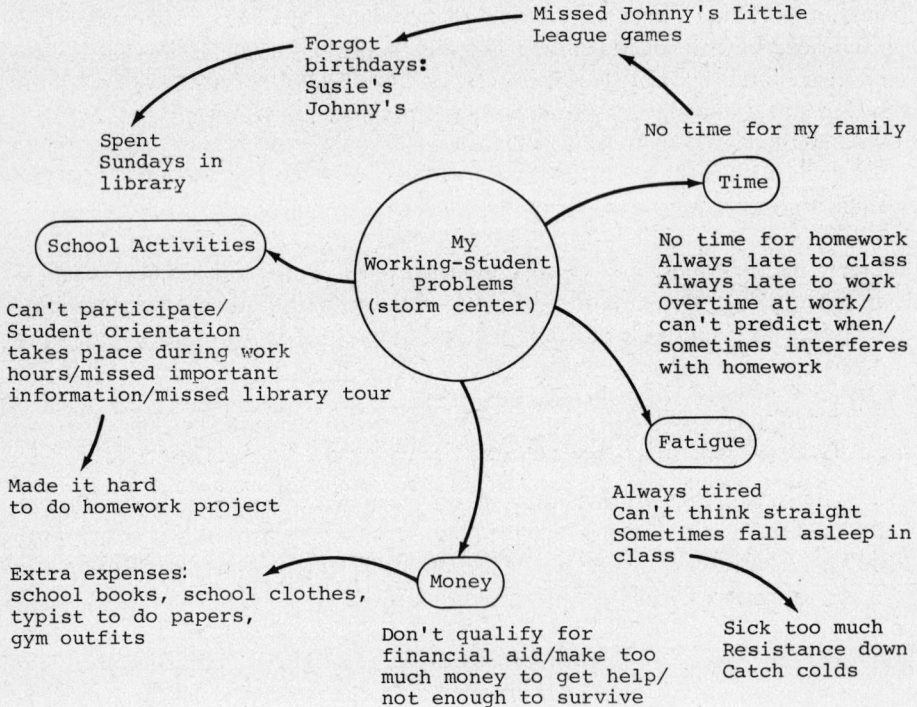

Figure 1

Keeping a journal is an ongoing way to generate ideas. If you record your thoughts and experiences as they occur, you will have an idea-book to refer to when you are searching for an essay topic or support for a paper. True, what you record in your journal will be stored in your brain as well, but usually an immediate written account will include many more details than a later version recalled from memory. (You will learn more about keeping a journal in Writer's Casebook #1.)

(3) Reading and observing

Reading and observing may help with a specific paper or with many papers if you make a point of recording your observations, important quotations, and summaries of key ideas in your journal. Although many students equate research with library work, you can just as effectively search for information by talking with friends and family, interviewing experts, writing query letters, and using questionnaires or polls to conduct surveys.

(4) Asking questions

Asking yourself certain questions will help you explore your subject in an organized fashion. *Journalistic questions*—Who? What? When? Where? Why? How?—provide an easily remembered frame for your investigation. These

Planning an Essay

questions fit the patterns of paragraph or essay organization and development that you will be studying and can help you decide how to organize and support your ideas. For example, asking what, when, and where something happened suggests *narration*, while asking why something happened or what caused it suggests *cause and effect*.

The student having problems with juggling work and school might begin a question session like this.

> Who has problems? I do but so do my family since they have to take up the slack. Who is responsible for these problems? No one unless it's me because I choose to go to school.

> What are the problems? Time, money, fatigue, getting homework in on time, making it to class and church and Little League and parents' night at school. What can I do about them? Manage my time better, take fewer classes.

> Why do I do it? Because I want to get ahead. Because I need a degree to receive promotions in my company. Because I enjoy my work and want to be the best.

Planning an Essay

Writing for Purpose and Audience   Exercise 1–1

NAME _____ DATE _____

For each exercise, write a short paragraph using the topic and information listed. Make your tone, materials, and method fit the purpose and audience given. Add or delete information as needed.

    EXAMPLE: Topic: dangerous driving during the 8 A.M. rush hour

        Information: weaving from lane to lane; speeding; driving while half asleep, drinking coffee and eating doughnuts, combing hair, putting on make-up; accidents increased 35 percent in one year

        Audience: City Council

        Purpose: to persuade the Council to launch a city-wide safety campaign

        The city's 8 A.M. rush hour is rapidly becoming the crush-and-crash hour because of dangerous driving habits. Drivers who are late to work make the freeway a speedway. They weave in and out of slower traffic, hopping from lane to lane, cutting belligerently in front of smaller vehicles and foolhardily in front of large trucks. Some make the front seat of their car their breakfast or dressing table and drink coffee, eat doughnuts, comb their hair, or put on make-up while driving. In the past year the number of accidents during this hour has increased 35 percent. A city-wide safety campaign is needed to educate our citizens about safe-driving habits.

1. Topic: cooking fried rice the Chinese way
   Information: *ingredients*—three cups of day-old rice, leftover chicken or beef, five green onions, two cloves of garlic, soy sauce, five tablespoons of cooking oil, three eggs; *tools*—wok or large frying pan and spatula; *method*—heat oil and garlic, stir-fry meat, then stir-fry rice, add soy sauce, scramble eggs in center of mixture, mix and add green onions, stir-fry
   Audience: amateur cooks
   Purpose: to explain a way to make leftovers a treat

© 1986 by CBS College Publishing. All rights reserved.

2. Topic: dealing with the complex demands of parenting
   Information: the need to provide both discipline and emotional support; the need to provide security but also to foster independent growth; the demands on one's personal time; the financial responsibilities, the anxieties, and the joys
   Audience: parents
   Purpose: to share the satisfaction and the frustrations of parenting

3. Topic: the football fanatic
   Information: owns every publicity product of favorite team from t-shirts to coffee mugs; can recite players' records; speaks of coaches as though they were long-time friends (or enemies); watches every game played in the NFL, USFL, or YFL; second-guesses draft choices for every major team; backseat referees for every game
   Audience: non-fans
   Purpose: to describe the phenomenon of football fanaticism

4. Topic: A–F grades at the elementary school level
   Information: pressure on children to compete, strain on young eyes from late-night study, penalties introduced into learning process, children influenced to study for the grade rather than for the love of learning, danger of burnout
   Audience: school board
   Purpose: to persuade the board to abolish A–F grades at the elementary school level

Planning an Essay

5. Topic: your reasons for buying a specific item (car, house, dishwasher, computer, and so forth)
   Information: supply your own
   Audience: a friend who plans to make a similar purchase
   Purpose: to persuade your friend to buy the item you chose

Narrowing Topics for Essays Exercise 1–2

NAME _____ DATE _____

Narrow each of these broad subjects to three topics suitable for short essays.

    EXAMPLE: Financial aid
          a. *filling out the paperwork, or how I earned my financial aid package*
          b. *the grant-work/study-loan formula for financial aid*
          c. *the myth of financial aid abuse*

1. Television violence
    a.
    b.

    c.

2. Required courses
    a.
    b.

    c.

3. Auto emissions regulations
    a.

    b.
    c.

4. Working your way through college
    a.
    b.
    c.

5. Small business versus big business
    a.

    b.

    c.

6. Motion pictures
    a.
    b.
    c.

Planning an Essay

7. Procrastinating
   a.
   b.
   c.

8. Bosses
   a.
   b.

   c.

9. Life goals
   a.
   b.
   c.

10. The private citizen and politics
    a.
    b.
    c.

© 1986 by CBS College Publishing. All rights reserved.

Generating Ideas by Brainstorming Exercise 1–3

NAME _____ DATE _____

Choose one of your narrowed topics from Exercise 1-2; then brainstorm for ideas. Add arrows, branches, circles, and so forth, as needed to emphasize the directions of your thoughts. Fill the page as quickly as you can.

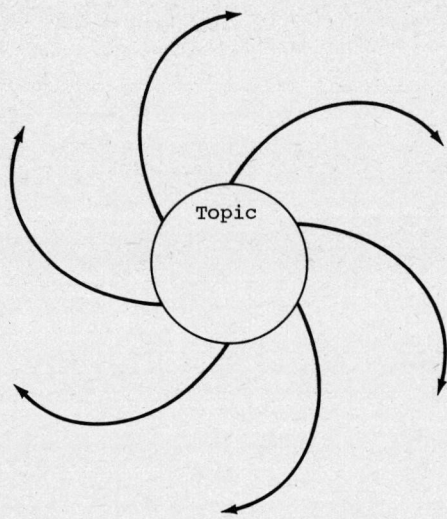

Planning an Essay

Generating Ideas with Questions Exercise 1–4

NAME _____ DATE _____

Use journalistic questions to explore each of these topics. Wherever possible, use your answers to generate more questions.

    EXAMPLE: Topic: Problems with telephone etiquette

        Who? *Most people. Male and female. Receptionists pressured by too many people demanding attention. Executives whose minds are on the reports they are writing or the decisions they are making.*

        What? *Mumbled speech. Failure to identify self. Abruptness. Placing callers on indefinite hold. What does bad etiquette lead to? Lost sales, lost good will, misinformation, wasted time.*

        And so forth.

1. Topic: The growing demand for personal computers
   Who?

   What?

   When?

   Where?
   Why?

   How?

2. Topic: Your feelings about exercise
   Who?

   What?

   When?

   Where?
   Why?

   How?

© 1986 by CBS College Publishing. All rights reserved.

3. Topic: Service in restaurants
   Who?

   What?

   When?

   Where?

   Why?
   How?

4. Topic: The rising costs of health care
   Who?

   What?

   When?

   Where?

   Why?

   What?

5. Topic: Do-it-yourself projects
   Who?

   What?

   When?

   Where?
   Why?
   How?

Planning an Essay

Review 1

Read the following statements carefully. If the statement is true, circle T; if it is false, circle F.

1. The essay form is short and tightly organized.   T   F
2. Both audience and purpose determine the tone of an essay.   T   F
3. Usually you must narrow assigned topics further.   T   F
4. Successful writing is process oriented.   T   F
5. Brainstorming means literally a storm of ideas.   T   F
6. Writer's block refers to the inability to put words on the page.   T   F
7. The writing process consists of planning, shaping, and writing and revising.   T   F
8. Research may include interviewing friends, conducting surveys, and writing letters of inquiry.   T   F
9. During the planning stage of writing, you discover and explore your topic.   T   F
10. Journalistic questions provide a convenient frame for your investigation.   T   F

Score _____

Check your answers against those in the back of the book. Deduct 10 points for each error.

The Writer's Casebook #1

Application: The Writer's Journal

A writer's journal is more than a log of events or dear-diary outpourings. Like a newspaper—the province of journalists—a writer's journal is a collection of stories, opinions, facts, hypotheses, observations, predictions, quotations, paraphrases, humor, tragedy, games, brief notes, and in-depth analyses. A journal is also the place to experiment with unfamiliar writing formats or patterns; to record events, ideas, and expressions for use in future papers; and to practice writing skills such as writing emphatic sentences (Chapter 8) or using parallel structures (Chapter 14).

A loose-leaf notebook that will allow you to insert leaves serves best as a writer's journal, but any notebook with plenty of paper will do. Write daily. The root of the word *journal* is *jour*, which means "day." Your writer's journal should record the day's events—what you see, think, feel, or learn— and should be written both during the day when things are happening and at the end of the day when you can sum up your impressions.

Your journal is also a good place to plan papers you must write for your English class or for other courses. Not all the ideas you discover by brainstorming, freewriting, or asking questions will be used in any one essay, but the unused ideas could contribute to some future project.

Generally, journal writing is quick writing. You have an idea; you quickly fill half a page, a page, or several pages with your thoughts; and you are finished—no laborious rethinking, correcting, and revising. However, occasionally you may want to use your journal as an experimental laboratory—a testing place for new writing techniques such as composing dialogue or achieving coherence through the use of parallel and balanced structures. Then you will work more carefully, and the words may come slowly.

Cases for Writing: Starting Your Journal or Being a Journalist

Case #1

Be the editor of a newspaper. Write an editorial on one or more of the incidents that happen on or off campus during the day. Emphasize opinion and speculation. (You may go to the editorial page of a newspaper for a model of this kind of writing.)

Case #2

Be an expert. Write a press release or interview yourself about something you learned in one of your classes—the reasons for the fall of the Roman Empire, the scientific method, the way to determine whether a difference is statistically significant, planning techniques for gathering material for a paper. Include all the details you can remember without referring to your text or class notes; put the information in your own words. (This exercise can provide effective reinforcement as you study various subjects.)

NOTE: You will find many other subjects and formats for writing as your journal progresses. However, describing everyday events in news story formats should help you begin by allowing you to use the familiar patterns and materials of the daily newspaper.

Shaping Your Material

2

Preview 2

A. For each pair of statements, circle the letter before the statement that seems more accurate.

1. a. A topic tree is an idea source, a collection of possible topics to refer to when you cannot decide what to write about.
   b. A topic tree is a way of grouping ideas about a subject.
2. a. You should always stick with your original thesis.
   b. You should begin with a tentative thesis and revise as necessary.
3. a. Your thesis may be a question, title, or phrase that will be developed further in the paper.
   b. Your thesis should be a declarative sentence.
4. a. A formal outline is a working plan for an essay.
   b. A formal outline is a blueprint for an essay.
5. a. In a formal outline indentions show coordination.
   b. In a formal outline indentions show subordination.

B. For each pair of statements, circle the letter before the one which could better serve as a thesis.

6. a. Should the graduated income tax be replaced by a flat-rate income tax?
   b. The graduated income tax should be replaced by a flat-rate income tax.
7. a. Harrison Candy Company, where good taste is our trademark.
   b. Harrison Candy Company does not live up to its good-taste trademark.
8. a. Computers are rapidly taking over in learning-assistance centers.
   b. Learning-assistance centers need to rely more upon computers.
9. a. Hazards on the road include reckless drivers, bad weather, and poor road conditions.
   b. Three types of reckless drivers are speeders, absent-minded dreamers, and drunks.
10. a. Frying Chicken My Way
    b. If you follow my secret recipe, your fried chicken will be the best.

Score _____

Check your answers against those in the back of the book. Deduct 10 points for each error.

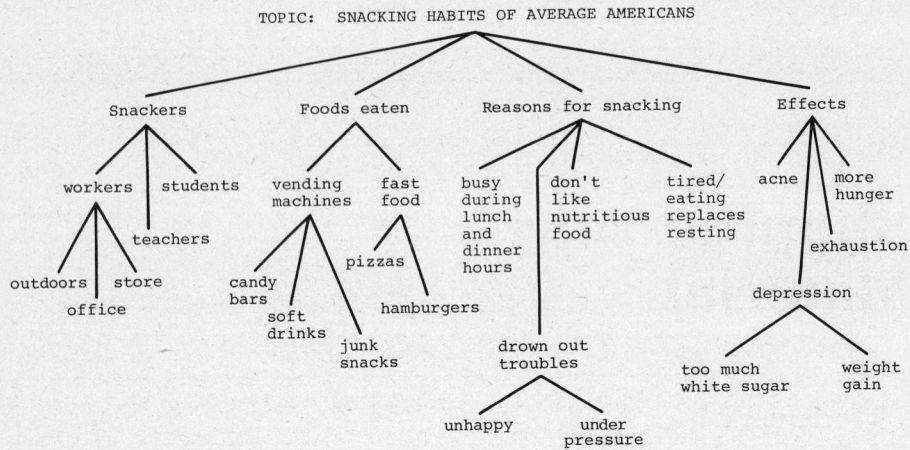

Figure 2

2a Grouping Ideas

Once you have a page or two of notes, you are ready to start choosing material for further development in your essay. To begin, you can use a topic tree to organize the ideas you discovered by brainstorming, freewriting, or questioning. First, head a sheet of paper with your narrowed topic. As you read through your notes, list the important categories or groups of ideas across the paper, directly under your topic, leaving plenty of room between listings. Then sort other ideas into appropriate groups, drawing lines to show relationships. A topic tree for the subject "snacking habits of average Americans" would begin like the diagram in Figure 2 and then continue until all the relevant notes from the planning stage are listed.

Building a topic tree helps you discover what subtopic you have the most ideas about. In the tree begun above, the most material so far appears under the two middle headings—"foods eaten" and "reasons for snacking"—but the fourth subtopic—"effects"—also has potential.

2b Developing a Tentative Thesis

A thesis is a statement of the main idea and the scope of your essay. The thesis should be the focus of your first paragraph and should be phrased as a declarative sentence—a sentence that declares or states something—rather than as a question. Both a promise to the reader and a plan for the writer, the thesis should include your narrowed subject and also a statement about that subject—an attitude, an opinion, a special perspective, the specific slant that you will adopt, or the position that you will defend in your essay.

Shaping Your Material

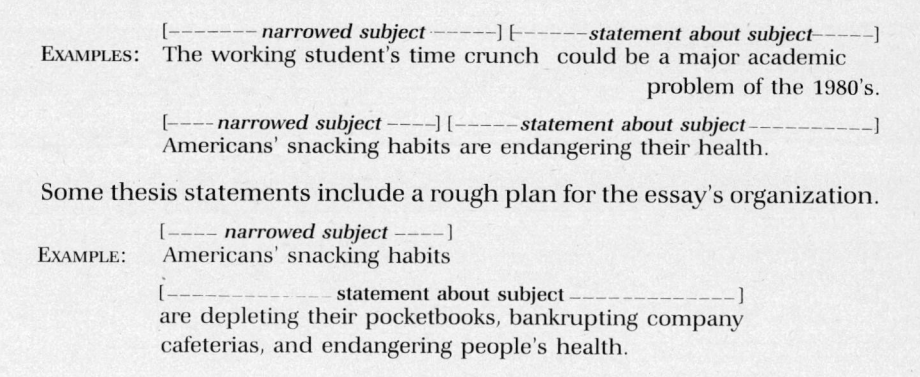

 [――――― *narrowed subject* ―――] [―――*statement about subject*―――]
EXAMPLES: The working student's time crunch could be a major academic problem of the 1980's.

 [――― *narrowed subject* ―――] [―――*statement about subject*―――――]
Americans' snacking habits are endangering their health.

Some thesis statements include a rough plan for the essay's organization.

 [――― *narrowed subject* ―――]
EXAMPLE: Americans' snacking habits
 [――――――*statement about subject*―――――――]
are depleting their pocketbooks, bankrupting company cafeterias, and endangering people's health.

This thesis leads us to expect the essay to explain Americans' snacking habits and then concentrate on three negative effects—depleted funds, bankrupt cafeterias, and endangered health—in that order. The writer would probably devote one or more paragraphs to each effect, being careful to give each equal emphasis.

The tentative thesis you compose as you shape your essay may change as the writing process continues. Like a proposal, the tentative thesis suggests an approach that will be tested as you continue writing and, perhaps, changed as you become more familiar with the possibilities and the limitations of your subject.

2c Preparing a Working Plan

An informal essay diagram, the working plan blocks out the main ideas to be covered and the general arrangement of the paper. It is somewhat tentative, and neither ideas nor structure are firmly fixed.

WORKING PLAN: *Head Nurse in a Maternity Ward*

THESIS STATEMENT: *Ten years from today I hope to be a head nurse in a maternity unit of a hospital, dedicating my life to the care of newborns and to the miracle of birth.*

Pursuing a career in nursing
  helping profession—my compassion for people and animals who are in pain
  making people well—importance of good health
  significant contribution—job worth doing
  long hours, hard work—my willingness to exceed duty
Being head nurse in a maternity unit
  challenge
  ability to supervise
  enjoy responsibility
  beliefs about the homelike atmosphere and nurturing attitudes of nurses that contribute to successful births

Working with newborns
   special appeal of red, wrinkled newborns
   helpless, trusting
   cry with entire body—arms and legs in motion,
   face—all mouth, wrinkled nose, eyes that are slitted folds
   sounds—coos, gurgles
Assisting with births
   excitement
   danger
   importance to child and family of first moments of life
   joy of birth—always new
   most important act on earth

2d   Preparing an Outline

While the working plan informally diagrams an essay, the outline is a formal blueprint for it. Because it requires more thought and care, the outline is more fixed, providing a firmer guide as you write.

The structure of the formal outline is prescribed. It uses Roman numerals, Arabic numerals, and uppercase and lowercase letters to show the order of presentation and the relationship of ideas.

EXAMPLE:
   I. First major division of your paper
      A. First secondary division
         1. First supporting example
            a. First specific detail
            b. Second specific detail
            c. Third specific detail
         2. Second supporting example
      B. Second secondary division
  II. Second major division of your paper

The ladder of indentions shows the logical system of subordination and also a progression from general to more specific information. In addition, the relationship of ideas is underscored by the use of *grammatically parallel terms* for topics on the same level. In other words, if the first major division of the paper is a noun followed by a prepositional phrase, all major divisions must be nouns followed by prepositional phrases. If one secondary division is a gerund phrase, all secondary divisions must be gerund phrases.

EXAMPLE OF PARTIAL OUTLINE WITH GRAMMATICALLY PARALLEL TERMS:

Title: Football Fanatics
Thesis: Football fanatics can be classified into three groups—fans of the team, fans of the game, and fans of betting.

I. Fans of the team
   A. Defending team
      1. Against prejudiced referees
         a. Bad calls
         b. Unjust penalties
      2. Against other fans
   B. Knowing the statistics
II. Fans of the game

- a, b: adjective plus noun
- 1, 2: prepositional phrases
- A, B: gerund phrases
- I, II: nouns followed by prepositional phrases

(Your instructor may ask you to complete this outline as a class exercise.) Keep in mind that no category may contain only one subdivision. If category II has an A, there must also be a B, and if category B has a 1, there must also be a 2. Each part may contain more than two divisions but never fewer than two.

Shaping Your Material   **23**

Identifying Thesis Statements   Exercise 2-1

NAME _____ DATE _____

Circle the letter before the most effective thesis statements in each group. Be prepared to defend your answer.

> EXAMPLE: a. Developing good work habits, the first task of the new employee.
> b. Developing good work habits is the first task of the new employee.
> ⓒ. Developing good work habits is a prerequisite for a new employee's success.

1. a. Gas utility rates rose 13.6 percent during the fall.
   b. The change in ownership of the gas utility contributed to an increase of 13.6 percent in rates during the fall.
   c. Consumers and officials were caught off guard by the 13.6 percent increase in gas utility rates during the fall.
2. a. Why did voters elect a pig to be County Commissioner?
   b. By a six-to-one-margin, voters elected Miss Piggy to be County Commissioner.
   c. The race for County Commissioner became a farce when voters elected Miss Piggy in a six-to-one landslide.
3. a. Financial aid packages for working college students must be on the Budget Committee agenda when the State Legislature meets.
   b. It was reported that financial aid packages for working college students will be on the Budget Committee agenda when the State Legislature meets.
   c. Financial aid packages for working college students—an important Budget Committee agenda item at the next meeting of the State Legislature.
4. a. Fees for auto emissions testing sparked protests this week.
   b. Citizens are for auto emissions testing, against testing fees.
   c. The city's charging fees for auto emissions testing may warrant citizens' accusations that city officials are profiting from the tests.
5. a. Numann's Department Store epitomizes excellence in customer service.
   b. Numann's Department Store, the epitome of excellence.
   c. Numann's Department Store claims in all its advertisements to offer customer service that is the epitome of excellence.
6. a. Not everyone can be a professional athlete, but everyone can enjoy some sport or exercise activity.
   b. Doesn't everyone enjoy some kind of sport or exercise activity?
   c. Interest in sports should be focused where it can do the most good—on being a participator rather than a spectator.
7. a. Computer-assisted tutoring is revolutionizing home-study.
   b. Computer-assisted tutoring would revolutionize home-study.
   c. Computer-assisted tutoring, a revolution in home-study.
8. a. Unlike the consumer of the 1970's, consumers in the 1980's are returning to bigger cars and more luxury items.
   b. Money is meant to be spent, according to consumers in the 1980's.
   c. The 1980's may see a new wave of consumerism, with buyers avoiding the economy-sized cars and practical selections of buyers in the 1970's and returning to bigger cars and more luxury items.

© 1986 by CBS College Publishing. All rights reserved.

9. a. Many public schools have adopted a computer-literacy requirement.
   b. Many public schools should adopt a computer-literacy requirement.
   c. Should public schools adopt a computer-literacy requirement?
10. a. The fifty-five-mile-per-hour speed limit is not always observed.
    b. The Highway Commission recommends withholding funds from communities with a poor record of enforcing the speed limit.
    c. If the Highway Commission withholds funds from communities with poor enforcement records, they will become motivated to enforce the speed limit.

Score _____

Shaping Your Material

Revising Thesis Statements Exercise 2-2

NAME _____ DATE _____

Compose an effective thesis statement by revising each of the following items extensively.

> EXAMPLE: Something should be done about all the junk employees are eating. *Candy, soft drink, and snack machines should be removed from the employee lounge and replaced with machines that dispense fresh fruit, juices, and milk.*

1. The first day on a new job can be an exciting experience.
Revision:

2. What are the police doing about safety for citizens who must travel the streets at night?
Revision:

3. The positive aspects of pet vaccination laws
Revision:

4. Adulthood definitely differs from childhood.
Revision:

5. Choosing a mate can be difficult.
Revision:

6. Feminist issues in athletics
Revision:

7. People need some freedom in addition to responsibilities.
Revision:

8. Why go to college?
Revision:

9. Where the dreams of life differ from its realities
Revision:

10. More must be done to help students who have small children.
Revision:

© 1986 by CBS College Publishing. All rights reserved.

11. Most Americans drive cars, but not all do it well.
Revision:

12. The boss who is never satisfied
Revision:

13. Waiting to have children can create problems.
Revision:

14. The cost of living is going up.
Revision:

15. My recipe for successful living
Revision:

Shaping Your Material 27

Writing Thesis Statements from Topics   Exercises 2–3

NAME _____ DATE _____

Narrow the general topics listed. Then write an effective thesis statement about each one.

> EXAMPLE: Topic: Grades
> Narrowed Topic: *Dr. Foss's intricate point system of grading*
> Thesis: *Dr. Foss's intricate point system of grading deserves an award for uniqueness.*

1. Topic: Happiness
   Narrowed Topic:
   Thesis:

2. Topic: Athletics
   Narrowed Topic:
   Thesis:

3. Topic: Friends
   Narrowed Topic:
   Thesis:

4. Topic: Community spirit
   Narrowed Topic:
   Thesis:

5. Topic: Students with children
   Narrowed Topic:
   Thesis:

6. Topic: Goals
   Narrowed Topic:
   Thesis:

7. Topic: People you have met
   Narrowed Topic:
   Thesis:

8. Topic: A movie you would like to see
   Narrowed Topic:
   Thesis:

© 1986 by CBS College Publishing. All rights reserved.

9. Topic: Working and going to school
   Narrowed Topic:
   Thesis:

10. Topic: Student finances
    Narrowed Topic:
    Thesis:

Shaping Your Material 29

Review 2

A. For each pair of statements, circle the letter before the statement that seems more accurate.

1. a. In a topic tree, lines are drawn to show relationships.
   b. In a topic tree, lines are drawn to separate unrelated thoughts.
2. a. A thesis is a statement of the general subject of an essay.
   b. A thesis is a statement of the main idea and scope of an essay.
3. a. In a formal outline all parts of each major division should be expressed in grammatically parallel terms.
   b. In a formal outline topics on the same level should be expressed in grammatically parallel terms.
4. a. A working plan is fixed and definite.
   b. A working plan is somewhat tentative.
5. a. Each category of an outline must have at least one subdivision.
   b. No category of an outline may contain only one subdivision.

B. For each pair, circle the letter before the more effective thesis statement.

6. a. Pet owners should be required to leash their animals.
   b. Should pet owners be required to leash their animals?
7. a. To improve its air quality, our city needs a program for testing auto emissions.
   b. A vote for auto emissions testing is a vote for clean air.
8. a. The city needs to install a traffic light at the corner of University Boulevard and Stadium Road.
   b. In 1984 forty-three accidents took place at the intersection of University Boulevard and Stadium Road.
9. a. The computer science lab might best be described as the brain bank.
   b. The Brain Bank, a good name for the computer science lab.
10. a. In buying a 4 × 4, you should consider size, price, and dependability.
    b. Buying a 4 × 4 requires much thought.

Score _____

Check your answers against those in the back of the book. Deduct 10 points for each error.

The Writer's Casebook #2

Application: Outlining to Test a Thesis

A common problem in developing a thesis is the temptation to keep it broad so that we will have no problem finding enough to say about it. Because an outline moves on a ladder of indentions from general to more and more specific statements, it can serve as a check on the narrowness of your thesis. If your Arabic-numeral and lowercase-letter subdivisions are only slightly less general than those headed by Roman numerals and uppercase letters, the thesis is too broad.

EXAMPLE: Thesis: There are three kinds of people in the world—the introvert, the extrovert, and the in-between.

    I. The Introvert
       A. The shy type
          1. Shy males
             a. Shy boys
             b. Shy men
          2. Shy females
             a. Shy girls
             b. Shy women
       B. The withdrawn type

Although we have used three levels of subdivision, the topics at all levels are still general. The thesis is therefore too broad.

Cases for Writing: Outlining with a Purpose

Case #1

Write outlines to test the narrowness of the following thesis statements. If the thesis is not narrow enough, revise it and test your revision by outlining.

a. Most people would benefit from an exercise program.
b. Basketball is a more exciting sport than football.
c. A liberal arts education is as important for business majors as for humanities majors.

Case #2

Outline an essay which you have written for this or another class. Use your outline to help you evaluate the essay in terms of the narrowness of thesis, the arrangement of materials, and the use of supporting materials.

Writing and Revising 3

Preview 3

Read the following statements carefully. If the statement is true, circle T; if it is false, circle F.

1. Essays should not use the first person, or "I," point of view. T F
2. Thesis and support is a type of essay structure. T F
3. A good writer can expect to make only minor corrections on the first draft. T F
4. An essay on the joys of parenting may devote several paragraphs to the frustrations as well. T F
5. You should draft your paper slowly and carefully, paying attention to each detail. T F
6. You write to be read; you revise to make what you have written more readable. T F
7. To begin revising, correct spelling, punctuation, and grammar. T F
8. The purpose of peer criticism is to help you identify problems, not to correct them. T F
9. A good thesis explains the writer's point of view but does not limit supporting evidence in any way. T F
10. Each supporting paragraph of an essay should be introduced by a thesis statement. T F

Score _____

Check your answers against those in the back of the book. Deduct 10 points for each error.

3a Using Thesis and Support

Thesis and support describes the general structure of most essays. A thesis-and-support essay begins with an *introduction,* which explains the direction of the paper and gives the thesis. The *body* of the essay supports the thesis in several paragraphs, each introduced by a *topic sentence* that summarizes the paragraph's main idea. The *conclusion* includes a restatement of the thesis and may sum up the support or give a final judgment on the subject.

NOTE: How long each of the three major parts of the essay will be depends upon the overall length required of the assignment. However, most short essays of one or two pages will devote one paragraph each to the introduction and conclusion and three or more paragraphs to the body.

A good thesis anchors your paper firmly in a specific attitude and point of view. (See Writer's Casebook #8 for more about point of view.) It also defines the limits of the supporting evidence you may draw upon and may even suggest a plan for the essay.

> Ten years from today I hope to be head nurse in a maternity unit of a hospital, dedicating my life to the care of newborns and the miracle of birth.

This thesis establishes a first-person, or "I," point of view. The writer limits the subject to professional goals ten years from now, leaving no room for discussion of next year's goals or of family or hobby plans. The thesis also projects four subtopics that will need to be supported or explained—pursuing a career in nursing, being head nurse in a maternity unit, working with newborns, and assisting with births.

3b Writing a Rough Draft

Do not expect to write a perfect paper the first time. The process of refining and perfecting cannot begin until you have tested your working plan by writing a draft.

The rough draft should be written quickly, and it should be written with the expectation of revising—perhaps several times. Your first thoughts may not be your best thoughts, but they will do when you are drafting.

Plan your work strategies as well as your writing strategies. Prepare your materials—notes, paper, pencils, erasers—and schedule your time. When writing a rough draft, some people prefer to impose a time limit of one or two hours. Do not worry about weak introductory and concluding paragraphs, errors, inconsistencies, and awkward phrasing. You will correct those problems when you revise.

Maellen wrote the following rough draft in an hour and ten minutes.

Becoming a Star

Why does a person choose what they do for a career? There are many answers to that question, and probably not many of them will be alike from person to person. I would like to tell you why I chose acting as a career.

As a child I was infatuated with movie and television stars. I would stay home all day and watch television while other kids went swimming or rode their bikes. I used to love to pretend I was one of those people.

I was on the show, living in their situations. Whenever a character got into some kind of problem or rejoiced over something terrific, I would do it right along with them. Marie Osmond was always my favorite performer. There was not a week that went by without me watching the Donny and Marie Show. I tried to do my hair like her's, I tried to dress like her, and I tried to smile like her. I remember one night after watching The Donny and Marie Show I spent about an hour in the bathroom, looking in the mirror, trying to smile like Marie Osmond. When that didn't work, I changed my affections to Lindsey Wagner who played on the Bionic Woman.

During the same time period as my infatuations with television and movie stars, I was modeling for a photographer down the street. She, Star Ockenga, was shooting pictures of children for two photography books she was later going to make. My posing for her inspired me to like acting, because I always had to act out a little scene for her pictures, for instance, one photography session when Star asked me and several other kids in the neighborhood to act out a funeral. We did, and while we acted Star took some excellent pictures. It was so much fun working with Star, and if I had to make a choice as to what was the most important influence that turned me to acting, I would say Star Ockenga.

Star mainly used my pictures for her books, but sometimes she would also put them in art galleries around Boston. When I was eleven years old, Star had my picture in one of Bostons bigger galleries. A man, also a producer, with the name of David Peters saw my picture. At the time, he was trying to cast a movie called Morning, Winter and Night. He needed a twelve year old looking female to play one of the leads. (Maxwell's first love as a boy). He called Star, and she in turn called my parents. After six weeks of them not knowing if they should even tell me or not, they did. I read for Mr. Peters and for many, more people all over New England, it seems everyone loved me but the finance director, who wanted a well-known name to bring in money. As it turns out, they were going to use Brooke Shields, but they never got enough money and so they never made the movie. But that is not the point. The point is that during that summer when all of this was going on--I loved it! I had never had a better time. After Star Ockenga this really made me want to act.

3c Understanding Revision

When you revise a paper, you "re-see" it from several points of view. You look at it from your point of view to see whether you have said what you wanted to say; from a general audience's point of view to see whether what you have said is clear and convincing; and from your specific audience's point of view to determine whether you have fulfilled its expectations—for example, the expectations of an academic audience that you observe the standards and conventions of American English.

(1) Revising for an audience

Comments from readers are especially helpful at this point. You write to be read; you revise to make what you have written more readable. In addition to your own careful scrutiny, peer and teacher criticism will help you to correct organizational problems that require the reader to backtrack; to pinpoint the places where summary, repetition, and stronger transitions are needed; and to eliminate problems with spelling, punctuation, and grammar.

(2) Strategies for revision

How you revise will vary from paper to paper; therefore, you need a repertoire of methods so that you can choose the one most appropriate to each task. A formal *outline* of the rough draft, if you did not use one to shape your materials, will help you check the structure of your paper to see where you have departed from your working plan, misplaced points, emphasized minor ideas, or deemphasized major ideas. (See 2d for an explanation of formal outlines.) Do not be afraid to experiment with the placement of paragraphs. Move them around, delete, and add during the early stages of revision until you find an arrangement that places emphasis where you want it and provides a logical progression of ideas.

Peer criticism may be formal or informal—part of a class activity initiated by your instructor or comments voluntarily sought (with your instructor's approval) from friends or classmates. In either case, the evaluation should focus on suggestions for improving communication. Do not allow your peer critics to make corrections or other changes for you. Your peers will learn from helping you identify problems, but you will not learn to avoid those problems until you have struggled through making the corrections yourself and, in the process, developed more effective strategies and better language habits.

The most useful *revision checklist* corresponds to the process of revision. First, survey the *whole essay* for problems with organization, thesis, and support. Then survey individual *body paragraphs* for topic sentences, development, and transitions; the *introductory paragraph*, to determine whether it is an interesting and effective preparation for the essay's subject; and the *concluding paragraph* for a summary of the essay's main points and a sense of closure or completion. Next check *sentences*. Look for a variety of sentence types and lengths, effective coordination and subordination, appropriate emphasis, use of active voice, and economy of expression. Consider *words* for accurate usage, a level of diction suited to the audience and purpose, concrete and specific language rather than vague clichés or jargon, and appropriate imagery. Review *tone and style*. Make sure that they fit both audience and purpose and that they are consistent throughout the paper. Finally, proofread carefully for errors in punctuation, grammar, and spelling.

3d Revising Your Drafts

(1) Revising the first draft

Since you can expect to write several drafts, focus on only a few areas of the revision process at a time. On the first draft concentrate on improving your organization, thesis, and support.

(2) Revising the second draft

Once you are satisfied with the larger elements of the essay, you can more easily identify problems with sentence structure, word choice, style, tone, and mechanics.

(3) Writing the final draft

The completed paper may be your third, fourth, fifth, sixth, or even seventh draft. Do not be surprised if it differs dramatically from the original version. The final draft of Maellen's paper about her choice of acting as a career retains only a few items from the original essay.

Another Star Is Born

What would make an adult play dress-up and make-believe in front of thousands of people? In other words, why does anyone choose acting as a career? Some say acting is a disease that can be inherited like hemophilia or caught like the measles. Others call it a destiny, written in the stars or ordained by the gods. I see acting as a rigorous but exciting way of life, and I was influenced to choose it as a career by childhood experiences, by my drama class, and by my actress-mother.

> New paragraph that focuses specifically on acting instead of careers in general

> Stronger thesis, outlining essay

As a child I was infatuated with movie and television stars. While other kids went swimming or rode their bikes, I would stay home and watch soap operas or old movies on television. I loved to pretend I was one of those gorgeous, rich young ladies. When they cried, I cried with them, being careful not to smear my black mascara and red lipstick. When they danced or sang, I danced and sang along, teetering precariously in my mother's high heels and trailing

> Paragraph retained from original but vagueness eliminated, details added, sentences combined, and errors corrected

her best gown behind me. Marie Osmond was always my idol. I never missed The Donny and Marie Show. I tried to do my hair like hers--shoulder length and curly--I tried to dress like her, even down to the hip-high mini skirts, and I tried to smile like her with a lot of teeth showing. I remember one night after watching The Donny and Marie Show, I spent about an hour in the bathroom, practicing my Marie Osmond smile in the mirror. I opened my mouth wide, showing all my teeth, tried to make slight dimples, and wished desperately for my eyes to twinkle. When that did not work (I looked more like Miss Piggy than Marie Osmond), I transferred my affections to Lindsey Wagner of The Bionic Woman.

    At about the same time my picture in a Boston gallery nearly led to my becoming a child star. David Peters, who was the producer of Morning, Winter, and Night, was looking for a twelve-year-old to play Maxwell Anderson's first love, and he thought I looked just like Hallie, the real-life sweetheart. I read for Mr. Peters and for many, many people all over New England. He loved me; they all loved me, except for the finance director. He wanted Brooke Shields to bring in the money. I lost the part but not my enthusiasm for acting; in fact, my taste of near-stardom left me totally stagestruck.   *Deciding her experiences as a model were only loosely related to acting, Maellen cut the paragraph about modeling and revised her account of her chance at becoming a child star.*

    Next came C.A.S.T.--Cibola Actors, Slaves, and Technicians--and Mrs. Kent, our high school drama teacher. You would think that a person who wanted to act would be a fearless extrovert, but I was shy and scared to death. Since I could not speak above a whisper, Mrs. Kent got me on stage first for a pantomine. Then I tried a monologue and then a dialogue. Soon I was acting in every production, designing costumes and sets, and promoting the shows. I was acting at last, and I loved it.   *New paragraph from material discovered during prewriting but not included in working plan*

    Mrs. Kent was not the only theater person to influence me. My mother once acted, and she raised me on stories of opening nights, backstage panic, and   *New paragraph from prewriting materials, not included in working plan* shows that must go on. Once Mom had laryngitis the day before the show opened. She swallowed honey and lemon by the gallon until she could speak in a low, raspy voice. Another time she tripped over the reviewer's feet during the show. Every story she told always made me tingle with anticipation, glee, or fright. And they all helped to make me want to act.

Someday I will be a star (I hope). My footprints will be in the cement outside Grummin's Chinese Theatre, and my picture will be on the cover of movie magazines. Meanwhile I will dream and work, knowing that the climb up is half the fun. But I will keep looking for more inspiration like Marie Osmond, Mrs. Kent, and my one-time actress mom and keep hoping that next time a big break comes, the finance director as well as the producer will like me better than Brooke Shields.

Concluding paragraph added, restating main idea and summarizing key points

Writing and Revising 39

Predicting Content from Thesis Statements Exercise 3-1

NAME _____ DATE _____

A. Circle the items that you would expect to find in a paper that develops the following thesis statements.

  EXAMPLE: Thesis: Chocoholism is a growing problem.
   ⓐ gorging myself on Milky Ways
   ⓑ a Hershey high
   c. salted peanuts between classes
   ⓓ M & M's before breakfast

1. Too many research paper assignments are turning me into a library squirrel.
   a. scurrying up and down the stacks
   b. storing facts in notebooks
   c. scolding anybody who gets in my way
   d. eating nuts day and night
   e. biting my fingernails
2. *The Odyssey* has all the ingredients necessary for a modern big-screen thriller.
   a. sex
   b. security of home and family
   c. blood and gore
   d. villains
   e. a happy ending
3. Lately the cost of outfitting students for college has been catching up with skyrocketing tuition.
   a. $3,500 for the computers now required by some colleges
   b. $1,000 for an electronic typewriter
   c. 10 cents for pencils
   d. $7.98 for bargain jeans
   e. $500 a month for an efficiency apartment
4. The best work habits emphasize maintaining a steady work pace, attending conscientiously to details, and tackling tasks in small rather than large chunks.
   a. all-night work sessions the night before a report is due
   b. leaving spelling and grammar for the secretary to correct
   c. beginning a major project as soon as it is assigned
   d. waiting until the office is quiet after hours to dictate letters
   e. making a daily work schedule
5. For some people the retirement years promise to be the best of their lives.
   a. the opportunity for travel
   b. no child-rearing responsibilities
   c. fixed income
   d. no job
   e. mature abilities and interests

Score _____

© 1986 by CBS College Publishing. All rights reserved.

Preparing a Working Plan   Exercise 3–2

NAME _____   DATE _____

Use this thesis and abbreviated brainstorming chart to prepare first a working plan and then a formal outline for an essay. Block out and outline subtopics and supporting materials that you think would fit into the various body paragraphs. Add or delete material as needed.

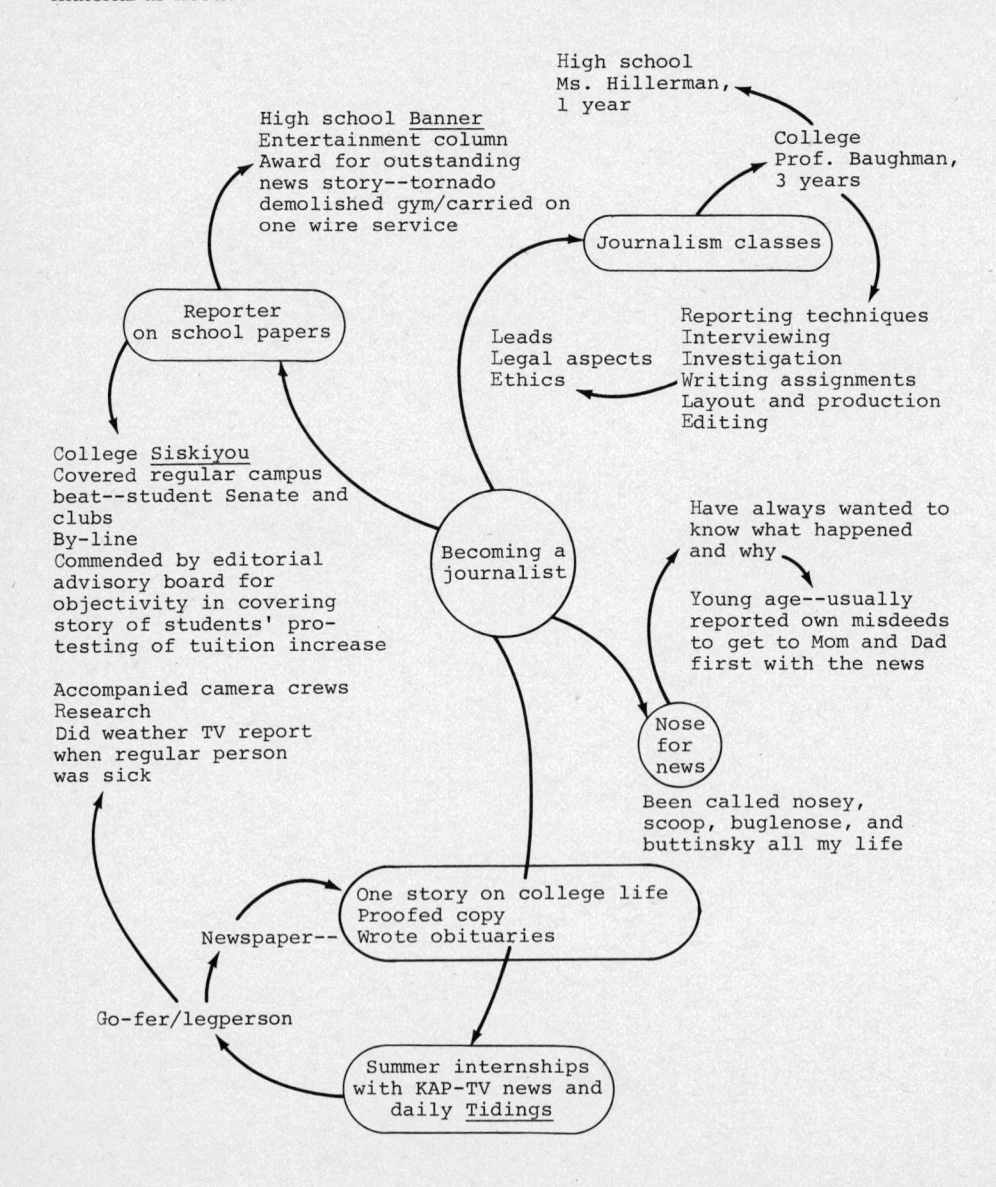

High school Ms. Hillerman, 1 year

High school Banner
Entertainment column
Award for outstanding news story—tornado demolished gym/carried on one wire service

College Prof. Baughman, 3 years

Journalism classes

Reporter on school papers

Leads
Legal aspects
Ethics

Reporting techniques
Interviewing
Investigation
Writing assignments
Layout and production
Editing

College Siskiyou
Covered regular campus beat--student Senate and clubs
By-line
Commended by editorial advisory board for objectivity in covering story of students' protesting of tuition increase

Accompanied camera crews
Research
Did weather TV report when regular person was sick

Becoming a journalist

Have always wanted to know what happened and why

Young age--usually reported own misdeeds to get to Mom and Dad first with the news

Nose for news

Been called nosey, scoop, buglenose, and buttinsky all my life

Newspaper—
One story on college life
Proofed copy
Wrote obituaries

Go-fer/legperson

Summer internships with KAP-TV news and daily Tidings

Writing and Revising   **41**

Thesis: To become a journalist in today's competitive market, one must have a nose for news, education, and experience: I have or am getting all three.

Working Plan:

Thesis Statement:

Formal Outline:

Thesis Statement:

© 1986 by CBS College Publishing. All rights reserved.

Score _____

Writing and Revising

Writing a Rough Draft Exercise 3-3

NAME _____ DATE _____

Plan and draft a paper on the following topic: why I chose _____ as a career. Prewrite using two or more strategies from Chapter 1. Then compose a thesis and arrange your materials in a working plan by outlining or blocking. After you have completed prewriting and arranging, your instructor may make drafting the first version of the essay an in-class writing assignment to accustom you to writing against the clock; however, if you write out of class, time yourself, allowing no more than an hour and twenty minutes for completion. You will need to use extra paper for this assignment, but record key points in the process on these pages. You will then have a handy reference page to guide you as you draft.

Prewriting Activity #1, Method:

Key ideas and support:

Prewriting Activity #2, Method:

Key ideas and support:

© 1986 by CBS College Publishing. All rights reserved.

Working plan or outline:

Thesis:

Score _____

Writing and Revising

Outlining to Revise   Exercise 3-4

NAME _____ DATE _____

Make a formal outline of the rough draft of Maellen's essay as it appears on pages 32 and 33. Then make suggestions for revision based on problems with support, organization, or emphasis revealed by the outline. When you have finished with Maellen's essay, follow the same procedure for your own rough draft of an essay on career choice (Exercise 3-3). Use additional paper for analyzing your own essay, but follow the basic pattern indicated on these pages, inserting additional body paragraphs as needed.

Outline: Paper title:

    Paper thesis:

      I. Infatuation with movie and television stars   (Topic of paragraphs #2 and #3)

          (Support)

     II. Model for photographer Star Ockenga   (Topic of paragraph #4)

          (Support)

    III. Audition for *Morning, Winter, and Night*   (Topic of paragraph #5)

          (Support)

Problems identified and solutions suggested:

Score _____

© 1986 by CBS College Publishing. All rights reserved.

Being a Peer Critic   Exercise 3–5

NAME _____ DATE _____

Be this student's peer critic. Evaluate the rough draft of her essay by answering the following questions. Do not rewrite parts of the essay yourself but give detailed advice for the writer's own revisions. In addition to responding to the questions, you may wish to make comments directly on the student's essay. After you have completed this task, your instructor may ask you to answer the same questions about a classmate's essay. Work carefully and compassionately, remembering that your aim as a peer critic is to inspire a better essay, not to drown your classmate's work in a sea of red ink.

Peer criticism of "Becoming a Star" by Maellen

1. What is the essay about? Does it have a clearly stated thesis? Could the thesis be improved? How?

2. How is the essay organized? Can you suggest any changes in the arrangement of paragraphs or materials within paragraphs?

3. Is the thesis adequately supported? Can you suggest any additions or deletions?

4. Are individual paragraphs effective? Does the introduction attract readers' attention and prepare them for the body of the essay? Are body paragraphs carefully organized to develop the ideas introduced in topic sentences? Does the conclusion restate the main idea and convey a sense of completion?

5. Is each sentence effective? Do you see any errors in sentence structure, grammar, or punctuation?

Writing and Revising

6. Are the words well chosen and well placed? Do you see any errors in spelling or usage?

7. Does any part of the paper need clarification? Can you suggest ways to eliminate the confusion?

8. What are the paper's major strengths? How can the writer build on those strengths?

9. What are the paper's major weaknesses? How can the writer correct those weaknesses?

© 1986 by CBS College Publishing. All rights reserved.

Writing and Revising

Review 3

Read the following statements carefully. If the statement is true, circle T; if it is false, circle F.

1. A good thesis narrows a subject but leaves the writer's opinion or attitude to be developed in subsequent sentences. T F
2. With enough practice you can expect to write a perfect paper the first time. T F
3. Write the rough draft quickly. T F
4. In revision, work from the largest unit—the whole essay—to the smallest units—words and punctuation. T F
5. The major job of the peer critic is to correct spelling, punctuation, and grammar. T F
6. The conclusion of an essay includes a restatement of the thesis and your final word on the subject. T F
7. The process of perfecting an essay should begin when you write the first word on the page. T F
8. First thoughts are best thoughts; therefore, stick with the basic ideas of the rough draft as you revise. T F
9. An essay is like a good recipe; revise it to your own taste, rather than to your audience's. T F
10. Use topic sentences to introduce supporting paragraphs. T F

Score _____

Check your answers against those in the back of the book. Deduct 10 points for each error.

The Writer's Casebook #3

Application: Charting a Course Through the Process of Writing

As you have worked through the first three chapters of this text, you have learned about and practiced various skills and techniques that make up the different phases of the writing process: planning, shaping, and writing and revising. Although these phases overlap and often even coincide, many writers find drawing up a plan of action helpful. You may backtrack many times as you move from finding a subject to handing in a completed paper, but the general direction and goal remain the same—a completed paper.

PHASE ONE: Finding something to say
    Brainstorming
    Freewriting
    Questioning
Narrowing the subject
Giving the subject direction (attitude, perspective, opinion)
Goal: Thesis sentence and raw materials for an essay

PHASE TWO: Shaping the material
    Organizing main ideas
    Selecting support
Goal: Outline or blocked plan

PHASE THREE: Drafting the paper
    Putting ideas into words, sentences, paragraphs
    Writing an introduction, body paragraphs, and conclusion
Goal: Rough draft

PHASE FOUR: Revising the draft (may be repeated several times)
    "Re-seeing" the paper through self-criticism, peer criticism, instructor criticism
    Refining structure, thesis, topic sentences, support
    Editing for errors in spelling, punctuation, and grammar
    Polishing to improve tone and style
Goal: Revised draft

PHASE FIVE: Preparing the final draft for submission
    Copying
    Adding finishing touches
Goal: Completed paper—the product

Cases for Writing: Processing Ideas

Case #1

Write a job description and a newspaper advertisement for your "dream" job. Then compose a letter explaining why you are qualified for the job in terms of your education, work experience, personality, motivation, ability to work with or to supervise people, and so forth. You may write from the perspective of your present situation and attainments or from a future perspective. Be sure to follow through on all parts of the writing process.

Case #2

You are a career counselor charged with advising new students about their career choices. Create a student to advise. Give that student a name, specific abilities and test scores, an interest profile, dreams, and ambitions. Then write a paper recommending a career that will be fulfilling to the student and will also offer significant opportunities for success in the 1980's and 1990's.

Writing Paragraphs 4

Preview 4

Fill in the blanks in each of the following sentences with words or phrases that best complete the thought.

1. In a long paragraph the middle paragraphs may be organized into subtopics, each introduced by _____ .
2. Repeating the patterns of words, phrases, or sentences to underscore the relationship of ideas is called _____ .
3. A _____ paragraph tells a story.
4. Process paragraphs explore _____ events happen.
5. Cause-and-effect paragraphs explore _____ events happen.
6. When you analyze by _____ , you classify or group several items.
7. You _____ something when you explain what it means.
8. A question may be used in the _____ of a paper to attract the readers' interest.
9. A _____ introduces the main idea of a paragraph.
10. Pronoun references, parallel structures, repetition, and transitional devices are ways of achieving _____ .

Score _____

Check your answers against those in the back of the book. Deduct 10 points for each error.

What is a paragraph?

Paragraph means literally "to write" (*graph*) "alongside" (*para*)—or in our modern sense of the word, to group together sentences about the same subject. When we paragraph, we indent the first of a group of sentences in which new ideas or new speakers are introduced, and each paragraph must be unified (about a single topic), coherent (logically organized), and well developed (filled with supporting information).

4a Charting Paragraph Structure

Many paragraphs are structured like small thesis-and-support essays. A *topic sentence* introduces the subject and provides direction for its development, middle or body sentences support the main idea, and a concluding sentence gives a sense of closure. In a long paragraph the middle sentences may be further organized into subtopics, each introduced by a *subtopic sentence*.

TOPIC SENTENCE (introduces main idea):
SUBTOPIC SENTENCE (selects first part of main idea for development):

SUPPORTING SENTENCES (develop topic):

SUBTOPIC SENTENCE (selects second part of main idea for development):

SUPPORTING SENTENCES (develop subtopic):
CONCLUDING SENTENCE (sums up and completes idea):

[University life in the Middle Ages mixed monastic restrictions with sometimes laughable, sometimes shocking license.] [The list of *thou-shalt-not*'s was lengthy.] Students were forbidden to speak any language other than Latin—no "vulgar" tongues such as French or English. They were not allowed to wear "dissolute" secular clothes such as puffed sleeves, red stockings, or pointed shoes. They were strongly discouraged from playing "insolent" games with balls or bats or with dice. And their smallest offenses were reported by paid informers, appropriately called "wolves." [On the other hand, the penalty for offenses was often laughable while some tolerated, if not exactly encouraged, behavior seems little short of licentious.] The one officially sanctioned amusement at many universities was drinking. Bribery was a way of life, although some attempted to curb excesses by stipulating that fees commonly paid to "honor and console" examiners be spent for the good of the whole. A typical penalty for being late to dinner, speaking French, or beating a servant was four gallons of good wine, to be paid for by the offender but enjoyed with his classmates. [If contradictions stimulate intellectual ferment, the fermentation of medieval university life would have resulted in a particularly intoxicating brew.]

4b Writing Unified Paragraphs

Paragraphs demonstrate *unity of subject* when they focus on and develop a single idea. Introducing information on a different or loosely related topic destroys unity and confuses the reader, as in the first version of the following paragraph.

CONFUSING: College students of the 1980's approach education like a business—with a plan, sophisticated resources, and drive. Most enter college with a major and a timetable firmly in mind. Many

Writing Paragraphs 53

of their parents, on the other hand, experimented during the first two years at college and even then could not make up their minds about a major and settled for a general studies degree or did not finish a degree at all. They arrive at school with computers in their trunks, two years of high school data processing in their background, and a summer of interning in a bank or corporation behind them. Such single-minded purpose can be almost frightening to their professors, who were educated in the laid-back campus atmosphere of the sixties and seventies. And they work hard, competing with an intensity born of big dreams and hard times.

UNIFIED: College students of the 1980's approach education like a business—with a plan, sophisticated resources, and drive. Most enter college with a major and a timetable firmly in mind. They arrive at school with computers in their trunks, two years of high school data processing in their background, and a summer of interning in a bank or corporation behind them. And they work hard, competing with an intensity born of big dreams and hard times.

Usually a topic sentence establishes the focus and limits the subject matter of a paragraph. Often the topic sentence will come at the beginning of the paragraph, establishing the "little-essay" structure shown in the paragraph about medieval university life earlier in this chapter. However, topic sentences may also come at the end of a paragraph, particularly when you want to lead the reader carefully to a controversial conclusion.

Executives in hundreds of large and small businesses were asked to identify the major deficiency of recent college graduates employed in their firms. Eighty-two percent cited writing skills. Clear, correct prose in letters, proposals, memos, and reports is essential to success in today's business world. Consequently, the Curriculum Committee recommends that six hours of business and technical writing be added to the requirements for a BBA.

4c Writing Coherent Paragraphs

A paragraph *coheres* or holds together when the writer organizes it logically and connects sentences with linking devices such as pronoun reference, repeated words, transitional expressions, or parallel structures. A paragraph may be unified but incoherent, as in the following example.

INCOHERENT (ideas arranged illogically): The Leaning Tower of Pisa, besides being one of the architectural wonders of the world, is also inseparably connected to the history of physics because of Galileo's famous experiment with falling bodies. Two spheres that Galileo threw from the upper platform of the tower dropped side by side and hit the ground at almost the same moment, thus disproving, once and for all, the belief of his contemporaries that heavier bodies must

<table>
<tr><td>COHERENT
(ideas arranged logically):</td><td>fall faster than light ones. One of the spheres was heavy, made of cast iron, and one was lighter, made of wood—a large difference in weight. Galileo simultaneously released the two spheres. By this simple experiment, Galileo established the important fact that independent of their weight, all material bodies fall with exactly the same speed.

The Leaning Tower of Pisa, besides being one of the architectural wonders of the world, is also inseparably connected to the history of physics because of Galileo's famous experiment with falling bodies. From the upper platform of the tower, Galileo simultaneously released two spheres, a heavy one made of cast iron and a lighter one made of wood. In spite of a large difference in weight, both spheres dropped side by side and hit the ground at almost the same moment. By this simple experiment, Galileo established the important fact that independent of their weight, all material bodies fall with exactly the same speed. He thus disproved, once and for all, the belief of his contemporaries that heavier bodies must fall faster than light ones. (Adapted from George Gamow, *Matter, Earth, and Sky*)</td></tr>
</table>

(1) Using pronouns to achieve coherence

Exact pronoun references link sentences and help maintain a consistent focus or point of view. (You will learn more about pronouns in Chapters 20 and 21 and more about point of view in Writer's Casebook #8 and Chapter 15a.)

<table>
<tr><td>INCOHERENT
(shifting view, inexact pronoun reference):</td><td>"The Pueblo Indian lives on the roof of the world. They are the sons of Father Sun, and with the Indian religion daily help the father to go across the sky. This is done not only for Indian people, but for the whole world. If we Indians were to cease practicing religion, in ten years the sun would no longer rise. Then it would be night forever."</td></tr>
<tr><td>COHERENT
(consistent view, exact pronoun reference):</td><td>"We are a people who live on the roof of the world; we are the sons of Father Sun, and with our religion we daily help our father to go across the sky. We do this not only for ourselves, but for the whole world. If we were to cease practicing our religion, in ten years the sun would no longer rise. Then it would be night forever." (Ochwiay Biano, quoted in Carl Jung, "The Pueblo Indian")</td></tr>
</table>

(2) Using parallel structure to achieve coherence

Repeating the patterns of words, phrases, and sentences underscores the relationship of ideas and helps chart the reader's path through a complex idea or train of thought. (You will learn more about parallel structure in Chapter 14.)

<table>
<tr><td>WITHOUT PARALLEL STRUCTURE:</td><td>Einstein was the freest man I have known. By that I mean that, more than anyone else I have encountered, he was the master of his own destiny. If he had a God, it was the God of Spinoza. Revo-</td></tr>
</table>

Writing Paragraphs   55

lution was never his aim, as the overthrow of authority was never his prime motivation. He was not a rebel, since any authority but the one of reason seemed too ridiculous for him to waste effort fighting against. He had the freedom to ask scientific questions, and his genius led him to ask the right ones. Fame may have on occasion flattered him, but he was never deflected from his purpose by it. He was fearless of time and to an uncommon degree, he did not fear death. (Adapted from Abraham Pais, *Subtle Is the Lord*)

WITH PARALLEL STRUCTURE:
(1, 2 parallel sentences):

(3, 4 parallel phrases):
(5, 6 parallel clauses):
(7, 8 parallel phrases):

Einstein was the freest man I have known. By that I mean that, more than anyone else I have encountered, he was the master of his own destiny. If he had a God, it was the God of Spinoza. ¹Einstein was not a revolutionary, as the overthrow of authority was never his prime motivation. ²He was not a rebel, since any authority but the one of reason seemed too ridiculous to him to waste effort fighting against. He had ³the freedom to ask scientific questions, ⁴the genius to so often ask the right ones. ⁵Fame may on occasion have flattered him, but ⁶it never deflected him. He was ⁷fearless of time and, to an uncommon degree, ⁸fearless of death. (Corrected version, Abraham Pais, *Subtle Is the Lord*)

(3) Repeating key words to achieve coherence

Repeating key words keeps readers on track by recalling and emphasizing important points.

WITHOUT REPETITION:

I passed all the other courses that I took at my University, except botany. This was because all students in that course had to spend several hours a week in a laboratory looking through a microscope at plant cells—something I could never do. This used to enrage my instructor. He would wander around the laboratory pleased with the progress all the students were making in drawing the involved and, so I am told, interesting structure of flower cells, until he came to me. I would just be standing there. "I can't see anything," I would say. He would begin patiently enough, explaining how anybody can see through a microscope, but he would always end in a fury, claiming I was just pretending my inability. "It takes away from the beauty of flowers anyway," I used to tell him. "We are not concerned with beauty in this course," he would say, "but solely with what I may call the 'mechanics' of flars." And I would say again that I wasn't able to see.

WITH REPETITION:

I passed all the other courses that I took at my University, but I could never pass botany. This was because all botany students had to spend several hours a week in a laboratory looking through a microscope at plant cells, and I could never see through a microscope. I never once saw a cell through a microscope. This used to enrage my instructor. He would wander around the laboratory pleased with the progress all the students were making in drawing the involved and, so I am told, interesting structure of flower cells, until he came to me. I would just be standing there. "I can't see anything," I would say. He would begin patiently enough, explaining how anybody can see through a microscope, but he would always end up in a fury, claiming that I could "too" see through a microscope but just pretended I couldn't. "It takes away from the beauty of flowers anyway," I used to tell him. "We are not concerned with beauty in this course," he would say. "We are concerned solely with what I may call the 'mechanics' of flars." "Well," I'd say, "I can't see anything." (James Thurber, "University Days")

Notice how the repetitions of the can-see/can't-see theme exaggerate the struggle between professor and student to the point of absurdity and provoke laughter—the writer's purpose.

(4) Using transitional words and phrases to achieve coherence

Transitions tie ideas together and show relationships. Like road signs, they guide the direction of readers' thoughts, telling them to expect an additional idea, a contrast, an example, a cause, or a summary.

WITHOUT TRANSITIONS: Stress is the spice of life. Stress is associated with all types of activity. We could avoid most of it only by never doing anything. Who would enjoy a life of no runs, no hits, no errors? Certain types of activities have a curative effect. They actually help to keep the stress mechanism in good shape.

WITH TRANSITIONS: Stress is the spice of life. Since stress is associated with all types of activity, we could avoid most of it only by never doing anything. Who would enjoy a life of no runs, no hits, no errors? Besides—as we have said earlier—certain types of activities have a curative effect and actually help to keep the stress mechanism in good shape. (Hans Selye, *Stress Without Distress*)

Some common transitions follow:

Words that signal transitions in time: *first, second, third,* and so forth; *soon; before; after; then; next; meanwhile; at the same time; later; when*

Words that signal transitions in space: *in front of, in back of, beside, next to, to the left, to the right, forward, behind, on the other side, north, south, east, west*

Words that signal transitions in action or process: *and; again; next; also; besides; finally; moreover; in addition; first, second,* and so forth.

Words that signal transitions between ideas: *however, nevertheless, but, yet, on the contrary, instead, on the one hand/on the other hand, because, since, therefore, consequently, of course, although, for example, for instance*

(5) Achieving coherence among paragraphs

Methods used to link sentences within paragraphs may also be used to link paragraphs. For example, the following paragraphs are linked by a transition, a pronoun, parallel sentence structure, and a repeated word.

Their triumph was not the winning of a battle, for this battle seemingly was not won by anybody; to all appearances it was simply a stalemate that wrecked two armies. Yet victory was in it. After it had been fought—because it had been fought—history came to a turning point. Indecisive tactically, the battle shaped all the rest of the war: meant at the very least, that the war now must be fought to a finish. There could no longer be a hope for a peace without victory. The great issues that created the war were going to be settled, at no matter what terrible cost. This fight was decisive.

Yet at the moment it did not look decisive. It looked like a stand-off, and the morning after the battle two exhausted armies lay on the field staring blankly over the silent guns, as if they were appalled by what they had done to each other. . . . (Bruce Catton, *The Army of the Potomac*)

4d Writing Well-Developed Paragraphs

Writers develop paragraphs by using specific instances to support the generalities introduced in the topic or subtopic sentences. The developmental sentences should fulfill the promises made in the topic sentence and therefore help the reader to understand the writers' main ideas, share their special perspectives or knowledge, "see" what they see, or retrace the thought processes that led to their conclusions.

Leaving gaps in the information that pose rather than answer questions results in inadequate development. You can test your paragraphs for unanswered questions by using the journalist's questions—the five W's + How: Who? What? When? Where? Why? How? If the information elicited by a question is pertinent to the topic, add it to develop your paragraph more fully.

INADEQUATE DEVELOPMENT: Exams make my college life a living purgatory. I suffer before each test, I suffer during the test, and I suffer after the test. I long for the release of graduation—my translation to a heaven of no college exams.

Who? me Who makes me suffer? Dr. Ferrar, Dr. Bowmer, Dr. Wilson What? exams What exams? geology, history, English, essay, multiple choice, true/false What about exams? living purgatory—suffering, agony, wailing, gnashing of teeth When? now When? before, during, and after tests Where? college Where do I suffer? in classrooms, library, dorm room Why? trick questions, exercises in total recall, memorizing footnotes How? suffer before test as I cram, burn midnight oil, stuff my head with knowledge; suffer during test as I fight against the clock to get everything down and to uncover information buried in my mind; and suffer after the test as I relive it and wait for my grade

REVISED TO FILL IN GAPS: Exams make my college life a living purgatory. Dr. Ferrar tortures me in Western Civilization I with his weekly "exercise in total recall." Dr. Bowmer tricks and teases with true or false questions about Shakespeare's histories that are never totally true or totally false. And Dr. Wilson terrorizes me in geology with questions over footnotes, tables, and appendices, all the while threatening with the whip of his impossible scoring system that could leave me with a minus score—worse off than if I had not taken the exam at all. I suffer before each test as I agonize over preparations—outlining, reciting, reviewing, cramming. I suffer during each test as I race the clock to finish five pages of fill-in-the-blanks in an hour or to unload all I know about the fall of the Roman Empire and the rise of nationalism in an hour and fifteen minutes. I suffer after the test as I relive the experience in my night terrors and wait for my grade. Might prayer for release from the "sin" of being a student speed graduation and my translation to a heaven of no college exams?

4e Using Patterns of Development

Patterns evolve from the materials used to develop or support ideas and from the way those materials are arranged. Frequently, experienced writers will use more than one pattern in a paragraph, and usually they will follow patterns unconsciously while responding to the demands of content. However, beginning writers should master each pattern separately, then practice until choosing and using effective patterns is automatic.

(1) What happened? (Narration)

Narrative paragraphs tell a story. Events are presented in chronological order—the order in which they occurred—and are unified by the single idea of what happened. Narrative paragraphs may or may not have topic sentences.

Narrative with a topic sentence

No one was more surprised than Aunt Ellen when her much-planned-for family reunion turned out to be a success. She watched as the family greeted each other warily—Brett wondering if Dan had forgotten their fight over Uncle Alvie's will, Irene hoping Grandmother Bryant had forgiven her for winning the blue ribbon for pickles at the State Fair. By the time Aunt Ellen had set the table, Vicki and Bonnie Ann had remembered their first square dances in the barn on Uncle Frank's farm, and Sylvester and Jason were reliving pranks they had pulled on stuck-up Cousin Priscilla. The yeast rolls were coming out of the oven when the sounds of Grandpa Lewis's deep laughter and Ruth's high-pitched titter reached the kitchen. With a sigh of relief, Aunt Ellen called the now happily reunited family to her feast, smiling secretly as they asked one another, "Why don't we do this more often?"

(2) What does it look like? (Description)

Descriptive paragraphs use details and comparisons to create word pictures. The more exact the details and comparisons and the more careful the arrangement of materials, the clearer the pictures. The paragraph below uses both physical details and comparisons to common objects to picture an immense desert landscape; the topic sentence, placed at the end of the paragraph, underscores the focus of the description—the sky.

Description
   The ride back to Santa Fe was something under four hundred miles. The weather alternated between blinding sand-storms and brilliant sunlight. The sky was as full of motion and change as the desert beneath it was monotonous and still—and there was so much sky, more than at sea, more than anywhere else in the world. The plain was there, under one's feet, but what one saw when one looked about was that brilliant blue world of stinging air and moving cloud. Even the mountains were mere ant-hills under it. Elsewhere the sky is the roof of the world; but here the earth was the floor of the sky. The landscape one longed for when one was far away, the thing all about one, the world one actually lived in, was the sky, the sky. (Willa Cather, *Death Comes for the Archbishop*)

(3) What are some typical cases or examples of it? (Exemplification)

An example is a specific instance, case, or model that illustrates, represents, or shows; supporting with examples clarifies a general statement and makes it seem more convincing. The questions in the following paragraph are all examples of the "fundamental life issues" mentioned in the topic sentence.

Exemplification
   Most of us stop at times—sometimes because of startling events, often out of sheer curiosity—and think seriously about fundamental life issues: What is life and why am I here? What is the place of life in this great universe? Is the universe friendly or unfriendly? Do things operate by chance or through sheer mechanism, or is there some plan or purpose or intelligence at the heart of things? Is my life controlled by outside forces or do I have a determining or even a partial degree of control? Why do men [and women] struggle and strive for their rights, for justice, for better things in the future? What do concepts like "right" and "justice" mean, and what are the marks of a good society? (Harold H. Titus, *Living Issues in Philosophy*)

(4) How did—or does—it happen? (Process)

Paragraphs developed by analyzing a process show how something works or how to do something. Usually organized in chronological or spatial order, they may fully describe stages of the process or briefly itemize instructions.

Process
   Planting a bare-root rose bush begins with selecting a suitable location—away from trees and shade; in light, loamy soil where the bush's roots can breathe and spread out. Then you dig. First, hollow out a large hole at least two feet across and three feet deep. Put one or two shovels of steer manure in the bottom of the hole and cover with a layer of soil. The fertilizer will give your rose's roots something to reach for, while the soil will keep them from being burned. Next fill the hole from your garden hose and let the rose's roots soak while the water seeps slowly into the ground. When the hole is empty and while the soil is still wet and sticky, build a mound of earth at the

center of the hole and set the rose on top of the mound. Firmly cover the bush's roots, but not the stem, with soil, tapping the earth with your hands and feet to eliminate air pockets. Water once again, and keep watering regularly for the next three months. You will be rewarded with tall, waxy canes; glossy leaves; and velvety, perfumed roses—breathtaking in the bud or in full bloom. (student)

(5) What caused it? What are its effects? (Cause and effect)

While process paragraphs explore *how* events happen, cause-and-effect paragraphs explore *why* they happen and what happens because of them. Usually a paragraph will focus on either the causes of an effect or the effects of a cause.

Causes of an Effect

Educational opportunities are closed for major segments of the society. Minority, lower-class, and female students face serious disadvantages: the teachers' attitudes, the counseling system, the tracking system, and the testing system. And all students must put up with irrelevant curricula that stifle the creative possibilities children bring to school and reinforce the inequities of social stratification that exist in the larger society. Access to higher education—important for occupational and social advancement—is sharply limited by social background. Students whose parents are well-educated and financially successful and who go to good high schools with good students are likely to be more successful academically than less advantaged students of comparable ability. Finally, the whole educational experience is systematically stacked against women students because a multitude of barriers stand in their way. (J. Victor Baldridge, *Sociology: A Critical Approach to Power, Conflict, and Change*)

Effects of a Cause

When the mill closed, the inhabitants of this small northwestern town thought the end of the world had come. For years the mill had been one of life's certainties. The high-pitched buzz of the saws cutting lumber and the pungent smells of wigwam burners incinerating mountains of sawdust had ruled the senses as surely as the mill itself ruled the pace of life. But then the impossible happened. The saws were still and the burners cold. The Safeway store closed first and then the Penney's branch. McDonald's dropped its plan for a new Golden Arches, and the city council rejected the mayor's proposal for a new traffic light. Within six months there were potholes in Main Street. Within a year grass grew between the cracks in the sidewalks, and wildflowers covered the cinders along the tracks of the town's railroad spur. (student)

(6) How is it like other things? How is it different? (Comparison and contrast)

When there are grounds for comparison between two subjects, development may emphasize similarities or differences or both. Grounds exist when subjects are of the same kind or share comparable parts, characteristics, or qualities. For example, you might meaningfully compare fast food with gourmet cuisine on the basis of cost, ingredients, diners, or calories, but you could not compare Persian carpets with redwoods or ice cream with pepper unless you can find a common ground to make the comparison meaningful.

When a paragraph is long or complex, the comparison may be organized point by point. In the following paragraph, Suzanne Britt Jordan contrasts fat and thin people on the basis of personality, food, and thought processes.

Comparison
> Some people say the business about the jolly fat person is a myth, that all of us chubbies are neurotic, sick, sad people. I disagree. Fat people may not be chortling all day long, but they're a hell of lot *nicer* than the wizened and shriveled. Thin people turn surly, mean and hard at a young age because they never learn the value of a hot-fudge sundae for easing tension. Thin people don't like gooey soft things because they themselves are neither gooey nor soft. They are crunchy and dull, like carrots. They go straight to the heart of the matter while fat people let things stay blurry and hazy and vague, the way things actually are. Thin people want to face the truth. Fat people know there is no truth. One of my thin friends is always staring at complex, unsolvable problems and saying, "The key thing is . . ." Fat people never say that. They know there isn't any such thing as the key thing about anything. Thin people believe in logic. Fat people see all sides. The sides fat people see are rounded blobs, usually gray, always nebulous and truly not worth worrying about. But the thin person persists. "If you consume more calories than you burn," says one of my thin friends, "you will gain weight. It's that simple." Fat people always grin when they hear statements like that. They know better. (Susanne Britt Jordan, "That Lean and Hungry Look")

Simple comparisons may be organized by subject. The first part of the paragraph develops one subject; the second part, the other.

Comparison
> Both sexes aspire to a physical ideal, but what is expected of boys and what is expected of girls involves a very different moral relation to the self. Boys are encouraged to *develop* their bodies, to regard the body as an instrument to be improved. They invent their masculine selves largely through exercise and sport, which harden the body and strengthen competitive feelings; clothes are only secondary help in making their bodies attractive. Girls are not particularly encouraged to develop their bodies through any activity, strenuous or not; and physical strength and endurance are hardly valued at all. The invention of the feminine self proceeds mainly through clothes and other signs that testify to the very effort of girls to look attractive, to their commitment to please. (Susan Sontag, "The Double Standard of Aging")

(7) What are its parts? (Division) Into what categories can its parts be arranged? (Classification)

When you analyze by *division*, you divide a single item into its component parts. When you analyze by *classification*, you classify or group several items by type, characteristics, or qualities.

Division
Baghdad when I first came to know it twenty years ago was a city with multiple identities. Surviving only in ruins and memories lingered Biblical Baghdad with its ghosts of Abraham, the Assyrians, and the Tower of Babel. In its place on one hand was dusty monotony, a city of sand-colored structures which if they had any charms at all, hid them in shady courtyards behind high clay walls. And on the other hand was an exotic Baghdad of labyrinthine, gaily colored bazaars—the souks—where coppersmiths and spice traders, tailors, shoemakers, cloth and carpet merchants, money changers and gold- and silversmiths offered their goods and services in narrow, covered alleys, haggling patiently, joking, cursing. (Adapted from Kurt Lanz, *Around the World with Chemistry*)

Classification
There are three types of psychologists involved in funded projects at the university. Psychologist Type A is a clinical psychologist. A works with people who have "psychological problems"—a student who complains that she is unable to study and feels depressed and lethargic or a worker who believes there is a widespread plot against him. Psychologist Type B is a physiological psychologist. B does not counsel patients but spends hours working in a laboratory, surrounded by complex and expensive pieces of equipment. B studies rats to understand more about how the brain controls and influences behavior and feelings. Psychologist Type C works with chimpanzees. C is trying to teach the chimpanzee to communicate with humans and appears to be succeeding. The chimpanzee not only communicates a fair number of its basic needs and wants to Psychologist C, but it also occasionally comments on matters in which it appears to be interested. (Adapted from John M. Darley et al., *Psychology*)

(8) What is it? (Definition)

To explain what a term means you begin with a simple, dictionary definition, identifying the class or group of things to which the item belongs and giving any distinguishing characteristics.

A googol is a finite number: 1 followed by a hundred zeros.

An *extended definition* probes further for meaning by employing other methods of development. The following paragraph uses narration, contrast, and example to extend the definition of *googol*.

Definition
Words of wisdom are spoken by children at least as often as by scientists. The name "googol" was invented by a child (Dr. Kasner's nine-year-old nephew) who was asked to think up a name for a very big number, namely, 1 with a hundred zeros after it. He was very certain that this number was not infinite, and therefore equally certain that it had to have a name. At the same time that he suggested "googol" he gave a name for a still larger number: "Googolplex." A googolplex is much larger than a googol, but is still finite, as the inventor of the name was quick to point out. It was first suggested that a googolplex should be 1, followed by writing zeros until you got tired. This is

a description of what would happen if one actually tried to write a googolplex, but different people get tired at different times and it would never do to have Carnera a better mathematician than Dr. Einstein, simply because he had more endurance. The googolplex then, is a specific finite number, with so many zeros after the 1 that the number of zeros is a googol. A googolplex is much bigger than a googol, much bigger even than a googol times a googol. A googol times a googol would be 1 with 200 zeros, whereas a googolplex is 1 with a googol of zeros. You will get some idea of the size of this very large but finite number from the fact that there would not be enough room to write it, if you went to the farthest star, touring all the nebulae and putting down zeros every inch of the way. (Edward Kasner and James R. Newman, "New Names for Old")

4f   Writing Special Kinds of Paragraphs

In addition to paragraphs that develop ideas, you will write paragraphs that introduce or conclude essays and paragraphs that provide transitions between ideas.

(1)   Writing introductions

An introductory paragraph should both acquire an audience for the essay—make potential readers want to see what you have to say—and prepare the audience for what follows—show your audience what you will write about. Often an introduction will include your essay's thesis statement.

Acquiring an audience may be automatic—the result of a simple, straightforward statement of a universally appealing subject, such as money or sex. But most of the time you will need to stimulate interest by providing an "interest catcher" that leads into your thesis. The readers' interest may be caught by introducing a *question* that they would like to see answered, a *quotation* or literary reference that fits your subject, a *definition* of a key term, an insightful *comparison*, an extreme or outrageous *opinion*, *images* or word pictures that help the readers visualize the subject, *anecdotes* that amuse or delight, or *background* information that highlights the importance of the subject. Here are some examples of paragraphs using these techniques.

Definition

Hypothermia is one of the leading killers of outdoorsmen, yet a surprising number of people know nothing about it. Hypothermia occurs when the body loses heat faster than it can be replaced. It is not, however, limited to cold weather situations. Hypothermia can occur even in mild climates: You may be drenched from a rain in 50 degree weather and be unable to retain body heat, or on a warm day you may lose body heat rapidly while standing in swimming trunks on a windswept ridge. [Anywhere you encounter wind, cold or wetness, you can encounter hypothermia.] Thesis statement (Anthony J. Acecrano, *The Outdoorsman's Emergency Manual*)

Images

I love candles and candlelight. The orange glow of a candle's flame changes a gloomy corner into a romantic haven, a so-so meal into a special dinner, and a lop-sided lump of dough and frosting into a birthday cake. Long, tapered candles in silver candelabra create an atmosphere of elegance, while giant, pine-scented candles in holly wreaths add cheerful notes to holiday celebrations. [Making your own candles to fit the mood and occasion is as easy as following these basic steps.] <u>Thesis statement</u>

Opinion and Quotation of Literary Reference

It would be nice if, in life, one didn't have to question the motives and behaviors of others, but [years of chess have taught me to be wary of the other fellow.] <u>Thesis statement</u> He always means well, by which I mean he *means* to win, and when he does, it is the wise loser who will study why. For, as Ovid said, it is allowable to learn from an enemy (even if he is an enemy only for the duration of the game). (Jerry Sohl, *Underhanded Chess*)

Background

It has long been known in maritime circles that many ships have disappeared in the area between Bermuda, Florida, and Puerto Rico. Some of the past disappearances may have contributed to the legend of the "Sea of Lost Ships" or the "Ships' Graveyard," located in the Sargossa Sea, part of which lies within the Triangle. Records concerning disappearing ships seem to indicate disappearances with increasing frequency since the 1860's possibly because of more detailed reporting. But it was some months after World War II that a startling incident occurred, suggesting that planes flying over the area could vanish from the sky for perhaps the same reason that ships had been vanishing from the sea. [This was the incident that gave the Bermuda Triangle its name.] <u>Thesis statement</u> (Charles Berlitz, *The Bermuda Triangle*)

Anecdote

"Ms. Elmhorst," Mr. Cobley said crisply, "I must speak with you." Until now I had thought I was performing splendidly as an American exchange teacher in a British school. As I watched my fourth-year students file out of class for the day, I was troubled by my supervising teacher's tone. The purpose of the exchange was to share the visiting teacher's culture with the host students; however, as Mr. Cobley explained, I had shared something I had not intended. "When you illustrated your two main points and held up two fingers—the middle and the index—with the back of your hand toward the students . . . well . . ." Here even this cool Briton hesitated. "That gives our students the same impression you would give your American students if you held up your single middle finger to emphasize one important point." Unintentionally I had made an obscene gesture to these fourth graders, and [in the process I had learned the importance of internationalizing my body language]. <u>Thesis statement</u> (Jeannie Elmhorst)

Questions and Comparison

[Algebra is just a variety of arithmetic.] <u>Thesis statement</u> Does that startle you? Do you find it hard to believe? Perhaps so, because the way most of us go through our schooling, arithmetic seems an "easy" subject taught in the lower grades, and algebra is a "hard" subject taught in the higher grades. What's more, arithmetic deals with good, honest numbers, while algebra seems to be made up of all sorts of confusing x's and y's. But I still say there's practically no difference between them and I will try to prove it to you. (Isaac Asimov, *Realm of Algebra*)

(2) Writing conclusions

A strong conclusion brings your essay full circle. While the introduction ushers readers into the special world of your essay, the conclusion ushers them out and back to their own larger worlds, often with some new idea, information, or insight. It reinforces the main idea, then reviews the main points, comments on results, or suggests future action or developments.

The conclusion to Margaret Halsey's essay about the "me generation," "What's Wrong with 'Me, Me, Me,'" reinforces her major idea that the cult of "me" is based on false ideas and then uses a quotation to underscore a final judgment.

> The current glorification of self-love will turn out in the end to be a no-win proposition, because in questions of personality or "identity," what counts is not who you are, but what you do. "By their fruits, ye shall know them." And by their fruits, they shall know themselves.

In *The Stress of Life*, Dr. Hans Selye concludes a discussion of stress with a summary of key ideas.

> In a nutshell, the response to stress has a tripartite mechanism, consisting of: (1) the direct effect of the stressor upon the body; (2) internal responses which stimulate tissue defense or help to destroy damaging substances; and (3) internal responses which cause tissue surrender by inhibiting unnecessary or excessive defense. Resistance and adaptation depend on a proper balance of these three factors.

And Vine Deloria ends her essay "Strangers on a Continent: An American Indian's View of America" with warnings for the future.

> I want to leave you with one message. You can slip and slide all you want on definitions, but you had better take a very close look, a very honest look, at your religion, your political system, the way you treat the immigrant, the way you treat the land. The day is coming when your definitions are going to fall apart. The longer we avoid social problems by redefinition, the longer the problems will continue to get worse and worse. As I look at America today, I feel that we are bringing on the apocalypse, that we are the chief agents of destruction. I see no way to stop it.

(3) Writing transitional paragraphs

Usually short, sometimes no more than a single sentence, transitional paragraphs signal the movement from one idea to the next. Instead of developing new material, these paragraphs reinforce ideas previously developed and prepare the reader for the information that will follow. They may provide a brief summary of preceding paragraphs, repeat a key idea, or ask questions that will be answered in succeeding paragraphs.

In *Realm of Algebra* Isaac Asimov uses two transitional paragraphs—a single-sentence comment and a short paragraph recalling an earlier statement—to help create a bridge between something his readers consider simple—arithmetic—and something they consider difficult—algebra.

? + 5 = 8

Now would you be surprised to know that we are already talking algebra? Well, we are. As soon as we begin using a symbol for an unknown quantity, we are in the realm of algebra. Most arithmetic books, even in the very early grades, start using question marks as I have been doing, and they're teaching algebra when they do so.

But this is just arithmetic, you may be thinking.

Exactly! And that is what I said at the start. Algebra is arithmetic, only broader and better, as you will see as you continue reading the book.

It teaches a way of handling symbols that is so useful in considering the world about us that all of modern science is based on it. Scientists couldn't discuss the things that go on about us unless they could use symbols. And even after they've done that, they couldn't handle the symbols properly unless they knew the rules that will be worked out in this book.

Writing Paragraphs

Unifying Paragraphs   Exercise 4–1

NAME _____ DATE _____

Circle the number of any sentence that does not belong in the following paragraphs. Then rewrite the paragraphs, maintaining unity of subject. Add, delete, or alter as necessary to write a complete, unified paragraph.

[1] My first day at Midstate University nearly made me quit school. [2] First, there were no spaces left in B parking lot, the only lot for which I had a sticker, and I wasted twenty-five minutes hunting for a metered space. [3] Fortunately, I did find a two-hour meter in a shady space where I didn't have to worry about my new paint job. [4] Then I pounded seemingly endless miles of concrete looking for my classes only to find that two had been moved and one canceled. [5] The only bright spot in my entire morning was the good-looking hunk who picked up my books when I dropped them for the sixth time. [6] Lunch brought a new low. [7] The lines at the Student Union lunch counter were so long that by the time I got my sandwich, it was time for class again. [8] But I did meet two girls from my old high school and made a date to see them later in the afternoon. [9] I was so relieved not to be alone any longer. [10] My afternoon chemistry class was a disaster. [11] The professor said that twenty percent of us would receive D's and F's. [12] I was glad, though, that he was an interesting lecturer. [13] Finally, I was five minutes late on my third trip to feed the parking meter and got a two-dollar ticket for my trouble. [14] Overall, the day was better than I expected.

Revision:

[1] On exam morning our formerly cheerful classroom appeared ominously like a hospital operating room. [2] The mellow, freshly painted walls had undergone a transformation in the night and now looked stark, glaring, and antiseptic. [3] The floor, already littered with papers and coffee cups, looked untidy, and I saw a cockroach scuttle away from a particularly unappetizing pile. [4] Along the south wall mesh screens, akin to prison bars, marred the sunlight. [5] Rows of chairs staggered in haphazard order around the prison-bare walls. [6] At one side of the room the chalkboard had been freshly scrubbed, and clean, white letters marked the times when the exam would

© 1986 by CBS College Publishing. All rights reserved.

begin and end. ⁷ In front of the chalkboard a long, white operating table was stacked with neat columns of white test pages and blue examination booklets—the instruments for extracting information from our brains. ⁸ Appropriately, I did not feel sick.

Revision:

Score _____

Writing Paragraphs   **69**

Writing Topic Sentences Exercise 4–2

NAME _____ DATE _____

Write topic sentences for the following short paragraphs in the spaces provided. If no topic sentence is necessary, write NTS in the blank space.

EXAMPLE: *The underground newspaper favors yellow journalism.*

Sensational headlines shout provocatively from the front page. Exposés, rumors, and gossip fill the stories. Advertisements for shocking products and amusements startle and occasionally captivate the reader.

1. _____

I leave work at 12:05 and sprint to the bus stop on the corner of Girard and Central. If the bus is on time, I bolt through the doors and jam my pass in the driver's face, hoping she will not dawdle over making change or taking directions from the other passengers. The fifteen-minute ride to the campus tries my patience as the bus stops and starts, picking up and letting off passengers. By the time we reach my stop, I am a nervous wreck, sorely in need of some exertion as I race to reach my 12:30 class on time.

2. _____

While full-time students are doing homework or relaxing, the working students are punching a time clock and logging in hours on the job. Late at night they do their homework, gulping down gallons of coffee to try to stay awake, and they often feel fragmented, torn between the demands of school and the equally important demands of the job. Yet the working students have advantages too. Often they know what they want and how to get it. Not for them are the soul-searching questions of the career counselor or the academic advisor, urging reluctant students to make up their minds about a minor. Nor do they have the worry, never far from the jobless students' minds, of finding a job after graduation. For the working students the challenge of getting an education may be greater, but the rewards are more tangible and more immediate.

3. An irregular expanse of rutted dirt and half-buried gravel, the south parking lot borders Industrial Park and straddles Corporation Drive. On wet mornings the lot is a bog of puddles. On dry, windy afternoons it rises in a choking, brown cloud and attacks the landscaping, burying green blades beneath miniature sand dunes. _____

_____

4. _____

Listen for key points in the meeting and summarize them. Do not try to write down every speaker's sentences verbatim, or you may miss important ideas or decisions while trying to remember unimportant words. If a presenter uses charts or makes notes on the chalkboard, write down highlighted information. Finally, listen for actions—votes taken or resolutions passed. Whatever the discussion, the outcomes of a meeting should be emphasized in your minutes.

© 1986 by CBS College Publishing. All rights reserved.

5.   On Tuesday Antonio has an appointment with the dentist after school. On Wednesday Monica goes to her ballet lesson at 2:30 and then has a 4-H meeting at the Fairgrounds at 4:00. Thursday morning brings my Spanish midterm at San Jose Community College, and Teresa, my youngest, sees her pediatrician in the afternoon. ___

Score _____

Writing Unified Paragraphs Exercise 4–3

NAME _____ DATE _____

Select appropriate details from the lists provided and write unified paragraphs to support the topic sentences. Add details if necessary.

Supporting Details

one eye on the clock	clock hands move swiftly
intense concentration	pen stumbles over page, spattering ink
fingers fly	relaxed breathing
slow motion of a nightmare	essay plan like race plan
mind wanders	distractions from other students
walking through the essay parts	sprint to finish conclusion
cramped muscles in hand	instructor at the finish line, urging us on

Topic Sentence: Writing an in-class essay is like running a race.

Supporting Details

finding babysitters	promotion
IRS audit	morning traffic
unexpected inheritance	balancing budgets
car repairs	raise in pay
coffee breaks	laid-back atmosphere
happy-go-lucky boss	sales meetings
vacations	surprise parties
deadlines at work and at school	sleep
examinations	

Topic Sentence: Success in life often depends upon coping with pressures.

© 1986 by CBS College Publishing. All rights reserved.

Supporting Details

shoppers charging down aisles
carts used as battering rams
assault on vegetables
waiting patiently in line
video game diversions for kids
pushing and shoving
scowls
browsing at the dairy counter

fighting over last package of porkchops
race to the check-out stand
tug-of-war over salami
courteous smiles
barked-out orders
watching someone go through the nine-item line with more than nine items

Topic Sentence: The supermarket at 6 P.M. is a battleground.

Score _____

Writing Paragraphs 73

Identifying Methods of Coherence Exercise 4–4

NAME _____ DATE _____

Identify the method or methods used to achieve coherence in each of the following paragraphs. Underline repeated words, transitions, and pronoun references. Bracket parallel structures.

> EXAMPLE: One day there came to the emperor's capital two clever rogues who declared that they were weavers. They claimed to weave a magic cloth of exceeding beauty and virtue. Their cloth, they vowed, would delight the eye and honor the wearer but it would also expose corrupt bureaucrats, for only those worthy of esteem and fit for office would be able to see the extraordinary clothes made from this extraordinary cloth. (Hans Christian Anderson, "The Emperor's New Clothes")

Method(s) _pronoun reference, repetition_____

1. Paradoxically, we tend to discover what we as individuals have to say by talking with others. Here, in the give-and-take of discussion we see our experiences in larger contexts: what seemed idiosyncratic or unimportant before now illuminates a general truth; what seemed obvious must now be defended; what seemed inexplicable now begins to make sense. Ideas come out of the dialogue we sustain with others and with ourselves. Without these dialogues, thoughts run dry and judgment falters. (Mina P. Shaughnessy, *Errors and Expectations*)

Method(s) _____

2. Science, more than anything else, was Einstein's life, his devotion, his refuge, and his source of detachment. In order to understand the man, it is necessary to follow his scientific ways of thinking and doing. But that is not sufficient. He was also a gifted stylist of the German language, a lover of music, a student of philosophy. He was deeply concerned about the human condition. (In his later years, he used to refer to his daily reading of *The New York Times* as his adrenaline treatment.) He was a husband, a father, a stepfather. He was a Jew. And he is a legend. (Abraham Pais, *Subtle Is the Lord*)

Method(s) _____

3. She took some of the clay that had started to be a big pot and thumped out a tortilla of it between her palms. Then she put the clay down in the base of the old bowl, which she was using as a form, and began to spin out a coil of clay for the sides. When the coil was long enough to go around the edges of the tortilla, she flattened it a little by slapping it with her palms. Next she took the flattened coil, tipped it on edge, and shaped it around the base of her jar, smoothing the joint with moistened fingers. Again and again she made more coils, one at a time, and built up the sides of the vessel until it was a deep bowl. (Adapted from Alice Marriott, *Maria: The Potter of San Ildefonso*)

Method(s) _____

4. Good and evil we know in the field of this world grow up together almost inseparably; and the knowledge of good is so involved and interwoven with the knowledge of evil, and in so many cunning resemblances hardly to be discerned, that those confused seeds which were imposed on Psyche as an incessant labor to cull out and

© 1986 by CBS College Publishing. All rights reserved.

sort asunder, were not more intermixed. It was from out the rind of one apple tasted, that the knowledge of good and evil, as two twins cleaving together, leaped forth into the world. And, perhaps this is that doom which Adam fell into of knowing good and evil, that is to say of knowing good by evil. (John Milton, *Aeropagitica*)

Method(s) _____

5. I decline to accept the end of man. It is easy enough to say that man is immortal simply because he will endure: that when the last ding-dong of doom has clanged and faded from the last worthless rock hanging tideless in the last red and dying evening, that even then there will still be one more sound: that of his puny inexhaustible voice, still talking. I refuse to accept this: I believe that man will not merely endure: he will prevail. He is immortal, not because he alone among creatures has an inexhaustible voice, but because he has a soul, a spirit capable of compassion and sacrifice and endurance. (William Faulkner, "On Accepting the Nobel Prize for Literature")

Method(s): _____

Score _____

Writing Paragraphs

Rewriting for Coherence Exercise 4–5

NAME _____ DATE _____

Rewrite the following incoherent paragraph to make it coherent. Pay attention to both sense (what the words mean) and sound (the smooth flow and pleasing arrangement of words). Delete details or alter sentences as necessary.

It brought to an end the brilliant and devastating career of Napoleon Bonaparte. The Battle of Waterloo was fought on June 18, 1815, twelve miles south of Brussels. But before that Napoleon had escaped from exile on the island of Elba following his earlier abdication in 1814. He escaped on March 1, 1815. His escape shocked the allies who had gathered in Austria for the Congress of Vienna to celebrate Napoleon's defeat and do diplomatic battle over carving up his empire. His second reign had lasted a Hundred Days and came to an end at Waterloo. The French rallied once again to his cause raising a striking force of 125,000 men, 70,000 of whom were veterans. Napoleon pursued his successor Louis XVIII into Belgium, hoping for a decisive victory before the allied armies, disbanded by his earlier defeat, could reassemble in full force. But he underestimated the deceptively unimpressive British commander, Wellington. He was outmaneuvered and outfought in a bloody battle that left a third of his troops dead and added a new expression to the English language: he met his Waterloo.

Score _____

© 1986 by CBS College Publishing. All rights reserved.

Writing Unified and Coherent Paragraphs   Exercise 4–6

NAME _____ DATE _____

Select sentences from the scrambled lists to compose unified, coherent paragraphs. Alter or delete sentences as needed.

    EXAMPLE: a. Without the stress of challenge and accomplishment, some retirees literally die of boredom.
                    b. We all need a little stress in our lives.
                    c. "Stress," according to Hans Selye, "is the spice of life."
                    d. We could all use some regular exercise too.
                    e. Stress from competition and difficulties in our careers can spur us on to greater accomplishments, causing many to realize their potential.

"Stress," according to Hans Selye, "is the spice of life." Without the stress of challenge and accomplishment, some retirees literally die of boredom. Without the stress of competition and difficulties in their careers, spurring them on to greater accomplishments, many workers would never realize their potential. We all need a little stress in our lives.

1. a. Should the work of kindergarten tots be graded A–F?
   b. When to grade and how much to grade pose dilemmas for many teachers.
   c. To some, grades may intimidate, impeding progress and creating learning blocks.
   d. Should children's creative work be evaluated and pigeonholed with a grade?
   e. To some, a grade may be a goal to strive for.
   f. College professors also agonize over assigning grades to students.
   g. Finding a balance between threat and challenge that will work for every child may be impossible.
   h. For some teachers grading is natural and easy.

2. a. Borrowings from French are so extensive that English-speakers can recognize literally thousands of French words without having studied the language.
   b. English should probably be called Franglish.
   c. English has also borrowed extensively from dozens of other languages.
   d. The languages began to mix in earnest after the Norman invasion of England.
   e. The proximity of France and England led inevitably to the exchange of ideas and words.
   f. In every age English-speakers have tasted, liked, and devoured French words literally by the mouthful.
   g. Borrowings from French include *lieutenant, beast, sabotage, camouflage, toilet,* and *à la mode.*

h. Borrowings from other languages include *exit, rodeo, soprano, blitz, kosher,* and *hula*.

3. a. College courses are now being offered on PBS television stations.
   b. The students can usually call their professor on a watts line during conference hours.
   c. Students watch weekly lectures, then send homework to their professors by mail.
   d. Credit for experience is another nontraditional way to earn a college degree.
   e. Exams are conducted and proctored on campus or at designated schools.
   f. Many students are now attending weekend colleges.

Evaluating Paragraph Development   Exercise 4-7

NAME _____ DATE _____

Identify the method or methods used in the development of each of the following short paragraphs. Evaluate the effectiveness of the development and, if necessary, make suggestions for improvement.

> EXAMPLE: Domesticated for nearly a thousand years, goldfish are still the most popular aquarium fish. The common variety, the comet, swims in countless home and school tanks. Exotic varieties such as the Veiltail Oranda challenge the fancier's pocketbook and skill.

Method(s) _*examples*_   Evaluation _*thin development/needs more examples or details*_

1.   A popular novel is often a literary hybrid. It crosses the proven techniques of classic literature with the proven plots of fairy tales. Strains of exoticism, sensationalism, and sensualism are added from the entertainment world, and the result is that hardy animal, the best seller.

Method(s) _____ Evaluation _____

2.   Math anxiety afflicts people of every age and every profession. First-grader René Anderson cries and trembles when asked to do sums. High school junior Ron Elac sits nervously in the back row, then ducks out as the teacher turns to the chalkboard to work on a problem with the x's and y's he cannot understand. Lawrence Carver, successful attorney and respected community leader, leaves balancing his checkbook to his accountant and turns over all tax cases to his partner. Monica Baca, talented administrator and holder of a BBA in office management, refuses a promotion when she learns it will add payroll computations to her duties. The disease is out of control and threatening the careers and well-being of literally millions.

Method(s) _____ Evaluation _____

3.   Math anxiety is a learning disease. Communicable and virulent, it may be caught in a classroom from teachers who are infected or who make mathematics seem mysterious, incomprehensible, and somehow threatening. It may be caught from friends who have tried and failed to understand the intricacies of fractions or factoring. Or it may be inherited from parents who are intimidated by their checkbooks or by IRS forms. The symptoms are easy to recognize—heavy dependence on a calculator, nervous reactions to new concepts, inability to recall information or to do simple computations on an exam. The cure takes slow, persistent effort; the willingness to make

Writing Paragraphs   **79**

mistakes; the patience to work through problems; and the determination to overcome all obstacles.

Method(s) _____   Evaluation _____

4.   On Monday I saw an accident take place on the freeway. It happened when I was on my way to work at 7:30. Two cars, a red Volkswagen Rabbit and a blue Toyota pickup, tried to change lanes at the same time. The Toyota collided with the right rear fender of the Rabbit, sending both cars spinning in front of oncoming traffic. I put on my brakes and just narrowly missed joining the pile-up.

Method(s) _____   Evaluation _____
                                             _____

5.   The atmosphere on the typical college campus has changed dramatically during the past twenty years. In the sixties discontent and unrest charged the air inside and outside the classroom. Then picket lines, rallies, and National Guardsmen were part of the campus scene. Now twenty years later campuses are quiet. Instead of picket lines there are lines at the financial aid windows. There is no time for rallies or need for National Guardsmen as students struggle with the problems of personal rather than national survival.

Method(s) _____   Evaluation _____
                                             _____

                                                          Score _____

© 1986 by CBS College Publishing. All rights reserved.

Developing by Patterns Exercise 4–8

NAME _____ DATE _____

Use the pattern listed in parentheses to develop the topic sentence. Revise or complete the topic sentences, as necessary, to match your own interests, knowledge, or experience.

> EXAMPLE: Topic Sentence: SQ3R outlines an effective "attack plan" for studying textbooks. (process)
>
> Development: *First, survey (S) the material to find out what the assignment is about. Then make a list of questions (Q) to be answered as you read. Next, read (1R) the assignment carefully, making notes and answering the questions you posed. When you finish reading, close the book and recall (2R) as much as you can remember of the information. Finally, review (3R) the assignment, paying special attention to any points that you had trouble remembering.*

1. Topic Sentence: For me, earning a degree is the beginning rather than the end of a dream. (definition)
   Development:

2. Topic Sentence: My two bosses both get things done, but one moves deliberately through her carefully organized world while the other works best in a continuing state of crisis and chaos. (comparison/contrast)
   Development:

3. Topic Sentence: Planning a party requires both a method and an instinct for fun.
   Development:

Writing Paragraphs 81

4. Topic Sentence: Joggers can be divided into several distinct groups.
   Development:

5. Topic Sentence: The best toys are those that stimulate imaginative play. (exemplification)
   Development:

Score _____

© 1986 by CBS College Publishing. All rights reserved.

Evaluating Introductions   Exercise 4–9

NAME _____ DATE _____

Rate the following introductions as effective or ineffective. Explain your answers.

> EXAMPLE: In this paper I will talk about my feelings about a subject I consider important. I will begin by discussing the subject; then explain how I once felt about it; then show how I changed my opinion; and finally, show what I feel now.
>
> Comment *ineffective/There is nothing to interest the reader and no statement of an actual subject.*

1. Susan hurried into class early, a dozen test booklets in one hand and a fistful of pens in the other. She chose her seat carefully—avoiding a place near the door where she would be disturbed by students' coming and going. She tried out one desk, then rejected it because of a glare from the window. She tried out another and settled in, spreading out her papers and putting the extra pens beneath the seat, where they could be grasped easily. She was ready for the biggest exam of her academic life.

Comment _____

2. Beethoven's Eroica symphony is startlingly different from his early music. It is mature, personal, almost spiritual.

Comment _____

3. What is a black hole? What colors are the stars? Is there life on Mars? How long will our sun continue to shine? These questions are all answered in an exciting new book called *Stargazing* by Hans Conrad.

Comment _____

4. I used to think our new company computer hated me. It waited until I had filled it with all the data about my accounts, then "burped," erasing my updates and filing the background information in some inaccessible, computer limbo. Then this summer I took a course in data processing that changed my entire outlook. I discovered that QX-T (affectionately dubbed Don Quixote by the office staff) is trying to be my friend while I am its worst enemy.

Comment _____

5. As the saying goes, "Too many cooks spoil the broth." This was proven recently when a simple experiment resulted in the destruction of the chemistry lab.

Comment _____

Score _____

Writing Paragraphs 83

Evaluating Conclusions   Exercise 4–10

NAME _____ DATE _____

Rate the following conclusions as effective or ineffective. Explain your answers.

EXAMPLE: In conclusion, let me say that we all lived happily every after.

Comment *ineffective/ The subject is not restated; the ending is too abrupt.*

1.   Is a turtle a fish? I imagine not. Fish do not breathe air, walk on four feet, or deposit their eggs on dry land. Turtles do.

Comment _____
_____

2.   On the other hand, I can see the other side of this question of smoking in public too. While it is true that smokers pollute other people's air as well as their own, it is themselves they are hurting most. And who has the right to tell people what to do with their own bodies?

Comment _____
_____

3.   The hidden curriculum has persisted in spite of equal-opportunity regulations and noisy public discussion. Girls still receive and respond unconsciously to cultural signals to leave math to the boys, to hide intelligence, to be pretty rather than smart, while boys are taught to value a pretty face more than an active mind and to look for a willing slave rather than a vigorous partner in a mate. To change the hidden curriculum, we must change the culture that produced it.

Comment _____

4.   Since I have never been to Chicago, my opinions about that city may not be worth much. However, for what they are worth, you have them. Overall, I would say it seems like a nice place to visit, but I wouldn't want to live there.

Comment _____
_____

5.   Will money soon be obsolete? Will direct-transfer bank cards replace checks? Will payday mean the day when your company computer signals a deposit to your bank computer and will payroll envelopes be a thing of the past? The answer is yes, and it may happen sooner than you think.

Comment _____
_____

Score _____

© 1986 by CBS College Publishing. All rights reserved.

Writing Special Paragraphs   Exercise 4–11

NAME _____ DATE _____

Write paragraphs to fit each of the special situations described.

> EXAMPLE: Write dialogue to illustrate the frustration of a mother speaking to an unresponsive child.
> *"How did it go at school today?"*
> *"OK."*
> *"Did you learn anything new?"*
> *"Yeah."*
> *"Well, what did you learn?"*
> *"Nothing much."*
> *"But you said you learned something."*
> *"Yeah."*
> *"What?"*
> *Shrug.*
> *"Go to your room."*

1. Write an introduction to a paper about how to have (or not to have) a good time on Friday night.

2. Write a transition paragraph to bridge the gap between a paragraph that extols the delights of junk food (or smoking or orgies of watching old movies on television) and a paragraph that decries the dangers.

3. Write a conclusion to a paper about good (or bad) study habits.

Student Writer at Work Exercise 4–12

NAME _____ DATE _____

The essay below has an introduction, three developmental paragraphs, and a conclusion. Examine each paragraph for effectiveness and write your suggestions for revision in the margins. Your instructor may ask you to revise one or more paragraphs on a separate page.

    Out of most average people I know, I must be one of the most lousiest students coming to the university. (At least I feel this way much of the time.) I have never been a good student. Ever since high school I do not do my studies, attend classes, nor do I set my priorities.

    Beginning each new semester, I am always a step ahead of myself. I read the following chapters and I make sure I know the material beforehand. Then, when the middle of the semester comes along, I begin to fall behind. I never read when I am supposed to, nor do I study consistently. Sometimes I honestly do not know how I pass my tests. I keep thinking to myself, I can do a lot better if I would only take the necessary time to study. Why I cannot sit down and study for a few hours is beyond me. I am always praying that I won't flunk out of school because I want to make it through school so I can make something out of my life.

    Next on my list of failures is not attending classes. This semester has been the worst for me. I have been ill on and off, and quite run-down and tired. Part of being tired is from poor sleeping habits. I can never fall asleep early enough at night, which makes it all the more difficult to wake up in the morning. It is not good to miss class because I miss important work, and consequently, if I miss more than four or five times, my grade drops down by one letter. This most certainly is not a good outcome, especially since my grades aren't that great to begin with. If I do not keep up with my grades, I will be on academic probation. This really messes me up because of my financial aid. Without the extra money and grants I get from financial aid, I could never continue on with college.

    Finally, but most harmful of all my problems is that I have no sense of priorities. I always forget that I should put extracurricular activities out of the way until I finish my homework. This is what causes me to fall behind the most. I could be in the middle of an assignment, and should a friend call me on the phone, I will stay talking for hours. Also, if my parents or anybody else for that matter, needs something done from me, I'll drop everything to go do it. I don't know if this is good or bad, but I feel as though I owe

© 1986 by CBS College Publishing. All rights reserved.

them the least of what I can do for them. Though, by the same token, I think they owe me the affability to let me study and do my work too. Either way, it seems like I lose out. If I do good for somebody else, I am rewarded with poor grades. Then too, there are certain commitments other than school that you just cannot avoid. All in all, I think I have a big problem on my hands.

I can only conclude that I better put my act together soon before I won't be able to repair my difficulties with college. They say realizing what you are doing wrong is the first step in repairing bad habits and faults. At least I do realize that much. My next step is to follow through with a lot of ambition and enthusiasm. As long as I keep a positive attitude, there is no reason for me to be a failure.

Score _____

Writing Paragraphs

Review 4

Fill in the blanks in each of the following sentences with words or phrases that best complete the thought.

1. Paragraphs demonstrate _____ when they develop a single idea.
2. A paragraph is _____ when it is logically organized.
3. _____ tie ideas together and show relationships.
4. _____ means developing an idea by giving typical cases or examples of it.
5. When you analyze by _____ , you divide a single item into its component parts.
6. A _____ reinforces the main idea of a paper, then comments on results.
7. Many paragraphs are structured like small _____ .
8. Exact _____ references link sentences and help maintain a consistent point of view.
9. _____ key words keeps readers on track by recalling and emphasizing important points.
10. To compare or contrast two subjects, you must first find _____ for comparison.

Score _____

Check your answers against those in the back of the book. Deduct 10 points for each error.

The Writer's Casebook #4

Application: Unity, Coherence, and Development in Essays

Like its individual paragraphs, an essay should be unified (regarding a single subject), coherent (logically organized), and well developed (filled with supporting information).

Just as the topic sentence controls paragraph unity, the thesis statement controls essay unity. No matter how interesting, information that does not fit within the scope and focus established by your thesis cannot be included in the paper. For example, a paper on the traumas of college life may include paragraphs on pre-exam nightmares or post-exam anxiety, but it should not include a paragraph on the delights of a well-executed chemistry experiment or of receiving an A from Professor "No-A's" Lee.

An essay coheres or holds together when two important conditions are met: (1) The paragraphs are ordered in a way that makes sense—that is, ordered chronologically for events that take place through time; ordered in space when setting is the focus; or ordered in terms of the importance of ideas. (2) The paragraphs are linked together with transitional devices such as pronoun reference, parallel structure, repetition, or transitional words and phrases. In a coherent essay, patterns of ideas, details, or facts are clear, easily discerned, and easily followed; the essay fits together and makes sense not only in its parts but also as a whole.

The amount of information needed to develop an essay well depends upon the scope of the thesis and the intended length of the paper. Two or three developmental paragraphs, each a hundred to a hundred and fifty words long, would probably be sufficient to develop a simple thesis such as "I am a junk food junkie." However, it would take more information and more developmental paragraphs to deal effectively with a subject such as "the frightening implications of Three Mile Island" or "the disadvantages of a world money system." Overall, if the demands of your subject lead you to write a half-page introduction, you should expect to fill at least a page and a half to two pages with supporting information; if your introduction is a page long, the supporting paragraphs should fill at least three pages and possibly more. Spatially, a well-developed essay resembles a balloon; however large it is, the proportions remain the same, and the beginning point is also the ending.

Cases for Writing: Writing Unified, Coherent, Well-Developed Essays

Case #1

Assume that you are an analyst for a computer dating service called Data Dating. Lately there has been an increase in dissatisfied customers. Jazz enthusiasts have been matched with Beethoven freaks; outdoors people with sit-by-the-fire types. You have been asked to explore the scope of the problem, isolate the causes, and recommend solutions. To accomplish this task, you have prepared case studies of both date-matching failures and date-matching successes. Write a paper on some single aspect or outcome of your study.

Case #2

In a surprise move the board of your company (or school) has decided to try a rank-and-file employee (or student) in the number one position—president—and you have been elected. Develop a slogan for your new administration, and write a paper about your implementation of that slogan.

Constructing a Logical Argument

5

Preview 5

A. Circle the letter before the sentence in each pair that is an argumentative thesis.

1. a. To computerize or not to computerize.
   b. To avoid being left behind by the competition, Atwood and Daughters must computerize.
2. a. Sixty-three percent of those surveyed agree that America should buy American.
   b. America should buy American.
3. a. Why should workers who smoke be allowed to pollute the air space of nonsmokers?
   b. To protect the rights of nonsmokers, the company should prohibit smoking on the job.
4. a. Dr. Suzanne Garcia is the best-qualified candidate for city council chair.
   b. Let's talk about the race for city council chair and the School Board's candidate, Dr. Suzanne Garcia.
5. a. It's wrong to allow senior citizens on fixed incomes to suffer from rising public utility costs.
   b. The state should subsidize the utility bills of senior citizens.

B. Circle the letter before the sentence in each pair that does *not* contain a logical fallacy.

6. a. The police arrested a prime suspect and charged him with the robbery.
   b. The police arrested the criminal and charged him with the robbery.
7. a. If you cannot ski, you should not move to Alaska.
   b. If you do not like snow, you should not move to Alaska.
8. a. You should vote "no" on Proposition 10 because the quality of our educational system is at stake.
   b. You should vote "no" on Proposition 10 because the measure will force the School Board to cut teachers' salaries.

> 9. a. When you stop overeating, I will listen to your complaints about my chain smoking.
>   b. We should both stop abusing our bodies and avoid smoking and overeating.
> 10. a. If handguns are regulated, fewer people will own guns.
>   b. If handguns are regulated, soon only criminals will have guns.
>
> **Score** _____
>
> Check your answers against those in the back of the book. Deduct 10 points for each error.

Argument is an *appeal to reason*. It uses factual information and analysis of that information to prove something and to convince the reader to accept the writer's point of view. Argument is central to the educational experience because it forces us to evaluate, test, revise, and express ideas as well as to consider conflicting opinions.

Because argument is rooted in facts, writing successful arguments entails writing effective exposition. Skills in organizing and presenting information clearly and in developing ideas fully are essential to convincing an audience that your opinion has substance and deserves careful consideration.

5a Planning Your Argument

Begin with a *debatable topic*—one about which people disagree. It need not be profound. "New students should be required to wear beanies during their first semester" will serve as well as an opinion on a major controversy, such as animal experimentation, if people have taken sides on the issue. However, statements of fact like "grass is green" are not debatable and therefore cannot serve as topics for argumentation.

Once you have a topic, *take a stand*: choose one side or the other of the argument and prepare to defend your choice. Your thesis will give your position in a single declarative sentence that asserts or denies something about the subject.

Define your terms. If you plan to prove that a rattlesnake makes the ideal pet, be certain to explain that your definition of *ideal pet* is one that requires little care, fits comfortably in your lap, and will frighten away potential burglars. Vague words—such as *wrong, bad, right, immoral*—that convey moral judgments should generally be replaced with more specific terms.

VAGUE: Censoring books is evil.
SPECIFIC: Killing a book is almost equivalent to killing a person. (paraphrase of John Milton, *Areopagitica*)

Consider your audience. If they lack any knowledge essential to their understanding your point, supply it. Also choose the language, evidence, and tone that your audience will find most convincing. Diatribes and an hysterical accusatory style, for example, will make most educated audiences reject your position immediately, whatever its merits. A reasonable tone and rational evidence will win you a fair hearing.

Your *evidence* should be verifiable facts or the testimony of experts in the field. Supporting opinions with more opinions will persuade no one.

OPINIONS: Tuition at our school should be lowered. None of the students can afford to pay it, and if the administration is not careful, there will soon be no student body left.

FACTS: Tuition at our school should be lowered. The new rate of $150 per credit hour means that the average full-time student, taking a fifteen-hour load, must pay $2,250 per semester in tuition alone. Eighty percent of the students at this institution receive some kind of financial aid, with an average grant of around $1,500 a year in a combination package of grants, work-study, and loans. This means that the average student on financial aid must still come up with $3,000 a year for tuition—plus money to pay for living expenses.

TESTIMONY: According to the registrar, more than five hundred students have requested that their transcripts be sent to other schools since the current increase in tuition went into effect. Of those students, 450 said they were transferring; 395 cited the high cost of tuition as the major cause for their leaving.

Be fair. Resist the temptation to strengthen your argument by distorting or slanting the evidence or by quoting out of context. If you are an advocate of nuclear weapons, for example, you would be distorting the evidence if you claimed Albert Einstein was a supporter because his equation $E = mc^2$ opened the way for physicists to study the conversion of mass to energy. Einstein was actually a pacifist, deploring violence of any kind.

Remember that you cannot argue in a vacuum. Argumentation assumes that there is an opposing side with advocates who believe in their position as much as you do in yours. *Dealing with the opposition's arguments* in a fair way is part of convincing your audience that you are a reasonable person, worthy of their attention, and that your argument is a reasoned one, arrived at after carefully considering the alternatives.

5b Shaping Your Argument

Arguments are constructed in two basic ways—*induction*, which moves from facts to conclusion, and *deduction*, which moves from conclusion to facts.

The basic pattern of the deductive argument is the syllogism, which presents the basic premises and the conclusion in a kind of chain of logic.

MAJOR PREMISE: All pens in that package are defective.
MINOR PREMISE: These pens are from that package.
CONCLUSION: Therefore, these pens are defective.

The syllogism establishes the grounds and sets the limits of the argument. The conclusion, which is your thesis, must follow from the premises; therefore, you must persuade your audience to accept your premises, either through the force of logic or by the weight of evidence.

If your position is especially controversial or difficult to establish, the inductive argument may be more effective. Induction begins with a hypothesis, which you may leave unstated or propose as a question. Then you present the evidence, being careful not to confuse the reader by raising additional questions. Finally, you make an *inductive leap*, based on the evidence, and draw a conclusion.

HYPOTHESIS: Is it going to rain?
EVIDENCE: The weather report predicts an 80 percent chance of rain.
The barometer is falling.
Dark clouds cover the sky.
The air feels damp and smells like rain.
CONCLUSION: I believe it will rain.

If your thesis is unpopular or improbable, you may wish to place it at the end of the paper so that you can approach it gradually. If you think the audience will probably agree with your thesis, state it at the beginning of the paper.

5c Writing and Revising Your Argument

Drafting an argument, like drafting any essay, should be done quickly to get your ideas down on paper. Then in addition to using general revision criteria, examine the draft for the special characteristics of arguments: Do you have enough evidence? Have you presented your evidence fairly? Have you dealt with the opposition? Is your essay inductive, deductive, or both? If you use deduction, does the conclusion follow logically from the premises? Does your discussion stay within the limits established by those premises? If you use induction, does your evidence include any confusing points? Is the inductive leap convincing?

In addition, examine your arguments for the indefensible flaws called *fallacies*. They may appear to be reasonable, but they rely upon emotional appeal or intellectual sleight-of-hand for their persuasive power. Some of the techniques of propaganda are identical to the fallacies listed here.

1. *Equivocation* means evading the issue. The evasion may entail a shift from a debatable point to another point that is easy to defend or that audiences commonly accept.

EXAMPLE: In *Hamlet* the grave digger answers Hamlet's question "What man dost thou dig it for?" with the equivocation "For no man, sir," thereby trying to evade the unpleasant task of telling the prince the grave is for the prince's sweetheart, Ophelia.

Constructing a Logical Argument

2. The *either/or fallacy* occurs when you reduce a complex issue with many sides to a simple issue with only two sides.

EXAMPLE: America: Love it or leave it. (1960's slogan aimed at those who opposed the Vietnam War)
If handguns are regulated, soon only criminals will have guns.

3. *Post hoc, ergo propter hoc* is a Latin expression meaning "after this, therefore because of this." It refers to the fallacy of saying that because one event immediately followed another event, the first event actually caused the second one.

EXAMPLE: I washed my car and then it rained. Washing my car causes it to rain.

4. *Begging the question* occurs when you state an opinion as though it were a fact, hoping to convince your audience that the issue has been decided irrefutably and your opinion proven.

EXAMPLE: You should vote "yes" on the bond issue because the money is for new schools and new roads. (It has not yet been established that new schools and new roads are needed.)

5. *Argument ad hominem* means attacking a person rather than an issue.

EXAMPLE: How can the President listen to Kissinger's recommendations on Central America? Kissinger wasn't even born in America. What can he know about American policies?

6. *The red herring fallacy* is named for the practice of dragging a red herring across a trail to distract dogs from their original quarry. In argument this fallacy occurs when the writer tries to distract the audience from the actual issue by introducing another subject.

EXAMPLE: This company has a good product, but the management supports radical causes.

7. *Tu quoque* means "you also." It occurs when the writer, instead of responding to the issue itself, accuses its advocate of not following his or her own advice.

EXAMPLE: You're telling me to watch my run-on sentences? Look at how many punctuation errors you make.

8. A *false analogy* oversimplifies; it suggests that because two things are similar in some ways, they are similar in other ways as well.

EXAMPLE: George is like a cat, intelligent and secretive. I'll bet he also is cruel and will play with his victims.

Constructing a Logical Argument

Identifying the Argumentative Thesis   Exercise 5–1

NAME _____   DATE _____

For each group of sentences, circle the letter before the sentence that is an argumentative thesis. If more than one alternative is argumentative, choose the better one.

EXAMPLE: a. The computer runs our office efficiently and dispassionately.
   (b.) The computer runs our office more efficiently and dispassionately than any office manager could.

1. a. Thousands of new jobs are opening in the computer field each year, and I am a computer science major.
   b. Computer science is the best major for the eighties because thousands of new jobs are opening in the field each year.
2. a. My pet rattlesnake Fang is an affectionate companion and an effective deterrent to burglaries.
   b. Rattlesnakes like my Fang make the best pets because they are affectionate companions and effective deterrents to burglaries.
3. a. Keeping cats and birds in the same house is prohibited by law in some states.
   b. People should not be allowed to keep cats and birds in the same house.
   c. Although keeping cats and birds in the same house is prohibited by law in some states, many pet owners disobey the law.
4. a. Censoring obscene books in a moral issue.
   b. Censoring obscene books is itself immoral.
   c. Does censoring obscene books restrict the freedom of thought?
   d. Censoring obscene books interferes with the development of critical thinking, an essential skill.
5. a. American education is not as poor as they say.
   b. Let's talk about what is right with American education.
   c. Educators should be concerned with building on the strengths as well as correcting the weaknesses of the American educational system.
6. a. Let me tell you about one person's experience with drinking coffee, and maybe you will not think it is so harmless after all.
   b. Coffee cans, like cigarette packages, should carry the warning that the product may be hazardous to one's health.
7. a. Portland needs to build a new bridge across the Columbia River.
   b. Portland built a new bridge across the Columbia River, and some people do not like it.
8. a. Teachers should be careful about the homework they give students.
   b. Should teachers be careful about the homework they give elementary school students?
   c. Teachers should not give homework to elementary school students.
9. a. Football has no place on the campus of a serious-minded school.
   b. Football on our campus brings in two million dollars a year.
   c. Because of the income it brings our school, football should be emphasized.
10. a. Is a turtle a fish?
    b. Although my opponent says a turtle is a fish, I maintain it is not.

Score _____

© 1986 by CBS College Publishing. All rights reserved.

Evaluating Evidence   Exercise 5-2

NAME _____ _____ DATE _____

Circle the letters before the items that could serve as evidence or support for each thesis. There may be more than one correct answer in each set. If none of the items could serve as evidence, do not circle any.

    EXAMPLE: Thesis: Tuition at our university should be raised.
                      (a.) The present tuition of $300 for a full-time load is far below the national average.
                      b. Students should not be allowed to get away with murder.

1. Thesis: The city should not build a new bridge to Westgate Heights.
   a. Bridges are ugly; they are offensive to the eye.
   b. A wildlife refuge—the winter home of ducks, geese, and cranes—would be destroyed by the construction.
2. Thesis: Snakes make delightful pets.
   a. Some people like snakes.
   b. Snakes are easy to take care of.
3. Thesis: The United States should allow American farmers to bring in cheap Mexican labor.
   a. The Mexicans deserve a chance.
   b. Americans do not want the jobs.
4. Thesis: Dr. Martinez assigns too much homework in Math 132.
   a. In the fall of 1984 he assigned 280 pages of problems.
   b. Over Christmas (between semesters!) he assigned the first chapter of the book we will use next semester in Math 161.
   c. I hate math, and the problems are too hard.
5. Thesis: Talking to plants may make them flourish or sicken, depending upon what you say.
   a. In the experiment we spoke softly to one group of begonias, and after ten days they were blossoming and sending out new shoots.
   b. We spoke harshly to another group of begonias, and after ten days they had withered.
   c. It stands to reason that living things will do better if they are happier.
6. Thesis: Christ, not Adam, is the hero of Milton's *Paradise Lost*.
   a. Adam falls but cannot redeem himself.
   b. It is appropriate that Christ should be the hero of a Christian epic.
   c. Christ fights the battles and wins the victories.
7. Thesis: Behaviorism dehumanizes people.
   a. It treats people like machines.
   b. The focus of behaviorism is measurable behavior.
   c. Internal processing, like thinking, is deemphasized or ignored.
   d. Programmed instruction—putting orders in; getting actions out—is a product of behaviorism.
8. Thesis: Christmas is not too commercialized.
   a. People buy because they want to, not because they have to.
   b. It is impossible to overdo such a joyous holiday.

Constructing a Logical Argument

    c. Many people still make their presents, showing their love with time and effort rather than with money.
    d. Most churches spend the holidays presenting plays and cantatas and reminding us of the true meaning of Christmas.
9. Thesis: Yazz is a better painter now than he was in the forties.
    a. His technique has matured, making his work more finished.
    b. His stylized figures are more distinctive.
10. Thesis: The battle was a defeat, not a victory.
    a. Six hundred soldiers were killed and two thousand injured.
    b. The enemy suffered minimal defeats.
    c. We abandoned our position the day after the battle because of insufficient strength left to defend it.
11. Thesis: Shirley Jackson's "The Lottery" more effectively exposes the traps of tradition than does Stephen Crane's "A Youth in Apparel That Glittered."
    a. In the story the lottery ritual is yearly, returning as surely and as naturally as "death and taxes."
    b. In the poem the young man's death is isolated, a single incident.
    c. The story makes me feel a chill in my bones.
12. Thesis: In a custody battle the major loser can be the child.
    a. The child is torn between two parents, both of whom he or she loves.
    b. Who can say what effect this trauma will have on the child's future?
    c. The child's security, rooted in stable relationships and confidence in caring adults, may be threatened.

Score _____

© 1986 by CBS College Publishing. All rights reserved.

Identifying Fallacies Exercise 5–3

NAME _____ DATE _____

Identify the fallacy or fallacies in the following passages. Then explain the problem in thinking represented by each fallacy.

> EXAMPLE: If a Catholic becomes President, soon the Pope will run the country. *either/or fallacy. The statement falsely suggests that there are only two alternatives, ignoring many other possibilities.*

1. Who are you to tell me to watch my step? You broke your leg last week.

2. Clinton Humperdinker left the party at 6:30 P.M. Victoria Van Pelter discovered her diamond necklace was missing at 6:35 P.M. Clinton must have taken it.

3. The defendant must be guilty. He had a wicked expression on his face, and he couldn't look the jury in the eye.

4. I have not broken the law because the law prohibits stealing, and I only borrowed the money; I'll pay it back next week.

5. My horoscope says today is my day for financial success; therefore, I can't miss if I invest in that new wildcat oil well.

6. It must be true. It's printed in the newspaper in black and white.

7. I won't buy any insurance because people who have insurance are always getting into accidents, and I don't want to have an accident.

8. Space is the New Frontier of the second half of the twentieth century. If Americans had not settled the West in the nineteenth century, the United States would not be

Constructing a Logical Argument

the country it is today. Therefore, we must move ahead into space or we might miss our destiny.

9. The fairly intelligent fly saw clusters of his peers gathering together on the window sill. He thought, "Look at all the flies. If everyone is there, that must be the place to be." (And he joined his friends on the flypaper.)

10. Frederico is really becoming the athletic type. He never misses the football games or the golf matches on television.

11. Sandy says I lied about paying her back on the first. I didn't lie. I told her I should have some money by the first. I didn't say I would give her any of it.

12. If I drop out of high school, I'll never get into college, and my life will be over.

Score _____

© 1986 by CBS College Publishing. All rights reserved.

Review 5

A. Circle the letter before the sentence in each pair that is an argumentative thesis.

1. a. Who can say how many house pets citizens in this country should have?
   b. Citizens in this county should not be limited by law to three house pets.
2. a. What this country needs is a flat income tax.
   b. Straight Talk About the Flat Income Tax.
3. a. Widmark Department Store should expand its floor space by 50 percent.
   b. The feasibility study showed that Widmark Department Store should expand its floor space by 50 percent.
4. a. The Garden Club was wrong not to become involved in the Beautify Rapid City Campaign.
   b. The Garden Club should become involved in the Beautify Rapid City Campaign.
5. a. No more than 1,200 wolves remain alive in the lower forty-eight states.
   b. Stronger measures must be taken to protect the 1,200 wolves remaining in the lower forty-eight states.

B. Circle the letter before the sentence in each pair that is *not* a logical fallacy.

6. a. I never use that tomato paste because the packaging is unattractive.
   b. I never use that tomato paste because I do not like the taste.
7. a. I washed my car so that it would rain.
   b. I washed my car, and it rained.
8. a. I used to like the group's music but not since their latest hit was used as the theme song of a violent movie.
   b. I like the group's music, but I wish they had not allowed their latest hit to be used as the theme song of a violent movie.
9. a. She broke a mirror, causing her to have seven years of bad luck.
   b. She broke a mirror, causing a repair bill of $75.
10. a. Those who disagree with this action should resign from the club.
    b. Those who disagree with this action could compose a minority opinion statement.

Score _____

Check your answers against those in the back of the book. Deduct 10 points for each error.

The Writer's Casebook #5

Application: Argument and Persuasion

In one sense all writing has a persuasive purpose. You persuade the reader to share your knowledge of a subject, to share your laughter at a joke, to share your perception of the breathtaking skyline of New York City at dawn or of the equally awesome horizons of Arizona mesas at sunset.
But argument involves a special kind of persuasion—convincing the reader to agree with you on some controversial issue—and to achieve this purpose, argument appeals primarily to reason rather than to emotion or self-interest.

Like all essay writing, however, argument does take place within the context of audience and purpose that we discussed in Chapter 1. Since your purpose is to persuade someone to share your views, your audience's needs, interests, values, and educational level will be important considerations in your selection of convincing arguments and evidence. Imagine, for example, that you are arguing to persuade a group of teachers to accept an alternative educational system. You would not choose as your major support examples of graduates of that system who are financially successful but academically deficient. Or if you are trying to persuade an employer to hire you, you would emphasize what you can do for the company, not what the company can do for you.

To persuade with argument or with any other kind of writing, keep in mind that your paper can only begin to accomplish its purpose when you have finished the final revision. The real test of effectiveness comes when an audience reads and reacts to what you have said.

The following basic pattern—only one of several possible patterns—is a simple but effective way to organize an argumentative essay.

Introduction
    Introduction of the controversy
    Sketch of background, immediate effects, or startling incident to involve the reader in the issue
    Thesis that takes a stand or gives the opinion you will argue for in the essay
Body
    Paragraph summarizing or highlighting the opposing view
    Supporting paragraphs (at least three)
        Topic sentence for each paragraph that presents one of your reasons or supporting points
        Developmental sentences that offer examples, details, facts, or proof by logical analysis

Conclusion
> Reiteration of your position
> Your final judgment—action that should be taken, advice to the reader

Cases for Writing: Taking a Stand

Case #1

Assume that you have been living in a town situated at the foot of a volcano (or over a fault in the earth) all your life. Although you have experienced occasional earth tremors, there has been no major disaster during your lifetime nor during that of your parents. Now scientists say that there is a 50/50 chance that your hometown will experience a major disaster before the end of the century. Considering this possibility, will you move? Argue for or against your moving.

Case #2

With the Surgeon General's comments on the dangers of cigarette smoking and subsequent findings that the smoke may also be a hazard to nonsmokers, many people have asked employers not to allow smoking in offices. For nonsmokers these no-smoking rules have the advantage of ensuring a healthy breathing atmosphere. For smokers the rules may make it difficult to stay at their desks for long hours. What do you feel is the fair solution? Should smoking be permitted or prohibited in offices? Or can you think of another alternative? Write an argument defending your position.

SECTION **II**

Composing Sentences

6
Building Simple Sentences

Preview 6

A. Underline and label the basic elements in the following sentences: subject (s), verb (v), direct object (do), indirect object (io), object complement (oc), subject complement (sc).

1. The spacecraft *Columbia* carried the first astronauts to the moon in July 1969.

2. Neil Armstrong was the first human being to walk on the moon.

3. The astronauts considered the moon "magnificently desolate."

4. They showed viewers pictures of the earth rising over the moon.

5. The moon orbits around the earth once in twenty-eight days.

B. Underline and label these elements in the following sentences: prepositional phrase, verbal phrase, absolute phrase, appositive, compound construction.

6. The Soviets' *Venera 9* gave scientists pictures of the surface of Venus, the bleak landscape ending many romantic dreams about the love goddess's special planet.

7. Blending heroic fantasy and science fiction, George Lucas's *Star Wars* encourages viewers to dream great dreams and attempt great deeds.

Building Simple Sentences

8. Someday we, the citizens of earth, may be citizens of the stars and space.

Score _____

Check your answers against those in the back of the book. Deduct 4 points for errors in Part A, 3 points for errors in Part B. A score of 80 percent or better indicates you can recognize basic sentence elements, but you will want to work through this chapter to gain more practice in building simple sentences.

A *sentence* is the basic unit of written expression. It expresses a complete thought, and it is grammatically independent, containing both a *subject* and a *predicate*.

6a Identifying the Basic Sentence Elements

The *subject* tells what the sentence is about; the *predicate* makes a statement or asks a question about the subject. The *simple subject* is a noun or a substitute for a noun while the *complete subject* includes all the words associated with the noun or noun substitute. The *simple predicate* is a verb or verb phrase while the *complete predicate* includes all the words associated with the verb as well as the words that follow it to complete the sense of the sentence.

[-----*complete subject*-----] [-----*complete predicate*-----]
The Italian scientist Galileo observed the rings of Saturn.
                     simple   *simple*
                     subject   *predicate*

[------*complete subject*------] [----------*complete predicate*----------]
Mars, the wandering planet, seems to move erratically through the sky.
simple   *simple*
subject   *predicate*

6b Constructing Basic Sentence Patterns

The most basic sentence, the *simple sentence*, consists of one complete subject and one complete predicate. We can build simple sentences according to five basic patterns.

(1) Subject and intransitive verb (s + v)

     s   *v*
The star exploded.

  s   *v*
Planets melted.

    s   *v*
Civilizations evaporated.

In each sentence the verb is *intransitive* because it does not transfer action from the subject to another noun or a noun substitute following the verb.

(2) Subject + transitive verb + direct object (s + v + do)

A *transitive verb* carries or transfers action to a noun or substitute for a noun in the predicate. The receiver of the action is called the *direct object*—that is, the object directly affected or touched by the action of the verb.

NOTE: To help find the direct object, use the whom/what test. Find the subject and verb; then ask the question: Whom or what? The word or word group that answers the question will be the direct object.

    s   *v*   *do*
We saw the explosion of a star. *(what?)*

    s   *v*   *do*
Rings encircle Saturn.   *(what?)*

      s   *v*   *do*
Captain Kirk struck Mr. Spock. *(who?)*

(3) Subject + transitive verb + direct object + object complement (s + v + do + oc)

This pattern builds on the one above (s + v + do) by adding an *object complement*, a noun or an adjective that follows the direct object and renames or describes it.

NOTE: If you can insert *to be* between the direct object and the noun or adjective that follows it, you have found an object complement.

    s   *v*   *do*   *to be* *oc (adj)*
Astronomers find large telescopes ∨ helpful.

               s   *v*   *do*   *to be* *oc (n)*
The Society of Planet Discoverers elected William Herschel ∨ president.

(4) Subject + linking verb + subject complement (s + v + sc)

Linking verbs (*be, seem, appear, feel, become,* and so forth) connect, or "link," the subject with a word or word group in the predicate that renames or describes it; this word or word group is called the *subject complement* because it adds to, or "complements," what we know about the subject. When the subject complement is an adjective (called a *predicate adjective*), it describes the subject. When the subject complement is a noun (called a *predicate noun* or *predicate nominative*), it renames the subject.

    s *v*   *sc*
Sirius is a blue star. *(predicate noun, renames subject)*

     s   *v*   *sc*
Betelgeuse looks red. *(predicate adjective, describes subject)*

    s   *v*   *sc*
Space dust clouds may become solar systems one day. *(predicate noun, renames subject)*

(5) Subject + transitive verb + indirect object + direct object (s + v + io + do)

This pattern also builds on the second pattern above (s + v + do) but adds an *indirect object* before the direct object instead of an object complement after it. An indirect object tells us "to or for whom" or "to or for what" the action in the sentence was done.

NOTE: Test for indirect objects by first applying the whom/what test to find the direct object; then ask the additional questions: To or for whom? To or for what? However, if the word or words that answer your question come after the direct object instead of before it, you have found a prepositional phrase instead of an indirect object.

        s   *v*   *io*   *do*
The scientists showed us the evidence. *(showed the evidence to whom?)*

     s   *v*   *io*   *do*
Technicians gave the equipment an overhaul. *(gave an overhaul to what?)*

But

      s   *v*   *do*   *prep phrase*
The astronomer donated his notes to the observatory.

6c Forming Questions and Commands

In the five basic sentence patterns just described, each sentence begins with the subject and then moves on to the verb. This standard word order may be varied when we ask questions or give commands.

(1) Forming questions

Most questions are formed by inverting the subject and verb or by beginning the sentence with an interrogative pronoun and then inverting the subject and verb.

NORMAL ORDER (**statement**):   Sirius is a blue star.
INVERTED ORDER (**question**):   Is Sirius a blue star?
INTERROGATIVE PRONOUN +   Why is Sirius a blue star?
INVERTED ORDER:

NOTE: With many verbs you will need to add an auxiliary and alter the verb form before you can invert. (The star exploded. → *Did* the star explode?)

(2) Forming commands

When the subject *you* of a command is left out, normal word order is altered.

NORMAL ORDER: You name the nine planets.
ALTERED ORDER: Name the nine planets. (The subject *you* is understood.)

6d Identifying Phrases and Clauses

Individual words may be combined into word groups called *phrases* and *clauses*.

(1) Identifying phrases

A *phrase* is a group of words that fit together or are related to one another in some way but form only part of a sentence. For example, a *prepositional phrase* is made up of a preposition, any modifiers, and the noun or noun substitute that is the object of that preposition. (See Chapter 20 for more about prepositions.) *Noun phrases* consist of a noun or noun substitute and all related modifiers; *verb phrases* consist of the main verb and all auxiliary verbs.

[-------- *noun phrase* --------] [--- *verb phrase* ---] [-- *prep phrase* --]
Modern astronomical science may have begun in Mesopotamia 4,000 years ago.

(Other kinds of phrases—the *verbal phrase* and the *absolute phrase*—will be discussed in Chapters 11 and 20.)

(2) Identifying clauses

A clause is also a group of related words. It contains both a subject and a predicate.

        subject   *predicate*
Many ancient astronomers believed in a geocentric universe.

     subject   *predicate*
The sun, moon, and stars were thought to travel around the earth.

When clauses such as the ones above can stand alone as complete sentences, they are called *independent clauses*. When they cannot stand alone as sentences, they are called *dependent clauses*; they "depend" upon an independent clause to complete their meaning.

	subject *predicate*
DEPENDENT CLAUSE:	When Galileo observed the satellites of Jupiter
	subject *predicate*
DEPENDENT CLAUSE:	Who first observed the satellites of Jupiter
DEPENDENT CLAUSE + INDEPENDENT CLAUSE:	When Galileo observed the satellites of Jupiter, he disproved the geocentric theory.
INDEPENDENT CLAUSE + DEPENDENT CLAUSE:	It was Galileo who first observed the satellites of Jupiter.

6e Building Simple Sentences with Individual Words

A *simple sentence* is a single independent clause containing a *subject* and a *predicate* and expressing a complete thought. To write richer, more meaningful simple sentences, you can add meat to the bones of the five basic simple-sentence patterns by building the sentences with words and phrases.

BASIC: The horse astonished audiences.
EXPANDED: Roy Rogers' horse Trigger, a silvery palomino, astonished audiences with his repertoire of tricks.

(1) Building simple sentences with adjectives and adverbs

Simple sentences may be expanded by adding *adjectives* and *adverbs*, *noun-adjectives*, and *verbals* (see Chapters 20 and 24).

Adjectives and adverbs may be added to describe, point out, emphasize, or qualify.

BASIC:	Westerns featured gunfights and hangings.
EXPANDED WITH ADJECTIVES:	Italian "spaghetti" Westerns feature raucous gunfights and gruesome hangings.
BASIC:	Fred Astaire danced through two decades of musicals.
EXPANDED WITH ADVERBS:	Fred Astaire danced smoothly and elegantly through two decades of musicals.
EXPANDED WITH ADJECTIVES AND ADVERBS:	Urbane Fred Astaire danced smoothly and elegantly through two glamorous decades of Hollywood musicals.

(2) Building simple sentences with nouns and verbals

Other single words—such as *nouns* that act as adjectives and *verbals*, forms of verbs that function as nouns or as modifiers—may also be used to expand simple sentences.

A *noun* functions as an adjective when it precedes another noun and describes or in some way qualifies it.

BASIC:	Films used effectively the sounds of guns and high-speed chases.
EXPANDED WITH NOUN-ADJECTIVES:	Gangster films used effectively the sounds of machine guns and high-speed auto chases.

Verbals include present and past participles, infinitives, and gerunds (see Chapter 20). When verbals are used to build simple sentences, they add variety to the sentence structure as well as descriptive details, explanation, or illustration to the content.

BASIC:	Julie Andrews was cast in *The Sound of Music*.
EXPANDED WITH INFINITIVE AND PARTICIPLE:	Exciting Julie Andrews was cast to star in *The Sound of Music*.

BASIC: At least six versions of *Dr. Jekyll and Mr. Hyde* have been filmed.
EXPANDED WITH PARTI- At least six spine-tingling versions of Dr. Jekyll's agonized
CIPLES AND GERUND: changing into Mr. Hyde have been filmed.

6f Building Simple Sentences with Phrases

Simple sentences may also be enriched by adding prepositional phrases, verbal phrases, absolute phrases, or appositives and by compounding.

(1) Building simple sentences with prepositional phrases

Prepositional phrases (prepositions plus any modifiers and their noun, pronoun, or noun-substitute objects) function as modifiers in a sentence. They act as adjectives or adverbs, depending upon the word the preposition is connected to by meaning.

Charlie Chaplin wore a mismatched suit with baggy pants but *adjective phrase*
tight-fitting vest and coat.   *describes noun*
                                                              suit
Mae West's words were breathed in a sultry, sensuous tone.   *adverb phrase*
                                                              describes verb
                                                              breathed

Like adjectives and adverbs, prepositional phrases describe, point out, and emphasize, but they can do so more fully than single words can.

BASIC: Mae West portrayed a woman.
EXPANDED WITH Sexy Mae West portrayed a worldly, perhaps street woman.
SINGLE-WORD
MODIFIERS:
EXPANDED WITH PREP- With her sensuous body and sultry voice, Mae West por-
OSITIONAL PHRASES: trayed a woman of the world and, perhaps, of the street.

(2) Building simple sentences with verbal phrases

Verbal phrases (participles, gerunds, or infinitives plus all their related modifiers, objects, or complements) serve the same functions in sentences as individual verbals.

Gerund phrases (verbal -*ing* nouns + related words) may serve as subjects, objects, or complements.

    subject   *subject complement*   *object of preposition*
Making a film means getting a chance at winning the world's adulation.

Infinitive phrases (to + base form of verb + related words) may be modifiers or nouns.

    subject   *n*   *adj*
To be a star is too often the dream to break hearts.

Building Simple Sentences

Participial phrases (present or past participle + related words) modify nouns or pronouns.

              adj   n
Fascinated by the animal's intelligence, the trainer rescued Benji from the pound.

                      n   adj
The trainer found him waiting forlornly at the pound.

Verbal phrases can enrich your writing, but be careful when placing them in your sentences. To avoid misplaced or dangling modifiers be sure that phrases are next to the words they modify (see 13e).

BASIC:	Tarzan beat his chest.
EXPANDED WITH SINGLE-WORD VERBAL:	Screaming, Tarzan beat his chest.
EXPANDED WITH VERBAL PHRASE:	Screaming the battle cry of the Great Ape, Tarzan beat his chest.

(3) Building simple sentences with absolute phrases

Absolute phrases modify an entire sentence or clause instead of a single word or phrase. Usually an absolute phrase is made up of a noun or pronoun plus a participial phrase, but sometimes an infinitive phrase may modify an entire sentence and, therefore, function absolutely.

His clothes shed in a phone booth, Superman sprang into the sky.
To tell the truth, I preferred the novel to the movie.

NOTE: The participle *being* may be omitted in an absolute phrase.

They filmed frantically, their money [being] almost gone.

Building with absolute phrases adds meaning and variety to your simple sentences.

BASIC:	Audrey Hepburn accepted the award.
EXPANDED WITH ABSOLUTES:	Her head high, her walk queenly, Audrey Hepburn accepted the award.

(4) Building simple sentences with appositives

Appositives are nouns or noun phrases that identify or give a new name to the words they follow. Appositives may be used with or without an introductory phrase (*such as, or, that is, for example, in other words*).

The floppy-eared canine star Benji makes everyone a dog lover.
Benji, the floppy-eared canine star, makes everyone a dog lover.
Animal stars, such as Lassie and Flipper, have huge fan clubs.

When appositives are used to enrich a sentence, they define, rename, identify, or clarify and also make the writing more concise.

BASIC:	The film was one of the first adult Westerns.
EXPANDED WITH APPOSITIVES:	The film *High Noon* was one of the first adult Westerns, <u>pictures dramatizing the dilemmas rather than exploiting the violence of the West</u>.

(5) Building simple sentences with compound constructions

Compound constructions occur when two or more words or phrases serve the same function and fill parallel positions in the sentence's structure. Parts of a compound may be joined with commas, with coordinating conjunctions (*and, but, or, nor, for, so, yet*) or with a pair of correlative conjunctions (*both/and, not only/but also, either/or, neither/nor, whether/or*).

<u>Young, inexperienced</u> Luke Skywalker could not control the Force. (compound adjectives, both describing the noun *Luke Skywalker*)

Chewbacca <u>yowled and maneuvered</u> the *Falcon* toward Endor. (compound main verbs)

<u>Not only the Wookies but also the Ewoks</u> supported the Alliance. (compound noun subjects)

Compounding can both expand sentences by adding details and information and eliminate wordiness by cutting down on repetition.

BASIC:	Four Marx Brothers starred in *Duck Soup*. The first was Groucho. The second was Chico. The third was Harpo. The fourth was Zeppo.
FIRST SENTENCE EXPANDED BY COMPOUNDING:	<u>Groucho, Chico, Harpo, and Zeppo</u> Marx starred in *Duck Soup*.

Building Simple Sentences   **113**

Identifying Subjects and Predicates   Exercise 6–1

NAME _____ DATE _____

In the following sentences underline complete subjects once and complete predicates twice.

EXAMPLE: Proxima Centauri is our nearest solar neighbor at 4.28 light-years away.
1. The Milky Way may be 10,000 million to 12,000 million years old.
2. The four rings of Saturn are made up primarily of ice particles.
3. The rings, like Saturn's ten satellites or moons, rotate about the planet.
4. The largest planet in the solar system, Jupiter contains around 70 percent of all planet matter.
5. Jupiter has been discovered to emit radio noise.
6. Two of Jupiter's satellites equal the planet Mercury in size.
7. The seventh planet from the sun, Uranus also is surrounded by rings.
8. As many as 100 billion stars make up the Milky Way.
9. Five hundred million galaxies are within range of Earth's telescopes.
10. The Andromeda Galaxy surpasses the Milky Way with 250 billion more stars.

                                                        Score _____

© 1986 by CBS College Publishing. All rights reserved.

Identifying Sentence Elements Exercise 6–2

NAME _____ DATE _____

Label the basic elements of the following sentences: subject (s), verb (v), direct object (do), indirect object (io), and subject complement (sc).

                        s   v   sc
EXAMPLE: Our solar system is part of a galaxy called the Milky Way.

1. Astronomers have counted five rings around Uranus.

2. Halley's Comet will return to Earth in 1986.

3. Comets' tails are actually luminous gases.

4. Many amateurs find astronomy a fascinating hobby.

5. Amateurs have given science some significant discoveries.

6. Some galaxies spiral outward from a luminous nucleus of interstellar gas and young supergiant stars.

7. Contracting stars may become solar systems with a central sun, planets, asteroids, and comets.

8. Earth most closely resembles Venus in size.

9. Some nineteenth-century observers considered Mars habitable.

10. In 1884 Percival Lowell charted a system of canals in the Martian deserts.

11. The canals resembled an irrigation system.

12. Speculation increased about intelligent life on Mars.

13. Alas, in 1976 *Viking I* sent us pictures of a lifeless Martian landscape.

14. Mars' polar ice caps are dry ice instead of frozen water.

15. No green Martians waved at us in the camera lens.

16. A hundred Martian tales instantly became obsolete.

17. Around the world science fiction enthusiasts wept.

Score _____

Building Simple Sentences   **115**

Identifying Sentence Patterns   Exercise 6–3

NAME _____ DATE _____

Identify the patterns of the following sentences by using the five basic sentence formulas: 1. (s + v), 2. (s + v + do), 3. (s + v + do + oc), 4. (s + v + sc), 5. (s + v + io + do).

    EXAMPLE: Some star systems emit radio signals.   *s + v + do*

1. Mercury is the closest planet to the sun.
2. Comets also orbit our sun.
3. Galileo gave the world proof of a heliocentric solar system.
4. An asteroid belt lies between Mars and Jupiter.
5. The Space Federation appointed an Earthwoman ambassador to Delta Cephei.
6. An amateur astronomer discovered the large asteroid Astraea.
7. From the moon Earth looks blue-green with a marbling of white clouds.
8. The Inquisition questioned Galileo's discoveries on religious grounds.
9. According to astrologers, the stars can tell us the future.
10. The four largest planets are gaseous.

1. _____
2. _____
3. _____
4. _____
5. _____
6. _____
7. _____
8. _____
9. _____
10. _____

                                                        Score _____

© 1986 by CBS College Publishing. All rights reserved.

Generating Basic Sentences   Exercise 6–4

NAME _____ DATE _____

Complete the following sentences by adding the sentence element or elements given in parentheses.

> EXAMPLE: Sol is (sc).
> _____*Sol is a star.*_____

1. The moon orbits (do)
_____

2. Space probes send (io, do)
_____

3. The spaceship landed (prepositional phrase)
_____

4. Early astronomers found (do, oc)
_____

5. Mars' canals are (sc)
_____

6. Space appears (sc)
_____

7. Someday humans will explore (do)
_____

8. Perhaps other beings will offer (io, do)
_____

9. Stargazers dream (prepositional phrase)
_____

10. Often science explodes (do)
_____

Score _____

Building Simple Sentences

Generating Basic Sentences   Exercise 6–5

NAME _____ DATE _____

Write two sentences using each of the basic sentence patterns listed.

    EXAMPLE: s + v + do
    A meteor grazed the hull of the starship.
    The sun gives light to the earth.

1. s + v

2. s + v + do

3. s + v + do + oc

4. s + v + sc

5. s + v + io + do

                                                                   Score _____

© 1986 by CBS College Publishing. All rights reserved.

Forming Questions and Commands Exercise 6–6

NAME _____ DATE _____

Rewrite each of the following sentences twice, altering normal word order in two different ways.

> EXAMPLE: No green Martians waved at us.
> *Did any green Martians wave at us?*
> *Wave at us, green Martians.*

1. Comets also orbit our sun.

2. An asteroid belt lies between Mars and Jupiter.

3. Halley's Comet will return to Earth in 1986.

4. Luke Skywalker fought Darth Vadar with a light saber.

5. The aliens have landed in New York's Central Park.

6. The War of the Worlds may have already begun on Earth.

7. The spaceship blasted the meteor hurtling toward Chicago.

8. NASA will launch the first interplanetary space probe by 1995.

9. Darth Vader's Death Star incinerated entire worlds.

10. The ship drifted, lost forever in space.

Score _____

Building Simple Sentences

Identifying Phrases and Clauses   Exercise 6–7

NAME _____ DATE _____

Identify phrases and clauses in the following exercise by marking independent clauses (IC), dependent clauses (DC), and phrases (P).

    EXAMPLE: __DC__ When the first starship reaches Andromeda.

_____ 1. In a clear, starlit sky.

_____ 2. Because stars are trillions of miles away.

_____ 3. Their light seems to twinkle.

_____ 4. The heliocentric or sun-centered model of the solar system.

_____ 5. Have observed planets, moons, asteroids, and comets.

_____ 6. Which we call the red planet.

_____ 7. Across the Milky Way, at the edge of the galaxy.

_____ 8. We lifted off.

_____ 9. Only 6,000 stars visible in the night sky.

_____ 10. When you wish upon a star.

_____ 11. The star may be a galaxy.

_____ 12. Blue, red, white, and yellow stars.

_____ 13. Exploded in a supernova.

_____ 14. Over the rainbow and into space.

_____ 15. If earth were the center of the universe.

_____ 16. To Alpha Centauri, 25,200,000,000,000 miles away.

_____ 17. Science fiction spaceships like the *Enterprise*.

_____ 18. They use warp-drive to travel faster than the speed of light.

_____ 19. Stars are born in space as well as in Hollywood.

_____ 20. After a red star exhausts its energy supply.

                                                                     Score _____

© 1986 by CBS College Publishing. All rights reserved.

Building Sentences with Phrases and Clauses Exercise 6–8

NAME _____ DATE _____

Build sentences from the phrases and clauses listed. Add words, as needed, but do not change the word groups provided.

> EXAMPLE: The distance. A light-year. That light travels in a year.
> *A light-year is the distance that light travels in a year.*

1. Medium-sized, yellow star. Named Sol. Our sun.

2. At the speed of light. 4.28 years. If a spaceship traveled to Proxima Centauri.

3. That travels for years. A small ship. Could be a boring experience.

4. 14 to 15 million degrees K. At the center of the sun.

5. Who dreamed of landing on the sun. Early, would-be space travelers. A world like the earth.

6. Freezing temperatures. When the sun collapses and becomes a white dwarf. The end of life on Earth.

7. From the sun. Is reflected. Moonlight. Instead of light from the moon.

8. Hide a stormy, hot surface. The clouds of Venus. Make the planet look soft and inviting.

9. Evidence of life and civilization. The famous Martian canals. Turned out to be natural formations.

10. Only one seems hospitable to human life. Nine planets in our solar system. The third planet from the sun.

Score _____

Building Simple Sentences

121

Building Simple Sentences with Individual Words Exercise 6–9

NAME _____ DATE _____

Build the following simple sentences by adding individual words such as adjectives and adverbs, verbals, and noun-adjectives.

    EXAMPLE: Clint Eastwood starred in Westerns.
    Versatile Clint Eastwood starred in many Italian "spaghetti" Westerns.

1. Dean Martin and Jerry Lewis were a team in the fifties.

2. Gene Kelly and Cyd Charisse starred in *Brigadoon*.

3. The Marx Brothers combined slapstick and insults.

4. Paramount is the attraction.

5. Producers measured potential with tests.

6. Esther Williams swam to music.

7. Bogart films are now considered classics.

8. Vaudeville gave Hollywood Charlie Chaplin.

9. Hitchcock produced thrillers.

10. John Travolta dances in musicals.

Score _____

© 1986 by CBS College Publishing. All rights reserved.

Sentence Combining: Building Sentences with Individual Words Exercise 6–10

NAME _____ DATE _____

Combine each of the following groups of short sentences into a longer simple sentence with modifiers. You will need to add, delete, and rearrange words.

> EXAMPLE: The star was a superstar. The star was enraged.
>
> The star walked off the set. The star was screaming.
>
> *The enraged superstar walked screaming off the set.*

1. There was a monster. The monster was gruesome. The monster looked like a snake. It hissed menacingly.
   _____

2. The movie depicted a fire. The fire was in a skyscraper. The fire was terrifying. The movie was *The Towering Inferno*.
   _____

3. She was a movie queen. Her name was Marilyn. She committed suicide. Her death was tragic.
   _____

4. The epic is science fiction. The epic shows the universe. It shows the universe to us. The universe is inhabited. The universe is exciting.
   _____

5. The films are being made today. Their type is horror. They use the occult. They use the occult to terrify.
   _____

6. The Western featured cowboys. The Westerns were made in Hollywood. The cowboys sang. The cowboys threw ropes. The cowboys fought with guns.
   _____

7. The crew ran the camera. The crew filmed scenes. They filmed Garbo. Garbo was temperamental. They filmed carefully. They were very careful.
   _____

8. They starred in movies. Their lives were legends. They lived luxuriously.
   _____

9. The performers wore greasepaint. The greasepaint was harsh. It pockmarked faces. This happened sometimes. It was unfortunate.
   _____

10. Stars took baths. Stars were glamorous. Some bathed in milk.
    _____

Building Simple Sentences

11. Walt Disney was astounding. He was innovative. He made stars. The stars were cartoon characters. They were cute.

12. Disney made film features. The features were animated. They were popular. The popularity was enormous.

13. *Animal House* was slapstick. It lampooned life. The life was at college. The life was in a fraternity.

14. They were a family. Their name was Von Trapp. They were being pursued. They were terrified. They hid. They remained silent.

15. The films are new. The films are about Superman. They have been rated PG. This is surprising.

© 1986 by CBS College Publishing. All rights reserved.

Identifying Phrases Exercise 6–11

NAME _____ DATE _____

Underline the phrases in the following sentences; then in the spaces provided at the right, identify the kind of phrases used: prepositional phrase (pp), verbal phrase (vbp), absolute phrase (abs), appositive phrase (app), and compound construction (cc). If there is more than one kind of phrase in a sentence, underline and identify each. One phrase may be a part of another phrase.

> EXAMPLE: Laurel and Hardy were contrasting but complementary comedians.
> *cc, cc*

1. With his horse Old Blue Tom Mix became one of the first cowboy stars. _____
2. Always ready to sing a Western song, the Sons of the Pioneers were often part of Roy Rogers's supporting cast. _____
3. Lash Larue, using his whip as often as his gun, usually wore black. _____
4. The Lone Ranger, still a folk-hero favorite, gave away silver bullets. _____
5. Many cowboy stars sang, rode, shot rustlers, and lassoed steers. _____
6. *The Great Train Robbery*, one of the first films with a story, was a Western. _____
7. His gun cocked, Gene Autry confronted the outlaws. _____
8. Wearing fringed shirts, pearl-handled guns, and ten-gallon hats, the cowboy stars dressed distinctively. _____
9. In the 1960's the era of the anti-hero reached the clean world of the Hollywood Western. _____
10. Clint Eastwood's made-in-Italy Westerns featured ruthless men, fierce struggles, and violent deaths. _____
11. To a generation remembering Hopalong Cassidy and Cisco Kid, the outlaw heroes offered a fresh perspective on a popular subject. _____

Score _____

Building Simple Sentences

Sentence Combining: Building Simple Sentences with Phrases Exercise 6–12

NAME _____ DATE _____

Combine each of the following groups of sentences into one simple sentence, adding a different kind of phrase in each part of the exercise as indicated.

> EXAMPLE: a. Prepositional phrases
>
> Too often Hollywood confuses Americans. Hollywood's impossible dreams confuse them.
>
> *Too often Hollywood confuses Americans with its impossible dreams.*

A. Prepositional phrases

1. Disaster films are spectacles. They have widespread appeal.

2. They depict massive destruction. Skyscrapers, airplanes, and cities are destroyed.

3. *On the Beach* portrayed the end. Life on earth ended. A global nuclear war preceded the end.

4. *Jaws* changes the old theme. The old theme is man against nature. *Jaws'* theme is nature against man.

B. Verbal phrases

5. In the 1930's the Motion Picture Association adopted a code. The code censored film content.

6. The code was upheld for twenty years. The code required certain things. According to the code, "good guys" must win and "bad guys" must be punished.

7. The code also imposed restrictions. Various forms of sex and violence were banned.

8. The code became obsolete in the 1960's. The code was replaced by a rating system.

C. Appositives

9. The science fiction film has matured since 1950. It is a product of the Age of Space and Technology.

© 1986 by CBS College Publishing. All rights reserved.

126   Composing Sentences

10. But earlier moviegoers also enjoyed space tales. They were the Flash Gordon serials.

11. Many films emphasize technological feats. The feats are flights to the moon and Mars or the invention of a time machine.

12. Some of the best films feature contact with alien beings. These films include *E.T., Close Encounters of the Third Kind,* and the made-for-television feature *V*.

D. Absolute phrases

13. Some disaster movies are also science fiction. Their catastrophes are the result of some technological advance.

14. The Planet of the Apes series explores a post-nuclear-war world. The apes have evolved as the new dominant species.

15. *King Kong* combines the horror and the disaster genres. The monster gorilla wreaks havoc throughout New York City.

16. *Star Wars* unites science fiction and fantasy. Its major battles are fought by knights with light sabers.

E. Compound constructions

17. Ian Fleming authored the James Bond novels. He transformed the modern spy story.

18. Early spy stories emphasized treachery. They emphasized blood. They emphasized the serious side of espionage.

19. Bond-type stories add romance to intrigue. They add glamour to danger.

20. Enemy agents are often women. The women are beautiful. The women are seductive.

Score _____

Review 6

A. Underline and label the basic elements in the following sentences: subject (s), verb (v), direct object (do), indirect object (io), object complement (oc), and subject complement (sc).

1. Hollywood rewrote the history of the West.

2. Roy Rogers became the prototype singing cowboy.

3. The audience makes a performer a star.

4. Disney gave the world animated features as well as Disneyland.

5. Hollywood still beckons glamorously to many would-be stars.

B. Underline and label these elements in the following sentences: prepositional phrase, verbal phrase, absolute phrase, appositive, compound construction.

6. The life-style of the movie colony has affected American culture, the luxury and extravagance setting trends and creating insatiable consumer appetites.

7. Tom Selleck, star of *Magnum P.I.* as well as a variety of adventure movies, epitomizes the older beach boy.

8. In addition to creating a bigger-than-life spectacle, making movies may involve financing a multimillion-dollar budget.

Score _____

Check your answers against those in the back of the book. Deduct 4 points for errors in Part A, 3 points for errors in Part B. A score of 80 percent or better indicates you can recognize basic sentence elements, but you should continue to practice building simple sentences.

The Writer's Casebook #6

Application: Showing Rather Than Telling

As you enrich basic sentences with words and phrases, you move from generalities to specifics. Telling about something in general terms rather than describing or showing it with specific details makes a subject seem remote and abstract—a disembodied idea rather than a real person or thing.

TELLING: Aunt Isabella was a kind and happy but extremely plump person who embraced us all in her ample arms.
SHOWING: Aunt Isabella measured sixty, quivering, chuckling inches around the middle, and there was not a one of us who had not been buried up to the ears in one of her great, pillowy hugs.
TELLING: Warren replied quickly and coldly.
SHOWING: Warren snapped back, and the temperature dropped to zero.
TELLING: The persuasive manner of the politician swayed the audience.
SHOWING: The senator scanned her audience, seeming to meet each eye and address her remarks to each person. Her back straight, her head high, she drove home points with the tip of a forceful finger, and her voice commanded the farthest corners of the huge auditorium. Soon the skeptical audience was nodding and applauding its approval.

In each of the examples the remote "telling" version has been rewritten to "show" by including specific descriptive details—all of which add more information to what the readers know and help them to create a mental picture.

To show rather than tell requires descriptive adjectives and adverbs and also descriptive nouns and verbs. General modifiers—like *nice, fine, good, bad, warm, cold, small, big*—will be less useful to you in showing your subject than modifiers that evoke immediate and definite images—like *blue, red, mountainous, freezing, lilliputian, nonchalant, wiry, foxy*. Similarly, the more specific the noun or verb, the more descriptive. For example, proper nouns often create a clearer picture than common nouns; *NYPD Sergeant Timothy O'Grady* suggests a large, brusque man, perhaps with a mild brogue and red hair, but *police officer* suggests at best a vague, uniformed outline. The workhorse verbs—such as *be, have, go,* and *do*—are less descriptive than verbs that are used less often but more specifically—such as *shuffle, hug, wrench,* and *scold*.

Enriching sentences with phrases can also change telling to showing and make the writer's point more precisely.

TELLING: Special effects can steal the show.
SHOWING: In fantasy epics like *Star Wars*, special effects, creating the sights and

sounds of space flight or of a battle with lasers, can steal the show and transform the imaginative world of ewoks and Death Stars into a new and more vivid reality.

Cases for Writing: Writing to Show

Case #1

You have traveled to the moon on a ship filled with scientists, adventurers, and star-gazing poets, but you are a land developer. You were sent to the moon at enormous expense by your company to examine the possibilities for development. Write a detailed account of your observations and speculations, showing rather than telling.

Case #2

Rewrite the following skeletal paragraph, enriching the bare bones of the ideas presented with descriptive words and phrases that show rather than tell.

> The cameras began shooting. The stars pasted on smiles. She smiled at him. He smiled at her. They leaned toward one another. His fingers touched her hair. Her lips trembled. The film broke. They sprang apart.

7
Building Compound and Complex Sentences

Preview 7

Revise the following basic sentences to include the construction indicated in parentheses. In the space at the right, identify the sentence you have built as compound (cd) or complex (cx). You may need to change words in the basic sentence or to add words or clauses.

1. Seeking a western route to India, Columbus did not "discover" America. (dependent clause—adverb) _____

2. Leif Ericson, or "Leif the Lucky," probably explored some part of North America around A.D. 1000. (dependent clause—adjective) _____

3. The Incas, Mayans, Aztecs, and many other native peoples were already here. (independent clause) _____

4. The Viking explorers called their discovery "Vinland." (dependent clause—noun) _____

5. Columbus actually landed in the West Indies. (dependent clause—adjective) _____

Building Compound and Complex Sentences 131

6. Columbus's voyage led to the exploration and colonization of the Americas by European countries. (independent clause) _____

7. Englishmen on a fishing voyage may have sailed almost as far as North America in the late sixteenth century. (independent clause) _____

8. Spanish explorers named the isthmus of Central America "Golden Castile" because of the gold ornaments worn by the inhabitants. (dependent clause—adverb) _____

9. The peoples now called Native Americans may have discovered the New World as long ago as 40,000 or 50,000 B.C. (dependent clause—adjective) _____

10. Columbus incorrectly identified the land found, as islands of the Orient and the people found, as Indians. (dependent clause—noun) _____

Score _____

Check your answers against those in the back of the text. Deduct 5 points for any sentence in which your expansion does not fit the model and 5 points for any incorrect identification of sentence type. A score of 80 percent or better means you understand the principles of sentence expansion discussed in the chapter, but even experienced writers will want to practice these principles further and work through the exercises.

7a Building Compound Sentences

In the last chapter you formed compound constructions by linking words and phrases that serve the same function in a sentence. Linking these parallel elements is called *coordination*. When you coordinate complete independent clauses—that is, simple sentences—the result is a *compound sentence*. Simple sentences may be coordinated to communicate addition, contrast, cause and effect, or a choice of alternatives, but in each case the sentences linked should be of equal importance.

(1) Using coordinating conjunctions

When coordinating conjunctions (*and, but, or, nor, for, yet, so*) are used to join independent clauses, a comma usually precedes the conjunction.

> The story of European explorations in the New World is one of rediscovery rather than discovery, for the American continents were already inhabited by their original discoverers.

> Columbus sailed from Europe in 1492, but the ancestors of Native Americans had walked across a natural land bridge from Asia tens of thousand of years before.

(2) Using conjunctive adverbs and other transitional expressions

Simple sentences of equal importance may also be linked by transitional expressions, such as *conjunctive adverbs*. Since the adverb or other transitional expression is not a true conjunction, we join the clauses with a semicolon, a stronger punctuation mark than the comma that precedes a coordinating conjunction. The transitional expression is usually preceded by a semicolon and followed by a comma.

> The Spanish court was interested in precious metals and jewels; consequently, Spanish exploration was also a treasure hunt.

> Columbus made four voyages to the New World; however, he returned to Spain in chains from the third voyage.

Commonly used transitional expressions include *for example, in fact, on the other hand,* and *for instance* and many conjunctive adverbs.

accordingly	furthermore	meanwhile	similarly
also	hence	moreover	still
anyway	however	nevertheless	then
besides	incidentally	next	thereafter
certainly	indeed	nonetheless	therefore
consequently	instead	now	thus
finally	likewise	otherwise	undoubtedly

NOTE: Unlike a true conjunction, a conjunctive adverb can occupy other positions in the sentence. The adverb both smooths the linking of the clauses and modifies the clause in which it is located, while the conjunction simply joins the clauses.

> The Spanish court was interested in precious metals and jewels; Spanish exploration was, consequently, also a treasure hunt.

Building Compound and Complex Sentences   **133**

(3) Using correlative conjunctions

Correlative conjunctions, pairs of joining words such as *not only/but also* and *either/or*, may also be used to form a compound sentence.
NOTE: Be careful not to omit any part of the correlative, such as *also* after *but*.

> Columbus not only sailed to the New World, but he also established colonies there.
>
> Either the ship would reach the Bahamas, or it would sink in the attempt.

(4) Using semicolons

Two closely related independent clauses may be joined with a semicolon.
NOTE: The first letter of the word that follows the semicolon will not be capitalized unless it is a proper noun or adjective.

> Ferdinand Magellan's ship *Victoria* was the first to sail around the world; Magellan, killed by hostile islanders in the Philippines, did not complete the voyage.
>
> The discovery of Australia began as a theory; Ptolemy calculated the need for a large southern continent to balance the weight of the heavy northern land masses.

(5) Using colons

A colon may be used between independent clauses for emphasis when the second clause explains or identifies something in the first clause.

> With no land in sight and the crew in mutiny, he gave his orders: the ship would sail on!
>
> After the third voyage Columbus's report may have been a calculated lie: he claimed to have found the terrestrial paradise in the Orient.

7b   Building Complex Sentences

A *complex sentence* consists of one *independent clause* and one or more *dependent clauses*. The major idea of the sentence is given in the independent or main clause; secondary points, in a dependent clause, which is linked to the main clause by a relative pronoun or a subordinating conjunction. For example, we might build a complex sentence from the major idea—"Columbus precipitated a full-scale European invasion of the New World"—and the minor idea—"He mistook the Bahamas for the Indies"—by introducing the minor idea with although.

secondary point—dependent clause
[Although he mistook the Bahamas for the Indies], [Columbus

main point—independent clause
precipitated a full-scale European invasion of the New World].

Making one part of a sentence dependent upon another part is called *subordination*.

(1) Using subordinating conjunctions and relative pronouns

Dependent clauses cannot stand alone as sentences. They must be placed at the beginning, at the end, or within an independent clause.

<u>When the Polos reached China</u>, they found a culturally and technologically advanced civilization.

Many Europeans did not believe Marco Polo's stories <u>because they seemed too fantastic to be true.</u>

The Polos, <u>who were merchants</u>, profited enormously from their expeditions.

Common subordinating conjunctions include the following.

after	before	rather than	until
although	even though	since	when
as	if	so that	whenever
as if	in order that	that	where
as though	now that	though	wherever
because	once	unless	while

Relative pronouns include *who* (*whose, whom*), *whoever* (*whomever*), *that, which, what, whatever,* and sometimes *where, when, whether, why,* and *how.*

(2) Using adjective, adverb, and noun clauses

Dependent clauses must serve a function in the main clause they are linked to. Clauses introduced by subordinating conjunctions function as adverbs, modifying an entire clause or part of it. Clauses introduced by relative pronouns may function either as adjectives or as noun substitutes. (See Chapter 20 for more about adjectives, adverbs, nouns, and pronouns.)

Adverb clauses may begin or end a sentence.

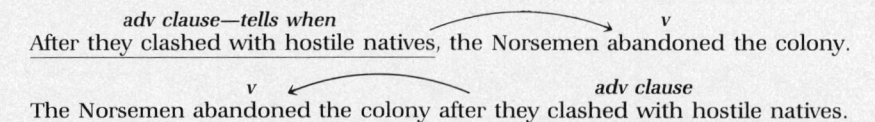

adv clause—tells when   *v*
<u>After they clashed with hostile natives</u>, the Norsemen abandoned the colony.

   v   *adv clause*
The Norsemen abandoned the colony <u>after they clashed with hostile natives</u>.

Adjective clauses usually follow the noun or pronoun they modify.

         n   *adj clause*
In 1001 Leif Ericson, <u>who was looking for timber</u>, settled on the northern coast of Newfoundland.

The Norsemen called their new colony "Vinland" because of the

     n   *adj clause*
wild grapes <u>that grew there</u>.

A *noun clause* may act as subject, object, or complement in the main clause.

Building Compound and Complex Sentences

        n clause—subject   *v*
<u>Who discovered America</u> is now a matter for debate.

Historians, archeologists, and minority groups are now

        n clause—direct object
debating <u>who discovered America</u>.

                n clause—obj of prep
The debate about <u>who discovered America</u> will go on and on.

(3) Using elliptical clauses

A subordinate elliptical clause leaves out some part of, or creates an ellipsis in, a dependent clause. If the meaning is clear from the context, the construction is considered acceptable.

    <u>Although [they were] frightened</u>, they sailed into the Straits.

    Columbus was more successful as an explorer <u>than [he was] as a leader</u>.

    He sought to enslave and exploit the native peoples <u>[that] he encountered</u>.

Building Compound and Complex Sentences

Building Compound Sentences Exercise 7-1

NAME _____ DATE _____

Combine each of the following sentence pairs in two different ways to make compound sentences.

> EXAMPLE: Marco Polo visited the Orient in the thirteenth century.
> He found a civilization far superior to that of Europe.
> *Marco Polo visited the Orient in the thirteenth century, and he found a civilization far superior to that of Europe.*
> *Marco Polo visited the Orient in the thirteenth century; unexpectedly, he found a civilization far superior to that of Europe.*

1. Marco Polo's story is almost like a fairy tale.
   He did not live happily ever after.

2. Kublai Khan welcomed Polo royally.
   The emperor made the Italian a government official.

3. Polo wrote about his experiences, leaving some things out to make the story believable.
   Most people still did not believe him.

4. His tales of burning rocks and liquid seemed absurd to medieval Europe.
   Today Polo's marvels of coal and oil are commonplace.

5. The Americas were named for Americus Vespucius, a Florentine.
   He may or may not have explored the coast of South America.

© 1986 by CBS College Publishing. All rights reserved.

6. Balboa called the Pacific the "Great South Sea."
   He waded in and claimed it for Spain.

7. The explorers may have been heroes.
   They may have been villains.

8. Some may have been interested in knowledge and communication.
   Most seemed preoccupied with plunder and conquest.

9. According to legend, Columbus's first voyage had been paid for with Queen Isabella's jewels.
   The success of all his ventures was measured in the hauls of gold and trinkets brought back.

10. The belated influence of Marco Polo was felt at the Spanish court.
    The sovereigns gave Columbus a letter to Polo's Khan, dead, no doubt, for 200 years by then.

Score _____

Building Compound and Complex Sentences **139**

Identifying Clauses Exercise 7–2

NAME _____ DATE _____

Underline each independent clause in the following sentences with a single line and each dependent clause with two lines. In the space at the right identify each sentence as simple (s), compound (cd), or complex (cx).

   EXAMPLE: Gulliver, who is Jonathan Swift's imaginative version of an explorer, has absurdly unbelievable adventures. _cx_

1. He arrives accidentally in Lilliput after being shipwrecked. _____
2. The Lilliputians are six inches tall; they call Gulliver the "Man-Mountain." _____
3. Gulliver agreed to give two hours' notice before he entered their capital. _____
4. The warning allowed the Lilliputians to stay safely indoors where Gulliver could not step on them. _____
5. It takes three hundred cooks to prepare Gulliver's meals, and one hundred waiters serve him. _____
6. In Brobdingnag, a land of giants, Gulliver himself is a Lilliputian. _____
7. The Brobdingnaggians treat Gulliver like a pet; they keep him in a box, and they play with him. _____
8. Then a bird carries Gulliver away in his traveling box, dropping him at sea. _____
9. Whether Gulliver is a barbaric Yahoo is the major concern of the Houyhnhnms, a race of rational horses. _____

Score _____

© 1986 by CBS College Publishing. All rights reserved.

Building Complex and Compound Sentences   Exercise 7-3

NAME _____ DATE _____

Combine the following sets of simple sentences to make complex or compound sentences. Change words or order as needed.

    EXAMPLE: Gulliver turned his back on his fellow humans. He was embarrassed by his relationship to the Yahoos.
    Because he was embarrassed by his relationship to the Yahoos, Gulliver turned his back on his fellow humans.

1. Some explorers may have had lofty motives. Most seemed intent on conquest.

2. Cortez defeated the Aztecs in just two years. He combined war and diplomacy.

3. Spain and Portugal argued over possession of the new lands. Each country had made important discoveries.

4. Pope Alexander VI arbitrated the dispute. He was Spanish.

5. The French and English searched for a Northwest Passage to the East. They explored North America in the process.

6. Peter the Great of Russia sent expeditions east in the eighteenth century. They named the Bering Sea and laid the foundation for Russia's claim to Alaska.

7. Thomas Jefferson dispatched Zebulon Pike to search for the headwaters of the Mississippi and the Red River. He sent Meriwether Lewis and William Clark to find a water route across the continent.

8. The Northwest Passage remained a puzzle until this century. The Norwegian explorer Roald Amundsen took a fishing boat west through the Arctic Ocean.

9. Amundsen was beaten to the North Pole by Robert E. Peary. Amundsen later discovered the South Pole.

Building Compound and Complex Sentences 141

10. In the second half of the twentieth century, both the United States and the Soviet Union have landed expeditions on the moon. Both have agreed not to claim sovereignty over space, the moon, or the planets.

_____
_____
_____

Score _____

Building Compound and Complex Sentences   Exercise 7-4

NAME _____ DATE _____

Expand the following skeletal paragraph by adding the elements indicated in parentheses. Change, add, or delete words as necessary.

> EXAMPLE: Magellan never completed his famous round-the-world voyage (dependent clause—adjective).
>
> *Magellan, who was killed by hostile natives, never completed his famous round-the-world voyage.*

    The world was an exciting place in 1492 (dependent clause—adverb). There were many enticing legends (independent clause). The earth was at last known to be round (dependent clause—adjective). No longer did explorers need to worry about falling off the edge of the earth. The earth was at last known to be round (dependent clause—adjective). They could confidently search for new lands (independent clause). The new world was indeed the pearl in the oyster (independent clause). Explorers conquered, colonized, and ruled (dependent clause—noun). It was a glorious time for the rugged individualists (dependent clause—adverb). They had found, as Columbus said, terrestrial paradise, Eden. However, the "discovered" peoples were less ecstatic (dependent clause—adjective). For them the Age of Discovery brought invasion (dependent clause—adverb). The conquerers destroyed the work of generations of Aztecs and Incas (dependent clause—noun). Paradise, it seems, was also hell (independent clause).

Building Compound and Complex Sentences   **143**

Review 7

Revise the following basic sentences to include the construction indicated in parentheses. In the space at the right, identify the sentence you have built as compound (cd) or complex (cx). You may need to change words in the basic sentence or to add words or clauses.

1. The explorers mapped the world. (independent clause)   _____

2. Ptolemy, an armchair Greek geographer, underestimated the size of the world. (dependent clause—adjective)   _____

3. Meeting a ship that had sailed north from San Francisco, Amundsen had successfully negotiated the Northwest Passage. (dependent clause—adverb)   _____

4. Today's explorers are scientists, exploring space, the oceans, and time, their exploration vessels their laboratories. (independent clause)   _____

5. Many hope the Space Age will be another Age of Discovery. (independent clause)   _____

6. They dream of a universe filled with people and treasure. (dependent clause—noun)   _____

7. In some science fiction, space captains, discovering a new world, conquer it, colonize it, and rule it. (dependent clause—adverb)   _____

8. Like Sir Francis Drake, they are out for adventure and plunder, with scientific discoveries and communications among races incidental at best, destroyed or forgotten at worst. (independent clause) _____

_____

_____

9. So far, however, space is a lonely place. (dependent clause—adjective) _____

_____

_____

10. The conqueror of the red planet, no matter which country, must look to Earth for praise, not to little green Martians. (dependent clause—noun) _____

_____

_____

Score _____

Check your answers against those in the back of the text. Deduct 5 points for any sentence in which your expansion does not fit the model and 5 points for any incorrect identification of sentence type. A score of 80 percent or better means you have a sound grasp of the principles of sentence expansion discussed in this chapter.

The Writer's Casebook #7

Application: The Comparison/Contrast Essay

In the sentences you have been building in this chapter, you have used conjunctions and transition words and an arrangement of clauses to show the relationship of ideas. For example, you may have used *but, however,* and *on the other hand* when the ideas in the clauses were contrasting or *and, moreover,* and *in addition* when the ideas were comparable, that is, showing similarities or likenesses. Also, to highlight the likenesses or differences, you joined the clauses in a single sentence.

> Some people believe Columbus discovered America, but others give credit to Leif Ericson. (compound sentence showing contrasting views)
>
> Although Columbus "sailed the ocean blue in 1492," Native Americans may have crossed the Bering Strait as long ago as 50,000 B.C. (complex sentence showing comparable action but making the first clause subordinate to and, therefore, less important than the second)

Building Compound and Complex Sentences

Often in academic writing you will be asked to compare and contrast ideas, books, people, and so forth. As in writing compound and complex sentences, you will need to adopt strategies for arranging and linking your materials that will emphasize the likenesses or differences you perceive.

When you are given a comparison/contrast assignment, first be certain you understand what is expected. Are you being asked to compare—that is, find likenesses? Are you being asked to contrast? Or are you being asked to do both? If you are not certain from the wording of the question, ask your instructor for a clarification.

Once you understand the assignment and have collected some materials, you need to choose a pattern of organization. If the subject and your approach to it are fairly simple, you may choose the *half-and-half* method. Divide the paper into two major parts: in the first part discuss one of the items you are comparing or contrasting, and in the second part discuss the other item. For example, the overall plan for a paper contrasting Columbus and Ericson as a discoverer of the New World might look something like this.

Half-and-Half Method

Introduction
LEAD-IN: Columbus and Ericson were both explorers.
THESIS: Their "discoveries" of America took place at different times and yielded different results.

Middle
ERICSON: He sailed around A.D. 1000, founded Vinland—a community that did not survive.
COLUMBUS: He sailed in 1492, thought he had found a direct passage to the Orient, but launched a wave of exploration and colonization.

Conclusion
FINAL JUDGMENT: Ericson may have been the first to discover the New World, but Columbus had more impact on history.

When the assignment or subject is more complex or your paper will be several pages rather than several paragraphs long, you can use a point-by-point method of organization. Organize materials by ideas; then discuss each idea in terms of first one and then the other of the items you are comparing.

Point-by-Point Method

Introduction
LEAD-IN: Columbus and Ericson were both explorers.
THESIS: Their "discoveries" of America took place at different times and yielded different results, yet neither can legitimately claim to have discovered America.

Middle

DATES:	Ericson sailed around A.D. 1000; Columbus, in 1492.
IMMEDIATE RESULTS:	Ericson founded Vinland; Columbus claimed discovery of direct route to Orient.
LONG-TERM RESULTS:	Vinland did not survive; Columbus's voyages launched a wave of exploration and colonization.
CLAIMS AS DISCOVERERS:	Neither truly "discovered" America; the Native Americans had already done that as long as 50,000 years earlier.

Conclusion

FINAL JUDGMENT:	Neither Columbus nor Ericson can truthfully be called the "discoverer" of America, but of the two explorers Columbus's impact on history was greater.

Cases for Writing: Comparing and Contrasting

Case #1

You have been given the chance to be part of the first interstellar flight to Alpha Centauri. The expedition is dangerous and will take at least fifteen years to complete. But the prospects are exciting. Scientists have picked up radio transmissions from the sixth planet of the star that we call Alpha-3. Write a paper in which you compare/contrast the advantages and the disadvantages of making the trip and make a decision about going or staying.

Case #2

You are an explorer. In your travels (by ship, time machine, spaceship, balloon, submarine, underground borer, and so forth) you discover a Utopia—an ideal society. Write a paper in which you compare/contrast your Utopia to our own world and decide whether to publicize your findings.

Writing Emphatic Sentences   8

> **Preview 8**
>
> Read the following sentence pairs carefully. Circle the letter before the sentence that more successfully emphasizes the content.
>
> 1. a. Some researchers claim that sports provide a practice arena for aggression, rather than a safety valve.
>   b. Sports provide a practice arena for aggression rather than a safety valve, according to some researchers.
> 2. a. Clear, cold, clean—the spring deserved its name, Blessing Waters.
>   b. The clear, cold, clean spring deserved the name Blessing Waters.
> 3. a. The day began in chaos, continued in chaos, and ended in chaos.
>   b. When the day began, everything was chaotic; as time went on, chaos continued, and by day's end chaos reigned supreme.
> 4. a. The computers were entered by a young hacker with the code name Captain Blood.
>   b. A young hacker with the code name Captain Blood entered the computers.
> 5. a. We wanted the tomatoes to grow fat and juicy; we watered them daily and fed them monthly, for that reason.
>   b. We wanted the tomatoes to grow fat and juicy; for that reason, we watered them daily and fed them monthly.
> 6. a. More cerebral but no less gory than the standard detective yarn, these mysteries are best sellers.
>   b. These mysteries are best sellers because they are more cerebral but no less gory than the standard detective yarn.
> 7. a. Duties of a President include managing the government, preparing the budget, and holding news conferences.
>   b. Duties of the President include holding news conferences, preparing the budget, and managing the government.
> 8. a. In the forties kids jitterbugged; in the eighties they breakdance; whatever the era, young people dislocate their spines with impossible contortions they call dancing.
>   b. Kids in the forties did the jitterbug while in the eighties they breakdance; in all eras dislocation of the spine during the contortions called dancing is a common malady of the young.

9. a. They decided to quit: to quit griping, to quit grumbling, to quit passing the buck.
   b. They decided to quit griping and to quit grumbling, and also to quit passing the buck.
10. a. That too much television adversely affects youngsters' social and mental development is a definite possibility.
    b. Too much television can adversely affect youngsters' social and mental development.

Score _____

Check your answers against those in the back of the text. Deduct 10 points for each error. A score of 80 percent or better means you have a good feeling for emphasis in English sentences, but even experienced writers will want to practice writing emphatic sentences by working through this chapter.

8a Achieving Emphasis Through Word Order

Where you place ideas in a sentence determines the amount of attention they will receive and, therefore, the degree of force they will carry. Altering normal sentence order and placing key points at the *beginning* or at the *end* of a sentence can help focus your readers' attention and, consequently, emphasize your ideas.

(1) Beginning with important ideas

Giving important ideas first ensures that busy, fact-oriented readers can grasp your meaning quickly. Business and technical (scientific) writing usually follows this pattern.

NOTE: Empty phrases like *It is a fact that, There is (are), It is interesting to note,* waste this strategic beginning position and should be avoided.

                                      key idea
UNEMPHATIC: It is clear that *IBM stock* is rising.
                          key idea
EMPHATIC: *IBM stock* is rising.

(2) Ending with important ideas

Saving important ideas for last allows you to dramatize them. Sometimes this dramatic positioning will be emphasized further by setting off or pointing out the key word or phrase with a colon or a dash.

> Running for political office in the 1980's requires an essential ingredient: money.
>
> Stanley plodded through the jungle with only one goal in mind—to find Livingston.

Sentences may also build in *climactic word order* toward a major idea or climax at the end.

> She is an attractive mother of three, a brilliant lawyer, a dedicated member of the club, and the best possible candidate for the club president.

NOTE: Avoid placing transitional expressions like conjunctive adverbs at the end of a sentence. Place them where they can best show the relationship between ideas.

LESS EMPHATIC: The storm roared menacingly overhead; no rain fell, however.
MORE EMPHATIC: The storm roared menacingly overhead; however, no rain fell.

(3) Departing from expected word order

The unexpected always catches our attention. Altering normal word order (subject + verb + object or complement) draws attention to the elements that are not where we expect them to be and makes the entire sentence more emphatic. However, since the effectiveness of the method depends upon its being unexpected, use it frugally.

> Slowly and faithfully plodded the tortoise; swiftly but erratically hopped the hare.

8b Achieving Emphasis Through Sentence Structure

Placing key ideas in main clauses and secondary ideas in modifying phrases and dependent clauses delineates the pattern of emphasis.

(1) Using cumulative sentences

In a *cumulative*, or *loose*, sentence structure, the main clause appears at the beginning of the sentence and modifiers follow it. Emphasis comes from the normal order of discovery; our expectations are met.

> The rain came in a wet, gray wall, sweeping across the mesa, churning the red clay into red mud, and turning dry arroyos into raging torrents of muddy water.

(2) Using periodic sentences

A *periodic sentence* unfolds differently from a cumulative sentence. Our expectations are frustrated, for the sentence begins with modifiers and ends with the main clause, but the unexpected alteration of normal order focuses our attention and builds suspense.

Sweeping across the mesa in a wet, gray wall; churning the red clay into red mud; and turning dry arroyos into raging torrents of muddy water—the rain came.

Marie Curie, after grueling months of hand-refining tons of uranium ore, finally isolated the new element radium.

8c   Achieving Emphasis Through Parallelism and Balance

Parallel structures add emphasis to language in much the same way that rhythm or repeated melodies add emphasis to music. The pattern made by the balanced or parallel parts, as well as by balanced punctuation, calls attention to any likenesses and/or differences you are seeking to emphasize. In a special type of parallel structure, the *balanced sentence*, all or some of the elements of two clauses will be mirrored, giving the writer an effective frame for comparison or contrast.

BALANCED INDEPENDENT CLAUSES: Ask not what your country can do for you; ask what you can do for your country. (John F. Kennedy, *Inaugural Address*)
PARALLEL PHRASES: Earth to earth, ashes to ashes, dust to dust. . . . (*Book of Common Prayer*)
PARALLEL WORDS: And now abideth faith, hope, charity, these three. . . . (I Corinthians 13:13, KJ)
PARALLEL WORDS: Why have women passion, intellect, moral activity—these three—and a place in society where no one of the three can be exercised? (Florence Nightingale, *Cassandra*)

8d   Achieving Emphasis Through Repetition

Although ineffective repetition sounds awkward, intentional repetition can emphasize key words or phrases. Repetition works especially well with parallel or balanced structures.

INEFFECTIVE: He lost the first match, but he still practiced, and still he kept working out, and he believed in himself still.
EFFECTIVE: He lost the first match; still he practiced, still he worked out, and still he believed in himself.

8e   Achieving Emphasis Through Active Voice

Usually the active voice of the verb is more emphatic because it fulfills our expectations by following normal word order: subject/actor + verb/action

+ object/receiver of the action. Passive voice, which reverses the order, should be used only when you wish to emphasize the receiver of the action.

ACTIVE: Tasmania has declared war upon Australia. (emphasis upon *Tasmania*)
PASSIVE: War has been declared. (emphasis upon *war*)

NOTE: Technical and business writers often use the passive voice when they want to emphasize what happened—that is, the results—rather than who made it happen.

Identifying Emphatic Sentences Exercise 8-1

NAME _____ DATE _____

Circle the letter before the more emphatic sentence in each pair. Be ready to explain the methods used to achieve emphasis in the sentences you choose.

EXAMPLE: a. There were two ways of doing things in my grandfather's view—his right way and everyone else's wrong way.

(b.) My grandfather saw two ways of doing things—his right way and everyone else's wrong way.

1. a. He finished Beethoven's Unfinished Symphony; he finished it magnificently, moreover.
   b. He finished Beethoven's Unfinished Symphony; moreover, he finished it magnificently.
2. a. Three things are necessary for happiness—good health, good friends, and hard work.
   b. To be happy, people need to have their health, they should develop good friendships, and they should work hard.
3. a. The Olympic Games were canceled in 1940 and 1944 because of the war.
   b. Because of the war, in 1940 and 1944 the International Olympic Committee canceled the games.
4. a. Some primitive life form may once have lived on Mars.
   b. It is possible that some form of primitive life may once have lived on Mars.
5. a. The national parks were created to provide attractive outings for tourists, to serve as public universities of nature, and to preserve our natural wonders.
   b. The national parks were created to preserve our natural wonders, to serve as public universities of nature, and to provide attractive outings for tourists.
6. a. From 1910 to 1914 the world's first airline provided town-to-town air service in Germany with a fleet of four Zeppelins.
   b. A fleet of four Zeppelins, making up the world's first airline, provided Germany with town-to-town air service from 1910 to 1914.
7. a. Over the river and through the woods to Grandmother's house, we go.
   b. We go over the river and through the woods to Grandmother's house.
8. a. He asked for justice, and justice is what he got.
   b. Justice he asked for, and justice he got.
9. a. She came, saw, and conquered.
   b. She came, she saw, she conquered.
10. a. It's good advice for boxers to "float like a butterfly, sting like a bee." (from Muhammed Ali)
    b. "Float like a butterfly, sting like a bee" is good advice for boxers.
11. a. Balloon buffoonery characterized the first years of lighter-than-air flight.
    b. The first years of lighter-than-air flight were characterized by balloon buffoonery.
12. a. There is certainly an obsession in American sports with winning.
    b. American sports are obsessed with one thing—winning.
13. a. Computer hackers scorn the uninitiated: "infidels," they are called.
    b. Because of the contempt and scorn that they feel for the uninitiated, computer hackers call them "infidels."

© 1986 by CBS College Publishing. All rights reserved.

14. a. The empty house was filled with mice—mice in the basement; mice in the attic; mice in the kitchen under the stove, behind the sink, and in the cupboards.
    b. There were mice everywhere in the empty house; the mice were in the basement; mice had set up housekeeping in the attic; and the stove, sink, and cupboards in the kitchen were filled with mice.
15. a. The Great Salt Lake—its shores ringed with sandy beaches, its air filled with the tang of salt, its piers crowded with gulls—makes desert-dwellers long for the sea.
    b. Desert-dwellers are made to long for the sea by the Great Salt Lake because its shores are ringed with sandy beaches, the air is filled with the tang of salt, and its piers are crowded with gulls.
16. a. An eagle dance is performed to give Pueblo warriors power in battle.
    b. Pueblo warriors perform an eagle dance to give them power in battle.
17. a. High fashion, high finance, and high living await in the Big Apple.
    b. There are high fashion, high finance, and high living awaiting in the Big Apple.
18. a. Succumbing to the temptation of a hot fudge sundae, I lost the battle of the pound; however, I had not lost the war.
    b. Succumbing to the temptation of a hot fudge sundae, I lost the battle of the pound; I had not lost the war, however.
19. a. I suffered through my POW rations of hardtack and water for two days.
    b. For two days I suffered with nothing to eat but hardtack and water, what you might call POW rations.
20. a. When I found that even POW rations caused me to gain another pound, I surrendered and pigged out.
    b. Unhappily, I surrendered and pigged out when it was found that even POW rations caused me to gain another unwanted pound.

Score _____

Writing Emphatic Sentences

Combining for Emphasis   Exercise 8–2

NAME _____   DATE _____

Combine each of the following sets of sentences into a single, emphatic sentence. Rearrange, add, or delete words as necessary.

> EXAMPLE: The depression of many elderly people is the cumulative effect of multiple causes. Their income and health have declined. Their friends are dying. Their children and grandchildren are too busy for them.
> *The depression of many elderly people is the cumulative effect of multiple causes—declining income and health, dying friends, and too-busy children and grandchildren.*

1. The expense of living is great. Only the expense of dying exceeds it.
   _____

2. The working woman often must have multiple personalities. At work she must be aggressive and authoritative. At home she must be nurturing. In the community she must be concerned and involved.
   _____
   _____
   _____

3. The spider spun slowly. The spider spun patiently. The spider waited for the fly. The fly was frivolous. The fly was unheeding.
   _____

4. The jogger was pursued by angry dogs. The jogger kept running.
   The jogger was insulted by bikers. The jogger kept running.
   The jogger was sideswiped by an automobile. The jogger kept running.
   _____
   _____

5. *The Lord of the Rings* is a fantasy epic. It was written by J. R. R. Tolkien. He was professor of Anglo-Saxon at Oxford.
   _____

6. The Everglades are located in Florida. The Everglades are made up of sawgrass prairies and swamps. They experience extremes of weather. In the summer there is flooding; in the winter, drought.
   _____
   _____

7. The manatee is a large aquatic mammal. It has flippers for forelimbs. It has no hind limbs. It is helpless on land.
   _____
   _____

© 1986 by CBS College Publishing. All rights reserved.

8. The manatee lives on seaweed and other water plants. It eats as much as 100 pounds of seaweed a day. It has to keep up its substantial weight. It may weigh as little as 450 pounds. It may weigh as much as 2,000 pounds.

9. There are 60 seconds left to play. The Lakers are one point behind. Jabbar has the ball. He dribbles. He zigzags. He slam dunks. The Lakers win.

10. Three household appliances are indispensable. Their invention marked the beginning of life on earth as we know it. One is the vacuum cleaner. Another is the dishwasher. And another is the refrigerator.

Score _____

Writing Emphatic Sentences

Revising for Emphasis Exercise 8–3

NAME _____ DATE _____

Rewrite the following paragraph in the space provided, changing unemphatic sentences into emphatic sentences. You may combine, add, delete, or alter as necessary.

    It is a fact that disciplinary problems in the home are usually dealt with powerfully by punishing the offender. Punishment is also a powerful way of dealing with disciplinary problems on the street and in the classroom. A child is spanked by a parent. A speeding driver is ticketed by a police officer. Extra homework is assigned by a teacher. Punishment has been administered to most of us, and punishment has been administered by most of us. But the question arises: what are its effects? B. F. Skinner, whose research in psychology is highly noted, has something to say on the matter. He says that punishment merely has the effect of suppressing the behavior, and it suppresses the behavior only in certain circumstances. The behavior may be continued by the person in the same way as before. Only when the punisher is present is the behavior changed. It is interesting to note that the side effects of punishment are often much worse than the behavior the disciplinarian sought to control. For example, it often happens that the punished behavior may actually increase rather than decrease. The punished child may learn to imitate, eventually becoming a child abuser, moreover. And often long-lasting and difficult to change are the emotional by-products of punishment. Punishment brings quick results, and that is why people punish, says Skinner. There is every reason to believe, however, that quick results are not always the same thing as long-term results.

Review 8

Read the following sentence pairs carefully. Circle the letter before the sentence that more successfully emphasizes the content.

1. a. The manatee is a placid but tasty creature; hunters, two- and four-legged, prey upon it, consequently.
   b. The manatee is a placid but tasty creature; consequently, two- and four-legged hunters prey upon it.
2. a. It says that a million-dollar lottery was won by Elizabeth Trimble, a secretary who had lost her job the day before.
   b. Elizabeth Trimble, a secretary who had lost her job the day before, won a million-dollar lottery.
3. a. Because of its raunchiness and obscenity, the film earned its "R" rating.
   b. Raunchy and obscene, the film earned its "R" rating.
4. a. Watching too much television can foster social withdrawal and mental apathy among young children.
   b. Symptoms of social withdrawal and mental apathy among young children can be fostered by the watching of too much television.
5. a. We may never realize our impossible dreams, but living the life of daily reality would be much less possible without them.
   b. Impossible dreams may never become reality, but reality may be impossible without them.
6. a. John F. Kennedy's charisma as a political candidate and later President consisted of two parts intelligence, one part money, and one part looks.
   b. John F. Kennedy's charisma as a political candidate and later President consisted of one part looks, one part money, and two parts intelligence.
7. a. Read to escape the past, to occupy the present, and to fortify yourself for the future.
   b. Reading will help you escape the past, it will also help you occupy your time in the present, and it will also help you become fortified for tomorrow.
8. a. There was a flash flood coming down the canyon, grinding boulders and snapping tree trunks.
   b. Down the canyon grinding boulders and snapping tree trunks came the flash flood.
9. a. Rain was promised by the storm, but it brought thunder.
   b. The storm promised rain but brought thunder.
10. a. The intellectual emptiness and garish imitations of life are pointed out by critics of the television wasteland as two major features of the neon-style landscape.
    b. Critics of the television wasteland point out two major features of the neon-style landscape: intellectual emptiness and garish imitations of life.

Score _____

Check your answers against those in the back of the book. Deduct 10 points for each error. A score of 80 percent or better indicates a good foundation for writing emphatic sentences.

The Writer's Casebook #8

Application: Emphasizing with Point of View

In writing sentences your arrangement of words will emphasize your point of view. For example, if you are writing about the gas company's recent increase in the customer's base rate and wanted to emphasize the increase, you would structure the sentence differently than if you wanted to call attention to the company itself.

> The Tri-State Gas Company has announced an increase of 50 percent in the customer's base rate, effective March 1. (The villains have been named! Let's write letters, take them to court, protest.)

> An increase of 50 percent in the customer's base rate will take effect March 1, according to Tri-State Gas Company. (The writer is more concerned about the increase itself than about who ordered it.)

In writing essays you also speak from a point of view. That perspective is an integral part of the message you communicate and determines the points you choose for emphasis as well as the way you organize your materials. You may write in the first person *I* or *we*, in which case the point of view is most often your own; that is, it is subjective, emphasizing your own beliefs, hopes, fears, background, and education. You may use the second person *you* when you want to emphasize the interests and concerns of your audience. (Business letters often adopt this perspective, with its emphasis on the customer. And so does this workbook!) You may write from a third-person point of view (*he, she, it, they*) when your message is objective—that is, object oriented, directed away from your personal interests and concerns, as in a lab report or a proposal. Or you may assume a role and write from a perspective completely different from your own.

Consider the following comments about Columbus's landing in the New World, each written from a different perspective.

FIRST PERSON, COLUMBUS:	I claim this heathen land, which I have discovered, for God and Spain.
SECOND PERSON, COLUMBUS TO RELUCTANT CREW MEMBER:	You will have gold and slaves when we land in the New World.
THIRD PERSON, OBJECTIVE:	Columbus landed in the Bahamas in 1492, claiming the island for Spain.
DIFFERENT ROLE—NATIVE AMERICAN:	The white devils invaded the island.

The following list illustrates the different points of view from which various writing assignments and tasks might be written.

1. First person: personal essays, reviews that emphasize your opinion or taste, business memos, reaction papers, creative writing, personal letters, journals

2. Second person: business letters (sales, collection, requests, congratulations, and so forth), instructions, some memos
3. Third person: reports (lab, business—especially formal, book, activity, observation, and so forth), interpretation, essay exams over content, analytical essays, summaries or précis
4. Different role: creative writing, some sociology exercises, journals

NOTE: Many academic assignments will call for the third-person, objective point of view in your writing.

Cases for Writing: Focusing In, or Writing from Where You Stand

Case #1

Assume that you are applying for the ideal job—the one you have always dreamed about. Write two letters concerning this job. First write a letter of application to the company or firm that advertised. Use the second person *you* and emphasize the benefits to the employer of hiring you. Then write a letter to a friend, using the first person *I* and emphasizing the benefits of the job to you.

Case #2

Imagine you are a staff writer for a local newspaper. First, investigate a controversial issue of significance to your community—such as whether or not to build a new courthouse, raise taxes to support education, or impose a curfew on teenagers. Second, write a news story about the dispute for the front page of the paper, maintaining an objective stance. Finally, write a column for the editorial page about your own opinion of the issue.

Writing Concise Sentences   9

Preview 9

Rewrite the following paragraph to eliminate unnecessary words, phrases, and sentences. Answers will vary.

    Spare-time hobbies are certainly leisure activities, things we do when there is nothing else to do and we want to fill up or pass the time away. But at the same time it is equally true that hobbies are activities pursued for the purpose of maintaining a good level of mental health and psycho-emotional well-being. It is a fact that many extremely busy and industrious people have managed to find time throughout the years to pursue or "ride" a hobby. Time was spared from matters of great importance by Churchill so that he could spend some time painting. Pipe organs were built by J. Edgar Hoover, whom everyone will remember, of course. Peter Marshall raised roses. He was a highly noted and well-thought-of Presbyterian clergyman. Meanwhile a well-thought-of Catholic clergyman, Cardinal Spellman, spent his spare time collecting stamps.

Score _____

Compare your answer to the one in the back of the text. Compute your score by adding one point for every word you are able to deduct. (Your score could exceed 100.)

    A *concise sentence* uses a minimum number of words to convey a maximum amount of meaning. Achieving economy in sentences begins with controlling diction, thereby reducing the number of words without reducing meaning.

Writing Concise Sentences   **163**

9a Eliminating Nonessential Words

Essential words are content words—words that convey major ideas. Nonessential words extend the length of the sentence without extending its content significantly. Essential words should be placed in the most important position in a sentence—that is, they should appear in the main clause as subject, verb, objects, or complements—and other words that make connections or show relationships should be kept to a minimum. Underlining essential words may help you rewrite wordy sentences.

WORDY (key words underlined):   It is my considered opinion that the <u>stress</u> we experience in our <u>competitive</u> society makes it especially <u>necessary</u> that each one of us has a leisure-time, just-for-fun activity—a <u>hobby</u>.

CONCISE: Stress in our competitive society makes hobbies a necessity.

(1) Deadwood

Eliminate deadwood, or empty phrases, such as *who are, which are, that is, there is, there are, it is, all things considered, it is a fact that, I feel, It goes without saying that, It is interesting to note that,* and so forth.

WORDY (deadwood underlined):   Some stamp collectors, <u>all of whom are called</u> philatelists, value cancellation marks, <u>which are</u> made by fancy stamping devices, <u>which are</u> the "killers" of the postal trade.

CONCISE: Some stamp collectors, or philatelists, value cancellation marks, made by fancy stamping devices, the "killers" of the postal trade.

WORDY (deadwood underlined):   <u>It goes without saying that there are</u> many collectors who simply look for the most attractive stamps.

CONCISE: Many collectors simply look for the most attractive stamps.

(2) Utility words

Eliminate utility words—all-purpose words like the abstract nouns *type, sort, thing,* and *aspect;* adjectives with general meanings like *important, interesting, nice,* and *fine;* and some common adverbs like *really, basically, very, rather,* and *actually.* Replace utility words with more meaningful words, or delete them.

WORDY (utility words underlined):   <u>Really</u> <u>interesting</u> are the rare <u>type</u> of stamps.

CONCISE: Most valuable are the rare stamps.

(3) Circumlocution

Eliminate circumlocution, or saying something in a roundabout (circling around) way.

WORDY: It is understandable that public figures who are under considerable pressure in their work lives should adopt activities for their leisure hours that will allow them to rest.

CONCISE: Understandably, public figures, pressured by career demands, adopt restful pastimes.

9b   Eliminating Needless Repetition

Intentional repetition will add emphasis to your writing, but unnecessary repetition makes your writing sound awkward and may distort its meaning. You can eliminate repetition by substituting a pronoun for a repeated noun, by using elliptical constructions, and by using appositives.

WORDY: Cardinal Spellman's extensive philatelic stamp collection is housed in a special museum donated by Cardinal Spellman's friend.

CONCISE: Cardinal Spellman's extensive stamp collection is housed in a special museum donated by his friend. (*Stamp collection* replaces redundant *philatelic stamp collection* and possessive pronoun *his* replaces repeated possessive noun *Cardinal Spellman's*.)

WORDY: The Spellman collection features mint domestic issues and Vatican City stamps. The smaller Benjamin K. Miller collection features U.S. stamps issued between 1847 and 1920. The Spellman collection is probably the most complete display in the United States.

CONCISE: The Spellman collection, probably the most complete display in the United States, features mint domestic issues and Vatican City stamps; the smaller Benjamin K. Miller collection, U.S. stamps issued between 1847 and 1920. (third sentence reduced to appositive, second sentence made elliptical by deleting repeated verb *features*)

Sentence combining may also be used to eliminate needless repetition, as well as to coordinate, to subordinate, and to eliminate deadwood.

WORDY: Philatelic treasures include a one-cent British Guiana stamp. It sold for $280,000 in 1970. Another treasure is an envelope with two one-cent Mauritius stamps. It sold for $380,000.

CONCISE: Philatelic treasures include a one-cent British Guiana stamp, which sold for $280,000 in 1970, and an envelope with two one-cent Mauritius stamps, which sold for $380,000. (first and third sentences coordinated as compound objects and second and third sentences subordinated as adjective clauses)

WORDY: The American Topical Association is made up of a special kind of stamp collector. To members of this society the interesting thing is topics. They collect stamps by topic. Topics include art, religious subjects, space, and birds.

CONCISE: Members of the American Topical Association collect stamps by topics, including art, religious subjects, space, and birds. (both repetition and unnecessary words eliminated through combining)

9c Tightening Rambling Sentences

A loosely structured sentence filled with repetition, unnecessary words, and tacked-on phrases and clauses requires thorough revision—that is, you must "re-see" major ideas and rewrite to create a stronger structure that adequately emphasizes those ideas. Your sentences will be stronger and more clearly focused if you remember to put main ideas in main clauses and, wherever possible, to use one word instead of several and phrases instead of clauses.

WORDY: In 1918 a stamp was printed, and it was airmail, but the airplane was upside down, and the stamp became famous.
CONCISE: A famous airmail stamp was printed in 1918 with the airplane upside down.
WORDY: The first official U.S. postage stamps, which were issued in 1847, were a five-cent stamp, which pictured Benjamin Franklin, and a ten-cent stamp, which pictured George Washington.
CONCISE: Issued in 1847, the first official U.S. postage stamps pictured Benjamin Franklin on a five-cent and George Washington on a ten-cent stamp.

Writing Concise Sentences   **167**

Eliminating Nonessential Words   Exercise 9–1

NAME _____   DATE _____

Eliminate deadwood, utility words, and circumlocution from the following sentences.

> EXAMPLE: Kiteflying, which can be a colorful and time-consuming hobby, at the present time probably originated in Asia in the vicinity of 3,000 years ago.
> *Kiteflying, a colorful and time-consuming hobby, may have originated in Asia around 3,000 years ago.*

1. One rather interesting aspect of kiteflying is the sport of kite fighting, which is really popular in Japan.

2. It is the object of the contestants to try to destroy each other's kites.

3. It is entirely possible to use a kite string coated with ground glass to cut the opponents' lines.

4. There are circular disks flown in a sort of train making up the Chinese dragon kite.

5. It is interesting to note that often the bamboo frames of Oriental kites are actually bent to form birds, insects, or various other kinds of shapes.

6. At one point in time Kazuhiko Asaba who happened to be from Japan flew 1,050 kites on one line.

7. As early as 1825 an English teacher, who was named George Pocock, built a kite that was actually strong enough to lift his daughter all of 300 feet in the air.

8. The same kite enthusiast was able to pull light carriages by means of kites at speeds in the vicinity of twenty miles per hour.

9. A particularly interesting kind of kite is the *barroletas*, which is flown to celebrate All Saints' Day in Guatemala.

© 1986 by CBS College Publishing. All rights reserved.

10. All things considered, kiteflying somewhere around the area of an electrical storm is basically quite dangerous due to the fact that lightening will actually travel down the wet line.

_____
_____

Score _____

Writing Concise Sentences   **169**

Eliminating Needless Repetition   Exercise 9–2

NAME _____ DATE _____

Revise this paragraph to delete unnecessary repetition as well as nonessential words or phrases.

> EXAMPLE: Numerous numbers of hobbyists raise various types of animals, which include canaries, goldfish, ants, even snakes.
> *Many hobbyists raise animals such as canaries, goldfish, ants, and even snakes.*

Fanatical enthusiasts have actually been raising animals for hundreds of years. These enthusiasts raise animals as hobbies. One group of enthusiasts, the Chinese, domesticated carp as long ago as a thousand years ago. Carp are the ancestors of the fish we now know as goldfish. The Chinese developed more than a hundred kinds or varieties of goldfish from mutants of the carp. Canary birds have been kept in confining cages since somewhere in the vicinity of the fourteenth century. Canaries may be the original birds in a gilded cage. The original wild canaries were gray-green and yellow. From these original canaries, fanciers have bred many truly exotic varieties of canaries. Fanciers have bred yellow, red, orange, peach, white, and variegated colors. Fanciers have bred canaries that sing with their mouths open and canaries that sing with their mouths closed. Fanciers have also bred birds with fluffy feathers, birds with sleek feathers, and birds with curly feathers. Other assorted hobbyists fill their homes with every type of a menagerie and assorted pens, cages, and tanks. Interestingly, ants are raised in farms. Gerbils are raised in elaborate mazes complete with every sort of toy. Pigeons are raised in lofts. Rare tropical fish are raised in elaborate saltwater aquariums.

Score _____

© 1986 by CBS College Publishing. All rights reserved.

Combining for Conciseness Exercise 9-3

NAME _____ DATE _____

Combine each set of sentences into one concise sentence.

> EXAMPLE: Some model builders work with matchsticks or toothpicks. These model builders have made detailed miniatures of famous buildings such as the British Houses of Parliament or the Taj Mahal.
> *Some model builders, working with matchsticks or toothpicks, have made detailed miniatures of famous buildings such as the British Houses of Parliament or the Taj Mahal.*

1. A model helicopter was built by Dieter Ziegler. Ziegler flew his helicopter across the English Channel in 1974.

2. Some model airplanes fly. These model airplanes are powered by miniature gasoline engines.

3. Model airplanes have flown to heights in the vicinity of 27,000 feet. Model airplanes have flown at speeds in excess of 200 miles per hour. Model airplanes have flown for periods as long as a full, round-the-clock, twenty-four-hour day and night.

4. Some model sailing ships can float. The models must first be balanced. The models must first be waterproofed.

5. Some model sailing ships are powered by electric motors. The motors run on batteries. The ships are guided by remote control.

6. More than 60 million Americans regularly and consistently feed wild birds. Feeding wild birds is the second most popular hobby or pastime in the United States.

7. There are 796 species or types of birds living in North America. Approximately 10 percent of the 796 species are regularly attracted to gardens. Garden visitors include finches, quail, jays, mockingbirds, chickadees, juncos, and hummingbirds.

Writing Concise Sentences **171**

8. Hummingbirds' ability to escape quickly and rapidly makes hummingbirds fearless. Hummingbirds are willing to investigate new sources of food. Hummingbirds will fight other hummingbirds for a place at a hummingbird feeder.

9. Bird lovers build houses for birds to nest in. Bird lovers build shelters for the birds to shelter in. Bird lovers fill yards with feeding stations or feeders. Some feeders will contain sunflower seeds for the finches. Some feeders will contain nectar for the hummingbirds. Some feeders will contain millet for the sparrows and doves. The bird lovers provide a veritable smorgasbord for birds.

10. Another very popular hobby is gardening. It goes without saying that gardening is America's most popular pastime. Gardening even outranks feeding wild birds.

Score _____

Revising Rambling Sentences   Exercise 9–4

NAME _____ DATE _____

Rewrite the following sentences to eliminate excessive use of subordination, coordination, and passive voice; awkward noun and prepositional phrases; ineffective repetition; and nonessential words. Answers will vary.

> EXAMPLE: Collectors are hobbyists, and they may be the most avid.
> *Collectors may be the most avid hobbyists.*

1. Collections may be worth a fortune or collections may simply have cost a fortune, but they may be beautiful or they may be simply intriguing while some may be odd, and some may be ridiculous.

2. Students of seashells are called conchologists and they have the oceans as well as the forests that they can search for specimens and there are in the area of 100,000 types or varieties that they can search for.

3. One shell, which is called the wentletrap, was at one point in time quite rare so that Chinese traders made cheap counterfeits of paste made of rice, but at this time the shells have become rather common with more found in collections and the counterfeits are rare and have become a precious collector's item.

4. Around 100 dolls were collected by Queen Victoria who is beyond a shadow of a doubt the most famous of the collectors of dolls.

5. Fancy-dress dolls of the seventeenth and eighteenth centuries were sometimes dressed in such fancy costumes that the dolls' presentation at court as though the dolls were debutantes was the result.

6. Buttons are collected by 50,000 Americans, and many of those Americans hold membership in the National Button Society, but the hobby or pastime actually achieved a degree of popularity in the nineteenth century, for it was then that charmstrings of buttons were extremely popular and girls often collected buttons.

Writing Concise Sentences   **173**

7. Collections for first editions of books by favorite authors are made by collectors of books who are called bibliophiles or sometimes the collections are made up of books with bindings and illustrations of great beauty.
   _____
   _____

8. Butterflies are caught in nets by collectors after which the butterflies are asphyxiated in a killing jar or after which the butterflies are dried until the butterflies can be mounted flat as specimens.
   _____
   _____

9. Beyond a shadow of a doubt the accumulation of enormous balls of string certainly ranks among hobbies that are quite odd.
   _____

10. Some other kinds of collections are made by people who make collections of cigar bands or who collect coins or who put together various varieties of snuff boxes or who try to find every imaginable kind of barbed wire.
    _____

                                                        Score _____

© 1986 by CBS College Publishing. All rights reserved.

Review 9

Rewrite the following paragraph to eliminate unnecessary words, phrases, and sentences. Answers will vary.

    In the vicinity of 5 million to 10 million citizens of the United States enjoy gathering collections of coins of various types. These Americans can be called numismatists, which is just another way of saying people who collect coins. Some numismatists look for coins for their collections according to all kinds of topics, and others choose items for their collection by metal and others by some specific type of design, and historical periods are the subject for collection by others. It goes without saying that a collection of coins from U.S. history might include the silver dollar called the Washington-Lafayette silver dollar, which was issued in 1900. The inclusion of the peace dollar of 1921 is also probable. At one and the same time some of the U.S. half-dollars that have been issued in commemoration of various events and of which there are forty-eight in existence might be included. An important commemorative half-dollar would be the 1892 half-dollar, which was issued to commemorate the World's Columbian Exposition.

Score _____

Compare your answer to the one in the back of the text. Compute your score by adding one point for every word you are able to deduct. (Your score could exceed 100.)

The Writer's Casebook #9

Application: Writing Concisely—Summaries and Abstracts

Writing concise sentences is essential when you summarize. A summary may contain as few as three sentences and thirty-five words or as many as twenty to twenty-five sentences and 300 words. The length will often, but not always, depend upon the length of the material being summarized. Often this material will be written, but occasionally you will need to summarize an oral presentation, such as a lecture, or an event, such as an experiment.

Summaries abstract information—that is, they are concerned with general outlines and principles rather than with specific applications or instances. Generally, a summary has three basic parts.

1. Statement of the key idea or thesis
2. Statement(s) about the support for the thesis, the methodology, and/or key subpoints
3. Statement of conclusions and implications

For example, the content of the preceding chapter might be summarized in these three sentences.

> Choose and arrange words in your sentences to emphasize key ideas. Place important points at the beginning or at the end of the sentence, use cumulative or periodic sentences, balance your ideas in parallel structures, repeat words effectively, or write in the active or the passive voice, depending on your purpose. Practice using the different methods for achieving emphasis by completing, identifying, combining, and revising exercises.

Cases for Writing: Writing It on the Head of a Pin

Case #1

Choose a textbook chapter that you have read recently. It might be for this class or for another course you are taking. Summarize the chapter in 100 words or less, being careful to include the three basic parts of a summary.

Cases for Writing: Playing the Expert or Doing It Your Way

Case #2

Your twin-engine Cessna has crash-landed on an uncharted South Pacific island. The natives have never seen an off-islander or an airplane before. They imagine the two of you are gods. You are able to repair the Cessna, but to get off the island you will need the natives' help to construct a runway. Assuming that somehow you have quickly learned their language, explain to the islanders why you need the runway and what they must do to help you.

Writing Varied Sentences   10

Preview 10

In the space provided explain how the writer of this paragraph alters the basic simple sentence and standard word order—beginning with the subject and verb—to achieve sentence variety. Refer to specific sentences by number.

¹Everyone has to eat. ²However, how Americans fulfill this basic need is as diverse as our mosaic population. ³In the Southwest every entree, including eggs, is garnished with red or green chili hot enough to blister your tongue. ⁴Dining in Hawaii, we can expect sweet-and-sour sauces and pineapple in every dish. ⁵Cooking country style in Pennsylvania may mean chicken stoltzfus in pastry squares, green beans in ham broth, and weiner schnitzel, while in Oregon, country style means sourdough biscuits, pan-fried steak, and green apple pie. ⁶Southerners, as everyone knows, eat grits and greens, and they fry their chicken in batter and spices. ⁷Texans barbeque their beef. ⁸Italian-Americans eat it in spicy meatballs covered with tomato sauce and swathed in pasta. ⁹And who hasn't heard of Cajun gumbos and crawdads? ¹⁰Obviously, one people's meat need not be another's poison: it could be a delicacy.

Score _____

Compare your answers to those in the back of the text. Compute your score by adding 10 points for each variation from the basic sentence and standard order that you identify.

Too many sentences of the same kind, length, and structure result in monotonous writing. Mixing sentence types can create interest and can also help you emphasize key points.

10a Varying Sentence Length

MONOTONOUS: Sourdough is dough soured by billions of microscopic yeast plants. It is used to leaven bread, biscuits, pancakes, or cakes. It was discovered by Egyptians about 5,000 years ago. Many people consider sourdough cooking to be both delicious and nutritious.

VARIED: Discovered by the Egyptians 5,000 years ago, sourdough—or dough soured by billions of microscopic yeast plants—can be used to leaven bread, biscuits, pancakes, or cakes. It is both delicious and nutritious.

10b Combining Choppy Simple Sentences

MONOTONOUS: The pioneers could not buy a fresh supply of yeast at the supermarket. They valued their sourdough starters. The starters were living, growing mixtures. They had to be fed and watered. They had to be properly cared for. The pioneers carried the starters across the plains in crock pots. The bread dish at nearly every meal depended upon sourdough. Some pioneers ate a lot of sourdough. Some old-timers were appropriately nicknamed "sourdoughs."

VARIED: Because they could not buy a fresh supply of yeast at the supermarket, pioneers valued their sourdough starters and carried them across the plains in crock pots. The starters were living, growing mixtures, requiring feeding and watering. But when properly cared for, the sourdough could be depended upon to leaven the bread dish at nearly every meal. Appropriately, after eating so much of it, some old-timers were nicknamed "sourdoughs."

10c Breaking Up Strings of Compounds

MONOTONOUS: Starving in the North American wilderness is almost impossible, yet many have starved. Around 30 million people are lost in the wilderness each year, and many of these die, for their unfed bodies become auto-cannibalistic, and they literally consume themselves. But no one need starve, and the wilderness is full of food.

VARIED: Although starving in the North American wilderness is almost impossible, many have starved. Around 30 million people are lost in the wilderness each year. Many of them die, as their unfed bodies become auto-cannibalistic, literally consuming themselves. However, no one need starve, for the wilderness is full of food.

10d Varying Sentence Types

MONOTONOUS: Lost hunters can feast instead of starve. Wilderness cuisine can be tasty. You must know, however, what to look for. You must also know how to prepare it. Some people like lemonade. A palatable variation can be made by mashing ants in water. Then use wild berries to sweeten the drink. A main course of grubs will keep you as plump as a grizzly bear. Grubs can usually be found in rotten logs or under rocks. Birch syrup is as sweet as maple syrup but spicier. It can be served over toasted insects. The result is a captivating dessert. It is like a wilderness M & M.

VARIED: Lost hunters can feast instead of starve. Wilderness cuisine can be tasty, but you must know what to look for and how to prepare it. Do you like lemonade? Mashing ants in water and sweetening with wild berries make a palatable variation. A main course of grubs, usually found in rotten logs or under rocks, will keep you as plump as a bear. And for a captivating dessert, try birch syrup. It will be as sweet as maple syrup but spicier. Served over toasted insects, it's a real taste treat—a sort of wilderness M & M.

10e Varying Sentence Openings

Rather than beginning each sentence with its subject, you may open a sentence with modifiers, with conjunctions or transitional expressions, or with an inverted appositive or absolute phrase.

SUBJECT OPENER:	Plants are edible.
SINGLE-WORD MODIFIER:	Happily, 120,000 plants are edible.
PHRASE:	According to botanists, 120,000 plants are edible.
CLAUSE:	Although many prefer animal food, 120,000 plants are edible.
CONJUNCTION:	But 120,000 plants are edible.
TRANSITIONAL EXPRESSION:	On the other hand, 120,000 plants are edible.
APPOSITIVE:	A boon to vegetarians, 120,000 plants are edible.
ABSOLUTE PHRASE:	Their abundance appreciated by vegetarians, 120,000 plants are edible.

10f Varying Standard Word Order

STANDARD:	I love tamales first and next to tamales sopaipillas.
INVERTED:	Tamales I love and, next to tamales, sopaipillas.
STANDARD:	The New England boiled dinner came out of the pot, perfect as usual.
INVERTED:	Out of the pot came the New England boiled dinner, perfect as usual.
STANDARD:	Posole requires long, slow simmering to accent the complementary flavors of chili and ham hocks.
SUBJECT SEPARATED FROM VERB:	Posole, to accent the complementary flavors of chili and ham hocks, requires long, slow simmering.

Writing Varied Sentences   **181**

Combining for Sentence Variety   Exercise 10–1

NAME _____ DATE _____

Combine sentences in the following groups to create a mixture of long and short sentences, including simple, compound, and complex sentences.

> EXAMPLE: Bread is the staff of life. It comes in a variety of types. My favorite is bagels.
>
> *Bread, the staff of life, comes in a variety of types. My favorite is bagels.*

1. Some commercial breads are not very nutritious. One manufacturer used sawdust to fill its dough. Another tested its bread. The bread had no nutritional value.

   _____
   _____
   _____

2. Many people store food for emergencies. They dehydrate vegetables, meats, and even butter. They pack the food in metal containers. They spray it with nitrogen. The food will last for twenty-five years.

   _____
   _____
   _____

3. Cooking with dehydrated foods requires special techniques. Cheese powder may be reconstituted simply by adding water. Reconstituted butter should sit for a day in the refrigerator before you use it. Bananas do not rehydrate easily. You will have to grind them up. Then you can cook them.

   _____
   _____
   _____
   _____

4. Preserving food was once a major problem. A chicken could be kept for as long as two days. First, it had to be cleaned, scaled, and coated with pepper. Meat had to be soaked in brine. It then had to be boiled for three or four days.

   _____
   _____
   _____

5. Keeping butter sweet demanded much more than putting it in the refrigerator. A brine had to be prepared of water, salt, and saltpeter. The butter was immersed in the brine. The butter kept. It was extremely salty.

   _____
   _____
   _____

Score _____

© 1986 by CBS College Publishing. All rights reserved.

Varying Sentence Types Exercise 10-2

NAME _____ DATE _____

Rewrite the following paragraph. Eliminate over-coordination by using a variety of sentence types. Delete, add, or rearrange words as necessary.

A nineteenth-century cookbook is of the same species as its twentieth-century descendant, but the substance of the nineteenth-century cookbook differs drastically from the substance of the twentieth-century cookbook. The twentieth-century cookbook gives the recipe for frying a chicken, and it concentrates on batter ingredients, and it gives pan temperatures, and it explains how to fry for an even, golden brown. The nineteenth-century cookbook starts with choosing and killing a young chicken, and it concentrates on judging the age of the chicken from its soft beak and unscaled legs, and it explains how to wring the neck, drain the blood, and clean out the entrails. The twentieth-century cookbook might give catsup as an ingredient of recipes, but the nineteenth-century cookbook gives a recipe for making catsup by the gallon. The one gives standard measurements and uses ingredients from the supermarket, and the other suggests a "pinch" of salt and calls for six peach leaves from the garden for a pot of boiling rice, and the nineteenth-century cookbook also provides recipes for making soap, wine, and toothpowder. Life in general may have become more complicated, but cooking at least is simpler.

Score _____

Writing Varied Sentences

Varying Sentence Openings   Exercise 10-3

NAME _____   DATE _____

Vary the opening of each of the following sentences in at least three ways. In each case, identify the method you use.

    EXAMPLE: Some food can be hard to eat.
    Unfortunately, some food can be hard to eat. (single-word modifier)
    When it slips off the fork, some food can be hard to eat. (clause)
    A challenge to get in your mouth, some food can be hard to eat. (appositive)

1. Spaghetti must be rolled on a fork or cut in little pieces.

2. Many people cannot cope with nibbling the ends of artichoke leaves.

3. Eating crab legs requires a special fork to pick out the meat.

4. Corn on the cob only poses a problem in public.

© 1986 by CBS College Publishing. All rights reserved.

5. Pomegranates, piñon nuts, and sunflower seeds are impossible to eat.

Writing Varied Sentences   **185**

Revising for Variety   Exercise 10–4

NAME _____ DATE _____

The following short essay lacks sentence variety and suffers from over-coordination. Rewrite the essay, combining to create different kinds of sentences and expanding or deleting to vary sentence length. You will also need to delete unnecessary words.

    A taste for chili may be inherited, or it may be acquired through diligent practice, but the proper way to assemble and eat a hot Mexican dinner is an art, and it must be learned.

    First, of course, comes the ordering, or you may prefer to cook your own. (Some of you prefer to cook your own. You should plan to spend several hours. Mexican dishes are time-consuming to prepare. They are delightful to consume.) The best dinner consists of samplings of many dishes. There should be some sour cream enchiladas. You will want a relleno. Its green chile center should be stuffed with mild cheese. Refried beans are a must. They should be liberally seasoned with garlic and onions. Spanish rice comes next. Your beef tamales must be made with masa flour. Don't forget carne adovada. The pork roast should be crusty on the edges. It should be well cooked. It should fall apart. Spicy guacamole is next. It should be eaten with fresh-fried corn chips. Boughten corn chips will not do. Add a liberal coating of red or green chile—or both!—to everything. Also add a basket of sopaipillas. Those are crisp, fluffy squares of deep-fried dough. You will also want a pitcher of iced tea. (You should never drink coffee with a Mexican meal). Now you are ready to begin eating.

    Let's hope the chili is the real thing and not the mixture with flour and usually reserved for tourists, for your first bite of the real thing should make you appreciate the iced tea. Coffee accents the heat of the chili; but iced tea soothes, and alternating bites with sips enables even the novice to enjoy the hottest dishes.

© 1986 by CBS College Publishing. All rights reserved.

Sopaipillas should be eaten throughout the meal like bread. You should resist the temptation to smear them with butter. You will be branded a tourist. Butter cannot sink into the crusty surface. It will slide around and drip. This makes it difficult for the sopaipilla to fulfill its major function. That function is scooping up stray morsels and mopping up chili. A few drops of honey will stick to the sopaipilla crust. The honey provides a welcome change for your burning tongue. A sopaipilla with honey is usually dessert. You won't have room for any more after your sumptuous Mexican dinner.

Review 10

In the space provided explain how the writer of this paragraph alters the basic simple sentence and standard word order to achieve sentence variety. Refer to specific sentences by number.

¹Although everyone has to eat, some people make eating an avidly pursued vice. ²Trenchermen or women, as these no-holds-barred eaters are called, have been known to consume gallons of ice cream in seconds and dozens of sandwiches in minutes. ³Have you ever wished for all the chocolates, doughnuts, or clams you can eat? ⁴Enter a contest. ⁵In every part of the country, voracious eaters compete for the dubious titles of Champion Corn Chomper or Mincepie Muncher of the Year. ⁶Bringing along a roll of antacids and a bottle of Pepto-Bismol, dozens of Texans enter annual jalapeño-eating contests. ⁷To Thomas Greene and Steve Meltzer have gone the titles for eating the most oysters (250 in 3 minutes, 56 seconds) and sausages (96 in 6 minutes); to Toll Nall and Steve Weldon, the titles for the most tortillas (74 in 3 minutes) and spaghetti (100 yards in 28.73 seconds). ⁸However, even the most pleasurable vice can be overdone. ⁹In 1977 a Frenchman, "Mangetout" or "Eats-Everything" Lotito, ate a bicycle. ¹⁰Its tires had been stewed and the metal, ground to filings.*

Score _____

Compare your answers to those in the back of the text. Compute your score by adding 10 points for each variation from the basic simple sentence and standard word order that you identify.

*From Norris McWhirter, *Guiness Book of World Records* (New York: Bantam, 1982), pp. 502–505.

The Writer's Casebook #10

Application: Process Analysis, or Analyzing What Happens

One major difference between process analysis and simple instructions is sentence variety. Compare the instructions and the analysis below. When you write instructions, you use short sentences, usually structured as commands. When you analyze a process, you use long as well as short sentences, statements and questions as well as commands, and a variety of sentence structures. Analysis employs a mixture of sentence types and patterns to add interest and to help you emphasize key points.

The key word in process analysis is *how*—how to do or make something, how something works, how events happen, how goals are achieved or destinations reached. Like instructions, analysis may direct a reader to perform actions, but unlike instructions, analysis is more than a list of steps. A process or purposeful series of actions is examined from every angle to see what happens, why it happens, how it happens, and what it looks like when it happens.

INSTRUCTIONS: To reconstitute dehydrated cheese for spreads

1. Add 2½ cups of ice water per cup of cheese powder.
2. Whisk until smooth.
3. Allow to sit in a cool place for several hours.

ANALYSIS: Dehydrated cheese forms a light powder that tastes and looks like a cheesy flour. To reconstitute it, begin by measuring 2½ cups of water for each cup of cheese powder. Plan the amount you will need carefully, remembering that restoring moisture also restores bulk. One cup of reconstituted cheese powder will make enough spread for cheese sandwiches for a family of twelve or enough hors d'oeuvres for a party of sixty. If you plan to use the cheese uncooked, make sure the water is cold enough to numb your fingertips or make your teeth chatter. Whisk the mixture together with quick, steady motions, continuing until it resembles a yellow sour cream. Allow the cheese to sit in a cool place, like a refrigerator or a crock pot in a cold stream, for several hours before using. The result will be a tasty spread—a bit sharper than the original and even yellower, like a cross between a squash and a carrot, but it will be delicious toasted on rye bread or mixed with reconstituted sour cream and layered on warm, fresh sourdough bread.

While clear instructions, when followed correctly, will enable you to duplicate actions, process analysis allows you both to duplicate the actions and to understand them. Process analysis is applicable to many subjects. For example, your biology professor might ask you to analyze the process of photosynthesis. Whatever the subject, decide first whether the series of actions it represents is best organized in the step-by-step pattern typical of written instructions or in stages. For example, you might discuss making a peanut-butter-and-jelly sandwich in steps because the actions involved are straightforward and simple. However, making sourdough bread is much more complex and time-consuming, and the procedure may be lost in the sheer number of steps. A simple solution would be to organize the many little actions into several stages: "growing" a sourdough starter, preparing the ingredients and tools for bread making, mixing the ingredients, rising and kneading, and baking.

The general structure of a process-analysis essay may vary with the discipline, but in many cases the following outline will provide a good starting point.

Introduction
Background or special circumstances to interest the reader
Thesis—statement giving the specific process to be analyzed

Middle
Explanation of materials, tools, and/or methods or principles involved
Step-by-step or stage-by-stage discussion of the process, including descriptive
    details, qualifications, implications, and examples

Conclusion
Final word, which could be a statement about the usefulness of the process or
    recommendations for the reader

NOTE: You may also use negative process analysis—that is, how not to do something, such as how not to make a banana nut cake or how not to get your candidate elected.

Cases for Writing: Showing How

Case #1

You are invited to a V.I.P. luncheon, where you will be sitting at the head table. You accept before you learn that the menu will include spaghetti (or crab legs or corn on the cob or raw fish)—something you find it either difficult or impossible to eat. Explain in a process-analysis essay how you overcome (or do not overcome) this potentially embarrassing situation.

Case #2

You have just stepped off a crowded bus in the heart of a city when you realize that you have left your purse (or wallet) with your life savings on the bus. It is winter. The streets are snowpacked, and the bus is already moving into the traffic. Write an analysis showing how you catch that bus to retrieve your property.

SECTION III

Solving Common Sentence Problems

Sentence Fragments   11

Preview 11

The following paragraphs contain several sentence fragments. Circle the number of each fragment and revise to complete the sentence.

¹ The plight of the Earth concerns everyone. ² From the eldest citizen, whose last breaths are hampered by pollution. ³ To the youngest citizen, whose future home is fast becoming a massive garbage scow. ⁴ Carrying the poisons of radioactive waste, toxic chemicals, and unbiodegradable residues endlessly through space. ⁵ Once taken for granted. ⁶ Clean water, clean air, and clean soil are now being recognized as our greatest heritage. ⁷ Once thought limitless, a vast cornucopia, forever replenished as we emptied it. ⁸ Our natural resources are now known to be limited. ⁹ And in many cases—such as petroleum, coal, and iron—irreplaceable.

¹⁰ Because many do care, are willing to sacrifice, and are not willing to give up. ¹¹ Laws to protect the environment are being enacted. ¹² And enforced! ¹³ Our consciences as well as our instincts for survival aroused by the dead fish of Lake Erie, the near extinction of the blue whale, the victims of mercury and radioactive poisoning, and the murky water flowing from our own kitchen faucets. ¹⁴ We are at last accepting our responsibilities. ¹⁵ To ourselves, to the future, and to the other living things that must share this planet with us.

Score _____

Check your answers against those in the back of this book. Deduct 5 points for an error in identification, 5 points for an error in correction. A score of 80 percent or higher demonstrates that you can identify and correct the kinds of fragments studied in this chapter.

A *sentence fragment* is a group of words punctuated like a sentence but lacking some element essential to completeness. A fragment may lack a subject, a verb, or a word or group of words needed to complete the sentence structure and thought.

Sentence Fragments

MISSING SUBJECT:	Have weathered another trying year.	*Who or what weathered the year?*
MISSING VERB:	The environmental defense forces.	*What did they do?*
MISSING INDEPENDENT CLAUSE:	As the ship *Rainbow Warrior* escaped from Siberia.	*What happened?*

Fragments leave readers with unanswered questions and speakers with their voices suspended in midair, waiting for the drop that comes with sentence completeness. (Reread the preview exercise outloud, one sentence at a time. Notice the way your voice drops significantly when there is a legitimate period but stays up or falls just slightly when there is a fragment.)

Fragments are major errors because they violate the boundaries of the sentence and confuse the reader. To complete a fragment, either add the missing part or attach the fragment to another word group in the paragraph.

ADDING SUBJECT:	Our ships and crews have weathered another trying year.
ADDING VERB:	The environmental defense forces have won.
ADDING INDEPENDENT CLAUSE:	As the ship *Rainbow Warrior* escaped from Siberia, Soviet ships and helicopters chased it.
ATTACHING RELATED WORD GROUPS:	The environmental defense forces have weathered another trying year.

Learning to recognize the different kinds of fragments will help eliminate these errors from your writing.

11a   Subordinate Clauses

A *subordinate*, or *dependent*, *clause* begins with a subordinating conjunction or a relative pronoun (see 7b) and includes both a subject and a verb. It cannot stand alone as a sentence but depends upon an independent clause for completeness. You can correct a subordinate-clause fragment in two ways: by attaching it to an adjacent independent clause or by deleting the subordinating conjunction or relative pronoun and, if necessary, providing an appropriate subject.

FRAGMENTS:	<u>When a river is polluted</u>. Life is disrupted for both the fish and the fishers. <u>Who are sustained and nourished by its waters</u>.
REVISION BY ATTACHING:	When a river is polluted, life is disrupted for both the fish and the fishers, who are sustained and nourished by its waters.
REVISION BY DELETING:	A river is polluted. Life is disrupted for both the fish and the fishers. Both are sustained and nourished by its waters.

11b Prepositional Phrases

A prepositional phrase is a modifier (see 6f and 20f). It follows a set pattern—beginning with a preposition, ending with an object, and including any number of modifiers in between. To correct a prepositional-phrase fragment, attach it to an adjacent independent clause that contains the word the phrase modifies.

FRAGMENT:	Nature strikes back. With volcanoes, hurricanes, and tornadoes.
REVISION BY ATTACHING:	Nature strikes back with volcanoes, hurricanes, and tornadoes.

11c Verbal Phrases

A verbal-phrase fragment results when a present participle (*writing*), past participle (*written*), or infinitive (*to write*) plus related objects and modifiers (*writing with a quill pen*) is punctuated as a complete sentence (see 20c). To correct the error, attach the verbal phrase to an adjacent independent clause or change the verbal to a finite verb and add a subject.

FRAGMENT:	To protest acid rain.
REVISION BY ATTACHING:	To protest acid rain, demonstrators climbed polluting smokestacks.
REVISION BY CHANGING:	Demonstrators protested acid rain.

11d Absolute Phrases

An absolute phrase modifies an entire sentence rather than a part of it and, therefore, is sometimes mistaken for a separate entity. It usually consists of a noun or pronoun, a participle, and any related modifiers (see 6f). To correct an absolute-phrase fragment, attach it to the sentence it modifies or change the participle to a finite verb.

FRAGMENT:	Earth's largest living thing is General Sherman. A giant sequoia weighing an estimated 2,145 tons.
REVISION BY ATTACHING:	Earth's largest living thing is General Sherman, a giant sequoia weighing an estimated 2,145 tons.
REVISION BY CHANGING:	The giant sequoia weighs an estimated 2,145 tons.
FRAGMENT:	The award for tallest trees goes to the California redwoods. Their heights being in excess of 350 feet with the champion being a towering 368 feet.
REVISION BY ATTACHING AND CHANGING:	The award for tallest trees goes to the California redwoods, which may grow in excess of 350 feet. The champion is a towering 368 feet.

11e Appositives

An appositive is a noun or noun phrase that follows the person or thing it modifies and identifies or renames the person or thing (see 6f). Correct an appositive fragment by attaching it to the modified word or word group.

FRAGMENT: The oldest living tree is a bristlecone pine. <u>The 4,600-year-old Methuselah of Wheeler Peak in California.</u>
REVISION BY ATTACHING: The oldest living tree is a bristlecone pine, the 4,600-year-old Methuselah of Wheeler Peak in California.

11f Compounds

When part of a compound predicate is separated from the rest of the sentence, the result is a fragment. To correct the error, rejoin the parts of the compound.

FRAGMENT: In 1970 amendments to the Clean Air Act limited new-factory pollution. <u>And provided for national ambient air quality standards.</u>
REVISION: In 1970 amendments to the Clean Air Act limited new-factory pollution and provided for national ambient air quality standards.

11g Incomplete Clauses

Since fragmentation results from incomplete sentence structure rather than from sentence length, it is possible to have a very long or a very short fragment. If you suspect you have written a fragment, analyze the sentence structure; then add, delete, or modify words to create a complete independent clause.

FRAGMENT: <u>In October, 1948, a killer smog, compounded of factory smoke and river fog and trapped by an air inversion, settling over Donora, Pennsylvania, to kill twenty people before rain dissipated the pollutants.</u>
REVISION BY CHANGING VERBAL TO FINITE VERB: In October, 1948, a killer smog, compounded of factory smoke and river fog and trapped by an air inversion, settled over Donora, Pennsylvania, to kill twenty people before rain dissipated the pollutants.

NOTE: Fragments may be acceptable in some writing—such as literature, journalism, and advertising—but only when they are intentional and serve a purpose. Generally, college writers should avoid fragments.

Sentence Fragments **195**

Revising Fragments Exercise 11–1

NAME _____ DATE _____

Underline the fragments in the following sentence pairs. Then revise each fragment in two ways: first by attaching it to the complete sentence and second by adding to it the necessary sentence elements or by altering the words found in it.

EXAMPLE: Outreigning any other order.

Dinosaurs dominated the earth for 100 million years.

a. *Outreigning any other order, dinosaurs dominated the earth for 100 million years.*

b. *Although outreigning any other order, the giant reptiles probably fell victim to widespread climatic changes*

1. Pleistocene extinctions include a variety of giant mammals. Such as bear-sized beavers, long-horned bison, saber-toothed tigers, and mammoths.

2. Although we no longer find representatives of the ten-to-twenty-inch-high *eohippus*, or dawn horse. It did not die out but developed gradually into today's *equus*, a full-sized horse.

3. The greatest threat to wildlife today is not the hunter's gun. But rather the tractor, the bulldozer, and the chainsaw that destroy the natural habitat.

4. Their natural habitat disappearing as wilderness turns into housing developments and their natural food supply diminishing as modern sanitation practices promote the "cleanup" of scavengers' food. The California condors face extinction.

© 1986 by CBS College Publishing. All rights reserved.

5. On the other hand, some species may actually benefit from this destruction. Those that did not thrive in the original habitat.

6. When the old forests were cut down. The number of white-tailed deer and cottontail rabbits increased.

7. Technology has endangered many plant species. By allowing pests to migrate.

8. An invasion of Chinese fungus attacked American forests. Killing within fifty years all the large chestnuts on the East Coast.

9. Nature's harshest lessons come too late. For example, the extinction of the passenger pigeons, whose population of 2 billion in the 1880's made them seem indestructible, a limitless supply for food and sport.

10. Today a hundred large animals face extinction. As well as tens of thousands of spiders, insects, and plants.

Score _____

Sentence Fragments

197

Revising Subordinate-Clause Fragments Exercise 11–2

NAME _____ DATE _____

Circle the numbers preceding any fragments you find in the following paragraphs. Then rewrite the paragraph in the space provided, revising errors.

[1] Although the bald eagle has been protected by federal law since 1940. [2] Only 50,000 bald eagles remain in the country. [3] That chose the bird as its national symbol in 1782. [4] Most of the remaining eagles live in Alaska. [5] Where the relatively undisturbed habitat offers them sanctuary and the garbage dumps afford these timid hunters a ready supply of food. [6] But the population continues to decline. [7] As wilderness gives way to farms and cities and pollutants invade their food supply. [8] The eagles are forced from their traditional eyries. [9] While the number of eaglets in the surviving nests declines.

Revision:

Score _____

© 1986 by CBS College Publishing. All rights reserved.

Revising Verbal Fragments   Exercise 11-3

NAME _____ DATE _____

Circle the numbers preceding any fragments you find in the following paragraphs. Then rewrite the paragraph in the space provided, revising errors.

¹ To save the grizzlies. ² Some hunters have suggested a moratorium on killing the huge beasts. ³ However, the very fierceness that helped name these bears prejudices their case. ⁴ Making people fear them and advocate extermination in self-defense or in defense of livestock. ⁵ One possible source of the word *grizzly* is the Old English *grislic*. ⁶ Meaning "horrible" or "demonlike." ⁷ Even one scientific name for the bear, *Ursus horribilis*, suggests the terror the creature inspired in early settlers. ⁸ Provoked, no doubt, by invasions of territory or threats to their young or food supplies. ⁹ Grizzlies chased explorer Lewis of the Lewis and Clark Expedition into the Missouri River, treed frontiersman Kit Carson, and scalped mountain man Hugh Glass. ¹⁰ Called "devils in fur coats." ¹¹ Grizzlies have inspired a healthy respect and an unhealthy antipathy.

Revision:

Score _____

Sentence Fragments   **199**

Revising Absolute-Phrase Fragments   Exercise 11–4

NAME _____ DATE _____

Circle the numbers preceding any fragments you find in the following paragraph. Then rewrite the paragraph in the space provided, revising errors.

¹ One early attempt at conservation ended in tragedy for the mule deer of the Kaibab North Plateau. ² The well-intentioned planners, including President Theodore Roosevelt, having failed to take into account the prolific reproduction rate of the species. ³ They established the Grand Canyon National Game Preserve. ⁴ All hunting banned within its precincts. ⁵ Natural predators such as mountain lions, bobcats, and wolves systematically exterminated. ⁶ The result was a phenomenal growth in the herd. ⁷ Its numbers increasing within less than twenty years from 3,000 to 30,000. ⁸ Eventually tens of thousands of deer starved or died of disease. ⁹ Their range, permanently damaged by over-grazing.

Revision:

Score _____

© 1986 by CBS College Publishing. All rights reserved.

Revising Appositive Fragments   Exercise 11-5

NAME _____ DATE _____

Circle the numbers preceding any fragments you find in the following paragraph. Then rewrite the paragraph in the space provided, revising errors.

[1] A recent, highly successful environmentalist organization is called Greenpeace. [2] An environmental defense force that intervenes in environmental emergencies around the world. [3] Greenpeace sends its five ships to confront violators. [4] Those who pollute the oceans or slaughter harp seals and whales. [5] People who do not give up. [6] Greenpeacers, protesting the slaughter of baby harp seals, have been harassed and jailed in Canada. [7] A country that had set the kill quota for one year at 180,000. [8] Greenpeacers in Europe were shot at and threatened with fire hoses while demonstrating against acid rain. [9] An industrial by-product that is rapidly destroying European forests. [10] But the work goes on.

Revision:

Score _____

Sentence Fragments   **201**

Revising Other Fragments: Predicates, Prepositional Phrases, and Incomplete Clauses Exercise 11-6

NAME _____ DATE _____

Circle the numbers preceding any fragments you find in the following paragraphs. Then rewrite these paragraphs in the spaces provided, revising errors.

[1] The harp seals—like the passenger pigeons and the buffalo before them—are hunted commercially. [2] And slaughtered by the tens of thousands in a single hunt. [3] The best prices are paid for the white pelts of newborns and the silky fur of the few-weeks-old pups called "beaters." [4] Therefore, the hunts take place in the seals' spring birthing grounds. [5] And focus on the pups, who are systematically clubbed to death. [6] But the pressure from environmentalists and the outraged public has had an impact. [7] Has reduced the 1984 harvest to 20,000 seals. [8] And, equally important, has reduced the world demand for seal pelts.

Revision:

[1] Coping with the depletion of fossil fuels has led to a major controversy. [2] Over nuclear energy. [3] Public debate over the building of nuclear power plants has intensified, heating to the level of public protest. [4] And even of physical violence. [5] Supporters cite the need for a new energy source. [6] For energy to run our factories and light our homes without polluting our already endangered air. [7] Opponents warn of the hazards. [8] Of the inadequacy of safeguards, of the poor safety record of nuclear plants, of the difficulties of storing radioactive waste. [9] And the debate goes on.

Revision:

© 1986 by CBS College Publishing. All rights reserved.

[1] Our beautiful blue-green world, millions of years in the making, often abused and taken for granted, but also celebrated by our poets, revered by people of good will, and defended by dedicated partisans. [2] A planet hosting billions of living organisms, each species part of an ecosystem made up of plants, animals, and the physical environment, interacting with one another according to complex patterns of relationships, often so delicately balanced that disturbing a single component may destroy the entire system. [3] Perhaps humanity will have better luck than the dinosaurs.

Revision:

Score _____

Sentence Fragments

Generating Sentences from Fragments Exercise 11-7

NAME _____ DATE _____

Decide whether the word groups listed below are complete sentences or fragments. Mark the complete sentences with a C in the space provided on the left. Mark the fragments F and, without changing any words, use them as starting points for generating complete sentences.

    EXAMPLE: __F__ When Mt. St. Helens erupted in 1980.
When Mt. St. Helens erupted in 1980, sixty people were killed, and millions of trees were mowed down like so many wooden toothpicks.

_____ 1. If the horse replaced the automobile as transportation.

_____ 2. The thunderheads, building over the mountains.

_____ 3. Save the whales!

_____ 4. Conserving energy.

_____ 5. For example, the ladybug and the praying mantis.

_____ 6. The Clean Air Act of 1963, amended in 1970.

_____ 7. Because people of good will everywhere care enough to act.

_____ 8. And follow the example of Israel in developing solar energy.

_____ 9. With the cooperation of many hunters who care about wildlife management.

_____ 10. Then we will all survive.

© 1986 by CBS College Publishing. All rights reserved.

Solving Common Sentence Problems

_____ 11. The most endangered of all species.

_____ 12. Who daily consume a variety of poisons in the food they eat, in the water they drink, and in the air they breathe.

_____ 13. Pelting the eastern seaboard with gale-force winds and torrential rains.

_____ 14. Colonizing the moon and Sol's other planets.

_____ 15. Biting an angleworm in half, the bird ate the fellow raw.

_____ 16. Old Man Willow, who despised all living things that walk free on two legs upon the Earth.

_____ 17. To preserve wildlife species in zoos.

_____ 18. Black bees with gilt surcingles, buccaneers of buzz.

_____ 19. Out of the soup and into the sauce.

_____ 20. The question whether large ocean animals are more intelligent than humans.

Score _____

Review 11

The following paragraphs contain several fragments. Circle the number preceding each fragment and revise to complete the sentence.

[1] While concerned citizens work to protect the Earth from human-made destruction. [2] The Earth itself threatens life from time to time with natural catastrophes. [3] Such as volcanic eruptions, earthquakes, tornadoes, and hurricanes. [4] These Earth-made disasters are awesome, uncontrollable, and incredibly destructive. [5] Far exceeding in power the blast of the first atomic bomb.

[6] Some of history's worst disasters have been caused by volcanoes. [7] Which have killed more than 200,000 people and countless other living organisms since the fifteenth century. [8] Mt. Pelée on Martinique Island, destroying the town of St. Pierre in 1902. [9] With 38,000 dead within minutes. [10] Mount Tambora, killing 12,000 in an 1815 eruption. [11] And releasing energy 6 million times greater than an atomic-bomb explosion. [12] More recently, eruptions in North America have claimed 247 lives and powdered thousands of square miles with volcanic ash. [13] Mt. St. Helens in 1980 and El Chichon in 1982. [14] Meanwhile other volcanoes in the Pacific Ring of Fire, like Mt. Shasta in California and Mt. Hood in Oregon, emit steam. [15] And rumble ominously, reminding inhabitants of nearby towns and forests that their tenancy may be temporary at best.

[16] The Earth shakes, quakes, or trembles perhaps a million times a year. [17] Most of the time, there is little or no damage. [18] But large quakes have exceeded even volcanoes in killing power. [19] With the heaviest tolls in the most densely populated regions of the world. [20] In this century the hardest hit has been China. [21] Losing 200,000 in 1920; 70,000 in 1932; and 240,000 in 1976. [22] In 1970 nearly 67,000 died in a Peru quake. [23] In 1976 23,000 in Guatemala. [24] And in the past twenty years Iran has lost more than 40,000 in four major earthquakes.

[25] The United States is the hardest hit by tornadoes. [26] With 700 reported yearly but with many more going unreported. [27] A large area of Kansas, Oklahoma, and Texas will see more than 200 tornadoes in a twelve-year period [28] Hence the name "Tornado Alley." [29] Like a snake hissing toward the Earth, a tornado swirls out of dense thunderclouds. [30] Then hits the ground with a roar, sucking up air, dirt, automobiles [31] Whatever is unfortunate enough to be in its path.

[32] The destructive power of hurricanes can be measured in both lives and property damage. [33] In 1979 Hurricane David went on a rampage through the Dominican Republic, Puerto Rico, and the southeastern United States. [34] Killing 2,000 and causing $2 billion in damage. [35] Six hurricanes in the past twenty

years have destroyed at least a billion dollars worth of property. [36] While killing more than 10,000 people.

[37] How do we cope with Nature in its violent moods? [38] By learning to predict disasters, by preparing for them as best we can, and by waiting for Mother Earth to smile again.

Score _____

Check your answers against those in the back of the book. Deduct 2.5 points for each error in identification or correction. A score of 80 percent or higher on the exercise indicates you have mastered the materials studied in this chapter. If your score is lower than 80 percent, ask your instructor to give you more work on fragments.

The Writer's Casebook #11

Application: Developing Essays with Examples

In this chapter your primary concern has been correcting fragments so that sentences are complete in both structure and content. At the same time you have been reading and revising paragraphs, many of which use examples as a way of developing ideas about nature and conservation. For instance, the Review exercise on the preceding page consists primarily of examples. If we delete the examples, we are left with just three sentences—a mere fragment of the original essay.

> While concerned citizens work to protect the Earth from human-made destruction, the Earth itself threatens life from time to time with natural catastrophes. These Earth-made disasters are awesome, uncontrollable, and incredibly destructive. How do we cope with nature in its violent moods?

Since examples comprise almost the entire content of this essay, it belongs to the pattern of development called *exemplification*. However, you will undoubtedly use examples in all your writing, regardless of your overall method of developing ideas.

An example names a specific instance of a general phenomenon. The closer an example is to real life—to real people, events, places—the more useful it will be. Be careful, therefore, to avoid vague examples or examples as general as the ideas to be developed.

General Idea	Vague Example	Less Vague Examples	Specific Examples
conservation issue	dangers to wildlife	commercial hunting of seals destruction of natural habitat	annual harvest of harp seals in Hudson Bay eagles forced from traditional eyries by pollution and land development

You may develop your paper with many short examples (as in the Review essay), one or two long examples, or a combination. A long example told in narrative form is sometimes called an illustration. Like a story, an illustration takes place through time, and it may include a time, a place, and dialogue to help you "show rather than tell."

GENERAL IDEA: Not all attempts at conservation have been successful.

ILLUSTRATION: One early attempt at conservation ended in tragedy for the mule deer of the Kaibab North Plateau. The well-intentioned planners, including President Theodore Roosevelt, failed to take into account the prolific reproduction rate of the species. They established the Grand Canyon National Game Preserve and banned all hunting within its precincts. Natural predators such as mountain lions, bobcats, and wolves were systematically exterminated. The result was a phenomenal growth in the herd. Within less than twenty years its numbers increased from 3,000 to 30,000. Eventually tens of thousands of deer starved or died of disease, their range permanently damaged by over-grazing.

Notice that the writer uses a number of short examples within the overall illustration. Theodore Roosevelt is an example of those who sponsored the preserve, and mountain lions, bobcats, and wolves are examples of natural predators.

Examples show or exemplify what you are writing about. They make your essay more credible because they offer evidence to support your thesis or main idea. They add to its completeness because they show what general statements only tell, enabling us to fill in the general outline with something we can see or hear or feel.

Cases for Writing: Using Examples

Case #1

Changes are taking place so rapidly in our environment that practically everyone has seen major alterations in his or her lifetime. Explore the changes in your own immediate world—the city, town, or state you live in—by reading, talking to people, or simply remembering. Write a paper about how that world has changed physically in the past twenty years. Be sure to use specific examples that show rather than tell and to avoid sentence fragments.

Case #2

Assume that you are an investigative reporter working for the *Daily News*, a paper whose editors have a strong sense of civic responsibility. You have been assigned to investigate pollution in your community to see whether any company, person, or group is posing serious threats to the health of people, animals, or plant life. Make your investigation; then write a feature story about your findings. You may need to do some library research to be able to write about the specific damages caused by pollutants such as automobile exhaust, factory smoke, chemical insecticides, and so forth.

Comma Splices and Fused Sentences

12

Preview 12

Identify run-on sentences (comma splices and fused sentences) in the following paragraph by circling the number before a sentence that contains either of these errors. Then add punctuation or words as necessary to correct the error.

¹ Philosophy, contrary to popular belief, is not an ivory-tower discipline dedicated to studying the dead thoughts of dead men, it is an intensely contemporary and intensely relevant subject with concerns that range from the clash of East–West political ideologies to the way we choose our mates and our art. ² The word *philosophy* comes from two Greek words, *philos* and *sophia* put together they mean "loving wisdom." ³ More generally, however, philosophy means the sum of our beliefs and principles. ⁴ In this sense everyone has a personal philosophy moreover, in every culture, group, and nation, members share some common philosophical ground. ⁵ In a very real sense, the crisis that many observers have identified in American society during the past twenty years is a philosophical crisis. ⁶ Our culture has become fragmented, it lacks the sense of purpose and shared goals of more single-minded societies. ⁷ George F. Keenan, diplomat and historian, has questioned whether a philosophically divided society such as ours can compete with the serious, disciplined, unified societies of China, the Soviet Union, or Japan. ⁸ This question, along with the more personal questions of who we are, why we are here, what we should do with our lives, concerns modern philosophers. ⁹ Literally, philosophy is a study of our life's goals and meaning philosophers are engaged in the important work of helping us understand ourselves.

Score _____

Check your answers against those in the back of the book. Deduct 10 points for an error in identification and 10 points for an error in correction. A score of 80 percent or better indicates you edit effectively for run-ons.

While sentence fragments are the result of too much end punctuation, *run-on sentences*—both *comma splices* and *fused sentences*—are the result of not enough end punctuation. The names of these errors are descriptive. Instead of being separated with periods or other acceptable end punctuation, independent clauses are spliced or joined together with commas or fused together without any punctuation at all.

These errors involve sentence structure, not sentence length. They do not result directly from the writer's "running on and on" in the sense of writing a particularly long sentence (although trying to cram too much into a single sentence may result indirectly in your writing comma splices or fused sentences). It is possible to write a short run-on sentence, just as it is possible to write a long sentence fragment.

RUN-ON: Socrates died his ideas live on.

These six words constitute a run-on sentence, not because of length, but because they contain two complete independent clauses. We can analyze them in terms of the sentence structure and word relationships discussed in Chapters 6 and 20.

```
     n–subj   verb  poss pron  n–subj verb adv
    Socrates died/    his     ideas live on.
 [independent clause] [---independent clause--------]
```

An independent clause, you will remember, consists of a subject and a verb and can stand alone as a complete sentence. We can test our analysis by reading the groups of words separately and in reverse order.

<blockquote>
his ideas live on
Socrates died
</blockquote>

Both make sense as independent statements; therefore, they require end punctuation to separate them or the addition of other punctuation and connective devices to link them properly. The devices include connecting words such as conjunctions or conjunctive adverbs.

> Socrates died. His ideas live on.
> Socrates died; his ideas live on.
> Socrates died; however, his ideas live on.
> Socrates died, but his ideas live on.
> Although Socrates died, his ideas live on.

The Comma Splice

A comma splice occurs when two independent clauses are joined by a comma. A relatively weak punctuation mark, the comma can only interrupt; it cannot end or complete. However, because we are paying attention to the close relationship of ideas or because we mistake a conjunctive adverb such as *however* for a coordinating conjunction, we are sometimes tempted to place a comma where a stronger punctuation mark belongs.

COMMA SPLICE: Socrates taught by questioning, he urged his students to question their beliefs. (closely related ideas)
COMMA SPLICE: He was charged with corrupting the youth of Athens, moreover, he was found guilty. (conjunctive adverb)

To correct comma splices, we must add punctuation or words that will accurately show both the relationship between the ideas and the structure of the sentence. For example, in the comma splices above the close relationship between the ideas and the division between the independent clauses would be appropriately indicated by a semicolon, changing each comma splice to a compound sentence. How you correct a comma splice depends upon content (what it means) and style (what it sounds like).

12a Period

Revise a comma splice by using a period when the independent clauses are not closely linked, when they are long enough not to sound choppy, and when the comma splices a broken quotation.

COMMA SPLICE: Plato's *Republic* envisions an ideal state in which philosophers are kings, poets, on the other hand, have no place in Plato's Utopia.
REVISED: Plato's *Republic* envisions an ideal state in which philosophers are kings. Poets, on the other hand, have no place in Plato's Utopia.
COMMA SPLICE: "Poetry feeds and waters the passions instead of drying them up," Plato writes, "she lets them rule, although they ought to be controlled, if mankind are ever to increase in happiness and virtue."
REVISED: "Poetry feeds and waters the passions instead of drying them up," Plato writes. "She lets them rule, although they ought to be controlled, if mankind are ever to increase in happiness and virtue." (*The Republic*, X)

12b Semicolon

Revise a comma splice with a semicolon when the two clauses are of equal importance but closely related in content or structure and you wish to emphasize the connection.

COMMA SPLICE: In Plato's ideal state there would be no private property, there would be no family, except the family of the state as a whole.
REVISED: In Plato's ideal state there would be no private property; there would be no family, except the family of the state as a whole.

Also revise with a semicolon when the clauses are linked by a conjunctive adverb.

COMMA SPLICE: Plato believed private property and families were a cause of dissension, however, Aristotle called them valuable sources of happiness and natural affection.

REVISED: Plato believed private property and families were a cause of dissension; however, Aristotle called them valuable sources of happiness and natural affection.

12c Coordinating Conjunction

Revise a comma splice by adding an appropriate coordinating conjunction when the clauses are closely related but the relationship needs clarification.

COMMA SPLICE: In the sixteenth century Sir Thomas More wrote his *Utopia* in Latin, he felt Latin was a more universal and permanent language than English.
REVISED: In the sixteenth century Sir Thomas More wrote his *Utopia* in Latin, for he felt Latin was a more universal and permanent language than English. (addition of *for* to show causality)
COMMA SPLICE: *Utopia* is philosophical like Plato's *Republic*, at the same time it is romantic like the popular adventures of explorers such as Vespucci.
REVISED: *Utopia* is philosophical like Plato's *Republic*, but at the same time it is romantic like the popular adventures of explorers such as Vespucci. (addition of *but* to show contrast)

12d Subordinating Conjunction or a Relative Pronoun

Revise a comma splice by adding an appropriate subordinating conjunction or relative pronoun when the clauses are not of equal importance.

COMMA SPLICE: More's ideal state follows Plato in abolishing private property, More's narrator defends private property.
REVISED: Although More's ideal state follows Plato in abolishing private property, More's narrator defends private property. (The addition of the subordinating conjunction *although* subordinates the first clause to the second, creating one complex sentence.)
COMMA SPLICE: More was executed in 1535 for refusing to recognize Henry VIII as head of the English church, More had previously been Lord Chancellor.
REVISED: More, who had previously been Lord Chancellor, was executed in 1535 for refusing to recognize Henry VIII as head of the English Church. (The addition of the relative pronoun *who* subordinates the second clause to the first, creating one complex sentence.)

12e Using Comma Splices Effectively

A comma splice may be permitted in some very rare cases, such as with short, balanced clauses or with tag questions.

> Utopias are not made, they are dreamed.
> *Utopia* means "nowhere," doesn't it?

Comma Splices and Fused Sentences

The Fused Sentence

A fused sentence occurs when two independent clauses are run together without any punctuation. Perhaps less common than comma splices, fused sentences can often be found by reading a suspect passage out loud, listening for the stops and sharp drops in your voice, and then analyzing each word group found in this way to determine which are independent clauses. For example, if you read the following passage out loud, you will probably stop, with your voice dropping lowest, in two places—after *silver* and after the first *it*.

> More's Utopians accumulate enormous amounts of gold and silver however they do not treasure it they use it for chamber pots and prisoners' manacles.

Analyzing each of the word groups found in this way, we find that each is an independent clause.

poss n   n–subj   verb   adj   n–do   adj prep phrase
More's Utopians accumulate enormous amounts of gold and silver

conj adv pron–subj verb adv   verb   pron–do
however   they   do not treasure it

pron–sub verb pron–do   adv prep phrase
they   use   it   for chamber pots and prisoners' manacles.

Therefore, we need to add end punctuation at both dividing points.

> More's Utopians accumulate enormous amounts of gold and silver; however, they do not treasure it. They use it for chamber pots and prisoners' manacles.

Fused sentences, like comma splices, can be corrected in four ways.

12f Period

Add a period between clauses to create two separate sentences.

FUSED SENTENCE: More used his *Utopia* as a vehicle for criticizing the ills of his own society the evils of contemporary England are systematically chronicled and corrected.

REVISED: More used his *Utopia* as a vehicle for criticizing the ills of his own society. The evils of contemporary England are systematically chronicled and corrected.

12g Semicolon

Add a semicolon between clauses.

FUSED SENTENCE: To prevent later disappointment, More's Utopians advocated prospective spouses' examining each other unclothed however, the examination was to be chaperoned.

REVISED: To prevent later disappointment, More's Utopians advocated prospective spouses' examining each other unclothed; however, the examination was to be chaperoned.

12h Comma/Coordinating Conjunction

Add a comma and an appropriate coordinating conjunction between clauses.

FUSED SENTENCE: More corrected society's ills in his *Utopia* later writers amplified those ills in anti-Utopias.
REVISED: More corrected society's ills in his *Utopia*, but later writers amplified those ills in anti-Utopias.

12i Using Subordination

Subordinate one clause to the other by adding an appropriate subordinating conjunction or relative pronoun.

FUSED SENTENCE: Orwell's *Nineteen Eighty-Four* envisions a state controlled by all-powerful Big Brother it is probably the best known of the anti-Utopias.
REVISED: Orwell's *Nineteen Eight-Four*, which is probably the best known of the anti-Utopias, envisions a state controlled by all-powerful Big Brother.

Comma Splices and Fused Sentences   **215**

Correcting Comma Splices I Exercise 12–1

NAME _____ DATE _____

Identify comma splices in the following sentences. If the sentence is a comma splice, rewrite it, correcting it in two of the four possible ways. If it is correct as it stands, write C beside it.

> EXAMPLE: Normative ethics concerns finding principles to live by, it may also involve examining why people act as they do.
>
> *Normative ethics concerns finding principles to live by. It may also involve examining why people act as they do.*
>
> *Normative ethics concerns finding principles to live by; it may also involve examining why people act as they do.*

1. Codes of conduct are necessary to keep my "freedoms" from infringing upon your "rights," some of these rules are conscious, some are unconscious.

2. Codes should be based on consideration of individual happiness as well as social usefulness, shouldn't they?

3. Although some people believe that moral actions contribute to the goodness of the world, others believe that moral actions are those that bring about the greatest good in the situation.

4. Some choose nature as their guide in ethics, nature, they believe, will ensure the survival of the fittest.

© 1986 by CBS College Publishing. All rights reserved.

5. Should we let nature take its course, should we trust that whatever *is* is right?

6. Be not concerned with right and wrong, the conflict between right and wrong is the sickness of the mind. (Adapted from Seng-Ts'an)

7. "Nature and history do not agree with our conceptions of good and bad," say Will and Ariel Durant, "they define good as that which survives and bad as that which goes under."

8. To many, right is person-affirming, wrong is person-denying.

9. Immanuel Kant emphasized the need for good will, he said, "Nothing can possibly be conceived in the world, or even out of it, which can be called good without qualification, except a Good Will."

10. Moral laws, according to Kant, should come from within, not from outside, moreover, they should be based on the principle of humanity as an end, never a means.

Score _____

Correcting Comma Splices II Exercise 12–2

NAME _____ DATE _____

Identify comma splices in the following student paragraph; then rewrite the paragraph to eliminate the errors. Base your method of correction on both the relationship of the clauses and the style of the paragraph.

> EXAMPLE: Should I tell my aunt her new hat is ugly, should I "tattle" on my brother Phil?
> *Should I tell my aunt her new hat is ugly? Should I "tattle" on my brother Phil?*

Is honesty always the best policy? Many people have asked this question, however, few have answered it satisfactorily. "The truth never hurts," my mother always told me, "Be like Washington who couldn't tell a lie." The idea sounds good, it has the advantages of being simple, easy to remember, and definite. The problems start when we try to put the rule into practice. Taking an exam last week, I happened to glance at the student next to me, he was copying answers from a crib sheet he had hidden in his sleeve. What did I do, what should I have done? Probably what I should have done was to tell Dr. Otero about the cheating, what I actually did was to look away and go on with my own test. Also last week my friend Angelo asked my opinion of the girl he is dating. As it happens, I grew up with Rhonda, there are few people I like less, but what I said to Angelo was, "She's pretty, I hear she's smart too." On Saturday I stopped at the Palomino Club after work, the happy hour was in full swing. I met a good friend from high school, consequently, I forgot about my date with Barbara. What did I tell Barbara? Did I say, "Barbara, I was having such a good time at the Palomino Club that I forgot about our date"? Not a chance! I said, "Barbara, I had to work late." I can't decide whether I'm basically immoral or just smart.

Score _____

© 1986 by CBS College Publishing. All rights reserved.

Correcting Fused Sentences I Exercise 12–3

NAME _____ DATE _____

Identify fused sentences in the following exercise items. If the item is a fused sentence, rewrite it, making the correction in two of the four possible ways. If the sentence is correct as it stands, write C beside it.

> EXAMPLE: East is East West is West never the twain shall meet. (Adapted from Rudyard Kipling)
> *East is East, and West is West, and never the twain shall meet.*
> *East is East; West is West. Never the twain shall meet.*

1. Value systems are the basis for many important decisions what we do and why we do it are a function of what we value.

2. The West tends to emphasize the physical world of the senses the East more often looks beyond the senses to another kind of reality.

3. To the Occidental thinker competitiveness may be positive because struggle and the survival of the fittest are accepted as conditions of living.

4. To the Buddhist, desire and striving bring suffering therefore, competition is negative.

5. The Westerner loves life for its own sake living is an end in itself.

Comma Splices and Fused Sentences

6. For the Hindu the goal of life is release from the circle of rebirths this cycle is the result of *karma,* the law of sowing and reaping.

7. The Japanese have adopted many elements of Confucianism and Buddhism they have also adapted those elements to the Japanese culture.

8. Traditionally Japan has emphasized conformity and authority however, those traditions were seriously challenged by contact with the West after World War II.

9. According to Ruth Benedict, the West is typified by the "guilt culture" we rely on the development of conscience and inner control to keep individuals in line.

10. The East, on the other hand, contains many "shame cultures" people are controlled by the fear of losing face.

Score _____

© 1986 by CBS College Publishing. All rights reserved.

Correcting Fused Sentences II Exercise 12–4

NAME _____ DATE _____

Identify fused sentences in the following paragraphs adapted from William Ouchi's *Theory Z*. Then rewrite the paragraphs to eliminate the errors. Choose your method of correction based on both the relationship of the clauses and the style of the paragraph.

> EXAMPLE: Motivating higher production among Japanese employees demands different methods than in the West the people have different values.
>
> *Motivating higher production among Japanese employees demands different methods than in the West. The people have different values.*

Executives of an innovative American company with plants in Japan determined to make a thorough study of Japanese workers they wanted to design a plant that would combine the best of the East and West. In their study they discovered that Japanese firms almost never make use of individual work incentives and that piecework or even individual performance appraisal is not tied to salary increases the American executives concluded that rewarding individual achievement and individual ability is always a good thing.

   In the final assembly area of their new plant, long lines of young Japanese women wired together electronic products on a piece-rate system the more you wired, the more you got paid. About two months after the plant's opening, the foreladies approached the plant manager. "Honorable plant manager," they said humbly as they bowed, "we are embarrassed to be so forward however, we must speak to you all of the girls have threatened to quit work this Friday" (to have this happen, of course, would be a great disaster for all concerned.) "Why," they wanted to know, "can't our plant have the same compensation system as other Japanese companies? When you hire a new girl, her starting wage should be fixed by her age therefore, an eighteen-year-old should be paid more than a sixteen-year-old moreover, every year on her birthday, she should receive an automatic increase in pay. The idea that any one of us can be more productive than another must be wrong none of us in the final assembly could make a thing unless all of the other people in the plant had done their jobs right first. To single one person out as being more productive is wrong it is also personally humiliating to us." The company changed its compensation system to the Japanese model. (Adapted from William Ouchi, *Theory Z: How American Business Can Meet the Japanese Challenge*)

Score _____

Correcting Run-on Sentences in Student Writing Exercise 12–5

NAME _____ DATE _____

Identify and correct run-on sentences, both fused sentences and comma splices, in this student paper.

Money—The Root of All Evil?

Like many people I have always heard and believed that "the best things in life are free." I have always appreciated sunsets and flowers, I even make my Christmas presents every year to avoid losing the true spirit of Christmas in shopping-center commercialism. Money to me has always been somehow embarrassing, something nice people don't talk about however, after living from hand to mouth for four months during my first semester in college, my attitude has changed drastically. I now believe that money is not the root of all evil the lack of money is.

My money troubles began on the first day of school I was $300 short on my tuition. I had not read the fine print in the catalog that said, "Tuition subject to change without notice." To make up the difference, I got a workstudy job in the Registrar's office, but that job only added to my woes. The Registrar required all student workers to wear dresses or skirts, moreover, we had to wear high heels. The only clothes I had brought to school were jeans and sweatshirts, I don't own any high heels, it cost $22.50 for the one dress and $16.50 for the inexpensive shoes that I had to wear to work every day for a month until my parents could send me some other clothes from home.

Lack of money had an effect on my school work too. At the going rate of $2.00 a page, I could not afford to have my English papers typed, everyone knows that teachers grade typed papers higher. I also could not afford to buy published notes on the books we were to read consequently, unlike my classmates, I had to read entire books.

By not having any money, I missed out on a lot of fun. When my dorm roommate went to Purgatory to ski over Thanksgiving, I spent the holiday writing a term paper. While she enjoyed a night at the movies or the ice rink, I studied in the library. Of course, I could not tell anyone the real reason I did not join in on any of this fun I could not bring myself to say, "I can't go because I don't have any money," so I told them I wanted to study. As a result, I developed a reputation for being a "grind."

I think my experiences during my first semester at college prove that for a college student it's not money but the lack of money that is the root of all evil.

Score _____

Comma Splices and Fused Sentences 223

> **Review 12**
>
> Identify run-on sentences (comma splices and fused sentences) in the following paragraph by circling the number before any sentence containing an error. Then add punctuation or words as necessary to correct the error.
>
> [1] In his book *Walden*, Henry David Thoreau proposes a way of living and thinking that many people find attractive. [2] Being self-sufficient was central to Thoreau's philosophy at Walden Pond he built his own house and raised the food he ate. [3] "The mass of men lead lives of quiet desperation," he said, "what is called resignation is confirmed desperation." [4] Much of this desperation, he felt, was caused by society's emphasis upon "getting and spending." [5] To gain control of one's life, one must reject the materialism of modern life. [6] Once free of the struggle to acquire things, one would be free to live life, one would be freed of the human waste of time spent earning a living. [7] At Walden Pond Thoreau led a very simple life. [8] He swam in the pond, read books, wrote, he even spent time observing and writing the chronicles of a war between an army of red and an army of black ants. [9] Once he thought about purchasing a farm but rejected the idea when he realized the continual work and worries involved. [10] He avoided for most of his short life a regular job it is more natural, he felt, to work one month out of the year and live eleven than to work eleven and live one.
>
> **Score** _____
>
> Check your answers against those in the back of the book. Deduct 10 points for each error in identification and 10 points for each error in correction. A score of 80 percent or better indicates mastery of this topic.

The Writer's Casebook #12

Application to Writing: The Contemplative Paper

To correct run-on sentences requires not only a good grasp of sentence structure but also the ability to assess the relationships among ideas. Once you have identified a comma splice or a fused sentence, you must determine and evaluate the relationships among the ideas expressed as independent clauses before you can decide whether to correct the error by adding a period or a semicolon, by coordinating, or by subordinating. This kind of assessment requires systematic thinking.

Systematic thinking—analyzing to discover patterns, evaluating relationships among ideas, and making judgments—is also required, though on a much larger scale, when you write a paper about ideas.

Often in humanities courses you will be asked to write a paper that requires contemplation, or intense and systematic thinking about an event, problem, or idea—such as the philosophical issues posed in some examples in this chapter. A contemplative paper combines information with analysis and opinion. Before you write such a paper, you must first study the subject to learn the facts, then analyze the subject to understand its implications, and finally evaluate the subject in terms of your own beliefs and those of others.

Topics such as the following are frequently posed in philosophy, history, and literature courses: Evaluate Kant's categorical imperative. Is euthanasia humane or cruel? What are the implications of the People's Republic of China's recent rejection of Maoism? Compare the realism of Aristotle with the idealism of Plato. Consider the impact of Shakespeare upon subsequent generations of writers. Is *All's Well That Ends Well* truly a comedy?

An effective strategy for dealing with these questions in a paper makes contemplation an integral part of the prewriting process.

Prewriting/Contemplation
Step 1: *Learn* about the subject: read, ask questions, do research.
Step 2: *Analyze* the subject: determine its parts; consider what it is, what it is not; explore its causes and effects; compare it to other, similar actions, ideas, or events; determine how things happen.
Step 3: *Evaluate* the subject: Is it a good idea or a bad idea? Is it practical or impractical? Are the effects beneficial or harmful?
Step 4: *Apply* the subject: Does it have any meaning for you? Have you seen it working? Can you use it in your daily life? Does it affect you directly or indirectly?
Step 5: *Form an opinion* about the subject.

Once you have successfully contemplated the subject, you are ready to plan a paper about it. You may need to choose an approach, or your instructor may make an approach implicit in the assignment, but generally you will be asked to do one of the following.

Evaluate a view or thought.
    Find an answer to a problem.
        Compare or contrast ideas.
            Explore the bases or consequences of ideas or actions.
                Speculate about what might happen in a hypothetical situation.
                Apply an idea to your own life.

In each case the paper will follow the standard thesis-and-support pattern you are familiar with. Your opinion, arrived at through the process of contemplation, will form the basis for a thesis. What you learned when researching the subject and when analyzing, evaluating, and applying your research will form the basis for support.

Suppose, for example, that you were given the task of evaluating the school you attend. You might go to the school catalog for your research. There you might find the statement that your school is dedicated to educating the academically able and prepared, that it provides programs and support services primarily for accelerated learning, and that its curricula emphasize preparation for graduate school. From this information you might infer that your school has no interest in helping disadvantaged students succeed. You might then present the thesis that the school should be more concerned about providing equal opportunity to obtain quality education. As support you might cite comments in the school's statements of academic objectives about the role of the university in enlightening the mind to achieve an enlightened society. You might also draw upon your personal observations by claiming that some students need help to succeed and tying their need to lessons taught in your philosophy, political science, or sociology courses.

What a contemplative paper does *not* require is that you regurgitate everything you know about the subject by surveying all relevant facts in your paper. Instead, you must select the information from your store of knowledge that is most pertinent to your view or analysis.

Cases for Writing: Writing About Ideas

Case #1

Evaluate the view about money posed by the student writer in Exercise 12–5. Do you agree or disagree with the student's thesis? Does any evidence in the student's paper indicate that not all the results of her lack of money were bad? Discuss your opinion in the light of your own experiences or those of others.

Case #2

Consider some issue (such as censorship, violence on television, driving age, literacy, compulsory education, income tax) in the light of your own beliefs. Explain the foundations of your opinion, and support that opinion with examples from life.

Misplaced and Dangling Modifiers 13

Preview 13

Circle the number before any sentence in the following paragraph that contains a misplaced or dangling modifier. Then in the space provided at the bottom of page, rewrite those sentences.

¹ Glittering and glamorous, the public idolizes stars. ² While seen on the stage or screen, fans make their favorites the subject of dreams and myths. ³ Those who play villains are hated and derided, off the stage as well as on it. ⁴ Admired heroes are loved and imitated by people who are endowed with every virtue of the roles they play. ⁵ Part of this shared illusion or fantasy may be a direct function of the communal experience appropriate to drama. ⁶ The play or movie creates an emotional atmosphere that is infectious and seems to grow more intense increasing in number. ⁷ However, with an actor as one of the most popular presidents in history, one cannot help wondering if the spell of drama has supplanted reality.

Score _____

Check your answers against those in the back of the book. Deduct 10 points for incorrect identification and 10 points for incorrect revision. A score of 80 percent or better indicates that you understand the problem of faulty modification.

Misplaced Modifiers

When a modifier is separated from the word it modifies or when its placement blurs relationships, the result is confusion for the reader.

MISPLACED: In agony over his tragic life, the pins from his wife and mother's dress become weapons for Oedipus to gouge out his eyes.

Because the introductory phrase precedes *pins*, the sentence seems to say that inanimate pins were in agony.

REVISED: In agony over his tragic life, Oedipus uses the pins from his wife and mother's dress as weapons to gouge out his eyes.

13a Words

Avoid misplacing words by placing most modifiers directly before or after the words they modify and by placing certain modifiers (such as *almost, only, even, hardly, nearly,* and *just*) directly before the words they modify.

MISPLACED: Innocent and uncomprehending, Othello strangles Desdemona.
REVISED: Othello strangles innocent and uncomprehending Desdemona.

Avoid *squinting modifiers*, words placed so that they may modify either the word directly before or the word directly following.

SQUINTING: The role of Camille that everyone thought would suit Yvonne completely disgusted her. (Is she suited completely or completely disgusted?)
REVISED: The role of Camille that everyone thought would completely suit Yvonne disgusted her.
REVISED: The role of Camille that everyone thought would suit Yvonne disgusted her completely.

13b Phrases

Avoid misplacing phrases by placing verbal phrases near the words they modify and most prepositional phrases immediately following the words they modify.

MISPLACED: Tamburlaine rides in triumph through Persepolis, exalting in his power.
REVISED: Exalting in his power, Tamburlaine rides in triumph through Persepolis.
MISPLACED: *Everyman* is a medieval morality play that dramatizes every person's death and impending judgment with allegorical characters.
REVISED: *Everyman* is a medieval morality play with allegorical characters; it dramatizes every person's death and impending judgment. (Notice

that without the change to a compound sentence in the revision, the final clause might be misconstrued to mean that characters wreak judgment.)

Note: Some adverbial prepositional phrases can appear in different positions:

For a long time Hamlet plots his revenge. Hamlet plots his revenge for a long time. But be careful to avoid ambiguity: *Hamlet plans to revenge his father's death in his mind.* (Did the death take place in Hamlet's mind?)

13c   Subordinate Clauses

Avoid ambiguity by placing subordinate clauses near the words they modify.

MISPLACED: *Agamemnon* is the first play in the *Oresteia*, a dramatic trilogy which depicts the tragic homecoming of a king. (Only *Agamemnon* depicts the homecoming.)

REVISED: *Agamemnon*, which depicts the tragic homecoming of a king, is the first play in the *Oresteia*, a dramatic trilogy.

13d   Intrusive Modifiers

Avoid inserting modifiers intrusively between the parts of a verb phrase or between the parts of an infinitive.

AWKWARD: Hamlet will, if he ever decides to act, revenge his father's death.
REVISED: If he ever decides to act, Hamlet will revenge his father's death.
AWKWARD: To fully avenge his father's death, Orestes must kill Clytemnestra, his mother.
REVISED: To avenge his father's death fully, Orestes must kill Clytemnestra, his mother.

Dangling Modifiers

When the word modified is missing from the sentence, the modifier is left dangling.

Selling his soul to the devil, his life becomes a series of triumphs and pleasures. (Who sold his soul?)

To correct a dangling modifier, you may do one of two things.

1. Change the subject of the main clause.

   Selling his soul to the devil, Faustus enjoys his life of triumphs and pleasures.

2. Expand the dangling phrase to a subordinate clause.

   After Faustus sells his soul to the devil, his life becomes a series of triumphs and pleasures.

13e Verbal Phrases

A participial or infinitive phrase dangles when the word it modifies is implied rather than directly stated in the sentence.

DANGLING: <u>Surfeited with life's pleasures</u>, the consequences for eternity are forgotten. (Who is surfeited?)
REVISED: <u>Surfeited with life's pleasures</u>, Faustus forgets the consequences for eternity.
DANGLING: Power and pleasure seemed to carry Faustus's mind away from reality <u>to forget about a future in hell</u>. (Who forgot?)
REVISED: Power and pleasure seemed to carry Faustus's mind away from reality <u>so that he forgot about a future in hell</u>.

13f Prepositional Phrases

Prepositional phrases, which may serve as either adjectives or adverbs, dangle when there is no word in the sentence that they can reasonably modify.

DANGLING: <u>With hundreds of lines to memorize</u>, the role of Faustus is overwhelming. (Who must memorize the lines? The role cannot.)
REVISED: <u>With hundreds of lines to memorize</u>, Franklin was overwhelmed by the role of Faustus.
REVISED: <u>Because there are hundreds of lines to memorize</u>, the role of Faustus is overwhelming.

13g Elliptical Clauses

Elliptical clauses (clauses from which words have been omitted and must be inferred from the context) also dangle if the sentence lacks the word modified.

DANGLING: <u>While on stage</u>, no itch, ache, or desire to sneeze can be given in to. (Are the itch, ache, or desire on stage?)
REVISED: <u>While on stage</u>, the actor cannot give in to the desire to sneeze, scratch an itch, or soothe an ache.

Misplaced and Dangling Modifiers   **231**

Revising Misplaced Modifiers   Exercise 13–1

NAME _____ DATE _____

Identify and revise any misplaced modifiers in the following sentences. Rewrite the sentences to eliminate errors.

    EXAMPLE: The actor barely spoke above a whisper.
    The actor spoke barely above a whisper.

1. Longing for bright lights and excitement, acting is the profession Derek chose.

2. Demanding classes in the School for the Arts challenge the brightest with hours of homework and grueling exams.

3. By writing my own examination plays, the professors were impressed, and they gave me a higher grade.

4. Scared and shaking, the audience looked like an ocean of faces as I stepped on the stage.

5. I decided to after all enroll in the School for the Arts.

6. The actors decided that the play *Macbeth* was cursed when they read the rave reviews, but they changed their minds when Lady Macbeth broke her leg.

7. The play *Phèdre* is about a Greek Queen's tragic passion for her stepson, Hippolyte by Jean Racine.

8. Phèdre declares her passion during the King's absence.

9. When he returns, King Thésée is by the intervention of Phèdre's friend Oenone misled to believe that his son has attempted to seduce the Queen.

© 1986 by CBS College Publishing. All rights reserved.

10. Thésée curses his son who is said to be a son of the sea god with the wrath of Poseidon.

Score _____

Revising Dangling Modifiers Exercise 13-2

NAME _____ DATE _____

Revise each sentence with a dangling modifier by rewriting it twice—first, by changing the subject of the main clause and, second, by expanding the dangling phrase to a subordinate clause. Write C beside any sentence that does not contain a dangling modifier.

> EXAMPLE: When performed on the stage, its classical simplicity is impressive. (*Phèdre* is performed)
> *When Phèdre is performed on the stage, its classical simplicity is impressive.*
> *When performed on the stage, Phèdre is impressive in its classical simplicity.*

1. By pursuing her stepson, the gods were offended. (Phèdre is the pursuer.)

2. Fleeing from his father's wrath, Hippolyte is killed in a chariot accident caused by Poseidon.

3. Before taking poison, all is confessed by Phèdre.

4. Victimized by Aphrodite, Phèdre's passion is uncontrollable.

5. Though a play in the classical tradition, the playwright Racine departs from the usual focus upon male tragic heroes. (Racine wrote *Phèdre*.)

6. On the stage for most of the two hours, Phèdre's agony and struggle dominate the play.

© 1986 by CBS College Publishing. All rights reserved.

7. While based upon a Greek play by Euripides, the focus has shifted dramatically from Hippolyte to Phèdre.

8. Denying nature, the wrath of Aphrodite is earned when Hippolyte denounces his stepmother and all women.

9. By emphasizing the unnatural pride of Hippolyte, the Queen is made by Euripides to be an innocent victim in the battle between her stepson and the goddess of love.

10. By giving Hippolyte a sweetheart, Racine changes the emphasis from the unnatural pride of Hippolyte to the unnatural passion of Phèdre.

Score _____

Misplaced and Dangling Modifiers 235

Review 13

Circle the numbers before any sentence in the following student paragraph that contains a misplaced or dangling modifier. Then in the space provided at the bottom of the page, rewrite those sentences.

¹ Taking place in a small cemetery, the setting of James Galloway's play *Boot Hill Rosaries* is New Mexico in the late 1800's and early 1900's. ² The characters are people who have over a period of years and for a variety of reasons died and been buried in the cemetery. ³ The characters include the Gunslinger, the Scholar, the Young Bride, the Mexican Mother, the Fancy Lady, and the twelve nuns. ⁴ I play Belle, the Fancy Lady. ⁵ Belle tells her story of hard times, angry and insecure. ⁶ While a beginning actress, it was impossible to get parts in London, so she moved first to New York and then to New Mexico. ⁷ Marrying an alcoholic, she became a stage coach driver. ⁸ Later she left her husband and opened a bordello in Albuquerque. ⁹ While not accepted by society, the rest of her life is spent making money and being contented.

Score _____

Check your answers against those in the back of the book. Deduct 10 points for incorrect identification and 10 points for incorrect revision. A score of 80 percent or better indicates that you have mastered the problem of faulty modification.

The Writer's Casebook #13

Application: Cause and Effect—Analyzing the Causes of an Effect or the Effects of a Cause or Discovering the Links in the Chain

Correcting dangling or misplaced modifiers requires you to understand the cause-and-effect relationships of meaning in a sentence. You must recognize that the selection and arrangement of words in a sentence create a chain of meaning that can be broken by varying the selection or altering the word order. Writing a paper that analyzes the causes of an effect or the effects of a cause also calls upon you to discover meaningful chains in events, conditions, and situations.

When you are asked by your theater instructor to discuss the causes of audience laughter or by your history professor to discuss the effects of the Treaty of Versailles, you will need to use the cause-and-effect method of development discussed earlier for the paragraph (see Chapter 4) to write a longer paper. The basic method remains the same. Ordinarily you will focus either upon causes—that is, the origins of an event, condition, or situation—or upon effects—the results or consequences of that event, condition, or situation.

The introduction and thesis, like the topic sentence of a paragraph, can help you establish the focus for your paper. For example, you might be writing about the effects upon the average athlete of a college career devoted to sports rather than to studies. You could begin by identifying the condition to be explored—the athlete's devotion to sports and neglect of his or her education. Then in the thesis you could propose several major results to be explored in the paper, such as not graduating and not being trained for a career outside sports, and assess the overall effect upon the athlete.

Writing a paragraph and writing a longer paper using cause-and-effect development differ primarily in the depth of analysis and the quantity of support needed. The overall organization follows the beginning–middle–ending structure, basic to both the standard paragraph and the essay. Two possible applications of the pattern are outlined briefly below.

Analyzing Causes of an Effect
Introduction
    Identification of the subject—the effect whose origins will be explored
    Short anecdote, image, quotation, or example that will make your reader want to understand the causes
    Thesis that proposes to discuss causes
Body
    Support paragraphs (at least 3)
        Topic sentence for each paragraph that presents one cause for examination
        Developmental sentences that offer examples, details,

Analyzing Effects of a Cause
Introduction
    Identification of the subject—the cause whose effects will be examined
    Short anecdote, image, quotation, or example that will make your reader want to understand the effects
    Thesis that proposes to discuss effects
Body
    Support paragraphs (at least 3)
        Topic sentence for each paragraph that presents one effect for examination
        Developmental sentences that offer examples, details,

    facts, or explanation by log-   facts, or explanation by log-
    ical analysis   ical analysis
Conclusion   Conclusion
    Reminder of subject   Reminder of subject
    Your final word, comment, or   Your final word, comment, or
    judgment   judgment

Note: Be careful not to confuse cause and effect with process analysis, which focuses upon explaining how rather than exploring why.

Cases for Writing: Probing for Reasons and Pursuing Outcomes

Case #1

Imagine you are an amateur theatricals director. You have just opened for a two-week run of a popular musical (*Fiddler on the Roof, Hello Dolly, Gigi, South Pacific,* and so forth) when you receive the news that one of your lead performers has a broken leg. The role calls for several dance numbers, and the understudy is refusing to go on. Your anxiety is mounting as you explore all the possible effects of this ill-timed broken leg. Write a paper about what could happen, being careful to avoid misplaced or dangling modifiers.

Case #2

One of your friends has become a star (movies, television, rock, country-western, and so forth). You have been invited to a party at your friend's home (in Hollywood, New York, Nashville, and so forth). Attend the party and then write a letter to someone back home discussing the effects stardom has had upon your friend. Use descriptive modifiers in your paper, paying special care to their correct placement in the sentence.

Faulty Parallelism   14

Preview 14

Circle the letter before the sentence in each of the following pairs that illustrates effective parallelism.

1. a. In a speech before the Virginia House of Delegates, Alexander Hunter proved that a turtle is not a fish and that it is not an oyster.
   b. In a speech before the Virginia House of Delegates, Alexander Hunter proved that a turtle is not a fish, and he also made the turtle's not being an oyster a point.
2. a. Breathing evenly, using the diaphragm, and a healthy dose of self-confidence will help you project your voice.
   b. Breathing evenly, using the diaphragm, and having a healthy dose of self-confidence will help you project your voice.
3. a. Speech is silver, but silence is golden.
   b. Speech is silver, but silence is worth its weight in gold.
4. a. Eat your fill and drink what you want for true merriment.
   b. Eat, drink, and be merry.
5. a. School was behind us; the world was before us.
   b. We were leaving school behind; there was a big world waiting.
6. a. The more I talk, the less they listen.
   b. When I talk too much, people listen to me less.
7. a. It is best to remain silent when you are too sure that you are right and also when you know that you are wrong.
   b. There are two times to remain silent: when you know you're 100 percent right and when you know you're 100 percent wrong.
8. a. It's easier saying something than to do it.
   b. It's easier said than done.
9. a. We will carry on the fight for ERA in the schools, in the churches, in the streets, and in the homes.
   b. We will carry on the fight for ERA, taking our cause to the schools as well as to the churches and we will campaign in the streets and homes.
10. a. Speak softly but carry a big stick.
    b. Keep your voice down; your big stick will do the talking for you.

Score _____

Check your answers against those in the back of the book. Deduct 10 points for each error. You probably earned a very high score on this exercise; however, unless you can explain the parallelism in each correct answer, you should still study this chapter so that you can revise faulty parallelism in your own work.

Faulty Parallelism

Written items are said to be parallel when they share the same grammatical form or structure (see 6f and 8c). Making parallel the words, phrases, and clauses that serve the same function in a sentence helps the reader to see relationships among ideas and to follow a complex sentence structure. Effective use of parallelism can also contribute to your writing style—to smoothing or pacing the rhythm of your sentences so that they are pleasant to read and perhaps even more memorable.

When you are not certain whether items are parallel or do not understand the parallelism, you can gain a fresh perspective by rewriting the sentence so that the parallel items are lined up vertically, with the rest of the sentence forming a frame or base.

> Who does not know that a turtle has four legs;
>   that those legs have feet; (and)
>   that those feet are armed with claws, like a cat's
>   a panther's (or)
>   a lion's?
>
> *(From "Is a Turtle a Fish?," a speech made by Alexander Hunter during a debate in the Virginia House of Delegates)*

The diagram shows that there are two separate instances of parallelism in the sentence—the first of parallel clauses, each serving as an object of the verb *know*, and the second of parallel words, each serving as an object of the preposition *like*.

14a   Parallelism

(1)   Items in a series

Use parallelism for words, phrases, or clauses in a series.

> A turtle's feet are armed with claws, like <u>a cat's</u>, <u>a panther's</u>, or <u>a lion's</u>. (series of words, serving as objects of preposition *like*)
>
> A turtle has a tail, but he does not use it <u>to swing from the trees like a monkey</u>, <u>to swat flies like a mule</u>, <u>to wag like a dog</u>, or <u>to swim like a fish</u>. (series of phrases, modifying verb *use*)
>
> I submit, Mr. Speaker, <u>that a turtle is not a fish</u>, <u>that it is not even a relative of the fish</u>, and <u>that it should not be a concern of this House's Committee on Fish and Oysters</u>. (series of clauses, serving as object of the verb *submit*)

(2)   Paired items

Use parallelism for paired items joined by coordinating or correlative conjunctions, by commas, or by semicolons.

> <u>Right</u> or <u>wrong</u>, we must make a decision. (paired words joined by coordinating conjunction *or*)

The speaker kept eye contact not only <u>with people in the front row</u> but also <u>with people in the back row</u>. (paired phrases joined by correlative conjunctions *not only/but also*)

<u>Stronger than many</u>, <u>wiser than most</u>—Lincoln still gives hope to the oppressed. (paired phrases joined by a comma)

<u>The war was over</u>; <u>the house was still divided</u>. (paired clauses joined by a semicolon)

<u>Reading a book</u> is easier than <u>writing it</u>. (paired phrases compared with *than*)

14b Revising Faulty Parallelism

Rewriting a sentence with the series of paired elements matched vertically helps identify faulty parallelism.

>My audience walked out because I had not prepared my speech,
>   because I had nothing to say, and
>   because of my weak speaking voice.

Although each of the items begins with *because*, only the first two are parallel clauses; the last is a prepositional phrase. For the items in the series to be parallel, all must share the same grammatical form.

>My audience walked out because I had not prepared my speech,
>   because I had nothing to say, and
>   because I spoke too softly.

(1) Parallel elements

Avoid faulty parallelism by matching nouns with nouns, verbs with verbs, phrases and clauses with phrases and clauses of a similar type or structure, and so forth.

FAULTY: Annoying speech habits include saying "ah" or "you know," use of a monotone, and clearing the throat frequently. (*Saying "ah" or "you know"* and *clearing the throat frequently* are gerund phrases; *use of a monotone* is a noun phrase.)

REVISED: Annoying speech habits include <u>saying "ah" or "you know,"</u> <u>using a monotone</u>, and <u>clearing the throat frequently</u>. (three gerund phrases)

FAULTY: After I took a speech course, I had more confidence, could organize my thoughts better, and I also felt more compassion for boring speakers. (*Had more confidence* and *could organize my thoughts better* are predicates; *I also felt more compassion for boring speakers* is an independent clause.)

REVISED: After I took a speech course, <u>I had more confidence</u>, <u>could organize my thoughts better</u>, and <u>also felt more compassion for boring speakers</u>. (three predicates)

(2) Signals of parallelism

Avoid faulty parallelism by repeating the words that signal parallel structures, including articles, prepositions, *to*, or conjunctions.

FAULTY: Parallelism is used by David in the Psalms, by Martin Luther King in his "I Have a Dream" speech, and Kennedy in his Inaugural Address. (*By* introduces the first two items but not the third, breaking the parallel.)

REVISED: Parallelism is used <u>by</u> David in the Psalms, <u>by</u> Martin Luther King in his "I Have a Dream" speech, and <u>by</u> Kennedy in his Inaugural Address.

(3) Relative pronouns

Avoid faulty parallelism by repeating relative pronouns such as *who*, *whom*, and *which*.

FAULTY: The funeral speech Marc Antony gives in *Julius Caesar* and which I memorized in high school, is filled with parallel structures.

REVISED: The funeral speech, <u>which</u> Marc Antony gives in *Julius Caesar* <u>and which</u> I memorized in high school, is filled with parallel structures.

Faulty Parallelism   **243**

Identifying Parallels   Exercise 14-1

NAME _____ DATE _____

Identify the parallel sentence elements in each passage. Then in the space provided explain whether the elements are parallel words, phrases, or clauses and what function they serve in the sentence.

> EXAMPLE: Our tragedy today is a <u>general</u> and <u>universal</u> physical fear so long sustained by now that we can even bear it. <u>There are no longer problems of spirit</u>. There is only the question: <u>when will I be blown up?</u> (William Faulkner, *On Accepting the Nobel Prize for Literature*)
> *paired adjectives modifying noun fear*
> *paired clauses*

1. Discrimination against women, solely on the basis of their sex, is so widespread that it seems to many persons normal, natural and right. (Shirley Chisholm, *In Support of the Equal Rights Amendment*)

2. With this faith we will be able to hew out of the mountain of despair a stone of hope. With this faith we will be able to transform the jangling discords of our nation into a beautiful symphony of brotherhood. With this faith we will be able to work together, to pray together, to struggle together, to go to jail together, to stand up for freedom together, knowing that we will be free one day. (Martin Luther King, "I Have a Dream")

3. The energy, the faith, the devotion which we bring to this endeavor will light our country and all who serve it—and the glow from that fire can truly light the world. And so my fellow Americans: ask not what your country can do for you—ask what you can do for your country. (John F. Kennedy, Inaugural Address)

4. A man who is good for anything ought not to calculate the chance of living or dying; he ought only to consider whether in doing anything he is doing right or wrong— acting the part of a good man or a bad. . . . (Socrates, *Defense*)

5. The divine bards are the friends of my virtue, of my intellect, of my strength. They admonish me, that the gleams which flash across my mind, are not mine but God's. . . . So I love them. Noble provocations go out from them, inviting me also to emancipate myself; to resist evil; to subdue the world; and to Be. (Ralph Waldo Emerson, "The Divinity School Address")

6. But, in a larger sense, we can not dedicate—we can not consecrate—we can not hallow—this ground. The brave men, living and dead, who struggled here, have consecrated it; far above our poor power to add or detract. The world will little note,

© 1986 by CBS College Publishing. All rights reserved.

nor long remember what we say here, but it can never forget what they did here. It is for us the living, rather, to be dedicated here to the unfinished work which they who fought here have thus far so nobly advanced. It is rather for us to be here dedicated to the great task remaining before us—that from these honored dead we take increased devotion to that cause for which they gave the last full measure of devotion—that we here highly resolve that these dead shall not have died in vain—that this nation, under God, shall have a new birth of freedom—and that government of the people, by the people, for the people, shall not perish from the earth. (Abraham Lincoln, "Gettysburg Address")

Score _____

Faulty Parallelism **245**

Revising Faulty Parallelism   Exercise 14–2

NAME _____ DATE _____

Identify and correct faulty parallelism in the following sentences. Mark correct sentences with a C.

> EXAMPLE: Show rather than telling.
> *Show rather than tell.*

1. The world is divided between those making speeches and those who climb mountains.

2. Opinion about Lincoln's "Gettysburg Address" is still a mixture of admiration of its poetic qualities and criticism of its clichés.

3. We shall fight on the beaches, we shall fight on the landing grounds, we will make a stand in the fields and in the streets, we shall fight in the hills; we shall never surrender. (Adapted from Winston Churchill, 1940 speech in the House of Commons)

4. On August 28, 1963, the Reverend Martin Luther King, Jr., led a march from the Washington Monument, and it ended at the Lincoln Memorial.

5. Millions, those marching with King and those who watched on television, heard his "I Have a Dream" speech.

6. I have a dream that one day every valley shall be exalted, every hill and mountain shall be made low, the rough places will be made plain, and the crooked places will be made straight. (From Martin Luther King, Jr., "I Have a Dream")

7. The true use of speech is not so much to express our wants as conceal them. (Adapted from Oliver Goldsmith, *The Bee*)

© 1986 by CBS College Publishing. All rights reserved.

8. I love a natural, simple and unaffected speech. . . . a pithy, sinewy, full, strong, compendious and material speech. (Adapted from Montaigne, *Essays*)

9. The Association of Citizens for Sanity in Politics has recommended improving the 1988 presidential campaign by limiting its duration to the two weeks before the election, by allowing no candidates to spend more than they collect in contributions, and all political speeches would be shortened to five minutes.

10. I believe this government cannot endure, permanently half slave and with half of us enjoying freedom. (Adapted from Abraham Lincoln, "House Divided" speech)

Score _____

Faulty Parallelism 247

Sentence Combining for Parallelism Exercise 14–3

NAME _____ DATE _____

Combine the following sentences into a single sentence with parallel elements.

EXAMPLE: She spoke strongly. She spoke with conviction.
She spoke with strength and with conviction.

1. Famous speeches by Lincoln include his address on "The Presidential Question." He also made an important speech about slavery. It is generally called "The House Divided." "The Gettysburg Address" is the most famous of them all.

2. In 1961 and 1962 President John F. Kennedy confronted Nikita Krushchev. He confronted the Soviet Premier on the question of Berlin. Kennedy said that our presence in Berlin was an issue of national security. He also said that our access rights were based on law. They were not based on sufferance. He also expressed our determination to maintain those rights "at any risk."

3. I begin preparing for a speech days ahead. I have to make speeches in Speech 152, Public Speaking. I begin by thoroughly researching the subject. Then I organize the material. Practice and practice and more practice is the last step.

4. Robert Louis Stevenson gave us some good advice. He said to keep your fears to yourself. Sharing your courage with others, however, is important.

5. According to a Hindu proverb we can know people by four things. Their conversation tells us a lot about them. Their disposition is very revealing. We can learn a lot from their family. We also know people by their conduct.

Score _____

© 1986 by CBS College Publishing. All rights reserved.

Review 14

Circle the letter before the sentence in each of the following pairs that illustrates effective parallelism.

1. a. Some people use speech to communicate ideas; some, to conceal them.
   b. For some people speech is a means of communicating ideas while others conceal ideas with words.
2. a. The less you say, the less you must explain.
   b. If you get in the habit of saying little, you will not be faced with always explaining what you mean.
3. a. Tell them what you are going to say; say it; then tell them what you said.
   b. Begin by explaining your subject; then you can go into the subject in detail; and finally, the conclusion should include a summary of all that went before.
4. a. It was a new kind of textbook—by students and for students.
   b. The new kind of textbook used materials written by students, and student interests and language were emphasized.
5. a. Martin Luther King, Jr.'s, dreams included equality and brotherhood, and he also longed for peace.
   b. Martin Luther King, Jr., dreamed of equality, of brotherhood, of peace.
6. a. It's not whether you win or lose but how you play the game.
   b. It's not important whether you win the game or lose, but you should always be a good sport.
7. a. If you begin by making a sacrifice of yourself for your loved ones, in the end you will hate them.
   b. If you begin by sacrificing yourself to those you love, you will end by hating those to whom you have sacrificed yourself. (George Bernard Shaw)
8. a. Sincerity and dedication win our admiration, stir our feelings, and inspire imitation.
   b. We admire people who are sincere and dedicated because they stir up our feelings and make us want to imitate them.
9. a. Not preparing sets you up for failing.
   b. If you fail to prepare, you prepare to fail.
10. a. A turtle is no more a fish than an oyster is an ostrich.
    b. Just as a turtle is not a fish, ostriches and oysters are not the same thing.

Score _____

Check your answers against those in the back of the book. Deduct 10 points for each error. Be sure you can explain as well as choose the correct answer.

The Writer's Casebook #14

Application to Writing: The Classification Essay

Parallelism is integral to classification. When we classify, we organize things, people, or events into groups according to some shared characteristics. When we make sentences or parts of sentences parallel, we are organizing our ideas into comparable units and using grammatical structure to emphasize the comparison. For example, the following sentences classify people according to comparable behaviors. In the first sentence the writer uses parallel noun phrases, and in the second, verbals, to highlight the categories.

> Airplane passengers can be divided into three main categories: the hate-to-fly group; the can'-t-sit-still group; and the know-it-all group.

> In my ten years of secretarial experience, I have encountered three different types of bosses: the enthused, the unenthused, and the bemused.

Classifying actually begins with comparison and contrast. When you are asked to classify your classmates or teachers into groups, for example, you must first determine in what ways they are alike and in what ways they are different. Once you have discovered a pattern in the likenesses and differences, you can begin to classify, separating according to differences and grouping according to likenesses.

Classification is the counterpart of division. That is, in division we separate the parts of one thing into categories and examine them one category at a time. In classification we separate several things into groups or categories. In division, for example, we might divide the parts of a persuasive speech into the prologue, the statement, the proof, and the epilogue (Aristotle, *Rhetoric*, Book III). In classification we begin with several speeches and then divide them into groups according to content, purpose, or effect on the audience.

For example, we might start with a list of speeches.

"I Have a Dream"—Martin Luther King
"Is a Turtle a Fish?"—Alexander Hunter
"What Is Photosynthesis?"—Professor Norman Squires
"Acres of Diamonds"—Russell H. Conwell
"The Danger Signals of Fatigue"—Dr. Janette Hinkley
"Gettysburg Address"—Abraham Lincoln
"Cross of Gold"—William Jennings Bryant
"How to Play the Stock Market"—Yvonne Chavez
"Give Me Liberty or Give Me Death"—Patrick Henry
"In Support of the Equal Rights Amendment"—Shirley Chisolm
"Energy Address to the Nation"—Jimmy Carter

All are speeches but not all have the same purposes and content. In fact, four basic types are represented here: informative, inspirational, entertaining, and persuasive. With this classification system in mind, we are ready to group the speeches.

Informative

"What Is Photosynthesis?"
"The Danger Signals of Fatigue"
"How to Play the Stock Market"

Inspirational

"I Have a Dream"
"Gettysburg Address"

Entertaining

"Is a Turtle a Fish?"
"Acres of Diamonds"

Persuasive

"Cross of Gold"
"Give Me Liberty or Give Me Death"
"In Support of the Equal Rights Amendment"
"Energy Address to the Nation"

Notice that all the items in the list are covered by one of the categories; a classification system will not work unless it accounts for all the items being classified. Notice also that there is more than one speech in each category. Categories refer to groups of things rather than to individual examples.

A general outline for a classification essay would look something like this.

Introduction
    Lead-in—identifying the subject in general
    Thesis—naming the different categories into which you have divided
        your materials
Middle
    Developmental paragraph defining, describing, and giving examples of
    one category
    Developmental paragraph defining, describing, and giving examples of
    another category
    And so forth
Conclusion
    Reiteration of the categories
    Explanation of the significance of your classification system

Cases for Writing:
Classifying and Writing the Classification Essay

Case #1

Identify a number of speakers (teachers, politicians, ministers) whom you have heard. Then separate the speakers into categories on the basis of some shared characteristics such as speaking style, content, or body language. Write a paper about what you find, being careful to explain your categories carefully and to illustrate them fully.

Case #2

You are a television critic who has been assigned to write a column on the new season. To organize your discussion, you begin by grouping the shows by type—for example, sit-coms, soaps, detective/police yarns, and so forth. Then write the column, including evaluative comments and many specific examples.

Shifts and Mixed Constructions   15

> **Preview 15**
>
> Circle the number before any sentence in which you find a shift in tense, mood, person, voice, or number or a mixed construction. Revise each error by crossing out the incorrect word or words and writing the correct word or words above the line.
>
> ¹ What is play and why do people play? ² For many, play is when they practice physical and social skills. ³ When you were an infant, you played with brightly colored mobiles to develop eye and hand coordination. ⁴ As a toddler, play "hide and seek" and "dodge ball" to develop strategies for getting along with others. ⁵ Competition, which often makes adulthood a rat race, ten-year-olds learn to deal with it by running races and playing marbles. ⁶ As teenagers, more complex social interactions are learned in team play. ⁷ When human beings become adults, they continue to play—to relieve tension, to experience victory, to feel in control of life.
>
> **Score** _____
>
> Check your answers against those in the back of the book. Deduct 10 points for each error in identifying sentences with shifts or mixed constructions and 10 points for inadequate revision.

15a Shifts

Tense, voice, mood, person, and number are like ground rules. They may change from game to game or from writing task to writing task, but once laid down for a specific situation, they should be followed consistently. Shifting from one set of rules to another after the game or sentence or paragraph has begun confuses the participants—that is, the players and spectators or the writers and readers. Take, for instance, the following paragraph.

¹To play the game of parcheesi, you need two or more players, a game board, dice, and four markers for each player. ²First, roll the dice. ³The player with the highest number starts the play. ⁴They placed their markers on the starting place on the board. ⁵Then roll the dice again and they will advance their markers the number of spaces indicated on the dice. ⁶When the markers have reached home, the game has been won.

The shifts in tense, voice, mood, person, and number make this paragraph difficult to follow. Who rolls the dice—the implied *you* of sentence 2, rolling perhaps for all players, or the individual *player* of sentence 3? Do all players advance all their markers for every roll of the dice, as sentence 5 suggests? If so, what is the point of the game, since all will reach home together? Rewriting the paragraph to eliminate shifts clarifies its meaning.

> Playing the game of parcheesi requires two or more players, a game board, dice, and four markers for each player. First, each player rolls the dice. The player with the highest number starts the play. She places her markers on the starting place on the board. Then she rolls the dice again and advances a marker the number of spaces indicated on the dice. The player whose markers reach home first wins the game.

(1) Tense

Avoid tense shifts that do not follow a logical sequence. (See 22f for more about sequencing tenses.)

CONFUSED: The Monopoly player plans to buy Park Place but went instead "directly to jail" without "passing GO." (shift from present to past tense)

REVISED: The Monopoly player had planned to buy Park Place but went instead "directly to jail" without "passing GO."

REVISED: The Monopoly player plans to buy Park Place but goes instead "directly to jail" without "passing GO."

(2) Voice

Avoid shifts in voice when they confuse, mislead, or sound awkward. (See 22j–l for more about voice.)

CONFUSED: Soon after the chess game began, my rook was captured by my opponent. (shift from active to passive voice)

REVISED: Soon after the chess game began, my opponent captured my rook.

(3) Mood

Avoid a shift in mood if it sounds awkward or confuses the reader. (See 22g–i for more about mood.)

CONFUSED: Open by moving Pawn to rank four; then you should follow with Queen's Bishop to rank three. (shift from imperative to indicative mood)

REVISED: Open by moving Pawn to rank four; then follow with Queen's Bishop to rank three.

(4) Person and number

Person is a characteristic of pronouns and verbs that indicates the speaker's or speakers' position relative to the pattern of communication. First person (*I am, we are*) indicates the person or persons speaking; second person (*you are*), those spoken to; and third person (*he, she, it is* and *they are*), those spoken about.

I (first person) am talking to you (second person) about him (third person).

Number is a characteristic of nouns, pronouns, demonstrative adjectives, and verbs. The number of *game, she, this,* and *seems* is singular, indicating one. The number of *games, they, these,* and *seem* is plural, indicating more than one.

Faulty shifts in person or number are confusing. One common error is shifting from first or third person to second person.

CONFUSED: I enjoy playing Monopoly, but you can never tell how long a game will take. (shift from first to second person)
REVISED: I enjoy playing Monopoly, but I can never tell how long a game will take.

(See Chapters 21 and 23 for more about consistency in person and number.)

To avoid referring to an indefinite pronoun or noun with a sexist *his* or an awkward *his or her*, some writers will shift from third person singular to third person plural. A better solution is to revise the antecedent.

CONFUSED: Everyone who plays strip poker risks embarrassing themselves.
REVISED: All of those who play strip poker risk embarrassing themselves.

(5) Direct to indirect discourse

Direct quotations, the exact words of the speakers enclosed in quotation marks, constitute *direct discourse:* He said "Let's play." Paraphrase—telling "what," "that," or "how" and questioning "if" or "why" without using the exact words of the speaker—constitutes *indirect discourse:* He said that we should play. Shifts from one kind of discourse to another are unnecessary when they confuse or result in awkward shifts in tense.

MIXED: In *Underhanded Chess,* Jerry Sohl advises, "Always lose to a kung fu expert" and that it is often sporting to allow a sick friend to win.
REVISED: In *Underhanded Chess* Jerry Sohl advises, "Always lose to a kung fu expert or to a sick friend." (revised so that both quotations are direct)
REVISED: In *Underhanded Chess,* Jerry Sohl advises that the prudent player always loses to a kung fu expert and a compassionate player, to a sick friend. (revised so that both quotations are indirect)

15b   Mixed Constructions

The composition of a sentence is mixed when the different elements do not fit together logically or structurally. Notice what happens when we shuffle the parts of the following sentences.

The square labeled GO is	at the corner of the Monopoly board.
When I collect my $200,	I will put a hotel on my property, St. James Place.

Read from left to right, the elements of each sentence fit together and make sense. Read from top to bottom, breaking at the center line, they produce mixed constructions. The sentence on the left is mixed structurally, with an adverbial *when* clause attempting to serve as a subjective complement—the job, you will remember, of a noun or an adjective. The mixed sentence on the right is both awkward and illogical. St. James Place is at the center edge, rather than at the corner of the Monopoly board.

(1) Adverbial clauses

MIXED: When you are outmatched is the time for underhanded tactics, according to Jerry Sohl. ("When you are outmatched" as subject of verb *is*)

MIXED: According to Jerry Sohl, the time for underhanded tactics is when you are outmatched. (still mixed but the problem adverbial clause is now placed where we should find an adjective or noun subjective complement)

REVISED: According to Jerry Sohl, when you are outmatched, it may be time for underhanded tactics. (subject and verb added)

REVISED: According to Jerry Sohl, the time for underhanded tactics comes when you are outmatched. (verb changed to come, which, unlike be, may be completed by an adverbial clause)

(2) Objects

MIXED: The Rubik's Cube I received for Christmas four years ago, I finally solved it. (*It* merely substitutes for the real object, "Rubik's Cube. . . ."; placing the object first makes it appear to be the subject.)

REVISED: I finally solved the Rubik's Cube I received for Christmas four years ago.

(3) Independent clauses

MIXED: Pay Day players learn about making and spending money was what caused the student teacher to use the game in her economics class. ("Pay Day players learn about making and spending money" as subject of *was*)

REVISED: Because Pay Day players learn about making and spending money, the student teacher used the game in her economics class. (independent clause revised to dependent clause)

15c Faulty Predication

MIXED: Compulsive betting and drawing to an inside straight are the downfall of many poker players. (The *betting* and *drawing* cause the players' downfall rather than *being* the downfall.)

REVISED: Compulsive betting and drawing to an inside straight cause the downfall of many poker players.

MIXED: The popularity of computer games are being developed by the score in the 1980's. (Intervening modifiers lead to faulty predication. The predicate matches *computer games* instead of *popularity*.)

REVISED: Computer games are being developed by the score in the 1980's.

MIXED: Scrabble is where you make words from lettered tiles. (Incorrect use of *when* or *where* clauses results in faulty predication. In definitions *be* must be preceded and followed by nouns.)

REVISED: Scrabble is a game in which you make words from lettered tiles.

MIXED: The winnings may be high in some games, such as a hundred dollars a card in bingo. (A *faulty appositive* results in faulty predication. *A hundred dollars a card* is not a game but a winning.)

REVISED: The winnings, such as a hundred dollars a card in bingo, may be high in some games.

REVISED: The winnings may be high in some games, such as a-hundred-dollars-a-card bingo.

Shifts and Mixed Constructions   **259**

Revising Paragraphs for Shifts   Exercise 15–1

NAME _____ DATE _____

Rewrite the paragraphs to eliminate shifts in tense, voice, mood, discourse, person, or number. The number in parentheses at the beginning of the paragraph indicates the number of shifts to be corrected. Revisions will vary.

(8)   To have won at Trivial Pursuit, the player must combine a quick recall with a brain stuffed like an attic with useless but intriguing odds and ends. You begin the game, like many others, by rolling dice, but winning was less a matter of luck than of knowledge. The category of question may be determined by a roll of the dice, but what happens next depended upon the nimbleness of your brains. If they can recall within thirty seconds that Hot Springs of the Doves, New Mexico, changed their name to Truth or Consequences in 1950 or that J. R. R. Tolkein preferred *dwarves* to *dwarfs* as the plural of *dwarf*, roll again.

(12)   The Ungame is not a game in the usual sense. You cannot lose, and no one wins. The object of the play was sharing. They begin in a fairly standard way by rolling the dice and the markers are moved around a playing board. But there the resemblance to most games ends. The space you land on may have instructed you to go to Complaint Campground if you complained today or to explain your personal goals, likes, and dislikes. They might say, "I do not like to go camping." Or you could explain that your goal was to become a CPA. Because the object of the game is better interpersonal communication, the rules included being honest when you speak and being a good listener when others are sharing. The Ungame has often been used by teachers and by counselors to encourage exchanges in small-group situations. Some writing teachers will use it to generate topics for creative writing—for example, exploring what makes them happy or afraid.

Score _____

© 1986 by CBS College Publishing. All rights reserved.

Recognizing and Revising Mixed Constructions Exercise 15–2

NAME _____ DATE _____

Read the following sentences carefully and revise any mixed constructions. Two of the sentences are correct. Revisions of the others will vary.

> EXAMPLE: When I play Chinese checkers is my time to win.
> *When I play Chinese checkers, it is my time to win.*

1. Edmond Hoyle, the British authority on games, standardized rules of play is the reason we say that we play "according to Hoyle."

2. The game of checkers begun after dinner, she won it with a multiple capture by her king.

3. All-night pinochle games when I have to work the next day will be the death of me.

4. Whenever we played charades, we raided the trunks in the attic for costumes and props.

5. "Let's play a game," said the computer to the teenage hacker in *War Games* and then told him that war is an exciting game.

6. When you lose your favorite "glassie" is a reason to quit playing marbles "for keeps."

7. The origin of checkers may have originated in Egypt in 1600 B.C., or it may be a variation of chess.

8. Crossword puzzles, which appear regularly in 90 percent of the world's newspapers, are an American invention.

9. The *New York World* in 1913 is when the first "word-cross" appeared.

10. The high stakes, thirty-six times what the player bets, this is why so many people play roulette.

Score _____

Shifts and Mixed Constructions   **261**

Revising Paragraphs for Mixed Constructions   Exercise 15–3

NAME _____ DATE _____

Rewrite the following paragraphs to eliminate mixed constructions. The number in parentheses at the beginning of the paragraph indicates the number of mixed constructions to be corrected. Revisions will vary.

(5)   My cousin Jack taught me how to play Monopoly, and it was many years before I learned that our game was "according to Jack" rather than "according to Hoyle." In standard play, passing GO is when the players collect $200. In our game when we passed GO was the time we collected $200 and paid the banker, Jack, $100. The purpose of Monopoly, explained the rules, calls it a real estate game, with all the board property for sale to all the players. According to Jack's rules, the banker began play with a monopoly is the reason for the name of the game. The utility companies, the railroads, and the most expensive real estate, he owned them all. For ordinary players, like me, the object of the game was to keep from going bankrupt while paying Jack's high rents, taxes, and inflated utility rates and railroad fares.

(5)   The morality of the lessons taught by some games is questionable, such as Monopoly and Cattlemen. Victory in Monopoly is when one player can buy all the utilities or railroads and, therefore, charge the customer higher rates. Raising rents and forcing opponents into bankruptcy, the players are rewarded rather than penalized for doing these things. Cattlemen requires even more immoral activities. The players become land barons and jumping each other's claims is where they get their money. According to one educational psychologist, "Play is the classroom children love," and that the lessons learned at play are remembered longest. If the psychologist is right, the curriculum of play may need a thorough overhaul.

Score _____

Shifts and Mixed Constructions 263

Review 15

Circle the number before any sentence in which you find a shift in tense, mood, person, voice, or number or a mixed construction. Revise each error by crossing out the incorrect word or words and writing the correct word above the line.

¹ Only the more complex living species exhibit play behavior. ² What form the play takes is usually determined by the adults' need for skills, strength, and social organization. ³ For some, play hunting is important behavior, such as cats. ⁴ Puppies played at chasing and fighting. ⁵ Observe dolphins playing off the prow of a ship. ⁶ Maneuverability is developed by their antics, which is essential for survival and for escaping the dolphins' natural enemies, the sharks. ⁷ Humans, of course, play in highly complex ways to prepare for and cope with their future in a complex society. ⁸ Two years old is when symbolic play begins as children act out and explore future behaviors. ⁹ The freedom of expression found in play causes many to continue playing—at golf, at chess, at gardening, at dancing, at cards—throughout their lives.

Score _____

Check your answers against those in the back of the book. Deduct 10 points for each error in identifying sentences with shifts and mixed constructions and 10 points for inadequate revision.

The Writer's Casebook #15

Application: Shifting Focus or Mixing Opinions

As you saw in this chapter, unnecessary shifts in tense or person and mixed constructions such as faulty predication blur ideas and confuse the reader. They leave him or her with unanswered questions: When did this happen? Who is acting? What is done? Consistent use of tense, voice, mood, person, and number and the structural pattern of the sentence sharpen the focus, thereby clarifying meaning.

Similarly, shifting the focus of your thoughts or mixing opinions in an essay overall obscures meaning and weakens the idea structure of the paper. To avoid or correct this problem, test the strength of the basic pattern of ideas that underlies your essay. Take, for example, the following idea structure from a student essay on Monopoly.

THESIS:	Monopoly teaches dangerous lessons.
TOPIC:	It encourages exploitation.
TOPIC:	It discourages compassion for the underdog.
TOPIC:	It promotes a vigorous, aggressive style of business.
CONCLUSION:	Monopoly should be banned.

The first two topics provide strong support for the thesis, but the third blurs the focus, shifting from the negative to a neutral or even possibly positive view. As a result of this shift, the conclusion seems unusually harsh and unconvincing.

To check the idea structure of your essay, outline the major ideas as shown above. Then ask yourself the following questions: Does each topic follow from the thesis? Does each topic lead to the conclusion? Is the focus of each topic and the conclusion consistent with that of the thesis? Have I changed my opinion in any way? Have I moderated my opinion?

Sometimes you will find that the focus of your essay shifts or that its ideas are mixed because your views changed as you explored the subject further. In that case, you need to revise the idea structure of the paper to fit your new views. For example, the writer of the essay on Monopoly might revise as follows:

THESIS:	Monopoly mixes dangerous with useful lessons.
TOPIC:	On the one hand, it encourages exploitation and discourages compassion for the underdog.
TOPIC:	On the other hand, it promotes the vigorous, aggressive style that is needed for a successful career in business.
CONCLUSION:	I have mixed feelings about this game.

The following writing cases are related to this chapter's theme—games and play. As you write, pay special attention to choosing the appropriate tense, voice, mood, person, and number. Test individual sentences for consistency in structure, and test the idea pattern of the essay overall for consistency of focus and opinion.

Cases for Writing: Writing About Games and Play

Case #1

Although you are a busy college student, and possibly a busy job-holder as well, you probably still make some time for play. Examine your reasons for play and the forms that it takes. Do you consider these activities helpful or harmful to your studies and general well-being? Write a paper about your conclusions.

Case #2

Be a researcher. Study some games that are now popular. Do the games teach positive lessons, negative lessons, or both? Develop a scheme for evaluating the games you have studied. You might rank them by suitability for different age groups; give them one-, two-, or three-star ratings on the basis of educational value; or recommend that a group of games you consider unhealthy or dangerous be removed from the market.

SECTION IV

Using Words Effectively

16
Choosing Words

Preview 16

Underline and correct any problems that you see with word choice in the following sentences. If the sentence is effective as it stands, write C beside it. Assume that the sentences are written for a generally educated audience.

1. I am continuously losing my place in the report I am typing because of the continual noise in this office.

2. The novel is an interesting story about a good man who had a nice wife.

3. The dude is dating a fox.

4. The aroma of wet wool is rather unpleasant.

5. "One small step for man, one giant leap for mankind."

6. The letter of recommendation was highly complementary, complimenting the applicant's résumé.

7. It goes without saying that Monica, who is as fleet as a deer, won the race.

8. The company must computerize its records investmentwise.

9. We should elect a governor who understands that he is responsible to the people first, not to his party machine.

10. My reasons for attending school are different now from my reasons for starting school a year ago.

> 11. Cogitating on the tribulations of my state of incarceration, I determined to effect an unauthorized egress.
>
> 12. Dark clouds like giant, smudged desk pads, rumbled across the sky, blotting up the rain.
>
> **Score** _____
>
> Check your answers against those in the back of the book. Deduct 2 points for each error in identifying problems, 2 points for each error in correction, and 4 points for an error in identifying the correct sentence. A score of 80 percent or higher indicates skill in choosing the right word.

"The difference between the right word and the almost right word," writes Mark Twain, "is the difference between lightning and the lightning bug." Effective *diction*—or choosing words that are appropriate, accurate, and fresh—involves making careful distinctions among the many meanings of words, matching meanings to context, and considering the past as well as present use of words.

For example, the word *lightning* means literally the discharge of electricity from one cloud to another or between a cloud and the earth. Connotatively, or by association, it means incredible speed, awesome power, and perhaps even the wrath of God. In a formal context we might use *white lightning* to describe the electrical discharges in the sky; in an informal context we could use *white lightning* to mean a particularly potent and highly illegal drink. Used in the phrases *as fast as lightning*, or *with lightning speed*, the word has been overworked and lacks descriptive value. Used by Emily Dickinson in a poem that begins "The Lightning playeth," the figurative meaning of the word is fresh and communicates images.

Choosing the right word is a complex process—one that you are already involved in and one that will continue long after you finish this course. The guidelines that follow will help you develop some habits for the intelligent and thoughtful choice of words.

16a Appropriate Words

Choose appropriate words—words that fit your audience, the occasion you are writing for, and your purpose in writing.

(1) Audience/occasion

Adjust your diction to the different levels of language (formal, informal, and popular) that match your audience's expectations and the occasion for which you are writing.

Formal diction is appropriate when you are writing for educated audiences in situations that demand dignity and decorum. Formal writing uses words familiar to educated audiences, such as *malevolent* instead of *nasty*. It avoids contractions, such as *I'll* for *I shall*, and abbreviations, such as *trig* for *trigonometry*. Often formal diction calls for a neutral rather than a personal tone, using *one* or *we* instead of *I* and *you*.

Ralph Waldo Emerson uses extremely formal diction in *The American Scholar*.

> Our age is bewailed as the age of Introversion. Must that needs be evil? We are embarrassed with second thoughts. . . . The time is infected with Hamlet's unhappiness—"Sicklied o'er with the pale cast of thought."

Informal diction is at the opposite extreme. It is language appropriate to our daily conversation and includes colloquialisms (*tv* instead of *television*), slang (*grossed out* instead of *revolted*), regionalisms (*to jaw* instead of *to talk*), and nonstandard language (*theirselves* or *themself* instead of *themselves*; *ain't* instead of *am not, is not*, and *are not*).

William Faulkner uses informal diction to represent the speech of the characters in *Old Man*. The first speaker, a doctor, is distinguished from those that follow, the prisoners, by the degree of slang and nonstandard usage.

> "Good man," the mild man said. "Plenty of life in the old carcass yet, eh? Plenty of good red blood too. Anyone ever suggest to you that you were hemophilic?" ("What?" the plump convict said, "Hemophilic? You know what that means?" The tall convict had his cigarette going now, his body jackknifed backward into the coffinlike space between upper and lower bunks. . . . "That's a calf that's a bull and a cow at the same time."
> "No, it ain't," a third convict said. "It's a calf or a colt that ain't neither one."
> "Hell fire," the plump one said. "He's got to be one or the other to keep from drounding.")

Popular diction is the language of popular magazines, novels, and newspapers. It falls somewhere between formal and informal diction—using a conversational tone, colloquialisms, contractions, and the personal *I* or *you* but avoiding incorrect grammar, slang, and nonstandard language.

Malcolm X uses popular diction in his *Autobiography*.

> I looked like Li'l Abner. Mason, Michigan, was written all over me. My kinky, reddish hair was cut hick style, and I didn't even use grease in it. My green suit's coat sleeves stopped above my wrists, the pants legs showed three inches of socks. . . . So I went gawking around the neighborhood—the Waumbeck and Humboldt Avenue Hill section of Roxbury, which is something like Harlem's Sugar Hill, where I'd later live. . . .

The level of diction you use at any one time should vary with your audience and the occasion. It is just as inappropriate to say "Now is the time for festivities" when the situation calls for "Let's party" as to say "I can't dig it" when the situation calls for "I don't understand the concept." Usually, the appropriate level for your college writing falls somewhere between formal and popular diction. You are writing for a generally educated audience (your peers and your professors) in a semiformal situation (the college classroom). Therefore, you should use correct grammar and avoid slang or nonstandard usage. Whether you use technical language and an impersonal tone or a more natural sound depends upon the assignment.

(2) Purpose

Adjust your diction to your purpose in writing—that is, whether you want to *inform*, to *express personal feelings*, or to *persuade*.

Informative writing is primarily factual. It avoids words with emotional associations and often relies upon a third-person voice to maintain distance and objectivity.

> Shakespeare uses anaphora in Sonnet 64 to amplify his themes.

> Jane Austen writes about money, manners, and morals in *Pride and Prejudice.*

Personal writing is appropriate for journals, letters, and personal experience essays. It relies upon the first person *I* and *we* and uses words that describe feelings.

> Shakespeare's sonnet about Time makes me want to cry, but it teaches me to appreciate what I have today.

> Elizabeth is my favorite character in Austen's *Pride and Prejudice* because I enjoy her wit and I admire her strength.

Persuasive writing attempts to convince someone to do something or to accept something, such as your opinion about a subject or literary work. It may use first-, second-, or third-person voice and often emphasizes expressions suggesting logical connections *(consequently, although, therefore)*; words conveying judgments *(inexcusable, negligent, noble)*; and words suggesting comparisons *(preferable, better)*.

> Although both A. C. Partridge and Douglas L. Peterson use commas after Line 10 of Shakespeare's mutability sonnet, a dash seems more appropriate in terms of the sonnet's theme and structure.

> Students at this college would rather read *Don Quixote* than *The Odyssey* in English 220, Our Literary Heritage. We propose the change in the interests of general student motivation and of fairness to Hispanic students, whose cultural roots are virtually ignored in the course.

(See Writer's Casebook #16 to learn more about writing about literature to inform, to persuade, and to express feelings.)

16b Accurate Words

(1) Denotation/connotation

Choose words with the right denotative and connotative meanings.

The *denotation* of a word is its literal or dictionary meaning, what the word means without any emotional associations. If you use *prodigy* (precocious child) when you mean *protegé* (someone guided and helped by a patron), you have committed an error in denotation. Similarly, if you confuse *ascending* with *descending* or *pistol* with *pistil*, your sentences will not make sense because the word used is inaccurate.

> It was a right angel. (as opposed to a wrong angel, a follower perhaps of Satan?)
>
> The train crossed the trellis. (climbed the grape arbor?)

Choosing a word with the right denotation is the first step; making sure the word you choose has the right *connotation* is the next step. The connotative meaning of a word is the attitude we have toward it because of emotional associations. According to the dictionary, both *mopy* and *gloomy* mean the same thing—being in low spirits. However, although the words mean the same thing denotatively, they do not "feel" the same; that is, our emotional associations with *mopy* (a word that suggests a pouting, spoiled brat) are different from our associations with *gloomy* (a word that suggests a brooding, almost sinister mood). The words have different connotations.

Errors in connotation occur when you choose words that do not have the appropriate feelings associated with them. For example, telling a friend you are sorry his grandfather "kicked the bucket" would be a connotative error; although the expression means literally that he died, it does not "feel" either sympathetic or respectful.

(2) Euphemisms

Euphemisms are words with positive or neutral connotations that are used in the place of words with negative connotations. For example, a teacher might call a student who refuses to work an *underachiever*. Euphemisms can be dangerous when they hide ugly truths; for example, the evils of discrimination and the victimization of many minorities are effectively glossed over by the word *disadvantaged*.

Because euphemisms can be vague and confusing and also deceptive, you should avoid them in your writing unless to do so would be unnecessarily offensive.

(3) Offensive language

Out of common courtesy and respect for your readers, you will want to avoid words that will offend a segment of your audience. *Racial, religious, and ethnic* slurs, words that deride members of specific groups, violate the dignity of human beings and have no place in the writing of an educated person.

Sexist language is also offensive, insulting both men and women. Avoid using the names of animals to refer to members of the opposite sex, using degrading diminutives, and substituting body parts for people. Also be careful not to use *man* or *mankind* when you mean all humanity; *he* when you mean *he or she;* or words or word combinations that exclude either men or women from certain professions—such as *policeman, chairman, doctor/he, nurse/she,* and so forth.

Avoid *obscenities* and *profanity:* words that your audience may find disgusting, offensive, or repulsive. These words can be classified as informal diction and have no place in college writing.

(4) Specific versus general

Use specific words for clarity and support and general words for summary statements.

GENERAL WORDS: The buildings on this campus should be torn down and new ones built.
SPECIFIC WORDS: Hodgen Hall, Mitchell Hall, Oñate Hall, and Marron Hall should be torn down and replaced by the newly proposed Perovich Complex.

(5) Concrete versus abstract

Use abstract words sparingly and concrete words liberally. *Abstract* words—*injustice, honesty, happiness*—refer to ideas, qualities, or conditions that are perceived intellectually rather than physically. Writing that uses too many abstractions is often too vague to communicate much real information.

Concrete words, on the other hand, convey vivid pictures. They name "solid" things that readers can perceive with their physical senses of sight, hearing, taste, touch, and smell. Compare the following descriptive sentences, the first abstract, the second concrete.

ABSTRACT: She was a vision of loveliness, exuding innocence and beauty.
CONCRETE: Brown eyes laughing from under a thick fringe of lashes, a vivid olive complexion, masses of black curls—Rosalie was an enchanting gypsy.

The first description uses abstract words like *loveliness* that feel vaguely pleasant to us but convey no picture. The second description draws a portrait. When you find it necessary to use abstract words, be sure to follow them with concrete words to anchor the abstractions in reality.

You will want to mix some abstract words with concrete words in your writing. Notice how much more the second of the following quotations says about the abstraction "hope."

ABSTRACT: Hope is itself a species of happiness. *(Samuel Johnson)*
ABSTRACT AND "Hope" is the thing with feathers—
CONCRETE: That perches in the soul—*(Emily Dickinson)*

However, you should avoid *utility words*—abstract descriptors like *nice, interesting,* and *great* that seem appropriate everywhere but actually convey very little meaning. Always resist the temptation to use one of these words as a filler when you cannot think of a precise term.

VAGUE: Your paper is *interesting*.
BETTER: Your description of the experiences of a Protestant attending a Catholic school is both sensitive and entertaining.

16c   Fresh Language

Use fresh language—words that are original and vivid or are used in original ways.

STALE: The last straw breaks the camel's back. (English proverb)
FRESH: The last feather breaks the horse's back. (English proverb)

Words and expressions that were once fresh can become stale through overuse, and some expressions that were once stale can become fresh again through disuse. For example, when Shakespeare wrote *Hamlet*, the statement "to be or not to be: that is the question" was original, but four hundred years later it has been worn out by constant use and adaptation: "to censor or not to censor," "to compute or not to compute," "to fricasee or not to fricasee." However, some expressions in *Hamlet* seemed stale to sixteenth-century audiences. Elderly Polonius tells his son, who is leaving for Paris, to be "familiar, but by no means vulgar," to be true to "thine own self" and "thou canst not then be false to any man." In Shakespeare's time the advice was probably clichéd or trite, ready-made wisdom, which made the audience laugh at Polonius as a pedantic old fool. But modern audiences, to whom the expressions are fresh, often are impressed by Polonius's wisdom.

(1)   Jargon

Avoid using jargon—specialized or technical vocabulary—when writing for a general audience.

JARGON: The octave of the sonnet works by amplification toward the paradox in line eight, followed by a shift in the first line of the sestet toward diminution.
TRANSLATION: In the first eight lines of the sonnet, the emotional impact of the language and figures of speech builds toward the apparent contradiction in line eight; then there is a change in method beginning with line nine. Language and figures of speech are used to reduce the emotional impact.

Choosing Words

(2) Neologisms

Avoid neologisms or recently invented words that have not yet gained (and may never gain) wide acceptance.

UNACCEPTABLE: Timewise today has been a disaster.
UNACCEPTABLE: We must prioritize our goals and effectivize our schedule.

But

ACCEPTABLE: Computerize your office.
ACCEPTABLE: We need a software package that includes word-processing capabilities.

(3) Pretentious diction

Avoid pretentious diction—unnaturally elevated diction chosen to impress the reader.

PRETENTIOUS DICTION: I composed an epistle on my diversionary excursion.
REVISED: I wrote a letter about my vacation trip.

(4) Clichés

To determine whether an expression is overused, try it out on friends. If you can give your friends part of the expression and they can complete it, it is probably overused. Clichés come rolling off the tongue in complete and ready-to-use phrases, but fresh language comes one word at a time, unconnected to other words until you connect it yourself in your writing.

TEST: gone but not _____
       sadder but _____
       This isn't my cup of _____
       We're all in the same _____
       sly as a _____
       fleet as a _____
       It goes without _____
       Needless to _____
       It is interesting to _____
       tall, dark, and _____

16d Figurative Language

Use figurative language or imaginative comparisons to go beyond literal language. Figures should not be overused in college writing, but neither should they be avoided when they will help you communicate more effectively with your reader.

(1) Similes

Construct similes by comparing two essentially unlike items and by introducing the comparison with *like* or *as*.

SIMILE: I looked like Li'l Abner. (Malcolm X, *Autobiography*)
SIMILE: A face in the classroom suddenly lighted as if switched on by a bright idea. (imitation of sentence in Annie Dillard's *Pilgrim at Tinker Creek*)

(2) Metaphors

Construct metaphors by comparing two essentially unlike items but without using *like* or *as*.

METAPHOR: "Hope" is the thing with feathers—
That perches in the soul—*(Emily Dickinson)*
METAPHOR: The take-home exam is Dr. Ferrar's Iron Maiden, an instrument of torture with a pleasant shape.

(3) Analogies

Construct analogies by using a familiar object to explain an unfamiliar one.

ANALOGY: Reading a poem is like playing catch with a poet.
EXTENDED ANALOGY:
I traveled on, seeing the hill where lay
    My expectation.
A long it was and weary way.
The gloomy cave of desperation
I left on the one, and on the other side
    The rock of pride. *(George Herbert, "The Pilgrimage")*

(4) Personification

Use personification to give inanimate things or abstract ideas human attributes, feelings, or powers.

PERSONIFICATION: When I have seen by time's fell hand defaced
The rich-proud cost of outworn buried age;
(Shakespeare, Sonnet 64)

(5) Allusion

Use allusions to literature and the Bible to enrich your expression of feelings and express a moral attitude.

LITERARY ALLUSION: When the fraternity constructed the scavenger hunt for rush week, it played Poseidon to the freshmen's Odysseus. (refers to Poseidon's keeping Odysseus from finding his way home during his long years of travel and adventure)

Choosing Words

BIBLICAL ALLUSION: Faculty beat their swords into plowshares at a recent faculty Senate meeting. (refers to an Old Testament preparation for peace)

16e Ineffective Figures of Speech

Avoid ineffective figures of speech by deleting dead metaphors (ones that have been overused and call up no images); revising mixed metaphors (comparisons that combine incompatible images); revising strained metaphors (comparisons that do not work logically); and revising overblown imagery (pretentious imagery, akin to pretentious diction).

DEAD METAPHOR: He was green with envy.
MIXED METAPHOR: Standard English is a tool, dead in its coffin.
STRAINED METAPHOR: The lyrics were feathers wafting through the air on winds of music.
OVERBLOWN METAPHOR: The literary society was a flower garden, spreading its blossoms of literary works and sweet fragrances of poetic lines throughout the luscious garden of academe.

Choosing Words 277

Writing at Different Levels Exercise 16–1

NAME _____ DATE _____

Identify the level of diction at which each of the following sentences is written; then rewrite the sentence at another level and identify that level.

EXAMPLE: One must comprehend the literary allusions to appreciate fully an erudite work. *formal*
Students need to get ahold of the echoes from great lit before an egghead work can grab them. *informal*

1. You ain't seen nothin' yet. _____
   _____

2. When one reads, one enters the minds of a host of learned men and women. _____
   _____

3. Reading may be a charge, but writing's a blast. _____
   _____

4. One may not agree with what another person says, but one should defend to the death that person's right to say it. _____
   _____

5. "We cannot lightly dismiss these allegations," the Dean told the Board of Regents. _____
   _____

Score _____

© 1986 by CBS College Publishing. All rights reserved.

Writing for Purpose Exercise 16-2

NAME _____ DATE _____

Identify the major purpose of each passage as informative, personal, or persuasive. Then rewrite it to match the purpose given in parentheses.

> EXAMPLE: In *Wuthering Heights* Catherine Earnshaw marries Edgar Linton, the heir to Thrushcross Grange, instead of Heathcliff, her childhood sweetheart. *informative*
> (Rewrite to persuade.)
> *In Wuthering Heights the cause of all the trouble is selfish, self-centered Catherine, who marries for money rather than love.*

1. In *The Odyssey* Odysseus must battle the Cyclops, travel to Hades, and encounter the monsters Scylla and Charybdis to learn the self-control he needs when he leads the slaughter of his wife Penelope's suitors back in Ithaca. _____
(Rewrite to inform.)

2. When Ahab tries to kill the white whale in *Moby Dick*, all my sympathies are with the whale. _____
(Rewrite to persuade.)

3. James Joyce's *Ulysses* borrows a pattern and several themes from Homer's *Odyssey*. The parallels between characters and events were outlined by Joyce in notes for his epic. _____
(Rewrite to express feeling.)

Score _____

Choosing Words 279

Choosing the Right Denotation and Connotation   Exercise 16–3

NAME _____ DATE _____

Underline the word in parentheses that best fits the denotative or the connotative meaning suggested by the sentence.

> EXAMPLES: And the (angle, <u>angel</u>) said, "Behold!"
> The Satanic hero Heathcliff (<u>sneered</u>, smirked, smiled) at us.

1. The (eminent, imminent) scientist says a collision between Earth and a comet is (eminent, imminent).
2. The frosted glass is (transparent, translucent); the gauze curtains are (transparent, translucent).
3. Sharla's eyes (glowed, glittered, gleamed) with happiness, but Jennifer's (glowed, glittered, gleamed) with jealousy.
4. My favorite aunt is pleasingly (plump, fat, obese), but my cousin is distressingly (plump, fat, obese), and their dog is disgustingly (plump, fat, obese).
5. (Incriminating, recriminating) evidence was brought against the suspect, but he answered his accuser with (incrimination, recrimination).
6. We admired her (ingenious, ingenuous) invention and were also pleased by her (ingenious, ingenuous) admission that the idea was not hers alone.
7. The judges were highly (complimentary, complementary) about the (complimentary, complementary) colors in the room design.
8. Because we were envious, we told glamorous and (svelte, skinny, thin) Theresa she was (svelte, skinny, thin).
9. I am proud to say that, although I listened to the arguments, I remained (stubborn, inflexible, firm) and hung the jury.
10. If we had not (defused, diffused) the bomb, the gas would have been (defused, diffused) throughout the city.
11. The (odor, aroma, smell, stench) of a good meal made me forget the (odor, aroma, smell, stench) of the sewer I had inspected earlier.
12. The lines (diverged, converged) in many directions; the lines (diverged, converged) to a single point.
13. The (odor, aroma, smell, stench, scent) of Le Gui perfume is delightful.

Score _____

© 1986 by CBS College Publishing. All rights reserved.

Using Specific and Concrete Words Exercise 16–4

NAME _____ DATE _____

Rewrite the following sentences and sentence groups to eliminate inappropriate use of abstract or general words.

> EXAMPLE: On that day in June an important event occurred.
> *On June 5, 1981, I received my bachelor's degree.*

1. The book was interesting. Reading it was a nice experience.

2. It was the most unusual painting that I have ever seen. The colors were unusual. The composition was unusual. Even the frame was unusual.

3. The problem with this school is the administration.

4. What I like most about the city is all the exciting things there are to do.

5. Meet me on the corner afterward.

6. The scene is beautiful.

7. Happiness is great.

8. Our group advocates justice and truth and the American way.

9. His clothes did not fit, but he had an engaging face.

10. Too much loose talk can lead to disaster.

Score _____

Using Fresh Language   Exercise 16-5

NAME _____ DATE _____

Revise the following sentences to eliminate stale or awkward words and phrases. In the space provided identify usage problems as jargon, neologism, pretentious diction, or clichés.

> EXAMPLE: He was tall, dark, and handsome. *cliché*
> *He was six feet tall with black hair, olive skin, and a face like Michelangelo's David.*

1. Let's get down to brass tacks. _____

2. Weatherwise the outlook is coldish to warmish. _____

3. Having sinned, suffered, and repented, Garfield was a sadder but wiser cat. _____

4. After cogitating at length, I determined to embark upon a career as an attorney at law in the criminal justice system. _____

5. It goes without saying that we must explore all of our options and find a viable alternative. _____

6. The survivability of fads in clothes and music is limited timewise. _____

7. The importance of co-operative behavior in social hunting is emphasized in studies of large social carnivores such as the lion, cheetah, and wolf. _____

8. The demonstration of legerdemain proved a most welcome divertissement. _____

9. In terms of content and in terms of structure, the couplet following the three quatrains is the focal point of the poem, bringing together the key elements of the discursive argument. _____

10. That's the last straw, the bottom line, the point of no return; I'm down for the count and out like a light. _____

Score _____

Choosing Words **283**

Using Figurative Language   Exercise 16–6

NAME _____ DATE _____

Enliven the following weak sentences by using the figures listed. Be sure to use fresh comparison and fresh language.

>   EXAMPLE: He was a big man. (metaphor)
>   *He was an elephant of a man, a Dumbo with big feet instead of big ears.*

1. The horse ran around the track. (simile)

2. The workings of a computer are not so mysterious. (analogy)

3. The mosquitoes in Alaska are large. (metaphor)

4. George's wife thought he should eliminate his boss and take over the company. (literary allusion).

5. Sometimes it is better to be good to people who don't like you. (Biblical allusion)

Score _____

© 1986 by CBS College Publishing. All rights reserved.

Identifying Figurative Language   Exercise 16-7

NAME _____ DATE _____

Following is an abbreviated version of "The Barrio," written by Robert Ramirez, general manager for WFBN-TV in Joliet, Illinois, when he was an undergraduate in a composition class. Ramirez acknowledges "excesses" in the essay, but his use of figurative language can teach you much about using figures in your own writing.

Read the essay, underlining each figure you find. Then label the types of figures. Do you find an example of a mixed metaphor? Do you find examples of extended metaphor, personification, simile?

The train, its metal wheels squealing as they spin along the silvery tracks, rolls slower now. Through the gaps between the cars blinks a streetlamp, and this pulsing light on a barrio streetcorner beats slower, like a weary heartbeat, until the train shudders to a halt, the light goes out, and the barrio is deep asleep. . . .

Within the invisible (yet sensible) walls of the barrio, are many, many people living in too few houses. The homes, however, are much more numerous on the outside. Members of the barrio describe the entire area as their home. It is a home, but it is more than this. The barrio is a refuge from the harshness and the coldness of the Anglo world. It is a forced refuge. The leprous people are isolated from the rest of the community and contained in their section of town. The stoical pariahs of the barrio accept their fate, and from the angry seeds of rejection grow the flowers of closeness between outcasts, not the thorns of bitterness and the mad desire to flee. There is no want to escape, for the feeling of the barrio is known only to its inhabitants, and the material needs of life can also be found here. . . .

The color-splashed homes arrest your eyes, arouse your curiosity, and make you wonder what life scenes are being played out in them. The flimsy, brightly colored, wood-frame houses ignore no neon-brilliant color. Houses trimmed in orange, chartreuse, lime-green, yellow, and mixtures of these and other hues beckon the beholder to reflect on the peculiarity of each home. Passing through this land is refreshing like Brubek, not narcoticizing like revolting rows of similar houses, which neither offend nor please.

In the evenings, the porches and front yards are occupied with men calmly talking over the noise of children playing baseball in the unpaved extension of the living room, while the women cook supper or gossip with female neighbors as they water the *jardines*. The gardens mutely echo the expressive verses of the colorful houses. The denseness of multicolored plants and trees gives the house the appearance of an oasis or a tropical island hideaway, sheltered from the rest of the world. . . .

There are those, too, who for a number of reasons have not achieved a relative sense of financial security. Perhaps it results from too many children too soon, but it is the homes of these people and their situation that numbs rather than charms. Their houses, aged and bent, oozing children, are fissures in the horn of plenty. . . .

Decent drainage is usually unknown, and when it rains the water stands for days, an incubator of health hazards and an avoidable nuisance. . . .

The houses and their *jardines*, the jollity of the people in an adverse world, the brightly feathered alarm clock pecking away at supper and cautiously eyeing the children playing nearby, produce a mystifying sensation at finding the noble savage alive in the twentieth century. It is easy to look at the positive qualities of life in the barrio, and look at them with a distantly envious feeling. One wishes to experience the feelings of the barrio and not the hardships. Remembering the illness, the hunger, the feeling of time running out on you, the walls, both real and imagined, reflecting on living in the past, one finds his envy becoming more elusive, until it has vanished altogether.
© 1986 by CBS College Publishing. All rights reserved.

Back now beyond the tracks, the train creaks and groans, the cars jostle each other down the track, and as the light begins its pulsing, the barrio, with all its meanings, greets a new dawn with yawns and restless stretchings.

Score _____

Review 16

Underline and correct any problems that you see with word choice in the following sentences. If the sentence is effective as it stands, write C beside it. Assume that the sentences are written for a generally educated audience.

1. Michael pulled a B in chem and an A is psych.

2. My boss smirked kindly as he scrawled his elegant signature on the document.

3. When a doctor hires a nurse, he expects her to be a qualified health professional.

4. Mankind has made great strides in conquering disease.

5. When it appeared the bandits were intervening too much with travel, the friar interfered with the king, asking him to intercede.

6. It is interesting to note that the hero was tall, dark, and handsome.

7. The penultimate instructor inculcates precepts as well as concepts.

8. The instructor said the project was interesting but gave it a less-than-satisfactory grade.

9. My life was like a butterfly's—serene and beautiful—until I started swimming with the wrong school of fish.

10. Mt. St. Helens was extinct before it erupted.

11. The glazed window is translucent rather than transparent.

12. The chief perpetrator of nefarious activities in our fair city resolved to decimate competition by liquidating his competitor's warehoused assets.

Score _____

Check your answers against those in the back of the book. Deduct 2 points for each error in identifying problems, 2 points for each error in correction, and 4 points for an error in identifying the correct sentence. A score of 80 percent or higher indicates skill in choosing the right word.

The Writer's Casebook #16

Application to Writing: Writing Purposefully About Literature

In 16a.1 you studied how to adjust diction and viewpoint to fit three purposes: *informative, personal,* and *persuasive*. Your purpose determines not only your choice of words and the person of pronouns and verbs, but also the content of your paper. For instance, consider an assignment whose subject is literature. An *informative* paper about literature explains facts. It could relate the names and describe the personalities of the major characters. It could summarize the plot. Or it could go outside the work itself to talk about the author or the circumstances of composition.

> *The Odyssey* is an epic poem about the wanderings of the Greek hero Odysseus. After the Trojan War he and his men are swept off course as they try to sail home to Ithaca. They travel throughout the Mediterranean, encountering monsters like the Cyclops and powerful immortals like Circe the witch.
>
> Over the years Emily Dickinson became an eccentric, dressing all in white and seeing few people outside her family. She wrote poems like herself—intense, private, and sometimes wildly exultant.

A paper expressing *personal* feelings about literature concentrates upon your reactions—whether or not you like the work, whether it inspires or depresses you, whether you enjoyed reading it or found the task an impossible chore. In a paper emphasizing personal reactions, it is usually appropriate to relate the work in some way to your own life—to an incident that parallels one in a literary work or a feeling strongly similar or dissimilar to your own.

> I enjoyed reading Alexander Pope's *The Rape of the Lock*. The battle for Belinda's curl is entertaining. When the sexes battle with snuff and hairpins, I am reminded of a similar war between the girls and boys at Lincoln Elementary School, with Susie and Brian in the roles of Belinda and the Baron.
>
> I find it difficult to admire Penelope. Although our instructor called her the "archetype of the faithful wife," I am disturbed by her continual weeping. In Book One "she fell to weeping" (p. 12). In Book Four she sinks "down on the door sill of the chambers / wailing" (p. 14). And in Book Nineteen "tears flowed / until she had tasted her salt grief again" (p. 361).

Most papers about literature probably fall under the third category, *persuasive* writing. In such papers, the writer attempts to persuade the reader that a poem does or does not develop the *carpe diem* theme, that *All's Well That Ends Well* is or is not a comedy, that "Sailing to Byzantium" is or is not a better poem than Yeats's later "Byzantium." The paper, then, is based on judgments and uses the language and patterns of logic to make a case: Because this is so and this is so, but that is not so, we must conclude the following. . . .

> Although listed in anthologies of Shakespeare's works as a comedy and although discussed in terms of Bassanio's and Portia's comic romance, *The Merchant of Venice* is not a comedy: it is a tragedy. The fall of Shylock through his greedy demand for a pound of Antonio's flesh is as tragic as the fall of Macbeth or Othello.

Cases for Writing: Informing, Persuading, Reacting

Case #1

Write a summary of the plot or a reaction to the ending of one of your favorite novels, short stories, or plays. (See Writer's Casebook #9 for a review of summary writing.)

Case #2

Examine a short work of literature, such as Shirley Jackson's "The Lottery" or Nathaniel Hawthorne's "Young Goodman Brown," and try to determine what the author's main idea is. Then write a *persuasive* paper in which you use evidence from the work to support your contention.

Using the Dictionary 17

Preview 17

Use your dictionary to answer the following questions.

1. How many syllables are there in the word *judicial?*

2. What do the abbreviations *vi* and *vt* mean?

3. What is the origin of the word *depress?*

4. Who was the second earl of Essex?

5. When did Napoleon meet his Waterloo?

6. How large is Estonia?

7. Is the expression *a couple dozen* appropriate for formal use?

8. What adjective is formed by adding a suffix to *educe?*

9. What is the less preferred plural of *eisteddfod?*

10. What is an alternative past participle of *drip?*

Score _____

Check your answers against those in the back of the book. Deduct 10 points for each error. A score of 80 percent or higher shows you are able to find and read information in your dictionary.

17a Contents

The word *dictionary* comes from the Medieval Latin word *dictionarium*, which in turn comes from the Late Latin *dictio*, or *word*. *Dictionary* is divided into four syllables—*dic • tion • ar • y*—and has two accents, the primary accent falling on the first and the secondary accent falling on the second syllable. The *ti* combination in the second syllable is pronounced like the *sh* in *she*, and the *a* in the fourth syllable is pronounced like the *e* in *ten*. *Dictionary* is a noun that forms its plural by changing the final *y* to *i* and adding *-es*. A dictionary is a list of words, arranged alphabetically and including spellings, definitions, pronunciations, and other information. It may also be called a *lexicon*, although this synonym is not used as much as formerly. Dictionaries may cover the words in a specific language, show equivalencies of words in different languages such as Spanish and English, or list the special language of a profession such as medicine.

All this information is contained in a standard entry for the word *dictionary* in a standard, *abridged dictionary*—that is, a dictionary that includes commonly used words and brief descriptions of their meanings and usage. An *unabridged dictionary*, one that contains many more words, would give you more information, while a pocket or paperback edition would give you less.

17b Choosing

For college writing and study, you should have for reference a standard abridged dictionary, such as one of the college editions listed below. These dictionaries contain most of the words (usually around 150,000) you need to understand and use in writing for a generally educated audience. A pocket edition may be useful for carrying to class when you write an in-class paper, but it does not contain enough entries (only around 50,000) or enough information about those entries to take the place of your college dictionary. If your course of study includes a foreign language, you may also need a dictionary that lists English words, meanings, and pronunciation side by side with the words, meanings, and pronunciation of the foreign language. As you progress in your studies, you may also need to add to your collection of dictionaries one that lists the special language of the profession you are entering.

17c Abridged

Abridged dictionaries include *The American Heritage Dictionary of the English Language*, 2nd Coll. ed. (Boston: Houghton Mifflin, 1982); *The Random House College Dictionary* (New York: Random House, 1982); and *Webster's New World Dictionary*, 2nd Coll. ed. (New York: Simon & Schuster, 1980).

17d Using

To learn to use your dictionary, you must first gain entry into its special system of abbreviations and symbols. The *front matter*, which precedes the *alphabetical listing*, explains how the dictionary is organized and provides guidelines for reading entries and finding essential information, such as pronunciation keys. The format for the *entries*, the basic units of the alphabetical listing, may differ from dictionary to dictionary, but the information and parts contained are usually the same.

1. *Guide words* at the top of the page, giving the first and the last words on each page
2. *Entry word* in boldface, giving the spelling of the word and its syllabication: jug・gle, e・rad・i・cate (Variant spellings, such as the chiefly British spelling *judgement* for *judgment*, may follow the entry word or come at the end of the listing.)
3. *Pronunciation* (or pronunciations) in symbols keyed to a guide, usually printed at the bottom of the page or at the bottom of facing pages: er' ənd for *errand;* nän'sens, -sans for *nonsense*
4. *Parts of speech* (labels to indicate the grammatical function of a word), *plurals*, and *principal parts of verbs*
5. *Etymology*, or word origin and history: LL; ME *noun suyt* < Anglo-Fr. *nonsute* for *nonsuit*
6. *Meanings*, which may be organized with the most common use first as in *The American Heritage Dictionary* or with the oldest meaning first as in *Webster's New World Dictionary*
7. *Synonyms and Antonyms*
8. *Idiomatic usage*, the use of the entry word in set expressions such as *a far cry* and *cry out* for the entry *cry*
9. *Special labels* that indicate the level of language at which the entry word may be appropriately used or current practice in using the word
10. *General information* such as the names of people, including historical and literary characters (Andrew Jackson, Oedipus); the dates of historical events (the Boer War, 1899–1902); the population of cities (Denver, pop. 515,000); or the size of states (Texas, 267,339 sq. mi.)

The *end matter* of your dictionary may differ in content as well as organization. In some dictionaries this section contains lists of weights and measures; in some, an explanation of punctuation marks; and in some, pronouncing gazetteers, vocabularies of rhymes and given names, and lists of colleges and universities.

Using the Dictionary

Using Your Dictionary   Exercise 17–1

NAME _____ DATE _____

Fill in the blanks in the following exercises with information from your own dictionary. This exercise will help you get to know your dictionary and to gain practice in using it.

Which dictionary are you using?

Name _____

Edition, publisher, and date of publication _____
_____

1. Guide Words

What are guide words? _____
_____

Where are they found? _____

List the guide words on the pages on which you will find the following words.

egress _____   nonsense _____

rein _____   feud _____

cocksure _____   terror _____

sonnet _____   haut monde _____

unctuous _____   gnomon _____

2. Entry Words

What are entry words? _____

What information do they contain? _____

Write out the following words as shown in the entry listings of your dictionary; include syllabication and any special punctuation, capitalization, accents, or division between words shown in the boldface entry word. Correct, at the same time, misspellings and errors in word division written here.

gnosticism _____   frondescence _____

succinicacid _____   manicdepressive _____

smoothefaced _____   postnasaldrip _____

© 1986 by CBS College Publishing. All rights reserved.

paleozoic _____   Dick-test _____

adz _____   neuro-muscular _____

Use the entry words to help you correct the following word divisions. (See 33a for a summary of how and where to divide words.) Rewrite the words, placing hyphens at appropriate division points.

never-nev-   ap-
er land _____   ron _____

arabes-   happ-
que _____   y _____

know-   disengag-
ledge _____   ed _____

laur-   comm-
eate _____   ittee _____

3. Pronunciation

Find the pronunciation guides in your dictionary. Study the guides and also any information about pronunciation in the front matter until you understand the symbols used. Then write beside each of the following words the way your dictionary symbolizes the sound of the letter(s) underlined.

parrot _____   mirror _____   moor _____   cut _____

date _____   bite _____   cute _____   sanity _____

father _____   go _____   cure _____   focus _____

elf _____   law _____   point _____   off _____

meet _____   tool _____   plow _____   phone _____

agile _____   mention _____   thin _____   Vallejo _____

mesquite _____ she _____   tough _____   Vandyke _____

Write out the pronunciation in symbols of each of the following words. Pronounce the words, paying special attention to accents and sounds you have difficulty pronouncing. If there is more than one acceptable pronunciation, list and practice pronouncing both until you determine which one is preferable for the part of the country you live in. The more generally accepted pronunciation will be listed first.

Using the Dictionary

exigency _____   onomatopoeia _____

desultory _____   ingenuous _____

chaos _____   pathos _____

quiche _____   soiree _____

Oedipal _____   Jungian _____

4. Abbreviations

Find the master list(s) of abbreviations and symbols used in your dictionary and use it to determine what abbreviations your dictionary uses for the following.

transitive verb _____   past participle _____

obsolete _____   Late Latin _____

subjunctive _____   intransitive verb _____

noun _____   adjective _____

Greek _____   conjunction _____

5. Parts of Speech

Use the list of abbreviations you found to guide you in interpreting the part-of-speech label for each of the following words. Write the abbreviation and then write out the part of speech in the space provided. If a word may serve as more than one part of speech, list each abbreviation and write out each one.

astrakhan _____   canvass _____

frigid _____   frenziedly _____

of _____   oh _____

off _____   and _____

Meccan _____   rappel _____

6. Other Grammatical Forms

Plurals and Principal Parts of Verbs

Use your dictionary's alphabetical listings to find the form of each of the following words as indicated in parentheses. If there is more than one acceptable form listed in your dictionary, give both. Your dictionary will list the preferred form first.

cactus (plural) _____   moose (plural) _____

© 1986 by CBS College Publishing. All rights reserved.

prove (past participle) _____   alumnus (plural) _____

gallery (plural) _____   sing (past tense) _____

drink (past participle) _____   burst (present participle) _____

Comparative and Superlative Degrees of Adjectives and Adverbs

Write the comparative and superlative degrees of the adjectives and adverbs listed. Some dictionaries will not list some of these forms; if yours does not, explain why.

happy _____

well _____

free _____

good _____

lovely _____

fast _____

Derived words

Words formed from other words by adding suffixes may have their own entry or be listed under the main entry for the base form of the word, depending upon the importance of the word created in this way. Look up and write the words formed by adding the suffixes in parentheses to the words listed.

culpable (-ity) _____   explicate (-ory) _____

nonobjective (-ism) _____   labyrinthine (-ian) _____

picayune (-ish) _____   picnic (-ing) _____

happy (-ly) _____   infer (-ed) _____

repercussion (-ive) _____   infer (-ence) _____

7. Etymology

The history of a word is fascinating for two reasons. First, it shows us what an international language we speak; around four-fifths of the words in English were borrowed from other languages. Second, it can give us insight into the meaning of words or into the way meanings change in our language.

For each of the words on the left, list the language of origin, the word of origin, the meaning of that word, and the present meaning of the word.

Using the Dictionary

	Source Language	Source Word	Original Meaning	Current Meaning
deer				
kowtow				
animal				
nice				
starve				

Some words enter the language from trade names or people's names or as made-up words. Your dictionary will also give you information about the origin of these words. Give the sources for the following words; then give the meaning of the word.

sandwich _____

googol _____

quark _____

Watt _____

jabberwocky _____

8. Meanings

Dictionaries may list meanings with the most common, current meaning first or the earliest meaning first. Which way does your dictionary list meanings?
_____

What does this tell you that may be helpful when you use your dictionary?
_____

Use each of the following words in two short sentences, based on two of the meanings listed in your dictionary.

jack   a.
          b.

limb   a.
          b.

guard   a.
           b.

discount a.
             b.

© 1986 by CBS College Publishing. All rights reserved.

retreat   a.
          b.

9. Synonyms

Find a synonym or antonym as indicated in parentheses for the words underlined in the following sentences. Write the word you find above the original and make any other necessary changes in the wording of the sentence.

Napoleon's army retreated (syn) from Moscow.

Deliver (syn) us from his endless nagging.

I dislike his mannerism (syn) of peering at students over the rims of his glasses.

Write a preface (syn) that says "hello" to the readers.

The land was fertile (ant).

10. Idiomatic usage

When entry words are frequently used in set expressions, those expressions will often be listed and explained. Find an idiomatic expression for each of the following words (a) and use the idiom correctly in a sentence (b).

head   a. _____
            b. _____
motion   a. _____
            b. _____
inch   a. _____
            b. _____
difference a. _____
            b. _____
open   a. _____
            b. _____

11. Labels

Special labels are used in modern dictionaries to show levels of language or to give special information about current practices (such as whether the word is used now or whether a meaning is limited in some way). Determine from the front matter what labels your dictionary uses. Then find labels for the following words or meanings of words. (If no label is used, write "no label.") Labels for specific words will vary with the dictionary.

Using the Dictionary

ain't _____

fetch: "to fetch a blow" _____

groovy _____

ground: "to ground a wire" _____

grind: "a student who studies hard" _____

envelope: "enclosing membrane" _____

hast _____

Score _____

Using the Dictionary

Review 17

Use your dictionary to answer the following questions.

1. Is the word *judgmatic* appropriate for formal use?

2. How many syllables are there in the preferred pronunciation of *interest?*

3. What is the population of Guanajuato?

4. What is the preferred plural of *effluvium?*

5. When was Dwight Eisenhower president?

6. What is Pantagruelism?

7. How many ways can the sound represented by ə be spelled?

8. What is the origin of the word *intermontane?*

9. What is a slang use for the word *egg?*

10. What is an archaic past participle of *drink?*

Score _____

Check your answers against those in the back of the book. A score of 80 percent or higher shows you are able to find and read information in your dictionary.

Writer's Casebook #17

Application: Defining in an Essay or Exploring Meanings

According to the dictionary, a *definition* states the meaning or meanings of something or clarifies it, making it explicit, definite, distinct. In an essay as in the dictionary, definition involves meanings. But, instead of presenting a straightforward statement or list of statements, an essay may explore many dimensions of meaning—the meaning of the subject to you or to the world at large; its literal, denotative meaning or its nonliteral, connotative meaning; what it is or what it suggests. And the expanded definitions of an essay will try to clarify these meanings by showing rather than telling them.

In a definition essay, as in a definition paragraph (see 4e.8), we may define by examining components, by exploring relationships, by giving examples, or by describing what the subject is not. The focus of our definition may be public meanings or private meanings—meanings we share with the rest of the world or meanings that apply particularly to our own experiences or feelings.

An effective pattern of organization for a definition essay begins with the simplest and moves to the more complicated definitions.

Pattern	Plan for Student Essay
Introduction of subject to be defined	Introduction to "belonging"
Explanation of its importance to the writer	Explanation of the writer's need to belong
Thesis that establishes the focus of the definition	Thesis: To me belonging is as essential to life as food or air or water.
Body of Essay	Body of Essay
Dictionary, denotative, or formal definition	Dictionary definition of *belonging*
Negative Definition—what it is not	What it is like not to belong—no one to eat lunch with, tell about your grades, go to games with
Examples, analysis, identification and examination of parts	
Positive Definition—what it is	What it is like to belong—people glad to see you, invitations to parties, name chosen for partner activities
Examples, analysis, identification and examination of parts	
Conclusion—summary of definition	Conclusion: I would not feel alive if I did not belong somewhere.
Final comment offering a special judgment, insight, or perspective	I wish I belonged.

Cases for Writing: Definitions and Dictionaries

Case #1

You are the sponsor for a family of refugees. As part of the acculturation process, you are introducing them to various American customs and holidays. Explain the meaning of some custom (such as trick-or-treat on Halloween) or holiday (such as Thanksgiving, Valentine's Day, or the Fourth of July). Include both public and private meanings in your explanation.

Case #2

Choose from the dictionary a common word that interests you (for example, *medicine* or *ink*). Write out in coherent prose the information that you find in the abbreviations, symbols, and listing. Then critique this experience. What did the exercise teach you about the dictionary? Did you learn anything about the word that you did not previously know?

Building a Vocabulary 18

Preview 18

Underline and correct errors in usage in the following sentences. If a sentence contains no errors, write C beside it.

1. The best scholar, the valetudinarian, spoke at her high school's matriculation exercises.

2. Irregardless of our pleas, he said his decision was irrevocable.

3. I have been reading Sandburg's autobiography of Abraham Lincoln.

4. *Hydrophobia* means a fear of high places.

5. The fission in the earth opened rapidly, as the vault in the rock slipped.

6. From this prospective the view is magniloquent.

7. The witches' brew bubbled in their chaldron.

8. The passage must be performed loudly—fortissimo.

Score _____

Check your answers against those in the back of the book. Deduct 5 points for errors in identification and 5 points for errors in correction. A score of 80 percent or higher indicates good vocabulary skills. As you work through this chapter, concentrate on techniques for building your various vocabularies.

The English language is filled with both treasures and traps for writers. The treasures are a rich vocabulary—several hundred thousand words with histories that span dozens of languages. But like the splendors of a pharaoh's tomb, the treasures come with traps—erratic spelling, resulting from diverse word origins and language changes; multiple meanings, whether drastic or subtle; and a multitude of rules, patterns, and associations to remember.

Your college dictionary, as you discovered in the last chapter (17b), covers around 150,000 words; your own writing and reading vocabularies may already include from 10,000 to 100,000 words. Yet learning new words—what they mean, how to use them, and how to spell them—is an integral part of the educational process. To improve your vocabulary, you must first understand your strengths and weaknesses in this area.

18a Analyzing

You actually have not one but four vocabularies, one for each context within which you know words. Your *speaking vocabulary* consists of the several hundred words you use in conversation. Your *writing vocabulary*, the words you use in essays and on examinations, is larger, from 10,000 to 45,000 words. And your *reading vocabulary* is larger still, varying with the individual college student from 50,000 to 100,000 words. Finally, there is your *guess vocabulary*, words whose meanings you can infer from context.

None of these vocabularies increases automatically, merely as a function of living. You must work intelligently and systematically at increasing your word power.

18b Building

A major part of your learning power depends upon the words you know. Words communicate ideas; without knowing the right words, it is difficult to understand, conceive, or communicate ideas. For example, suppose your psychology professor makes these statements.

> As information hits the system, your senses actually store it very briefly in the sensory information storehouse. If it is visual information, it is stored in the iconic register for approximately a quarter of a second. It is then either erased, or it is read off by the short-term memory store for further processing. If the information is given meaning, it becomes stored in long-term memory.

To understand what the professor is saying about information processing, you must first understand new terms, such as *sensory information storehouse* and *iconic register*, and new uses for old terms, such as *meaning, memory*, and *processing*. If you have not added special vocabulary words to the list of words you recognize, complex ideas and the knowledge they represent are closed to you as surely as if they were written in a foreign language. Moreover, if you do not make these terms part of your writing vocabulary by learning both how to use and how to spell them, at examination time you will not be able to communicate to your professor what you know.

18c Avoiding Ineffective Vocabulary Building

Memorizing lists of difficult words without considering the differences among your several vocabularies will do little to increase your word power. Moreover, it may result in errors in language usage. For instance, you may use words like *languished* or *metempsychosis*, which belong in your reading vocabulary, in your daily conversation.

Building a Vocabulary

Using Roots, Prefixes, and Suffixes Exercise 18-1

NAME _____ DATE _____

One way English acquires new words is by adding prefixes and suffixes to word roots. Learning some of these word building blocks will enable you to make intelligent guesses about the meanings of words formed in this way.

A. Use your dictionary to find the meanings of the following word roots. You may have to study word etymologies.

1. graph
2. psycho
3. thermo
4. crypto
5. techno

6. bio
7. geo
8. spir
9. gram
10. pneuma

B. Use your dictionary to find the meanings of the following prefixes and suffixes.

1. -ology
2. para-
3. -atic
4. -ic
5. -osis

6. re-
7. con-
8. -ation
9. -y
10. -al

C. Use the roots, prefixes, and suffixes that you found to help you determine the meaning of the words listed. First, make an intelligent guess; then check your answer in your dictionary. After you are certain that you understand the meaning, use the word in a sentence.

                Meaning   Example

1. graphology

2. parapsychology

3. geothermal

4. cryptogram

5. biotechnology

© 1986 by CBS College Publishing. All rights reserved.

6. pneumatic

7. respiration

8. conspire

9. technographic

10. pneumograph

11. graphic

12. geology

13. cryptographic

14. geography

15. psychosis

16. spirograph

Building a Vocabulary

17. biogeography

18. thermal

19. thermogram

20. psychology

Score _____

Inferring Meaning Exercise 18–2

NAME _____ DATE _____

Your guessing vocabulary will expand quickly if you develop the habit of using context to infer meaning—that is, to try to figure out the meaning of a word you don't know from the meanings of the surrounding words that you do know.

In the following exercise first "guess" at the meanings of the words underlined. Then check your guesses by consulting your dictionary. Finally, demonstrate your understanding of the word by using it in a sentence.

> EXAMPLE: The speech was apt, fitting the needs of a graduating class exactly.
>   a. guess: *suitable*
>   b. dictionary: *unusually suited*
>   c. sentence: *Your answer was apt, giving the advice they needed.*

1. Time, which antiquates antiquities, and hath an art to make dust of all things, hath yet spared these minor movements. (Sir Thomas Browne, *Hydriotaphia, Urn-Burial*)
   a. guess:
   b. dictionary:
   c. sentence:

2. He was convinced (as he afterwards told me) that I must be a Yahoo, but my teachableness, civility, and cleanliness astonished him; which were qualities altogether so opposite to those animals. (Jonathan Swift, *Gulliver's Travels*)
   a. guess:
   b. dictionary:

   c. sentence:

3. Clark was a sophisticated urbane political creature with a sort of country-club, Hamiltonian distaste for mass man. (Tony Hillerman, *The Fly on the Wall*)
   a. guess:
   b. dictionary:
   c. sentence:

4. Be careful that you do not commend yourselves. . . . [I]t is fulsome and unpleasing to others to hear such commendation. (Sir Matthew Hale, *On Conversation*)
   a. guess:
   b. dictionary:
   c. sentence:

5. [I]t was the Greek belief that the spirits of the dead found no rest till their obsequies had been performed. (Charlotte M. Yone, *The Battle of Thermopylae*)
   a. guess:
   b. dictionary:
   c. sentence:

Building a Vocabulary 311

6. Her voice was not unsteady, but her mind was in all the perturbation that such a development of self, such a burst of threatening evil, such a confusion of sudden and perplexing emotions, must create. (Jane Austen, *Emma*)
   a. guess:
   b. dictionary:
   c. sentence:

7. Helen was still asleep and as I crawled between the sheets beside her I was still wallowing in my Yuletide euphoria. There wouldn't be much work tomorrow; we'd have a long lie—maybe till nine—and then a lazy day, a glorious hiatus in our busy life. (James Herriot, *All Things Bright and Beautiful*)
   a. guess:
   b. dictionary:
   c. sentence:

   a. guess:
   b. dictionary:
   c. sentence:

8. Read not to contradict and confute, nor to believe and take for granted nor to find talk and discourse but to weigh and consider. (Francis Bacon, *Of Studies*)
   a. guess:
   b. dictionary:
   c. sentence:

9. I had much rather the speculative and quick-sighted should complain of my being in some parts tedious, than that anyone, not accustomed to abstract speculations, or prepossessed with different notions, should mistake or not comprehend my meaning. (John Locke, *An Essay Concerning Human Understanding*)
   a. guess:
   b. dictionary:
   c. sentence:

   a. guess:
   b. dictionary:
   c. sentence:

10. Arbus . . . [did not have] Warhol's narcissism and genius for publicity. (Susan Sontag, *On Photography*)
    a. guess:
    b. dictionary:
    c. sentence:

Score _____

© 1986 by CBS College Publishing. All rights reserved.

Review 18

Underline and correct errors in usage in the following sentences. If a sentence contains no errors, write C beside it.

1. Gluttony is the result of too much gluten in the diet.

2. The materfamilias both earns a living and raises her family.

3. When her painting received critical acclaim, she became notorious.

4. The point you are making is disputatious.

5. Microeconomics concerns large factors in the economy; macroeconomics, small factors.

6. When you travel abroad, prepare for every contingent.

7. The purpose of the town forum is for citizens to focalize the citizens' concerns and then focus on specific problems.

8. The prologue at the end of the play bore no relation to the plot.

9. When you have finished the marketing study, dissimilate the results to every company office.

10. The disease is communicative, so the patient has been placed in quarantine.

Score _____

Check your answers against those in the back of the book. Deduct 5 points for errors in identification and 5 points for errors in correction. A score of 80 percent or higher indicates good vocabulary skills, but you should continue to use the techniques practiced in this chapter to build your vocabularies.

The Writer's Casebook #18

Application to Writing: The "Inkhorn" Style

While you are adding many new words to your reading vocabulary, you will want to add some of them to your writing vocabulary as well. However, using too many of the longer and more complex words you are learning could lead to a cumbersome, pretentious writing style. In fact, many of the multisyllabic words compounded of Latin and Greek roots, prefixes, and suffixes are what writers hundreds of years ago called "inkhorn" terms. The name suggests their origin in musty manuscripts rather than living language.

Telling a friend in conversation that you wish to "elucidate a moot point" would be an inappropriate use of language for the level and purpose involved. Similarly, informing your history professor that your paper about the Civil War concerns "the antebellum events that precipitated the hostilities" would be inappropriate because the big words do not actually communicate any more meaning than your saying that you are writing about events leading up to the Civil War.

Generally, avoid multisyllabic, "inkhorn" words in your writing unless you are certain they contribute significantly to meaning. (An exception is technical terms such as *geothermal* and *psychosis*, for which we do not have equivalent expressions.)

Cases for Writing: Exploring Words

Case #1

Assume the pose of a "vocabulary-word-dropper" (akin to a name-dropper). Write an account of your day's activities in the most pretentious language you can muster. Then underline the most difficult words, and use your dictionary to discover their origins. What languages contribute the majority of these terms? How can you recognize and avoid pretentious "inkhorn" language?

Case #2

Use the front and back matter in your dictionary as well as the alphabetical listings and sources to learn something about the history of the English language. What are its origins? How is it related to other European languages? How have historical events and movements affected the language? As we use it today, is *English* an appropriate name for this language? Write a paper about your findings.

Improving Spelling   19

Preview 19

Underline and correct spelling errors in the following sentences. If a sentence contains no errors, write C beside it.

1. Within site of the building cite the officer sighted me for an incorrect lane exchange.

2. The basic criteria for joining this club is committment.

3. Let your conscious be your guide.

4. The written greivance was noticably irrational.

5. The valevictorian was congradulated at her high school's graduation exercises.

6. The error in the accounts of the multimillionaire's heir made the banker's hair turn white as he gasped for air.

7. Before we can beautyfy our nieghborhood, we must first rectyfy the mistakes of the zoning commision.

8. There are six Nancies and two Maria's in our club.

9. The Foxes scored two points in the final seconds of the game, beating they're number one rival, the Oxes.

10. Her three sister-in-laws each borrowed three cupfuls of sugar.

Score _____

Check your answers against those in the back of the book. Deduct 2 points for errors in identification, 3 points for errors in correction. A score of 80 percent or higher is an indication of good spelling skills, but you will still want to work through this section to review some principles basic to improving spelling.

19a Spelling/Pronouncing Words

1. Watch for vowels in unstressed positions: *soldier, reluctance, maharaja, geometric, crimson*.
2. Watch for silent letters: *ptomaine, wreck, isle, rhapsody, reign, gnash, grime, debt, receipt*.
3. Watch for words that contain letters or syllables not pronounced in informal speech: *restaurant, secretary, government, except*.
4. Be aware of variant forms of the same word: *three, thirteen* (changes in roots); *prescribe, prescription* (change from one part of speech to another); *sing, sang, sung* (principal parts of irregular verbs); *elf, elves* (change in plural); *traveled, travelled* (more than one accepted spelling).
5. Learn words that sound alike but are spelled differently: *air, heir, err; aisle, isle, I'll; idol, idle, idyll*.

19b Spelling Rules

Learn spelling principles. (Individual exercises will present some of these principles. Also, many dictionaries will include an essay on spelling.)

19c Spelling Skills

1. Learn commonly misspelled words.
2. Make your own list of words you commonly misspell.
3. Uncover patterns in your misspellings, such as problems with plurals or -ible/-able endings.
4. Fix each word in your mind by using memory devices; for example, you might remember that *separate* contains the vowel sequence e, a, a, e by associating the vowels in the word with a series of words—*eat, ate, ate, eat*—or a sentence—*Earnest also agreed earnestly*.
5. Pronounce words carefully, being careful to give each sound its full value and not to include any extra letters or leave out any necessary ones.
6. Learn to use the dictionary to find words that you cannot already spell by (a) approximating the spelling (for example, *idil* for *idyll*) and (b) searching through each possible spelling given in the pronunciation key for an individual sound (such as a, e, i, o, u, and y for ə in *idyll*).

Using *Ie/Ei* Exercise 19–1

NAME _____ DATE _____

Follow the principles summarized below to fill in the blanks in the following words with ie or ei. Use your dictionary to check for exceptions.

> PRINCIPLE: Use i before e except after c or when pronounced ay as in *neighbor* and *weigh*.
>
> EXAMPLES: th*ie*f, fr*ie*nd; rec*ei*ve, dec*ei*ve; n*ei*gh, *ei*ght
>
> EXCEPTIONS: *either, seize*, and so on

1. conc __ ve
2. y __ ld
3. l __ sure
4. for __ gn
5. sl __ gh
6. fr __ ght
7. sc __ nce
8. c __ ling
9. defic __ nt
10. fr __ nd
11. n __ ce
12. w __ rd
13. bel __ ve
14. consc __ nce
15. misch __ f
16. sh __ k
17. v __ n
18. n __ ther
19. conc __ t
20. perc __ ve

Score _____

Words Ending in *E* and *Y* Exercise 19–2

NAME _____ DATE _____

Follow the principles summarized below to add suffixes to words that end in *e* and *y*. Use your dictionary to check for exceptions.

> PRINCIPLES:
> 1. Keep e before a suffix that begins with a consonant: *late/lately, same/sameness*. (Exceptions: *argument, truly, judgment, abridgment*)
> 2. Drop e before a suffix that begins with a vowel: *traverse/traversed, move/movable*. (Exceptions: *changeable, courageous*)

1. whole (-ly) _____
2. tire (-some) _____
3. judge (-ing) _____
4. bone (-less) _____
5. disgrace (-ing) _____
6. hope (-ful) _____
7. bone (-ed) _____
8. entice (-ment) _____
9. notice (-able) _____
10. hope (-ing) _____
11. imagine (-able) _____
12. mile (-age) _____
13. disgrace (-ful) _____

14. singe (-ing) _____
15. game (-ly) _____
16. judge (-ment) _____
17. peace (-able) _____
18. curve (-ature) _____
19. grieve (-ance) _____
20. home (-less) _____
21. acre (-age) _____
22. abridge (-ment) _____
23. peace (-ful) _____
24. love (-able) _____
25. home (-y) _____

> PRINCIPLE: Change y to i when a suffix begins with a consonant unless a vowel precedes the y: *happy/happily*. When the suffix begins with a vowel or the base word is a proper name, keep the y: *play/played, Mary/Marys* (Exceptions: *say/said, day/daily*)

1. beauty (-fy) _____
2. supply (-ed) _____
3. accompany (-ist) _____
4. Kennedy (-s) _____
5. enjoy (-ment) _____
6. gay (-ly) _____
7. mercy (-less) _____

8. dry (-er) _____
9. phony (-est) _____
10. showy (-er) _____
11. body (-ly) _____
12. copy (-ist) _____
13. toy (-ing) _____
14. sally (-ed) _____

Improving Spelling

15. gay (-ety) _____
16. carry (-ed) _____
17. play (-er) _____
18. military (-ism) _____
19. dewy (-ness) _____
20. sally (-ing) _____

21. defy (-ant) _____
22. embody (-ment) _____
23. baby (-hood) _____
24. defy (-ing) _____
25. try (-ed) _____

Score _____

© 1986 by CBS College Publishing. All rights reserved.

Spelling Plurals Exercise 19-3

NAME _____ DATE _____

Use the following principles as well as your dictionary to form the plurals of the words listed.

1. Form most plurals by adding -s (*books, cats*) or -es if the word ends in a sibilant, or any of the -s sounds (*brushes, buses, boxes*).
2. Form some plurals of words that end in f or fe by changing f to v and adding -es (*wife, wives*); form others by simply adding -s (*chiefs*); and form some either way (*hoofs, hooves*).
3. Form the plurals of common nouns that end in y preceded by a consonant by changing -y to -i and adding -es (*candies*). If the -y is preceded by a vowel, just add -s (*days*).
4. Form the plurals of some words that end in o preceded by a consonant by adding -es (*tomatoes, heroes*); form others, especially words associated with music, by adding -s (*pianos, altos*). If the o is preceded by a vowel, add -s (*radios*).

1. soprano _____   8. Mary _____
2. lash _____   9. belief _____
3. monkey _____   10. echo _____
4. twenty _____   11. dwarf _____
5. self _____   12. studio _____
6. potato _____   13. leaf _____
7. roof _____

5. Form the plurals of compound nouns by making the major word plural (*chairpersons, fathers-in-law*).
6. Learn some irregular plurals, and rely upon your dictionary (*woman/women, child/children, foot/feet*).
7. Form the plurals of some foreign nouns according to principles in those languages. Check your dictionary when in doubt (*thesis, theses; medium/media; phenomenon/phenomena; index/indices; cherub/cherubim*).
8. Use the same form for the plural and the singular of some nouns, particularly the names of fishes, birds, and mammals (*moose, sheep, quail*).

1. analysis _____   7. genesis _____
2. notary public _____   8. stimulus _____
3. aphis _____   9. alga _____
4. elk _____   10. ox _____
5. minutia _____   11. alumna _____
6. datum _____   12. criterion _____

Score _____

Review 19

Underline and correct spelling errors in the following sentences. If a sentence contains no errors, write C beside it.

1. Great literature echos with the exploits of heros.

2. During the sales campaign the canvaser slept in a canvass tent.

3. The psychologist could of charged $100 an hour.

4. The shiek's son stayed with us as a foriegn exchange student.

5. The composite photograph looked like a counterfeit.

6. Nomes dwell underground and gaurd thier treasures.

7. In our liesure time we must bridge the gaps in our general knowlledge.

8. Add three cupsful of sugar to the mixture.

9. On a lonely aisle in the South Pacific, I'le wonder through isles of cocanut palms.

10. The alga on the acquarium glass made it difficult to see the fishes—guppies, swords, catfish, and neons.

Score _____

Check your answers against those in the back of the book. Deduct 2 points for errors in identification, 3 points for errors in correction. A score of 80 percent or higher is an indication of good spelling skills. Continue to practice the principles for improvement outlined in this chapter.

The Writer's Casebook #19

Application to Writing: Editing for Spelling

Finding and correcting spelling errors in your writing may require some special techniques, particularly if you find yourself making the same errors over and over again. If you carefully proofread your papers and still cannot find your errors, you may be reading what you meant to write rather than what is actually on the page, or poor spelling habits may be causing incorrectly spelled words to appear to be correct.

Editing for Spelling Techniques
1. Read your paper out loud, slowly pronouncing each syllable of each word and giving full force to every vowel and consonant sound. Common errors caused by sloppy pronunciation may be caught in this way—such as *goverment* for *government* or *restraunt* for *restaurant*.
2. Keep a list of problem words—words that you misspell frequently or words whose spellings you find confusing, such as those with silent letters like *rhinoceros* or *Wednesday*. Check your papers carefully against this list.
3. Read the paper backward, starting with the last word and ending with the first. This technique will help you to concentrate on individual words without being distracted by the overall context.
4. Read the paper through quickly, underlining possible problems, such as *ie/ei* combinations, plurals, or homophones. Then look up each underlined word in your dictionary, being careful to check the definition as well as the entry word. Remember that many dictionaries list nonstandard spellings like *alright* for *all right*, and also the minor difference of one letter may make a major difference in meaning, as in *compliment* or *complement*.

Cases for Writing: Writing About Spelling

Case #1

Edit one or more of your papers for spelling errors, and analyze the problems you find. Was the error caused by a silent letter? A forgotten spelling rule? A homophone? Then write a paper discussing your spelling problems overall and developing a strategy for correcting those problems.

Case #2

Some problems with erratic English spellings are caused by our practice of borrowing words from other languages. Often we retain the meaning and the spelling, even though English has a different way of representing the sounds that make up the word; for example, we borrowed the word *beau* from French, retaining the French spelling of the long sound of *o*. Or we may keep the meaning and the original spelling but change the pronunciation of a word, retaining, for example, the initial *k* in the Dutch borrowing *knapsack* but not pronouncing it.

Use your dictionary to explore the spelling problems caused by borrowing words from other languages. Write a paper about your findings.

SECTION V

Understanding Grammar

20
Identifying the Parts of Speech

Preview 20

Label the part of speech of each underlined word in the following paragraph: noun (n), pronoun (pro), verb (v), adjective (adj), adverb (adv), preposition (prep), conjunction (conj), interjection (int).

The "final frontier," space has inspired dreams and stimulated the imagination for centuries. In the second century the Greek cynic Lucian wrote humorously of a lunar voyage on man-made wings, and Greek, Persian, and Hindu myths often depict flights to impossibly fabulous heavens. However, after Galileo observed the moon through his telescope in the seventeenth century, fantasies became science fiction, fictive accounts that speculated sometimes meaningfully about space travel. Cyrano de Bergerac, who spun tales of flights to the moon and the sun, first suggested rocket propulsion, and Edward Hale, another popular writer, explored the possibilities of a space station or satellite in his book, *The Brick Moon*. Alas, by the time *Apollo II* landed the first humans on the moon, the dreamers were already trekking through the stars. The frontier had moved.

Score _____

Check your answers against those in the back of the book. Deduct 2 points for each error in identification. A score of 80 percent or higher demonstrates understanding of the materials in this chapter.

323

In Section II: Composing Sentences, you learned to build effective sentences by combining individual words and groups of words in meaningful ways (Chapters 6 and 7). Learning how the different elements of a sentence function in relation to one another will help you understand the basic grammar, or principles, of sentence structure.

Words may be classified into eight basic parts of speech according to their functions in a sentence: *nouns, pronouns, verbs, adjectives, adverbs, prepositions, conjunctions,* and *interjections.* The dictionary lists the part of speech for each word defined, but you can also determine which class a word belongs to by examining what the word does in a sentence.

20a Nouns

Nouns are "name" words; they name people (*Neil Armstrong*), places (*Luna*), things (*spacecraft*), ideas (*myth*), actions (*spacewalk*), and qualities (*magnificence*).

Nouns may be subdivided into *proper nouns,* which name a specific person, place, or thing (*Astronaut Edwin Aldrin, Tranquility Base, Apollo II*); *common nouns,* which name a nonspecific person, place, or thing (*astronaut, moonbase, spaceflight*); *mass nouns,* which name uncountable quantities (*time, sand*); *abstract nouns,* which name intangible ideas or qualities (*pride, lunacy*); and *collective nouns,* which name a group unit (*crew, team*).

Landing in the powdery *dust* (mass) of the *Sea of Tranquility* (proper), the *crew* (collective) of the lunar *module* (common) performed a *feat* (abstract) that some considered "a giant *step*" (common) and others, an *act* (common) of *lunacy* (abstract).

20b Pronouns

Pronouns ("for-nouns") take the place of or stand for nouns, which are called pronoun *antecedents,* or "ones that go before." Like nouns, pronouns may be divided into different types. *Personal pronouns* stand for a person (*I, you, he, she, it, we, they,* and the other words derived from these pronouns). *Indefinite pronouns* stand for unspecified people or things (*everyone, anybody, all, none, many*). *Reflexive pronouns* and *intensive pronouns* end with *-self* and refer back to the subject or emphasize a noun or another pronoun (*myself, yourself, herself,* and so forth). *Relative pronouns* introduce dependent clauses (*which, what, that, these,* and *those*). And *reciprocal pronouns* denote mutual relationships (*each other, one another*).

Acting like lunar tourists, *they* (personal) photographed *one another* (reciprocal), acquainted

Identifying the Parts of Speech   **325**

    reflexive
    themselves with the bleak landscape, carried away as souvenirs all items, such as
           relative personal
    rocks and dust, that they wanted to take back to Earth, but littered the landscape
      demonstrative   *relative indefinite*
    with those, such as used urine bags, that no one wanted to take home.

20c   Verbs

Verbs express action or show a state of being.

          action
    The astronauts slipped on glass spherules in the lunar soil.
     state of being
    The soil was slippery because of millions of tiny glass spherules.

Verbs that show state of being—such as *be, seem, become, appear,* and *feel*—are called *linking verbs* because they connect, or "link," the subject with its complement, a word that renames or describes it.

                     linking
    With the *Apollo II* flight the moon became part of our world.

Main verbs identify the action or state of being while *auxiliary verbs* (sometimes called helping verbs) combine with main verbs to make up *verb phrases,* indicating tense, voice, mood, necessity, possibility, or willingness.

                            verb phrase
                        [aux   main verb]
    As many as 500 million people may have listened to broadcasts of the lunar
                         verb phrase
                   [aux   main verb]
    landing. On television Armstrong could be seen as he stepped onto the moon's

    surface.

Auxiliaries include *will, would, shall, should, may, might, can, could, need (to), ought (to), must,* and forms of *be* and *have.*

A *verbal* is a part of a verb that cannot function alone as the main verb of a sentence but may serve other functions. For example, the verb participle *landing* would require the addition of an auxiliary verb such as *be* or *were* before it could be used as the main verb of a sentence: The spacecraft *is landing* on the moon. But without the auxiliary the verb part or verbal could function as an adjective or as a noun.

    adj modifying noun gear   *noun as object of prep* during
    The landing gear functioned safely during the moon landing.

There are three basic kinds of verbals: *infinitives, participles,* and *gerunds.*
    1. Infinitives consist of the base form of the verb preceded by *to: to fly, to land, to collect.* They function in sentences as adjectives, as adverbs, and as nouns.

Moon rocks were more than mementos to treasure. (adjective modifying noun *mementos*)

Students were eager to study them. (adverb modifying adjective *eager*)

To own a moon rock is still a scientific status symbol. (noun as subject of verb *is*)

2. Every verb has two *participles:* a *present participle*, which ends in *-ing (flying, landing, collecting)*, and a *past participle*, which may end in *-ed (landed, collected)* or may have an irregular form *(flown)*. Combined with various auxiliary verbs, the participles form the base for a variety of main verb tenses: The ship *was landing*. . . . ; the astronauts *had collected*. . . . But used alone in a sentence, participles often act as adjectives, modifying nouns.

Awed, the astronauts watched the Earth rise over the moon. (adjective modifying noun *astronauts*)

The rising Earth was a blue-green sphere on the horizon. (adjective modifying noun *earth*)

3. Participles may also function as nouns.

With the lunar landing the unknown became the known. (present participle as object of preposition *with*; past participles as subject and complement of verb *became*)

The *-ing* verbal is used so frequently as a noun that it is called a gerund, or sometimes a *verbal noun.* The gerund can serve any of a noun's functions in a sentence—as object of the preposition, as in the example above, or as subject and direct object, as in the following sentence.

Unfortunately, Armstrong's walking on the moon ended for all time lovers' fantasizing about a lunar paradise. (subject and direct object, respectively, of verb *ended*)

NOTE: Like other nouns gerunds may be modified by possessive forms.

20d Adjectives

Adjectives modify nouns or pronouns. Most are *descriptive*, showing a quality or picturing a characteristic. When a descriptive adjective is formed from a proper noun, the adjective also is considered "proper" and must be capitalized.

On the Martian horizon Earth looms blue-green in a red sky.

Other kinds of adjectives limit or qualify, rather than describe: articles *(a, an, the)*; possessive adjectives *(my, your, his, her, its,* and so forth); demonstrative adjectives *(this, that, these, those),* interrogative adjectives *(which, whose, what)*; indefinite adjectives *(another, each, both, many, any,* and so forth);

Identifying the Parts of Speech

numerical adjectives (*one, two, first, second,* and so forth); relative adjectives (*what, whatever, which, whichever, whose, whosever*).

NOTE: Many of these words function as pronouns when they stand alone in a sentence but as adjectives when they precede nouns.

indefinite   *demonstrative*   *relative*   *article numerical*
Each member of that *Apollo II* team whose destiny made them the first Earth

article   *possessive*
people to walk on the moon was spellbound by his experience, wondering,

interrogative
"Which planet will we conquer next?"

20e Adverbs

Adverbs modify verbs, adjectives, or other adverbs. They answer the following questions: "How?" "Where?" "When?" "To what extent or what degree?"

v   *adv*
The Space Age began frenziedly with a race between the United States and the Soviet Union. (How?)

adv   *v*
Then in October, 1957, the Soviets orbited *Sputnik I.* (When?)

adv adv   *v*
Very soon *Sputnik II*, carrying the first space dog Laika, joined *Sputnik I* there in Earth orbit. (To what degree? When? Where?)

adv   *adj*
NASA's first attempt to orbit a satellite was shockingly disastrous. (To what extent?)

20f Prepositions

Prepositions relate nouns or noun substitutes to other words in a sentence. The structural pattern of a prepositional phrase is simple and usually does not vary in written expression: preposition + modifiers (optional) + object.

prep obj
FOR EXAMPLE: in orbit

prep modifier obj
OR: in stable orbit

Notice the underlined prepositions and prepositional phrases in the following sentence.

prep obj   prep obj   *prep obj prep*
By January of 1958 the United States joined the Soviet Union in space with the

modifiers   obj
first Explorer satellite.

Here is a list of common prepositions.

about	beside	in regard to	regarding
above	between	in spite of	since
across	beyond	inside	than
after	by	into	through
against	concerning	like	throughout
along	despite	near	to
among	down	of	toward
around	during	off	under
as	except	on	underneath
at	for	onto	until
as well as	from	out	up
because of	in	outside	upon
before	in addition to	over	with
behind	in back of	past	within
below	in front of	per	without
beneath			

20g Conjunctions

Conjunctions join single words, phrases, clauses, or complete sentences. Coordinating conjunctions *(and, but, or, nor, for, so, yet)* join words or word groups of equal grammatical rank—that is, that serve the same function in the sentence.

During the early days of the space race, the United States <u>and</u> the Soviet Union struggled to be the first <u>or</u>, if second, claimed to be the best.

Correlative conjunctions *(either/or, neither/nor, not only/but also, not/but)*, which are always used in pairs, also join equals.

The Soviet Union orbited <u>not only</u> the first artificial satellite <u>but also</u> the first space lab.

Subordinating conjunctions *(since, because, although, if, when, after, while, before, unless, once,* and so forth) join word groups in such a way that one becomes subordinate to or dependent upon the other.

<u>Although</u> we were behind at the beginning of the space race, the United States caught up <u>when</u> Neil Armstrong became the first human being to set foot on the moon.

20h Interjections

Interjections are single words that express emotion, surprise, awe, or chagrin. They may be punctuated alone with an exclamation point, or they may be set off in a sentence with commas, but they do not have a syntactic or structural function in the sentence.

Identifying the Parts of Speech

"Wow! Oh! Whoopee! Oops!" The astronauts enjoyed leaping in the low gravity of the moon, but then, alas, it was time to return to Earth.

NOTE: Some words may be used as more than one part of speech, depending upon their function in a sentence. For example,

prep   *conj*
For thirty years the Soviets and the United States have competed in space, for each wishes to be thought superior in technology and progress.

Or

n   *v*
The might of a nation might be measured by its scientific accomplishments.

When in doubt, check the dictionary for the part of speech that matches your specific use of a word.

Identifying the Parts of Speech   **331**

Identifying Parts of Speech   Exercise 20-1

NAME _____ DATE _____

In the following sentences label the part of speech of each word noun (n), pronoun (pro), verb (v), adjective (adj), adverb (adv), preposition (prep), conjunction (conj), and interjection (int).

                   n   v   prep n prep adj   n
   EXAMPLE: White walked in space for twenty-one minutes.

1. The first human in space was a Soviet cosmonaut, Yuri A. Gargarian.

2. He quickly flew one orbit of the Earth in an hour and forty-eight minutes.

3. Although the first woman, Valentina V. Tereshkova, was not launched until 1962, she flew longer and further than Gargarian as her ship, *Vostok 6*, orbited the Earth forty-eight times in seventy hours.

4. Tereshkova also holds records for the highest altitude, 143.5 miles, and highest speed, 17,470 miles per hour, that any Earthwoman has attained. Viva Tereshkova!

5. Unfortunately, the United States did not put its first woman into space until twenty years later when Sally Ride joined the crew of a space shuttle.

6. While scientists conquer the space that we can see, artists explore the space that we can imagine.

7. The voyages of the *Starship Enterprise* may be nearly as famous as the voyages of *Columbia* or *Eagle*, and more people may remember the names Kirk and Spock than remember Alan Shepard and Yuri Gargarian.

8. George Lucas brought romance and high adventure to space tales with his series of *Star Wars* movies.

© 1986 by CBS College Publishing. All rights reserved.

9. *Star Wars* and *Battlestar Galactica* added alien menaces to the imaginative world of space, while *E.T.* transformed the usual space monsters into lovable friends.

10. Why reach for the stars?

11. Why, stars make up our dreams and our future.

Score _____

Identifying the Parts of Speech   **333**

Using Parts of Speech   Exercise 20–2

NAME _____ DATE _____

Fill in the blanks in the following paragraphs with appropriate words. Indicate the parts of speech of the words you use in the spaces provided at the right, using the abbreviations already given.

EXAMPLE: A [a]*long* time ago, in a [b]*galaxy* far, [c]*far* away. . . .   a. *adj* b. *n*
c. *adv*

   The fine sand blew hard over the [1] _____ of Tatooine. The wind   1. _____
seemed to come [2] ____ everywhere at once, typhooning in spots, swirl-   2. _____
ing [3] _ devilwinds here, hovering in stillness there, without [4] _____ or   3. _____
meaning.   4. _____
   A road wound across the [5] _____ plain. Its nature changed con-   5. _____
stantly, at one [6] _____ obscured by drifts of ochre sand, the [7] ___   6. _____
moment swept clean, or distorted by [8] _ heat of the shimmering air   7. _____
above it. [9] _ road more ephemeral than navigable, yet a [10] ____ to be   8. _____
followed, all the same. For [11] _ was the only way to reach the [12] _____   9. _____
of Jabba the Hutt.   10. _____
   Jabba was the [13] _____ gangster in the galaxy. He had his   11. _____
[14] _____ in smuggling, slave trading, murder; his minions scattered   12. _____
[15] _____ the stars. He both collected and invented [16] _____ , and his   13. _____
court was a den of [17] _____ decay. It was said by some   14. _____
that [18] ____ had chosen Tatooine as his place of [19] _____ because   15. _____
only in this arid crucible of [20] _ planet could he hope to keep   16. _____
his [21] ___ from rotting away altogether—here the parched [22] ___   17. _____
might bake his humor to a festering brine.   18. _____
   In any case [23] _ was a place few of kind spirit [24] ___ knew of, let   19. _____
alone approached. It was [25] _ place of evil.   20. _____
   21. _____
   22. _____
   23. _____
   24. _____
   25. _____

From *The Return of the Jedi*, the novel.

                                                                Score _____

© 1986 by CBS College Publishing. All rights reserved.

Writing Sentences Exercise 20-3

NAME _____ DATE _____

Generate sentences using the words listed below. Add and arrange words as needed.

    EXAMPLE: off, rocket, blast, Earth 6:22 P.M.
                  The rocket will blast off from Earth at 6:22 P.M.

1. planets, by, explored, people, intrepid

2. becomes, science, fact, fiction, often

3. kids, for, be, star, wish

4. space, by, inhabited, will, monsters

5. gravity, moon, leap, because, low

6. first, jumped, over, cow, moon

7. mission, worlds, explore, starship, new

8. man, where, go, before, no

9. space, lost, years, easy, be

10. possible, interplanetary, Mars, travel, will

11. Earth, colony, escape, lunar, overcrowding

12. moon, who, rights, own, mineral

13. dump, moon, waste, we, nuclear

14. heaven, hell, space, which, like

15. life, worlds, friendly, other, hostile

Score _____

Review 20

In the following paragraph label the part of speech of each underlined word: noun (n), pronoun (pro), verb (v), adjective (adj), adverb (adv), preposition (prep), conjunction (conj), and interjection (int.).

In popular imagination space is a glorious frontier for exploration and adventure. We think of endless worlds with exotic creations, where we can intrepidly meet new challenges and valiantly fight new battles. Lizard people, luminous creatures of energy and light, sapient animals, angels, and demons populate the space of our dreams. But, alas, the universe of science fact often seems mundane beside the universe of science fiction. As *Viking I* showed us, there are no canals and no little green Martians on the red planet. Our nearest neighbor in the solar system, Venus, hides 885-degree temperatures and barren deserts behind its apparently lush cloud cover instead of a watery, edenic paradise. With current methods of propulsion, it would take a spaceship 115,000 years to reach Proxima Centauri, our nearest solar neighbor.

Score _____

Check your answers against those in the back of the book. Deduct 2 points for each error in identification. A score of 80 percent or higher demonstrates that you have mastered the materials in this chapter.

The Writer's Casebook #20

Application: Narration—Telling It As It Happened, or Relating Events in an Essay

In this chapter, as you studied parts of speech, you also read examples and completed exercises that asked you to think about the exploration of space. Both as fact and as fantasy, space travel stimulates our imaginations.

In fact, stargazers have been writing stories about it for hundreds of years. Although writing fiction belongs properly to the study of creative writing, expository writing still has a place for narration. Its proper use is explored in this casebook application and practiced in the writing cases that follow.

To narrate means to relate a story or to tell what happened. In a paragraph, narration may be used to structure and develop a brief anecdote (a short, amusing incident that helps to fix the reader's interest) or to emphasize a point. Usually a narrative paragraph supports some larger purpose of the complete essay—for instance, to inform, to persuade, to explain. The scope and focus of the narration are determined by the purpose it serves.

In a narrative essay, however, the story itself controls structure. If the story has a surprise ending, such as winning the sweepstakes after losing your job or helping a neighbor, you will probably want to give your readers a "blow-by-blow" account, dramatizing the key events leading up to the surprise at the end. On the other hand, the story may be more memorable because of your reaction to the events rather than because of the events themselves; for example, you may have experienced the same first-day-of-school jitters as any other college student, but you were amused rather than nervous or frightened. Your perspective would probably result in a narrative built on summaries and commentary rather than on a cinematic dramatization of events.

Usually your narrative will include the following elements.

A beginning in which you set the scene—locate the event in time and space and introduce your actor or actors

A middle in which you follow the progress of the event chronologically, often including descriptive details and dialogue

An ending in which the event is completed and/or commented upon

Although the narrative essay relates actual rather than imagined events, you will use some of the techniques of the fiction writer. For example, you will choose a perspective, or viewpoint, from which to tell your story; often you will use the first-person or "I" viewpoint, the story as told by the participant or identified observer: "I saw her swing the ax. I screamed as it split my head." Sometimes you may prefer to remain anonymous and tell the story in the third person: "She swung the ax. The victim screamed as it split her head." You will also set a scene by using specific details to create a stage on which the action can take place and use dialogue to help your readers hear as well as see what is happening. (You probably won't remember the exact words said, but you can approximate.)

Cases for Writing: Reliving Events, Reporting the Facts, and Telling Tales

Case #1

Recall, as accurately as you can, the events of a space-shuttle launch or landing, a moonshot, or some other major scientific event that you have observed on television or in person. Retell some part of the action in a narrative essay focusing upon what you considered to be the essence of the event. Write in the first person, or assume the role of a reporter assigned to cover the event.

Case #2

You are an amateur astronomer. Studying the western sky at evening with your rooftop telescope, you have discovered a previously unrecorded comet. For several weeks you track its progress along the horizon; then with the help of your home computer, you chart its course. To your amazement, you find that it is on a collision course with Earth. Write a narrative about discovering the comet, about what happens when you attempt to warn the world, or about what happens when the collision takes place.

Nouns and Pronouns 21

Preview 21

Underline and correct problems with pronoun case and reference in the following paragraph.

Thirty years ago the usual image for a multicultural America was a melting pot. They came from many lands to lose theirselves, their accents, and their native customs in a well-stirred American broth. This allowed them to adopt instead a rather fractured version of English and a history that had begun a scant two hundred years before. Warren is a typical case. The child of German immigrants, he was raised between World Wars I and II when they frowned upon Germans. Therefore, Warren was encouraged by his parents to be thoroughly American. "Its a new country with new ways," they said. Him learning English, going to school, being like the others were important. The old ways, their family's history, the German language were forgotten. He grew up, therefore, with only the shallow new roots of their family's brief American experience to give meaning to the struggles of life. Warren died in Germany during the Battle of the Bulge, hating them as much as any other 100 percent GI Joe hated them.

Score _____

Check your answers against those in the back of the text. Deduct 5 points for each error in identifying and 5 points for each error in correcting a problem. A score of 80 percent or better indicates mastery of the materials in this chapter.

338

Case

Nouns, or name-words (see 20a), and pronouns, words that stand for nouns (see 20b), serve many different functions in a sentence: they may be subjects, direct objects, indirect objects, subjective complements, objective complements, objects of prepositions, verbal objects, or verbal subjects. They may rename or reidentify other nouns or pronouns, indicate possession, or show emphasis. To indicate these different functions, nouns and pronouns may change in form, or *case*.

English has three cases: *subjective, objective,* and *possessive*. Nouns and most pronouns change form only in the possessive case: *the anthropologist's hypothesis, anyone's guess*, for instance. But some pronouns change in all or more than one case.

Subjective	I	you	he, she, it	we	they	who, whoever
Objective	me	you	him, her, it	us	them	whom, whomever
Possessive	my	your	his, her, its	our	their	whose
	(mine)	(yours)	(hers)	(ours)	(theirs)	

The possessive case is discussed fully in Chapter 28. (Your instructor may ask you to study Chapters 21 and 28 together.) The discussion in this section focuses upon the pronouns that change for more than one case.

21a Using the Subjective Case

The subjective case can be used as the subject of a verb, the subject of a noun clause, a subjective complement, and an appositive to the subject (a word that renames or reidentifies it).

subject
Ansel Adams and she photographed the Anasazi ruins at Mesa Verde.

subject complement subject of noun clause
The student archaeologist wished it had not been he who broke the pre-Columbian pot.

appositive
Both scientists, the "dig" supervisor and I, agreed on the dating of the mole fetish.

NOTE: Common practice permits the less formal "It's me" or "It's him" in everyday speech or informal writing. However, in academic writing be careful to use the subjective case for complements of the verb *be*.

21b Using the Objective Case

The objective case is used for objects, subjects of an infinitive, and appositives to an object.

direct object
Our cultures shape us, subtly but forcefully.

indirect object
The Native Americans' folklore gives them a deep appreciation for living things.

object of preposition
Hispanic legends weave an enchanted world around me.

object of verbal infinitive
A sixty-foot totem pole stands beside the Haida chief's doorway to remind him of the tribe of his lineage.

subject of infinitive
The curandera told her to drink a tea made from herbs.

appositive
Many of us immigrants retain the customs of our native lands.

21c Using the Possessive Case

The possessive case is used before a noun or a gerund (a verbal noun) to show ownership.

possessive
Their favorite Greek dessert is baklava, made with layers of pastry, nuts, and honey.

modifies gerund
Her cooking brings back memories of Naples and my grandmother's spice-scented kitchen.

Some possessive pronouns—*his, hers, mine, ours, yours,* and *theirs*—may be used alone.

Yours is a rich heritage of music, art, and history.

The rare eagle Kachina doll is his.

21d Correcting Common Errors: Case

Use the subjective pronoun *I* for subjects and subjective complements and the objective pronoun *me* for all objects.

COMMON ERROR: Me and Monica fried squash blossoms for appetizers.

subject
REVISED: Monica and I fried squash blossoms for appetizers.
COMMON ERROR: Between you and I we have collected a dozen tales about Old Coyote.

object of preposition
REVISED: Between you and me we have collected a dozen tales about Old Coyote.

Distinguish carefully between possessive pronouns and look-alike or sound-alike contractions: *your/you're, its/it's, their/they're, whose/who's*. When in doubt about which form to use, test the sentence by inserting the complete pronoun and verb of the contraction. If the sentence makes sense, use the contraction. If the sentence does not make sense, use the possessive pronoun.

> During the Creation of the Earth, Eagle used its/it's feathers to make the trees and shrubbery.

TEST: During the Creation of the Earth, Eagle used it is feathers to make the trees and shrubbery. (The sentence does not make sense, so the correct form is the possessive pronoun.)

CORRECT: During the Creation of the Earth, Eagle used its feathers to make the trees and shrubbery.

> NOTE: *Theirselves, hisself,* and *its'* are nonstandard forms and should be avoided.

(1) Words left out

To clarify the function and, therefore, the case of a pronoun, add left-out but understood words, particularly after *than* or *as*.

COMMON ERROR: Beatian knows more parts of the Navajo Blessing Way ceremonies than me.

LEFT-OUT WORDS ADDED: Beatian knows more parts of the Navajo Blessing Way ceremonies than me (know).

REVISED: Beatian knows more parts of the Navajo Blessing Way ceremonies than I.

COMMON ERROR: Our uncle taught Beatian more than I.

LEFT-OUT WORDS ADDED: Our uncle taught Beatian more than (our uncle taught) I.

REVISED: Our uncle taught Beatian more than me.

(2) *Who* and *whom*

Use *who* and *whoever* for subjects and *whom* and *whomever* for objects. Within a clause the case of the pronoun depends upon its function in the clause, not the function of the clause in the sentence.

COMMON ERROR: Eskimos share their food with whomever is in need.
                                              subject of clause
REVISED: Eskimos share their food with whoever is in need.

COMMON ERROR: I wonder who Hispanic culture influences more, men or women.
                     object of verb influence
REVISED: I wonder whom Hispanic culture influences more, men or women.

To determine the case of *who* when it appears at the beginning of a question, use a personal pronoun to answer the question. The case of the pronoun answer will also be the case of *who* in the question.

COMMON ERROR: Whom did you say wrote *Beyond the Melting Pot?* (*They* wrote it. *subject*)
REVISED: Who did you say wrote *Beyond the Melting Pot?*

Pronoun Reference

Pronouns take the place of nouns—that is, they eliminate the need to repeat a noun over and over again. Compare the following sentences.

WITHOUT PRONOUNS: The Native Americans most people call Navajos call the Navajo Dinee, or "the People."
WITH PRONOUNS: The Native Americans we call Navajos called themselves Dinee, or "the People."

Using pronouns improves the style, or sound, of the sentence and also the pattern of emphasis.

21e Making Pronoun References Clear

Most pronouns take their meaning from an *antecedent*, a noun or noun phrase that "goes before" and names a person, place, thing, or idea. Therefore, the relationship between the pronoun and its antecedent must be clear.

> The rain converted itself abruptly into a flurry of popcorn snow. It rattled off Jim Chee's uniform hat, bounced down the collar of his uniform jacket, and made him shiver. (From Tony Hillerman, *People of Darkness*)

In the first sentence *itself* refers to *rain; it* at the beginning of the second sentence, to *snow;* and *his* and *him,* to *Jim Chee*. The order of the words in the sentence—pronouns following the nouns they refer back to—makes the meaning clear.

21f Revising Ambiguous or Vague Pronoun References

When a reader has trouble finding the antecedent of a pronoun, the sentence should be revised.

(1) Pronouns should not refer to more than one antecedent

Make sure the antecedents of problem pronouns like *this, that, which,* or *it* are clear.

AMBIGUOUS: The Navajo policeman took out his pen and completed the report. Then he put it in his pocket and it in his briefcase.
REVISED: The Navajo policeman took out his pen and completed the report. Then he put the pen in his pocket and the report in his briefcase.
AMBIGUOUS: Lieutenant Leaphorn radioed Sergeant Jim Chee that he had been called back to Window Rock and he would have to handle the Yazzi case alone. This did not exactly thrill him.

Nouns and Pronouns 343

REVISED: Lieutenant Leaphorn radioed Sergeant Jim Chee that Leaphorn had been called back to Window Rock and Chee would have to handle the Yazzi case alone. Working alone on the Yazzi case did not exactly thrill Chee.

(2) Pronouns should not refer to remote antecedents

AMBIGUOUS: In 1863 General Carleton determined to confine the Navajo to a reservation in eastern New Mexico. He sent Kit Carson to force the People to move from their ancestral lands. But the Dinee were a part of their lands. Black Mesa and Navajo Mountain were sacred to them. They would not leave the places where their ancestors had entered the Fourth World and the Beautiful Mountain, where they were to take shelter during the destruction of the Fourth World and do the Sun Way that would prepare the way for the Fifth World. To break their spirit, he burned their hogans, destroyed their secret caches of food, and cut down their ancient groves of peach trees.

REVISED FINAL SENTENCE: To break the People's spirit, Kit Carson burned their hogans, destroyed their secret caches of food, and cut down their ancient groves of peach trees.

(3) Pronouns should not refer to nonexistent antecedents

AMBIGUOUS: The Long Walk of 8,000 Navajo to Bosque Redondo is still remembered bitterly. They tell stories about the hardships of the three-hundred-mile death march.

REVISED: The Long Walk of 8,000 Navajo to Bosque Redondo is still remembered bitterly. Descendants of the survivors tell stories about the hardships of the three-hundred-mile death march.

NOTE: Indefinite pronouns like *everybody, somebody, nobody, many,* and *some* do not require antecedents. When other pronouns such as *I* and *you* have a clear meaning, they also may not need stated antecedents.

Nouns and Pronouns 345

Identifying Pronouns and Case   Exercise 21–1

NAME _____ DATE _____

Underline the pronouns in the following paragraphs and identify the case of each one.

object
EXAMPLE: Hispanics enjoy a cultural heritage that makes <u>them</u> special.

The fastest-growing minority group in the United States, Hispanics are proud of having maintained their culture and their language in the face of pressures for acculturation. "We see America as a mosaic of many peoples rather than a melting pot for one people," an Hispanic leader described his attitude. To him and to millions of Hispanic-Americans, cultural identity is a both/and proposition. They are both Hispanic and American. They speak both Spanish and English. They share the heritage of Independence Hall and Thanksgiving, and at the same time, they remember that Santa Fe was a thriving center for Hispanic arts and government before the Mayflower dropped its anchor in Plymouth Harbor.

Hispanics share history, customs, and usually religion, and theirs is a rich heritage. The conquistadores, the Penitentes, folk medicine administered by curanderas, Our Lady of Guadalupe set many Hispanics apart from Americans whose ancestors entered the New World via Ellis Island or came west in covered wagons and even separate Hispanic Catholics from other Roman Catholics. At the same time Hispanics have shared elements of their culture with the rest of the country. Who has not enjoyed a taco, a burrito, or a bowl of chili? To whom is a rodeo, a corral, or a lasso unfamiliar? Whose childhood memories do not include Zorro, pinatas, and "La Cucaracha"?

© 1986 by CBS College Publishing. All rights reserved.

Hispanic culture has given us luminarias, biscochitos, and posole at Christmas; Spanish-mission and adobe-hacienda architecture; mariachi bands; and literature of the land and its people, like Rudolfo Anaya's *Bless Me Ultima*.

Score _____

Nouns and Pronouns

Correcting Errors in Case Exercise 21-2

NAME _____ DATE _____

Find and correct any errors in pronoun case in the following sentences. Write C beside any correct sentence.

                    Whose
    EXAMPLE: Who's life-style includes kayaks and ice houses?

1. Eskimos, whom we know are related to the Mongolians, call themselves the "real people."

2. One hunting device, the frozen spring bait, fascinated the researchers and I.

3. The trap springs itself inside the animal's stomach when it's ice and fat coating melts.

4. They're warm, fur parkas also help combat subzero temperatures.

5. Eskimos have greater tolerance for cold than us.

6. The importance of snow in their lives is demonstrated by them giving specific names to different kinds of snow.

7. Whomever pictures all Eskimos as living in ice igloos is mistaken.

8. Caribou-hide tents and sod houses constitute their traditional shelters.

9. However, modern Eskimos, who we can find in Denmark, Canada, the Soviet Union, or Alaska, often live in wood-frame houses or even in high-rise apartment buildings.

10. The museum estimates that you're ivory carving of a bear is Dorset art from an Eskimo subculture that flourished six hundred years ago.

11. Us studying the Eskimo languages revealed a complex, extremely detailed word structure.

12. The northern lights, the quiet tundra, and the need for medical care lured Dr. Antonio Candello and I to the Eskimo village of Gambell.

© 1986 by CBS College Publishing. All rights reserved.

13. The people appreciated us coming, but many preferred they're shaman's spells and potions to our medicines and treatment.

14. The shaman had the advantage of providing spiritual as well as physical relief to the patients who he treated.

15. One winter an elderly man who's cancer was terminal died.

16. No one was more surprised than us to see our Eskimo helpers knocking a hole in the wall of the hospital.

17. The temperature had dropped to it's lowest in two weeks.

18. Still, the other patients in our small hospital ward encouraged the vandals: "Its not big enough. Make the hole bigger."

19. We soon learned that the workers' hole was preparation for them removing the dead body.

20. If the body were taken out through a hole, which was later closed up, the spirit of the dead man could not find its way back and harm whomever remained in the hospital.

21. Me and the doctor busied ourselves with piling blankets on the patients, while the local shaman chanted spells.

22. Us giving them orange juice and keeping them warm probably kept half the patients from dying of pneumonia.

23. However, the shaman received their thanks and we had to endure they're pitying us for not knowing more about the proper medicine of burials.

24. But we soon worked out a compromise with the shaman, who we then took everywhere on our rounds: he treated the spirits and we treated the bodies.

Score _____

Nouns and Pronouns

Sentence Combining with Pronouns   Exercise 21-3

NAME _____ DATE _____

Combine the pairs of sentences using the word or words in parentheses. Add, delete, or alter the sentences as necessary.

> EXAMPLE: The Amish are a religious people.
> They have developed a distinct culture. (who)
> *The Amish are a religious people who have developed a distinct culture.*

1. The Amish are named for their leader Jakob Ammann.
   He was a Swiss Mennonite bishop. (who)

2. Ammann's followers emigrated to North America because of persecutions.
   Their beliefs included "shunning" the excommunicated and baptizing adults. (whose)

3. Old Order Amish live in self-contained communities in Pennsylvania, Ohio, and Indiana.
   Tourists find the Old Order Amish picturesque. (whom)

4. Amish women must cover their heads with small lace caps in religious services.
   They wear long black dresses and shawls. (who)

5. Amish men also wear black.
   They do not cut their beards.
   Their position as head of the household is absolute. (and, whose)

6. The Old Order Amish live the back-to-the-earth dream of many modern intellectuals.
   Modern technology has bypassed the Old Order Amish.
   The intellectuals long for the simple life. (who, whom)

© 1986 by CBS College Publishing. All rights reserved.

7. The Old Order Amish do not use electricity to light or heat their homes.
   They do not use tractors to work their fields.
   Their life-style has changed little in a century. (neither/nor, whose)

8. But life is far from grim for these devout people.
   They seem untouched by the stresses of modern life.
   They seem untouched by the diseases of modern life. (who, and)

9. The Amish love Christmas.
   I love Christmas.
   They celebrate with a love feast of candlelight and cookies. (who, as much as)

10. The Amish are pacifists.
    Their religious teaching requires them to abstain from all government as well as any military service.
    They believe in Christlike love as a basis for all actions. (who, whose)

Score _____

Nouns and Pronouns   **351**

Finding Pronouns and Antecedents   Exercise 21-4

NAME _____ DATE _____

Underline pronouns in the following paragraphs. Circle the antecedents.

> EXAMPLE: The (Iroquois) were a major military force in the sixteenth and seventeenth centuries. <u>They</u> supported the British against the French in numerous battles.

When the European settlers moved west from the Atlantic Seaboard, they encountered a League of Nations: the Mohawk, Cayuga, Oneida, Seneca, and Onondaga. Called collectively the Iroquois, or "Real Adders," these nations lived in established settlements and organized their social and political life around complex, interlocking circles and clans and sechems. Individual families were headed by a matron who controlled property and directed work. While men hunted and cleared land for farming, women raised crops of maize, beans, and squash—the "Three Sisters" of Iroquois agriculture.

With the coming of the Europeans, the Iroquois began nearly two centuries of constant warfare. Sometimes they fought against the settlers, sometimes with them. Always the names of war chiefs like Cornplanter and Joseph Brant were feared and respected on the frontier.

                                                                    Score _____

© 1986 by CBS College Publishing. All rights reserved.

Revising for Pronoun Reference Exercise 21–5

NAME _____ DATE _____

In the following sentences, underline any pronoun reference that is ambiguous. Then revise the sentence in which the reference occurs.

> EXAMPLE: The Black Civil Rights movement of the 1950's laid the groundwork for many minorities to demand equal rights in the 1960's. <u>Their</u> centuries-long struggle for freedom continues today.
> *Blacks' centuries-long struggle for freedom continues today.*

1. The significant role played by blacks in exploring the New World is realized by few people today. They, including most notably the Southwest explorer Estevanico, contributed to the expeditions of Columbus, Balboa, Cortes, and many others.

2. Slave traders delivered at least 15 million African slaves to the New World, but millions more died during capture or on the slave ships. This lives in the memories of many American blacks.

3. In 1790 nearly 20 percent of the population of the United States was black, which declined to around 10 percent less than two centuries later.

4. Harriet Tubman was heroine of the Underground Railroad movement, which smuggled more than 70,000 slaves to freedom before the Civil War. Slaves were rescued from plantations, courtrooms, and even jail and guided to northern states or to Canada. She made 20 trips into the South and brought out more than 300 slaves.

5. During the Civil War Harriet Tubman served with the Union Army. They used her as a cook, nurse, scout, and spy.

6. On one of her underground trips Harriet Tubman rescued her parents. It was a crowning achievement and a personal triumph.

7. Another hero of the Underground Railroad was Frederick Douglass, who was also a friend of the famous abolitionist John Brown. Born a slave, he escaped in 1838 and became a leader of antislavery groups.

Nouns and Pronouns

8. Douglass's story, published in 1845, exposed the inhumanities of slavery and revealed the name of Douglass's former master. This nearly cost him his freedom.

9. British liberals bought Douglass's freedom. It allowed the leader to return to the United States and to begin publication of an abolitionist newspaper, the *North Star*.

10. Douglass advocated equality for women as well as for blacks. He participated in their first equal rights convention in 1848.

11. Modern black leaders have continued to struggle for justice in the face of personal danger. Founded in 1910, the NAACP emphasized legal rights and education but was viewed by some opponents as radical and dangerous. CORE, the Congress of Racial Equality, and SNCC, the Student Nonviolent Coordinating Committee, took the battle a step further with the nonviolent actions of sit-ins and Freedom Rides. During the course of the struggle, they have often been martyred.

12. The school desegregation decision in 1954 marked a turning point in the long battle for equal rights, which ironically led to even fiercer struggles.

13. In 1964 they murdered three volunteers who were helping register black voters in Mississippi.

14. Dr. Martin Luther King, Jr., civil rights leader and martyr, advocated nonviolence. Modeled on Gandhi's "creative disorder" tactics in India, the philosophy of nonviolence combined direct action with passive resistance to retaliation. Candidates for sit-ins or marches were trained to endure verbal and physical abuse. In spite of frequent arrests and threats, he held fast to the principle, "Love will be returned for hate."

15. King's famous *I Have a Dream* speech was given during the March-on-Washington demonstration in 1963. It became a rallying cry for equal-rights activists in every minority group.

16. King's nonviolent leadership was honored in 1964 when they gave him the Nobel Peace Prize. He was thirty-five years old, which made him the youngest person to receive the prize.

© 1986 by CBS College Publishing. All rights reserved.

17. King was assassinated by James Earl Ray on April 4, 1968. He was preparing to lead another march on Washington, the Poor People's Campaign.

18. With King gone, the Rev. Ralph Abernathy carried on, which resulted in a two-month encampment in the capital.

19. The black cultural structure in the United States has been described as essentially Euro-American. This is probably one result of their forced removal rather than voluntary immigration from Africa.

20. To rediscover his African heritage, author Alex Haley traced his ancestry in a book called *Roots*. That started a national movement to rediscover and appreciate our pre-American backgrounds.

Score _____

Nouns and Pronouns   **355**

Student Writer at Work   Exercise 21-6

NAME _____ DATE _____

Identify any problems with pronoun case or reference in the following student essay. Your instructor may ask you to revise the essay on a separate sheet of paper.

Once upon a time in the city of Zanzibar, there lived a man named Abdul and a man named Abdullah. He was a charming and helpful guy, so all the neighbors liked him. One day Abdul went to Abdullah and borrowed a cooking pot. He gave him one of his pots on the condition that he bring it back within a week.

After one week Abdul returned Abdullah's pot and with it another small pot. This amused Abdullah to see his bringing two pots instead of the one he had borrowed. But Abdullah was an honest man, so he said to Abdul, "My friend, all must remain on the up and up, between you and I, so I must tell you that your mistaken. I gave you only one pot."

Abdul then explained to him that when the pot was at his house, it gave birth to the small one. Abdullah had never heard of any pot giving birth, but he did not argue with Abdul for long. He accepted the two pots, and they're friendship was stronger than ever.

After a month or so Abdul went back to Abdullah's house to borrow another pot. He was so excited that he offered him the biggest pot in the house. Its the least I can do for a friend," said Abdullah, all the while thinking that this time the big pot would give birth to a big baby pot.

Abdul took the pot home. After two weeks he returned to Abdullah but instead of him carrying a big pot and a baby pot, he brought a sad story. "You're pot," he said, "that I borrowed, died a week ago." And he cried bitterly.

© 1986 by CBS College Publishing. All rights reserved.

Abdullah was furious. "There is no way a pot can die," he told him and demanded that he return his pot.

"All things that give birth die," said Abdul, "If the first pot can give birth to a baby pot, the second one can die."

A fight broke out, and they were never again the friendly neighbors they had once been.

Score _____

Review 21

Underline and correct problems with pronoun case and reference in the following paragraphs.

At the Summer Olympics in 1984 athletes from more than a hundred nations were greeted by Los Angeles residents who's ancestral roots were in those nations. Them greeting the visitors in costume, speaking the languages, and performing the native dances added to the atmosphere of good will. It also demonstrated a new feeling about cultures in this country. No longer a melting pot, the United States now prides itself on it's cultural diversity.

When Antonio Chavez went to school, they were not allowed to speak Spanish. Now his sons and daughters are taught by a bilingual teacher, which allows you to comment or ask questions in either Spanish or English. When Angela Liu immigrated from Taiwan in 1960, she discarded their native costumes for high heels and miniskirts. Now more than twenty years later, she again wears variations of the Manchu gown and the Japanese kimona to work at the university. Rose Pesata receives time off from her job to attend an important pow wow, and that enables her to be a more active participant in her own culture.

This new America has been called a salad bowl, a stew, a vast mosaic. Who should we thank for the transformation? Ourselves.

Score _____

Check your answers against those in the back of the book. Deduct 5 points for each error in identifying and 5 points for each error in correcting a problem. A score of 80 percent or better indicates mastery of the materials in this chapter.

The Writer's Casebook #21

Application: Putting Yourself in the Subject

The case of a noun or pronoun depends upon the relationship of the word to other words in the sentence. Putting yourself in a subject requires a similar analysis of relationships. Are you an actor or an object, a major or a subordinate factor, the possessor or the possessed? Is your involvement in the subject close or distant?

One difference between an essay that tells "about" a subject and an essay that shows the subject is the distance that writers maintain between themselves and their materials. One writer may hold the subject at arm's length, not willing to get involved or to examine the materials too closely, while another may dive in head first, trying to find a link between the topic and his or her own experiences. The following short paragraphs were written by the same student—the first before and the second after she had put herself in the subject.

A. Discrimination is still widespread in America today. Many members of minorities encounter it daily on the job or at school. It rears its ugly head in every aspect of American life.
B. "Aren't you smart for a little Mexican?" the old lady said with a pat on my hand. She had meant to be kind, but what she had sent me unconsciously was a very different message, one far from kind. She had shown me the closed sign of discrimination, and I knew for the first time that I was an outsider.

The first paragraph is abstract. It generalizes, talking around the subject without naming specifics. The second paragraph is specific and immediate. The reader grasps instantly that this writer knows her subject—that she is inside it and therefore has something worthwhile to say.

To put yourself in a subject, explore your relationship to it. Ask yourself a series of questions, perhaps following the journalistic formula (the five W's and How) discussed in Chapter 1:

What do I know about this subject? What have I heard? What have I seen? What have I felt?
Who do I know that might be involved? Am I involved? Are my friends? My family?
When did this or that happen? Does it happen all the time? How often?
Where would I go to see the subject? Is it nearby? Far away?
Why am I interested in this subject? Why is it important to me?
How does this subject concern me? How does it touch my life?

As you write the papers described in the following cases, pay special attention to the selection of noun and pronoun cases.

Cases for Writing: Writing About Culture

Case #1

What is your culture? Examine your background and life-style for the patterns of beliefs, customs, shared history, or shared viewpoints that make up your cultural perspective. Evaluate your relationship to the culture or cultures you are related to. Then write a paper exploring your identity as a member of a culture.

Case #2

Imagine that you have just arrived in the United States with your family. You have immigrated to enjoy the better life in the "Land of Opportunity," but you also have heard of some of the difficulties here. What advice will you give your son or daughter about becoming an American?

Verbs

22

Preview 22

Underline and correct any errors in verb form, tense, mood, or voice in the paragraph.

¹The history of politics in the United States has often been marked by violence. ²In 1801 a duel was precipitated between Aaron Burr and Alexander Hamilton by a campaign slur. ³Hamilton would be dead the next day, and Burr goes on to have led a military rebellion against the United States. ⁴An argument in the Senate in 1856 ended with Senator Charles Sumner laying on the floor. ⁵The Senator had been caned and permanently crippled by his opponent Rep. Preston Smith Brooks. ⁶Consider also the history of violence surrounding the United States Presidency. ⁷Andrew Jackson was the original shoot-from-the-hip President, as it was. ⁸Having won the Presidency in 1828, he had dealt with his enemies by horsewhipping, knifing, or shooting them. ⁹Four Presidents will be assassinated—Lincoln, Garfield, McKinley, and Kennedy—and a nearly successful attempt will be made to assassinate President Reagan by John Hinkley. ¹⁰In 1968 two political assassinations occur within the space of about two months—Martin Luther King, Jr., on April 4 and Robert F. Kennedy on June 6.

[11]But the United States is not alone. [12]Worldwide, political power is accompanied by political violence. [13]In this century alone more than fifty heads of state have been assassinated, their deaths often having precipitated war and further violence. [14]Probably many politicians wish they knew the risk before they had taken office. [15]But comes what may, there always seem to be those who are not only willing but also eager to take the risk.

Score _____

Check your answers against those in the back of the book. Deduct 2 points for errors in identifying problems, 3 points for errors in correcting. A score of 80 percent or higher demonstrates you understand the basic principles of verb usage.

Verb Forms

As you learned in Chapters 6 and 20, verbs are the part of a sentence that shows the action or condition of the subject. Verbs also change form to show the various tenses or times when those actions or conditions are taking place. For two tenses, simple present and simple past, a single word suffices: Time *marches* on. Time *marched* on. But for all other tenses and variations of tenses, two or more words are needed—a basic form of the verb and one or more auxiliary verbs.

Time will march on. (future action)
Time has marched on. (action begun in the past and completed in the present)
Time may be marching on. (possible continuing action)
Time did march on. (emphatic past action)
Time used to march on. (past action that no longer occurs)

Each verb has four basic forms, or *principal parts:* (1) a *base form,* which is also the present tense form of the verb; (2) a *present participle,* or *-ing* form, which is used with helping verbs to show ongoing action; (3) a *past* form, which is the simple past tense of the verb; and (4) a *past participle,* which is used with helping verbs to show various past tenses as well as passive voice.

Most verbs are *regular verbs.* They form their principal parts in the same way—by adding *-ing* to the base for the present participle and *-ed* or *-d* for the past tense and the past participle.

Base Form	Present Participle	Past	Past Participle
record	recording	recorded	recorded
learn	learning	learned	learned
happen	happening	happened	happened

Auxiliary verbs are added to the principal parts to show emphasis, condition, or time. Some common auxiliary verbs are *should, could, would, shall, will, may, might, can, do, did, used to,* and all the forms of the verbs *be* and *have.* (See Chapter 20 for a discussion of other functions of verb parts.)

22a Identifying the Principal Parts of Irregular Verbs

Irregular verbs also form the present participle by adding *-ing* to the base, but they form the past and past participle by changing the base, by changing vowels, by using endings other than *-ed* or *-d,* or in some cases by not changing at all.

Base Form	Present Participle	Past	Past Participle
sing	singing	sang	sung
buy	buying	bought	bought
burst	bursting	burst	burst

22b Using Correct Verb Forms

A dictionary, in addition to giving the spelling and pronunciation of a verb, will indicate its principal parts, either directly or indirectly. If only the base form is listed, the verb is regular and forms the past tense and past participle by adding *-ed* or *-d.* For an irregular verb, in addition to the base form, all the parts will be listed if they differ or only two parts if the past tense and past participle are the same.

write v. (past *wrote,* past participle *written,* present participle *writing*)
bet v. (past and past participle, *bet,* present participle *betting*)

Tense

Verb forms change to indicate changes in the tense or (roughly) time of the action or condition. There are three basic kinds of tenses in English: (1) *simple tenses,* which show the simple times of present, past, and future; (2) *perfect tenses,* which show "completed," rather than "flawless," actions; and (3) *progressive tenses,* which show ongoing actions.

Simple Tenses

Present	Historians see and record events.	*Progressive Tenses* Present progressive	Historians are seeing and are recording events.
Past	Historians saw and recorded events.	Past progressive	Historians were seeing and were recording events.
Future	Historians will see and will record events.	Future progressive	Historians will be seeing and will be recording events.

Perfect Tenses

Present perfect	Historians have seen and have recorded events	Present perfect progressive	Historians have been seeing and have been recording events.
Past perfect	Historians had seen and had recorded events.	Past perfect progressive	Historians had been seeing and had been recording events.
Future perfect	Historians will have seen and will have recorded events.	Future perfect progressive	Historians will have been seeing and will have been recording events.

22c Using the Simple Tenses

(1) The present tense

To form the present tense, use the base form of the verb *(write)* or, if the subject of the verb is a singular noun or third-person singular pronoun, add *-s* or *-es* to the base form (Virginia *writes*; she *writes*). Generally the present tense indicates actions happening now, but it may also indicate recurring action (she *writes* everyday); future action (she *writes* tomorrow); or an accepted belief, judgment, or fact (she *writes* brilliantly).

(2) The past tense

The past tense is one of the principal parts of a verb and is formed by adding *-d* or *-ed* to the verb base or by changing the base. The past tense indicates that something happened or recurred in the past but did not extend into the present: The Wright brothers *flew* for the first time. The Wright brothers *flew* every day for a week.

(3) The future tense

To form the future tense, add *shall* or *will* to the base form of the verb. The tense indicates the certainty or probability that some future action will take place: Justice *will prevail.* Our efforts for peace *will succeed.*

22d Using the Perfect Tenses

The perfect tenses show that one action or condition was or will be completed before another begins. To form the perfect tenses, follow the clue provided by their names—that is, for the present perfect tense, add the present tense of the helping verb *have* to the past participle of the verb (she *has finished*); for the past perfect tense, add the past tense of *have* to the past participle (she *had finished*); and for the future perfect tense, add the future tense of *have* to the past participle (she *will have finished*).

(1) Forming the present perfect tense

The present perfect tense shows actions that began in the past and extended into the present or that occurred at an unspecified past time: The reporters *have completed* their Watergate exposés, and the researchers *have begun* to trace the origins of Watergate morality in American politics.

(2) Forming the past perfect tense

The past perfect tense indicates a past action that was completed before another past action was begun—that is, the tense points "past the past"—or indicates an unfulfilled desire: Many Americans *had hoped* to avoid involvement in the Second World War. Those hopes *had flourished* before the Japanese bombed Pearl Harbor.

(3) Forming the future perfect tense

The future perfect tense shows that an action will be finished by a specific future time or that one future action will be finished before another future action begins: By 1998 the first manned spacecraft *will have landed* on Mars. By the time our children are grandparents, Earth *will have sent* an expedition to the nearest star.

22e Using the Progressive Tense Forms

The progressive tenses show ongoing action and are based upon the present participle, or *-ing* form of the verb. Again, the name of the tense holds a clue to its formation.

1. To form the *present progressive tense*, add the present form of the helping verb *be* to the present participle. Use the tense to show action continuing in the present: The conflicts in Central America *are escalating* steadily.

2. To form the *past progressive tense*, add the past tense of *be* to the present participle. Use the tense to indicate action that was ongoing or happened over a period of time in the past: Gunboat diplomacy *was making* the United States feared and hated.

3. To form the *future progressive tense*, add the future tense of *be* to the present participle. Use the tense to show future continuing action: Relations between China and the United States *will be warming* considerably during the next decade.

4. To form the *present perfect progressive tense*, add the present perfect form of *be* to the present participle. Use the tense for actions continuing from the past into the present: The budget deficit *has been skyrocketing* in recent years.

5. To form the *past perfect progressive tense*, add the past perfect form of *be* to the present participle. Use the tense to show a past action that continued until another past action began: Until he was exposed, President Nixon *had been enjoying* unprecedented popularity.

6. To form the *future perfect progressive tense*, add the future perfect form of *be* to the present participle. Use this tense for actions that will go on until a future time: By 1995 the Earth *will have been struggling* to survive the Nuclear Age for fifty years.

22f Using the Correct Sequence of Tenses

When there is more than one verb in a sentence, the tenses will change or stay the same, depending upon meaning and the relationship of the verbs. When verbs occur at the same time, they should be in the same tense.

past *past* *past*
When Carry Nation stood up, women cheered, but saloon keepers jeered.

The tense of verbs and verbals in independent clauses depends upon meaning.

past *future/passive*
Ms. Nation was a militant suffragette, but she will be remembered most for her
present
hatcheting of bars.

The tense of verbs and verbals in *subordinate (dependent) clauses* depends upon their relationship to the verb or verbs in the independent clause.

1. When the verbs in the independent clause show any tense except past or past perfect, meaning determines the tense of verbs in the subordinate clause.

present *past*
I understand that Ms. Nation's first husband was an alcoholic.
present *past*
She is a legend in temperate Kansas where in 1901, she wrecked her first saloon.

2. When the independent-clause verbs show past tense, the subordinate-clause verb will show past or past perfect tense.

past *past*
Carry Nation sold souvenir hatchets, which commemorated her "hatchetations,"
past
as she called her destruction of bar fixtures and stocks of liquor.

When the independent-clause verbs show past perfect tense, the subordinate-clause verb will usually show past.

> *past perfect*
> She <u>had</u> also <u>campaigned</u> against smoking and wearing tight corsets long before
> *past*
> doctors <u>pronounced</u> these practices health hazards.

3. When an infinitive shows an action that happens at the same time as the main verb, use the *present* form: *to* plus the base form of the verb.

> Ms. Nation *spoke* between acts at carnivals <u>to pay</u> her fines and <u>to build</u> a shelter for alcoholics' battered wives. (The speaking, paying, and building are happening at the same time.)

When an infinitive shows an action that happened earlier than the main verb or verbs, use the *perfect* form: *to have* plus the past participle.

> When prohibition <u>was passed</u> in 1920 Carrie Nation <u>was said</u> <u>to have been</u> a primary cause. (The cause came before the passing and the saying.)

4. Use the *present participle*—the *-ing* form of the verb—to show action happening at the same time as the verb (regardless of its tense). Use either the present or the present participle plus the past participle (the present perfect form) to show action happening before the verb.

> Firmly <u>gripping</u> her hatchet, Carry Nation <u>marched</u> into the saloon. <u>Having wrecked</u> the furniture, she <u>turned</u> her attention to the stock of liquor behind the bar.

Mood

Verbs show the attitude of the writer by their *mood*. When the writer is stating or questioning facts, the *indicative mood* is used: *The mass ascension of hot air balloons <u>began</u> at 7:45 A.M. When <u>did</u> the mass ascension of hot air balloons begin?* When the writer gives commands or makes direct requests, the *imperative mood* is used: *<u>Inflate</u> the balloons. Please <u>launch</u> your balloon.* When the writer expresses a wish or doubt or states something contrary to fact, the *subjunctive mood* is used: *If the balloon <u>were</u> not lighter than air, it would not rise. The rider insisted that the pilot <u>land</u>.*

22g   Using the Indicative Mood

The mood of most verbs in college writing is *indicative* because college writing usually deals with objective information—statements and questions about facts. No change in the verb form is needed to show the indicative mood, but a form of the helping verb *do* may be added for emphasis or to form a question.

> Hot air balloons fly at the mercy of the winds.
> Hot air balloons do fly at heights of 1,000 to 8,000 feet.
> Do hot air balloons fly at speeds greater than 12 mph?

22h Using the Imperative Mood

Instructions and process analysis as well as commands and requests are usually written with the verbs in the *imperative mood*. The mood is shown by using the base form of the verb and eliminating the subject. When the writer is included in the command or instruction, *let us* or the contraction *let's* precedes the verb.

> To make a hot air balloon, begin with a nylon air bag or envelope.
> Let's spend $40,000 on a specially designed balloon.

22i Using the Subjunctive Mood

The *subjunctive mood* has three different forms. The *present subjunctive* uses the base form of the verb, regardless of the subject: *My ballooning instructor recommended that I be a cross-country balloonist.* The *past subjunctive* has the same form as the past tense of the verb except that *be* becomes *were*, regardless of the number or person of the subject: *I wish I were as fearless as balloonist Maxie Anderson.* The *past perfect subjunctive* has the same form as the past perfect tense: *I wish I had known about the expense of maintaining a balloon before I bought one.*

Because subjunctive verbs often sound awkward, the indicative mood has almost replaced the subjunctive. However, there are three common situations in which writers still use the subjunctive mood.

1. In *that* clauses after words such as *ask, suggest, require, recommend,* and *demand*:

   > The frightened rider demanded that the balloon descend.

2. In contrary-to-fact clauses beginning with *if* or expressing a wish:

   > If I were a bird, I could sail through the sky every day.

3. In certain idiomatic expressions—that is, expressions peculiar to English and independent of any rules of grammar or logic:

   > If need be, we will set sail, as it were.
   > Come what may, they will attempt the round-the-world flight, and far be it from me to criticize world-famous balloonists.

Voice

Voice indicates the relationship of a verb to its subject. When the verb is in the *active voice*, the subject acts upon something. When the verb is in the *passive voice*, the subject is acted upon.

	actor	action	receiver of action
ACTIVE:	Navratilova	leads	the pack.

	receiver of the action	action	actor
PASSIVE:	The pack	is led	by Navratilova.

22j   Using the Passive Voice

Usually the most effective pattern for an English sentence is active: subject/actor + verb/action + direct object/receiver of action. This pattern is more emphatic, more economical, and often less awkward.

ACTIVE: Dr. J. left Larry Bird in his tracks, slammed the ball through the hoop, and shattered the backboard.
PASSIVE: Larry Bird was left in his tracks, the ball was slammed through the hoop, and the backboard was shattered by Dr. J.

The passive construction is longer and less emphatic than the active because the auxiliaries both add words and dilute action. In addition, readers must wait until the end of the sentence to discover what they needed to know first to be able to visualize the action—who is acting.

However, there are times when the passive voice is appropriate: (1) when we do not know or care who is acting, (2) when we want to emphasize the receiver of the action, or (3) when we need to place the actor at the end of a clause where we can easily add a modifier.

1. Wimbledon quarterfinalist Kathy Jordan was honored at the banquet.
2. Jerry Baker was traded to the Minnesota Vikings.
3. The longest jump of the Calaveras County Jumping Frog Jubilee was made by Ex Lax, who jumped 17 feet, 6¾ inches for its owner Bill Moniz.

22k   Changing from Passive to Active Voice

Change a sentence from passive to active by reversing the order of the actor and the receiver of the action, changing the verb to eliminate the *be* auxiliary, and deleting *by*, which often follows the passive verb. You may need to supply an actor if none is named in the passive construction.

Verbs 369

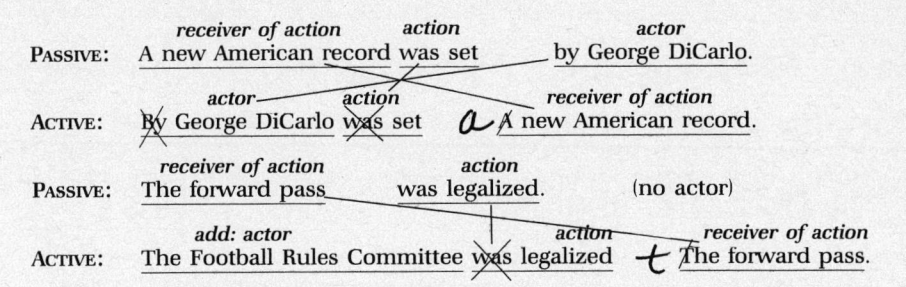

	receiver of action	*action*	*actor*
PASSIVE:	A new American record	was set	by George DiCarlo.

	actor	*action*	*receiver of action*
ACTIVE:	~~By~~ George DiCarlo	~~was~~ set	*a* ~~A~~ new American record.

	receiver of action	*action*	
PASSIVE:	The forward pass	was legalized.	(no actor)

	add: actor	*action*	*receiver of action*
ACTIVE:	The Football Rules Committee	~~was~~ legalized	*t* ~~T~~he forward pass.

22l Changing from Active to Passive Voice

Change a sentence from active to passive by making the receiver of the action the subject, by changing the verb to include the *be* auxiliary, and by putting the actor in a prepositional phrase, usually beginning with *by*, at the end of the sentence.

	actor	*action*	*receiver of action*
ACTIVE:	Patty Sheehan	won	a half-million dollar bonus.

	receiver of action	*action*	*actor*
PASSIVE:	*A* ~~a~~ half-million dollar bonus	(was) won	(by) Patty Sheehan.

Verbs

Making an Irregular Verb Chart   Exercise 22–1

NAME _____ DATE _____

Frequently as you edit and revise your papers, you will want to check on one of the principal parts of an irregular verb. To get a head start, you can make a verb chart. For each of the verbs for which a base form is listed, first write down the principal parts from memory. Then check your answers by using a dictionary. If there are alternatives, be sure to list them.

EXAMPLE:	Base Form	Present Participle	Past	Past Participle
	creep	*creeping*	*crept*	*crept*

Base Form	Present Participle	Past	Past Participle
1. awake			
2. be			
3. begin			
4. bite			
5. break			
6. bring			
7. burn			
8. catch			
9. choose			
10. come			
11. dive			
12. do			
13. drink			
14. eat			
15. feed			
16. find			
17. fly			
18. forget			
19. freeze			
20. give			
21. go			
22. grow			
23. have			
24. hear			
25. lay			
26. lie			
27. prove			
28. raise			
29. ride			
30. rise			

© 1986 by CBS College Publishing. All rights reserved.

Base Form	Present Participle	Past	Past Participle
31. run			
32. see			
33. set			
34. shake			
35. shrink			
36. sit			
37. speak			
38. spring			
39. stand			
40. strike			
41. swear			
42. take			
43. teach			
44. think			
45. throw			
46. wake			
47. wear			
48. win			
49. wind			
50. wring			

Score _____

Choosing the Right Verb Exercise 22-2

NAME _____ DATE _____

Fill in the blanks in the following sentences with the appropriate form of the verb in parentheses.

EXAMPLE: (repeat) Contrary to popular opinion, history does not *repeat* itself.

1. (repeat) Contrary to popular opinion, history has not _____ itself.
2. (repeat) Contrary to popular opinion, history is not _____ itself.
3. (teach) However, history has _____ us valuable lessons for the future.
4. (bend) Herodotus, an early Greek historian, occasionally _____ the factual records to include amusing tales.
5. (tell) He _____ about Egyptian sheep with huge tails, rolling along behind them on wheels.
6. (handicap) Early historians were _____ by the lack of a common time scale.
7. (use) Some _____ to measure history by Olympiads—the four-year intervals between Olympic Games.
8. (set) Others had _____ the beginning of history at the founding of Rome in 753 B.C.
9. (keep) The writers' lack of a clear idea of geography also _____ ancient records from being exact.
10. (triumph, fall, know) The location of some major battles in which kingdoms _____ or _____ is still not _____ .
11. (see, influence) St. Augustine, who _____ human events as God's way of revealing His will, has _____ generations with the *City of God*.
12. (be) Medieval histories _____ often chronological tables of events from the Creation to the present.
13. (find) Researchers have _____ elements of folklore and oral epics in the *Anglo-Saxon Chronicle*.
14. (become, chose, fit) Documentation had _____ important by the fifteenth century, but writers often _____ information according to whether it _____ their special biases.
15. (deal) In his popular *Book of Martyrs*, John Foxe _____ with acts of heroism and faith.
16. (give) Little space is _____ to history in the political writings of the eighteenth-century *philosophes*.
17. (seek) They _____ to promote the idea of all intellectual, cultural, and artistic history's progressing toward the Enlightenment of their own time.
18. (lay) In the nineteenth century Leopold Von Ranke, called the father of modern historical method, _____ the foundations of current study.
19. (bring) He _____ the use of original historical documents rather than biased earlier histories to its present stage of importance.
20. (lie) In terms of method and emphasis, modern historical study, since Ranke, has _____ somewhere between the social sciences and the humanities.

Score _____

© 1986 by CBS College Publishing. All rights reserved.

Forming Tenses Exercise 22-3

NAME _____ DATE _____

Rewrite the sentences, changing the verbs to each of the tenses listed. (See example on p. 363.)

1. present   *Kingdoms <u>crumble</u>, but ideas <u>live</u> on.*
    past
    future
    present perfect
    past perfect
    future perfect

    present progressive
    past progressive
    future progressive

    present perfect progressive

    past perfect progressive

    future perfect progressive

2. present   *Time <u>flies</u>, and progress <u>creeps</u>.*
    past
    future
    present perfect
    past perfect
    future perfect
    present progressive
    past progressive
    future progressive
    present perfect progressive

    past perfect progressive

    future perfect progressive

Score _____

Verbs **375**

Using the Tenses Exercise 22–4

NAME _____ DATE _____

Write a sentence for each verb listed, using the verb tense in parentheses. Then rewrite the sentence, changing the verb to a different tense. Write the tense of the second sentence in the space provided.

    EXAMPLE: support (past perfect progressive)

        a. *Until the death of their leader Tecumseh in 1813, the confederation of northern tribes had been supporting the British.*

        b. *(past perfect)*
          Until the death of their leader Tecumseh in 1813, the confederation of northern tribes had supported the British.

1. win (present perfect)
   a.
   b.

2. steal (past progressive)
   a.
   b.

3. agree (present progressive)
   a.
   b.

4. know (future perfect)
   a.
   b.

5. prove (present perfect progressive)
   a.
   b.

                                Score _____

© 1986 by CBS College Publishing. All rights reserved.

Sequencing Tenses   Exercise 22–5

NAME _____ DATE _____

Choose the appropriate form of the verbs in parentheses.

   EXAMPLE: The vote for women _had been_ (had been, has been) a major women's rights issue until the Nineteenth Amendment _was_ (had been, was) ratified in 1920.

1. In most countries voting rights ____ (are coming, come) first, then women ____ (have won, win) the right to hold political offices, and finally they ____ (gained, gain) access to those offices through _____ (having won, winning) elections.

2. Because Susan B. Anthony ____ (had been, was) a leader in the women's suffrage movement, the Nineteenth Amendment __ (was, is) known as the Anthony Amendment.

3. After the Revolution the first state to give women the right to vote _____ (had been, was) New Jersey, but the right ____ (had been, was) withdrawn in 1807.

4. _____ (Having included, Including) women's suffrage in their constitution, Wyoming _____ (becomes, became) the first state to grant women full voting rights.

5. Thailand _____ (grants, granted) women the right _____ (to vote, to have voted) in 1932, _____ (becoming, having become) the first country in Asia with a universal suffrage law.

6. After World War II the United Nations _____ (was encouraging, encouraged) equal rights when the General Assembly unanimously _____ (had supported, supported) a resolution that ____ (calls, called) for universal suffrage.

7. The Universal Declaration of Human Rights, _____ (having been adopted, adopted) in 1948, ____ (called, calls) for "universal and equal suffrage."

8. Swiss women _____ (were not, had not been, were not being) enfranchised for federal elections until 1971.

9. But in the Middle East advances _____ (have come, came) most slowly.

10. Iran, which ____ (had given, gave) women limited voting rights in 1949 and 1963, _____ (has withdrawn, withdrew) many privileges since the Khomeini revolution.

11. The United States ____ (lags, lagged) behind Great Britain in _____ (giving, having given) women full access to public office.

12. But with Geraldine Ferraro's vice presidential candidacy in 1984, the United States ____ (takes, took) another step toward electing a woman President.

Score _____

Identifying Mood   Exercise 22-6

NAME _____ DATE _____

Underline the verbs in the following sentences. Then in the space at the end of the sentence, indicate whether the verbs are in the indicative (IN), imperative (IM), or subjunctive (SUB) mood.

    EXAMPLE: Let's play ball.   *IM*

1. Juniel Farthing's college coach recommended that she set her sights on a career in professional basketball. ___ , ___
2. The once all-male world of playing fields and locker rooms has been desexed and desegregated. ___ , ___
3. No longer do women find themselves relegated exclusively to the cheering section; they are on the field as athletes and in the locker rooms as sports reporters. ___ , ___
4. She took the hurdle as if it were a molehill. ___ , ___
5. Lean into the turn as though you were holding up a wall. ___ , ___
6. Sports and exercise have played an important role in education since the ancient Greeks required six- and seven-year-old boys and girls to begin a life-long program of physical conditioning. ___ , ___
7. Develop a healthy body and have a suitable vessel for a healthy mind. ___ , ___
8. The Persian Empire required that each boy be delivered to the state for physical training at age six. ___ , ___
9. She wished that she were as strong as the Spartan girls. ___ , ___
10. Gymnastics became a key part of physical education in the nineteenth century when Harvard, Amherst, and Yale built gymnasiums on their campuses. ___ , ___

                                                    Score _____

© 1986 by CBS College Publishing. All rights reserved.

Writing Active and Passive Verbs Exercise 22-7

NAME _____ DATE _____

Fill in the blanks in the following short paragraphs with the appropriate form of the verb in parentheses. Identify the verbs as active (A) or passive (P) in the space provided at the right.

EXAMPLE: Ski masks *are worn* (wear) by cross-country skiers to protect the face from frostbite. ___P___

Golf [1] _____ (originate) by the Scots, who [2] _____ (play) the game with religious fervor. This devotion [3] _____ (discourage) somewhat by King James II. He [4] _____ (ask) Parliament to deemphasize the game so that more time [5] _____ _____ (devote) to archery, an important sport for national defense.

1. _____
2. _____
3. _____
4. _____
5. _____

Football [6] _____ (often compare) to the gladiator sports of ancient Rome. The frequent deaths and injuries [7] _____ (encourage) the comparison but no more so than the behavior of the fans. Favorite teams [8] _____ (idolize); stars [9] _____ (worship). Success in the arena [10] _____ (bring) multi-million-dollar playing contracts and equally lucrative advertising endorsements. But defeat [11] _____ (turn) the crowd savage, eager for blood and heads.

6. _____
7. _____
8. _____
9. _____
10. _____
11. _____

Soon boxing [12] _____ (may outlaw) in Great Britain, where the ancient sport [13] _____ (revive) in 1719. The risks of brain damage and other injuries [14] _____ (cite) by the British Medical Association as reasons for the campaign to ban the sport. Moreover, eleven professional boxers [15] _____ (kill) in the ring since 1949.

12. _____
13. _____
14. _____
15. _____

Robert Coover's novel *Baseball* [16] _____ (parody) baseball history and America's tendency to deify sports heroes. A board game of baseball [17] _____ (invent) by the main character, J. Henry Waugh. Played with three dice and complex charts, the game [18] _____ (obsess) its creator, whose life [19] _____ (absorb) by the make-believe players' lives. His grasp on reality [20] _____ (sever) by Coover's special version of baseball fanaticism.

16. _____
17. _____
18. _____
19. _____
20. _____

Verbs **379**

Tennis [21] _____ (introduce) at a garden party in Wales in 1873. Its inventor, Walter C. Wingfield, [22] _____ (patent) the game in 1874, calling it Sphairistiké. Matches [23] _____ (play) on an hourglass-shaped court with a rubber ball and an oval racket. A seven-foot net [24] _____ (divide) the court. The first Wimbledon tournament [25] _____ (held) just four years after the game's introduction.

21. _____
22. _____
23. _____
24. _____
25. _____

Score _____

© 1986 by CBS College Publishing. All rights reserved.

Sentence Combining Exercise 22–8

NAME _____ DATE _____

Combine the following sentence pairs into single sentences. Avoid unwarranted shifts in voice.

> EXAMPLE: The Olympics were begun in Greece more than 2,700 years ago as part of a religious festival honoring Zeus. The Greeks held the Games regularly for more than 1,000 years.
>
> *The Greeks began the Olympics more than 2,700 years ago as part of a religious festival honoring Zeus, and they held the Games regularly for more than 1,000 years.*

1. A single 200-yard race was run by the original Olympic contestants.
   Today contestants compete in twenty-one sports in the Summer Olympics and six sports in the Winter Olympics.

2. The ancient Greeks halted wars between feuding city-states to hold the Olympic Games.
   Even time was measured in terms of the four-year intervals, called Olympiads, between the Games.

3. In modern times the Games have been halted instead of the wars, with no Olympics held in 1916, 1940, and 1944.
   Most recently, boycotts of the Moscow and Los Angeles Olympics have been caused by political concerns of the rival United States and Soviet Union.

4. In 1936 Adolf Hitler usurped the Berlin Games to stage a propaganda fete for his Nazi ideology.
   Aryan supremacy would have been proven, he believed, by German victories.

5. However, the Games were dominated by a black athlete from the United States, Jesse Owens.
   Records were set or equaled by Owens in the 100-meter dash, the 200 meters, the 400-meter relay, and the broad jump.

Verbs

6. Six women were included in summer competition for the first time in the 1900 Paris Games.
   Thirteen women competed in the first Winter Games in 1924.

7. Olympic rules require men to compete with men and women with women in most events.
   Competition between men and women is allowed only in equestrian sports, yachting, and shooting.

8. In the 1912 Games Native American Jim Thorpe easily won the pentathlon and decathlon.
   He is considered by many to be the greatest athlete of all time.

9. Thorpe was stripped of his medals in 1913.
   It was learned that he had accepted $2 a game for playing baseball prior to the Olympics, thereby losing his amateur status.

10. Thorpe's medals were posthumously restored by the International Olympic Committee in 1982.
    His children had campaigned twenty-nine years for the restoration.

Score _____

© 1986 by CBS_College Publishing. All rights reserved.

Revising for Ineffective Voice Exercise 22-9

NAME _____ DATE _____

Rewrite the following paragraphs in the spaces provided, revising for ineffective use of active or passive voice. The sentences have been numbered for easy reference. Revisions will vary.

A. ¹The language of the sports world exudes action and catastrophe. ²A game is never simply lost by the losers. ³They are blitzed, steamrollered, or throttled by the winners. ⁴Balls are not hit by players. ⁵They are smashed, belted, ripped, slammed, clouted, clashed, and hammered. ⁶Adding to the picture of general mayhem, sportswriters borrow from the vocabularies of war correspondents and mystery writers. ⁷In a baseball game, outfielders are hit by an artillery barrage. ⁸In golf the favorite murders the field, digs graves, and leaves bodies in the basement. ⁹A high point in hysteria was reached by one analyst who hailed a Supreme Court ruling on college football as "the beginning of the end of life on Earth as we know it."

B. ¹Although ample coverage is given by the media to the major sports, little serious attention is paid to the intriguing world of minor (or minuscule) sports. ²While football, basketball, horse racing, and baseball are focused upon by the majority of fans, other equally devoted enthusiasts train their frogs to leap, their armadillos to race, and themselves to balance on a log, floating in a mill pond, and to roll the log with their feet. ³Champions are given birth by these unheralded sporting events and reputations are made or broken.

C. [1]Boomerang throwing, for example, boasts world championship matches, and a distance record of 370 feet is held by New Yorker Al Gerhards. [2]Ten International Championships for log rolling have been won by Jubiel Wickheim, who has rolled for 2 hours and 40 minutes before falling off. [3]Frog-jumping meets are held annually at the Calaveras County Frog Jubilee in Angels Camp, California. [4]And the skies of Albuquerque, New Mexico, are filled with hot air balloons each October as balloonists race slowly across the city, competing on race courses that no one but they can see.

Score _____

Review 22

Underline and correct any errors in verb form, tense, mood, or voice in the paragraph.

¹The place of sports in higher education is often being questioned. ²Ever since football was described by an incredulous college president as "agitating a bag of wind," the lines of battle, as it was, have been drawn. ³Sports enthusiasts will cite the benefits of athletic programs to the students. ⁴Play football to build character, we were told. ⁵Team spirit, sportsmanship, and competitiveness are all supposed to be developed by sports, and school pride and spirit are boosted by successful teams. ⁶The alumni's demands that their schools' teams are winners and the schools' need for the alumni's money are also advanced as reasons for having supported college athletics. ⁷Opponents, on the other hand, lamented the waste in human financial resources. ⁸Even a modest program might have costed hundreds of thousands of dollars, and a major program would of cost millions. ⁹Many are being disturbed by the distortion of values by athletics and athletics boosters. ¹⁰The emphasis upon winning games rather than having passed tests is raised to a level of mania by some coaches, who would have placed football first in the player's college experience. ¹¹The exploitation of young people, many of whom will never have graduated because of their devotion to sports rather than to studies is also protested by opponents. ¹²As the NCAA scrambles to enforce rules and penalize violators, the question is remaining. Do sports have a place in higher education?

Score _____

Check your answers against those in the back of the book. Deduct 2 points for errors in identifying problems, 3 points for errors in correcting them. A score of 80 percent or higher demonstrates mastery.

The Writer's Casebook #22

Application: Choosing Tenses in Essay Writing

The best rule to follow in writing essays as in writing individual sentences is to choose verb tense according to meaning. However, several special cases are worth remembering.

A. When you are writing about the composition of literature or about events that take place in literature, you should write in the present tense—even if the author lived a hundred years ago and wrote in the past tense.

> In *Death Comes for the Archbishop* Willa Cather writes about Archbishop Lamy, who struggles with the powerful, charismatic Father Martinez to establish a more orthodox Catholicism in the Southwest.

B. When you write about general truths or beliefs, you should write in the present tense to show that truths or beliefs are timeless.

> Members of the Society for Creative Anachronism claim to believe that the Earth is flat and that space journeys are elaborate hoaxes. However, the Earth is actually pear-shaped, and space exploration is a reality.

C. When you write about experiences, you have a choice of main tenses. You may write primarily in the present or primarily in the past, but whichever tense you choose, you must use it consistently throughout your paper. Changing from one tense to another confuses the reader.

CONFUSED: I walked into the State Capitol Building with my portfolio under my arm and a tape recorder in my pocket. I was climbing the stairs of the rotunda, going toward the pressroom, when I see the would-be assassin. He is wearing a loose-fitting suit and shielding his weapon, which looks like sticks of dynamite, under his jacket.

REVISED (past tense): I walked into the State Capitol Building with my portfolio under my arm and a tape recorder in my pocket. I was climbing the stairs of the rotunda, going toward the pressroom, when I saw the would-be assassin. He was wearing a loose-fitting suit and shielding his weapon, which looked like sticks of dynamite, under his jacket.

REVISED (present tense): I walk into the State Capitol Building with my portfolio under my arm and a tape recorder in my pocket. I am climbing the stairs of the rotunda, going toward the pressroom, when I see the would-be assassin. He is wearing a loose-fitting suit and shielding his weapon, which looks like sticks of dynamite, under his jacket.

Cases for Writing: Using Different Styles and Tenses

Case #1

Exercise your stylistic muscles. Choose an action that you know how to perform well, such as sharpening a pencil, pumping gas into your car, or washing windows. Then write about the action in three different styles for three different purposes. First, write in the imperative mood to instruct a reader to perform the task. Second, write a description of yourself performing the action; use the active voice and report each step. Third, report in the passive, formal style on the completed project; explain what was done and how it was done, but pay little or no attention to who did it.

Case #2

Investigate the beliefs of some group that interests you, such as the Sierra Club, the YMCA, or NOW. Then write a paper to explain those beliefs, being careful to choose the appropriate verb, tense, mood, and voice.

Agreement 23

Preview 23

Find and correct any errors in agreement in the following sentences.

1. Stress, including the pressures, anxieties, pollution, and pace of modern life, pose a major problem for health.

2. How well our bodies survive the demands we make on them depend upon how we fuel them—nutrition.

3. A fight or shock drain the system of Vitamin C.

4. There is more indoor work and lack of sunshine taking its toll on the body.

5. Probably the majority in our country is deficient in one or more essential daily food requirements.

6. Every one of those who are reading this sentence need to assess their own nutritional needs.

7. The amount of vitamins and minerals you need vary with the kind of life we lead.

Score _____

Check your answers against those in the back of the book. Deduct 10 points for each error in correction. A score of 80 percent or higher shows you understand the principles of agreement.

When subjects and verbs or pronouns and the words they refer back to correspond in number, case, gender, or person, we say that they "agree." Agreement underscores the relationships among elements in a sentence. Observing the conventions of agreement is necessary for coherence—the logical linking of ideas—and sense—the effective communication of meaning to a reader.

CONFUSED: Each of us—busy students, mothers, fathers, teachers, workers—often forget an important fact: they are what we eat. (The subject *each* is singular, but the verb *forget* is plural. The sentence begins with the indefinite, singular pronoun *each*, then switches to third person plural *they*, then switches again to first person plural *we*.)

REVISED: All of us—busy students, mothers, fathers, teachers, workers—often forget an important fact: we are what we eat. (The number of the first subject has been changed to plural to match the verb and to avoid an awkward construction. Pronouns in the second sentence have been matched.)

23a Making Subjects and Verbs Agree

Both subjects and verbs show the characteristic of *number*—that is, they have different forms for singular and plural. Therefore, to be consistent, we should use singular subjects with singular verbs and plural subjects with plural verbs.

> Junk food produces the "junk" of fat and cellulite deposits.
> Nutritious foods build strong bones and muscles.

NOTE: Although the *-s* or *-es* ending of a subject denotes the plural number (vitamin*s*, pastri*es*), the *-s* or *-es* ending of a verb denotes the singular number (eat*s*, munch*es*, i*s*, ha*s*).

The form of present tense verbs depends upon the *person* as well as the number of the subject. If the subject is the writer (first-person singular *I*) or the writers (first-person plural *we*), the verb will take the base form without an *-s* or *-es* ending.

> I serve yogurt at all meals, and we give our children yogurt popsicles.

Similarly, if the subject is someone addressed directly by the writer (second-person *you*) or people or things written about (third-person plural *they*), the verb will take the base form.

> You eat apricots daily, but they fill up on cookies and candy.

However, third-person singular subjects—a single person or thing that is written about—will take the *-s* or *-es* form of the verb. Third-person singular subjects include singular nouns; the personal pronouns *he*, *she*, *it*, and *one*; and many indefinite pronouns such as *each*, *everyone*, and *somebody*.

Nutritionist Yvonne Gallegos urges snackers to replace candy bars and chips with raisins and fruit.
She also feels that everyone needs delicious as well as nutritious foods.

NOTE: In addition to the present tense, the perfect and progressive tenses may require changing verb form to match subject number or person. In these cases the form of the auxiliary verbs *have* and *be* changes; the past or present participle does not.

The cafeteria manager has thrown out all white sugar, and the cooks have replaced it with natural honey.
The students are feeling better, and classroom performance is improving.

(1) Intervening prepositional phrases

The number of words that come between the subject and the verb does not affect the number of the verb.

ERROR IN AGREEMENT: A nutritious breakfast including toast, bacon, orange juice, and eggs promote efficiency and energy at work.

REVISED: A nutritious breakfast including toast, bacon, orange juice, and eggs promotes efficiency and energy at work. (*Breakfast* is the subject, not the list of foods.)

REVISED: Toast, bacon, orange juice, and eggs, which make up a nutritious breakfast, promote efficiency and energy at work. (The subject has been changed to the foods.)

(2) Compound subjects

Compound subjects joined by *and* usually take plural verbs.

ERROR IN AGREEMENT: Liver and wheat germ supplies B vitamins

REVISED: Liver and wheat germ supply B vitamins.
(The compound refers to separate foods, rather than to one dish.)

However, when the compound refers to a single person or thing or when *each* or *every* precede the compound, use the singular verb.

ERROR IN AGREEMENT: Bread and butter are a wholesome snack when made with whole wheat flour and real butter, and each slice of bread and pat of butter provide energy for play or work.

REVISED: Bread and butter is a wholesome snack when made with whole wheat flour and real butter, and each slice of bread and pat of butter provides energy for play or work. (The first compound refers to something we eat as a single dish rather than separately—a bite of bread, a lick of butter, and so forth. The second compound is limited by the word *each* to consideration of one *slice* or *pat* at a time.)

Compound subjects joined by *or, nor, either/or,* or *neither/nor* take a singular verb if both subjects are singular and a plural verb if both subjects are plural. When the number or person is mixed, the verb agrees with the nearest subject.

ERROR IN AGREEMENT: Brewer's yeast or wheat germ supply needed iron, while beans or meats such as beef supplies protein.
REVISED: Brewer's yeast or wheat germ <u>supplies</u> needed iron, while beans or meats such as beef <u>supply</u> protein.
ERROR IN AGREEMENT: Sour fruits or buttermilk are said to aid in the absorption of iron.
REVISED: Sour fruits or <u>buttermilk is</u> said to aid in the absorption of iron.
REVISED: Buttermilk or sour <u>fruits are</u> said to aid in the absorption of iron.
ERROR IN AGREEMENT: Neither Dr. Jarvis nor I recommends synthetic vitamins.
REVISED: Neither Dr. Jarvis nor <u>I recommend</u> synthetic vitamins. (The first person singular pronoun is the closest subject; it always takes the base form of the verb.)
REVISED: Neither Dr. Jarvis nor <u>I can recommend</u> synthetic vitamins. (The addition of the auxiliary verb *can* eliminates the awkwardness caused by making the verb agree with *I*.)

(3) Indefinite pronouns

Indefinite pronouns (pronouns that do not refer to specific people or things) may be either singular or plural. Common singular indefinite pronouns include *each, either, neither, anything/something/everything, anyone/someone/everyone*, and *anybody/somebody/everybody*. These pronouns take the singular verb.

ERROR IN AGREEMENT: Every one of Dr. Jarvis's folk remedies have been tested for years.
REVISED: <u>Every one</u> of Dr. Jarvis's folk remedies <u>has been tested</u> for years. (Every remedy has been individually tested.)

Some indefinite pronouns—*both, many, few, several*—take the plural verb, while others—*some, all, any, most, much*—may take a plural or a singular verb, depending upon the meaning of the subject.

ERROR IN AGREEMENT: Many is the afflictions of those who ignore nutrition.
REVISED: <u>Many are</u> the afflictions of those who ignore nutrition.
ERROR IN AGREEMENT: Some of our daily pains is the result of poor nutrition, and most of our chronic fatigue are caused by dietary deficiencies.
REVISED: <u>Some</u> of our daily pains <u>are</u> the result of poor nutrition, and <u>most</u> of our chronic fatigue <u>is caused</u> by dietary deficiencies. (*Some* refers to *pains* and, therefore, takes a plural verb, while *most* refers to the singular *fatigue* and, therefore, takes a singular verb.)

(4) Collective nouns

A collective noun—like *audience, class,* or *group*—is a "group" noun. It is singular in form but refers to a group of people or things that may act together as a unit or separately as individuals.

ERROR IN AGREEMENT: The audience applaud the denouncing of white sugar as "poison."
REVISED: The audience applauds the denouncing of white sugar as "poison." (The audience acts together in agreement.)
ERROR IN AGREEMENT: The group disagrees about the value of ginseng root.
REVISED: The group disagree about the value of ginseng root. (The group members are acting separately because of their disagreement.)

Expressions of amount are also treated as collective nouns. They take a singular verb when they comprise a single unit and a plural verb when they refer to several parts.

ERROR IN AGREEMENT: Three-fourths of his meal were empty calories.
REVISED: Three-fourths of his meal was empty calories. (We are considering the three-fourths as a single unit rather than one-fourth at a time.)
ERROR IN AGREEMENT: The majority of workers in our office suffers from chronic fatigue because of poor nutrition.
REVISED: The majority of workers in our office suffer from chronic fatigue because of poor nutrition. (The workers who are part of this majority are looked at one at a time; they "suffer" as individuals.)

(5) Singular subjects that have plural forms

Some nouns may end in -s but have a singular meaning. Words like *obstetrics, ethics, athletics, statistics,* and *gymnastics* are described in the dictionary as plural nouns—that is, nouns that may be singular or plural depending upon the context. For example, *ethics* is singular when it refers to a branch of philosophy but plural when it refers to the principles underlying a particular course of action.

Biomedical Ethics is a required course of study for all health science majors.
The ethics involved in publishing research data are complex.

Other plural nouns with singular meanings include *news, measles, mumps, rickets, physics, economics,* and *aerobics.*

ERROR IN AGREEMENT: Rickets are a vitamin-deficiency disease caused by too little Vitamin D in the diet and the resulting inadequate absorption of calcium.
REVISED: Rickets is a vitamin-deficiency disease caused by too little Vitamin D in the diet and the resulting inadequate absorption of calcium.

Titles of individual works are also treated as singular, even if their form is plural.

Secrets of Health and Beauty is a book by Linda Clark.

(6) Inverted verb order

Verbs must agree with subjects, even if the subjects follow the verbs.

ERROR IN AGREEMENT: As breakfasts go, so go the morning.

REVISED: As breakfast goes, so goes the morning. (The subject of the second *goes* is *morning;* the number of the subject and verb of the introductory clause was changed to maintain a balance.)

NOTE: Words like *there* and *here*, which sometimes introduce sentences, cannot serve as subjects. They are adverbs whose use in this position signal us that the writer has inverted the normal order of the sentence, placing the subject after the verb.

NORMAL ORDER: Adelle Davis and Dr. D. C. Jarvis are noted advocates of nutrition as preventive medicine.
INVERTED ORDER WITH ERROR IN AGREEMENT: Here is Adelle Davis and Dr. D. C. Jarvis, noted advocates of nutrition as preventive medicine.
REVISED: Here are Adelle Davis and Dr. D. C. Jarvis, noted advocates of nutrition as preventive medicine.

(7) Linking verbs

Linking verbs, you will remember, connect a subject with a word or words in the predicate that describe or rename the subject—the subjective complement. The verb will agree with the subject, even if the number of the subjective complement is different.

ERROR IN AGREEMENT: According to Nobel Prize winner Dr. Linus Pauling, the key to preventing the common cold are large doses of Vitamin C.
REVISED: According to Nobel Prize Winner Dr. Linus Pauling, the key to preventing the common cold is large doses of Vitamin C. (The verb agrees with the singular subject *key* rather than with the plural subjective complement *doses.*)
REVISED: According to Nobel Prize winner Dr. Linus Pauling, large doses of Vitamin C are the key to preventing the common cold. (The verb agrees with the plural subject *doses* rather than with the singular subjective complement *key.*)

(8) Relative pronouns

Often a relative pronoun is the subject of a dependent clause. However, the relative pronouns *who, which,* and *that* do not change form to show number; their number is determined by their antecedents—the nouns or pronouns they refer back to. The verb, then, agrees in number with the antecedent.

ERROR IN AGREEMENT: Dr. D. C. Jarvis is only one of those who has advocated nutrition as preventive medicine.
REVISED: Dr. D. C. Jarvis is only one of those who have advocated nutrition as preventive medicine. (The antecedent of *who* is the plural *those* rather than the singular *one.*)
REVISED: Dr. D. C. Jarvis is one who has advocated nutrition as preventive medicine. (Because of deletions, the antecedent of *who* is now the singular *one.*)

NOTE: When a verbal, a verbal phrase, or a clause serves as subject, use the same verb you would use if a noun or nouns occupied those slots in the sentence.

COMPOUND VERBAL PHRASES AS SUBJECTS: Eating liver and drinking milk provide the protein and B vitamins you need to get through the stress of exams. (The verb is the same as it would be if *liver and milk* were the subjects.)

NOUN CLAUSE AS SUBJECT: What you eat at breakfast determines your blood sugar and energy levels all morning. (The verb is the same as it would be if *your breakfast* were the subject.)

COMPOUND NOUN CLAUSES AS SUBJECT: What you eat and what you don't eat are both important to your health. (The verb is the same as it would be if *vitamins* and *minerals* were the subjects.)

23b Making Pronouns and Antecedents Agree

Antecedents, you will remember, are the words that pronouns refer back to. Pronouns must agree with their antecedents in number (singular, plural), person (first, second, third), and gender (masculine, feminine, neuter).

ERROR IN AGREEMENT OF NUMBER: The Food and Drug Administration publishes minimum daily requirements of many vitamins and minerals, but they do not always support their figures with evidence.

REVISED: The Food and Drug Administration publishes minimum daily requirements of many vitamins and minerals, but it does not always support its figures with evidence. (The antecedent, *The Food and Drug Administration*, is singular rather than plural, necessitating a change from plural *they* and *their* to singular *it* and *its* and also a change in the number of the verb in the second clause from *do* to *does* to agree with the new subject *it*.)

ERROR IN AGREEMENT OF PERSON: You, the consumer, must beware of using drugs to mask the effects of our poor diet.

REVISED: You, the consumer, must beware of using drugs to mask the effects of your poor diet. (First-person *our* has been changed to second-person *your*.)

REVISED: We, the consumers, must beware of using drugs to mask the effects of our poor diet. (The antecedent *you* has been changed to first person *we*, necessitating changing the number of the noun appositive to the plural *consumers*.)

ERROR IN AGREEMENT OF GENDER: Every one of the students tested needed to add potassium to his diet.

REVISED: Every one of the students tested needed to add potassium to his or her diet. (Both male and female students were tested. At one time the masculine *his* would have been correct in this construction because the masculine pronoun was felt to include both sexes in the same way as *mankind* was felt to include the entire human race. However, just as *humankind* is replacing *mankind,* pronoun references are becoming increasingly exact, specifying both sexes when both are meant.)

REVISED: All of the students tested need to add potassium to their diet. (For those who find *his or her* awkward, rewriting the sentence with a plural antecedent may be helpful.)

(1) More than one antecedent

Generally, pronouns follow the same principles for agreeing with compound antecedents that verbs follow for agreeing with compound subjects.

1. If the compound antecedent is joined by *and,* the pronoun, like the verb, will usually be plural. The two exceptions occur when the compound refers to a single unit (liver and onions) or to one person (my doctor and advisor on health matters) and when *each* or *every* precedes the compound.

ERROR IN AGREEMENT: The FDA and AMA may emphasize drugs, but it cannot deny the importance of vitamins and minerals.

REVISED: The FDA and the AMA may emphasize drugs, but they cannot deny the importance of vitamins and minerals.

ERROR IN AGREEMENT: Each vitamin and mineral has their special place in the nutrition process, as my nutritionist and eating expert demonstrate with their research.

REVISED: Each vitamin and mineral has its special place in the nutrition process, as my nutritionist and eating expert demonstrates with her research. (*Each* makes the first compound singular and calls for a singular pronoun, while the second compound refers to a single person who fills both the roles.)

2. If the compound antecedent is joined by *or* or *nor,* the pronoun will be singular when the parts of the compound are singular and plural when they are plural, but when the number of the compound is mixed, the pronoun will agree with the closer antecedent.

ERROR IN AGREEMENT: Neither Vitamin K nor Vitamin E have had their day in court.

REVISED: Neither Vitamin K nor Vitamin E has had its day in court. (Singular antecedents joined by *nor* call for a singular verb and a singular pronoun.)

ERROR IN AGREEMENT: Neither the skeptical doctors nor the skeptical researchers have supported one's doubts about the importance of these vitamins.

REVISED: Neither the skeptical doctors nor the skeptical researchers have supported their doubts about the importance of these vitamins. (Plural antecedents call for a plural pronoun.)

ERROR IN AGREEMENT: Either the university's nutritionists or Adelle Davis are presenting their ideas about proper eating habits.

REVISED: Either the university's nutritionists or Adelle Davis is presenting her ideas about proper eating habits. (The verb and the pronoun have been changed to agree with the nearest subject, *Adelle Davis*, but the result is awkward.)

REVISED: Either Adelle Davis or the university's nutritionists are presenting their ideas about proper eating habits. (Changing the order of the compound allows us to use the plural pronoun, which in this case sounds less awkward.)

(2) Collective noun antecedents

If the meaning of a collective noun antecedent is singular, use a singular pronoun. If the meaning is plural, use a plural pronoun.

ERROR IN AGREEMENT: The vegetarian group encouraged their members to grow soybean sprouts as a meat substitute.

REVISED: The vegetarian group encouraged its members to grow soybean sprouts as a meat substitute. (The members act together as one group.)

ERROR IN AGREEMENT: When sweetwort, a brew of barley sprouts and honey, was served by Captain Cook, the crew passed its cups.

REVISED: When sweetwort, a brew of barley sprouts and honey, was served by Captain Cook, the crew passed their cups. (The crew members act individually.)

(3) Antecedent indefinite pronouns

Use singular pronouns if your antecedent is a singular indefinite pronoun and plural pronouns if your antecedent is a plural indefinite pronoun.

ERROR IN AGREEMENT: Each of these chemical additives should be carefully tested to determine whether they will do harm to our bodies.

REVISED: Each of these chemical additives should be carefully tested to determine whether it will do harm to our bodies. (*Each*, not *additives*, is the antecedent.)

NOTE: Since agreement is a matter of relationships among sentence parts, revising for subject-verb agreement may lead to further revising for pronoun-antecedent agreement and vice versa. (See examples above.) You should be aware of the overall pattern of agreement within your paragraphs.

Agreement

Making Subjects and Verbs Agree Exercise 23–1

NAME _____ DATE _____

Underline subjects, then choose the correct verb from the pair in parentheses.

EXAMPLE: America with its fastfood heavens on every corner *is* (is, are) overfed and undernourished.

Although the supply of different kinds of foods ___ (is, are) abundant in the United States, many Americans including the richest and the poorest ___ (is, are) literally starving. Often excess weight ___ (hides, hide) serious deficiencies in essential nutrients. Chubby children, bloated from too many soft drinks and too much candy, or the tired office worker, caught in the coffee-and-doughnuts trap, ___ (continues, continue) eating because the body's hunger mechanism ___ (continues, continue) to signal unfulfilled needs. But often that need and very real hunger ___ (is, are) answered by more potato chips, chocolate cake, or ice cream.

As much as one-third of the population ___ (lacks, lack) sufficient calcium to build and maintain strong bones and teeth and sufficient Vitamin C to fight colds and infections. Most women, who experience menstruation, ___ (does, do) not absorb enough iron from their diets. Nearly every one of us ___ (consumes, consume) too many empty calories and too few nutrients.

Score _____

© 1986 by CBS College Publishing. All rights reserved.

Revising Faulty Agreement Exercise 23-2

NAME _____ DATE _____

Find any errors in subject-verb agreement in the following sentences. If you find an error or errors, revise the sentence in two ways: first by changing the verb to match the subject and second by changing the subject to match the verb. If the sentence is correct, write C beside it.

EXAMPLE: The question of whether to take supplements and what kind to take are debated continually.
   a. *The question of whether to take supplements or what kind to take is debated continually.*
   b. *The questions of whether to take supplements and what kind to take are debated continually.*

1. In the past either doctors or the Food and Drug Administration have discouraged supplementing our diets with mineral and vitamin tablets.
   a.

   b.

2. Today, although the debates goes on, more of our medical community seems interested in using dietary supplements.
   a.

   b.

3. Neither the foods we eat nor the soil we grow them in have maintained the high level of nutrients common a hundred or even fifty years ago.
   a.

   b.

4. According to researchers, 95 percent of our foods has been processed in some way.
   a.

   b.

5. Any one of us have the potential for consuming thousands of unnatural chemicals that are added to our food to preserve it, flavor it, color it, or stabilize it.
   a.

   b.

Agreement 399

6. Our campus doctor and health officer now recommend vitamins rather than aspirin or pain remedies to students suffering from headaches or chronic fatigue.
   a.

   b.

7. Refining and bleaching flour removes most of the essential nutrients and results in the styrofoam product called white bread.
   a.

   b.

8. Unfortunately, foods high in sugar and starch are cheap and plentiful, while those high in protein and other nutrients are more expensive.
   a.
   b.

9. Vitamin A and Vitamin D is essential to health; however, large doses of thousands of units daily, sometimes taken as a remedy for illness, is toxic.
   a.

   b.

10. The Food and Nutrition Board disagrees about the amount of Vitamin A the public requires, but the membership agree on the importance of the vitamin.
    a.

    b.

Score _____

© 1986 by CBS College Publishing. All rights reserved.

Using Appropriate Verbs Exercise 23–3

NAME _____ DATE _____

Underline subjects or antecedents and subjects; then choose the correct verb from the pair in parentheses.

> EXAMPLE: Dietetics <u>*is*</u> (is, are) the science of applying the principles of nutrition to planning and preparing meals.

1. Eating delicious, well-cooked meals __ (is, are) both a necessity and a pleasure.
2. There _____ (comes, come) Ben C. Harris, author of *Eat the Weeds*, and Martha Oliver, author of *Add a Few Sprouts*.
3. Dr. Linus Pauling is only one of those who _____ (believes, believe) in the preventive powers of Vitamin C.
4. Washing and boiling _____ (destroys, destroy) the Vitamin C in vegetables.
5. The major problem with the American evening meal __ (is, are) the size and the hour.
6. The size and the hour __ (is, are) the major problem with the American evening meal.
7. What some people recommend eating and what they actually eat often _____ (differs, differ) dramatically.
8. The person above all others who _____ (needs, need) B vitamins is the person under stress.
9. The biggest news from our school's cafeteria and snack bar __ (is, are) the addition of sprouts to the salad bars and the elimination of french fries and onion rings from the menu.
10. There _____ (has, have) been an appeal from the dean of students and a petition from Student Senate to include health foods in the cafeteria menu.

Score _____

Revising Faulty Agreement   Exercise 23-4

NAME _____ DATE _____

Circle the number of any sentence in the following short paragraphs that contains an error in subject-verb agreement. Then cross out the incorrect verb and write the correct verb above it.

                                                is

EXAMPLE: ⓔ What inspires confidence ~~are~~ results.

¹ The importance of some vitamins have been known for a long time.   ² Dr. James Lind, an eighteenth-century doctor, was the first to use Vitamin C in the form of lemon juice to combat scurvy among British sailors.   ³ Some of the medical profession has prescribed Vitamin E for patients since the 1930's.   ⁴ And niacin or Vitamin B-3, which were discovered in the nineteenth century, have been acknowledged for decades as a cure for the disease pellagra.

⁵ The claims for the curative power of Vitamin C is extraordinary.   ⁶ Dr. Linus Pauling is one of those who has made promoting the use of Vitamin C a vocation.   ⁷ He concentrates upon its preventing the common cold and recommends a dose of 500 mg at the first sneeze or sniffle.   ⁸ What others claim for this vitamin in the way of cures and powers are much more dramatic.   ⁹ It has been used to treat glaucoma, lead poisoning, mononucleosis, hepatitis, arthritis, ulcers, lockjaw, hay fever, and slipped discs.   ¹⁰ Polio, whooping cough, snake bite, and tuberculosis—each have, we are told, responded to massive doses of Vitamin C.

¹¹ The major problem with Vitamin C are the many ways it can be lost from food and from the body.   ¹² Most Vitamin C is eliminated from vegetables when we prepare them for eating.   ¹³ The 100 mg of Vitamin C from your morning glass of orange juice is lost milligram by milligram as fights, cigarettes, coffee, and shock of inflation drains it from the body.

© 1986 by CBS College Publishing. All rights reserved.

¹⁴ There is still people who doubts the effectiveness of Vitamin C supplements. ¹⁵ Fortunately, from natural sources they can get the same effect as a massive dose of supplements. ¹⁶ All they have to do to duplicate the 1,000-mg-per-hour dose recommended by some as a cold remedy are to drink ten glasses of orange juice an hour.

Score _____

Agreement   **403**

Choosing the Right Pronouns   Exercise 23-5

NAME _____   DATE _____

Underline the antecedent in each sentence; then choose the correct pronoun from the pair in parentheses.

   EXAMPLE: In *Folk Medicine*, a book about the home remedies common in Vermont, <u>Dr. D. C. Jarvis</u> writes about *his* (his, their) discoveries.

1. Dr. Jarvis's book has delighted millions with __ (its, his) down-to-earth remedies and simple "horse sense."
2. Vermonters, he found, value foods such as cider vinegar for ____ (its, their) medicinal as well as nutritive qualities.
3. The AMA has not taken an official position on folk medicine. __ (It, They) warned, however, of the dangers of putting off medical treatment in cases of serious illness.
4. The farm family made apple cider vinegar from whole apples gathered in __ (its, their) orchard.
5. The family put two teaspoons of vinegar in ____ (its, their) water glasses at dinner to aid digestion.
6. Each of the cows in the barn had been given a dose of vinegar on __ (its, their) feed.
7. Neither the pregnant cows nor the pregnant woman had been spared __ (her, their) daily, potent helping of apple cider vinegar.
8. The family also used apple cider vinegar as __ (its, their) major external medicine.
9. The family rubbed the vinegar directly on ____ (its, their) skin to combat ringworm, shingles, impetigo, poison ivy, and even varicose veins.
10. Another bonanza for eating and curing was found in honey as well as the honeycomb. Farm families used __ (it, them) instead of white sugar for cooking and instead of drugs such as antihistimines to cure respiratory problems.
11. Bedwetting and arthritis are chronic afflictions, a purgatory for many. ____ (It, They) respond to regular doses of honey.
12. An ideal snack on the farm was stone-ground whole wheat bread and honey. __ (It, They) provided needed energy in the form of useful (not empty) calories and also twelve important minerals.

                                                              Score _____

© 1986 by CBS College Publishing. All rights reserved.

Revising for Agreement   Exercise 23–6

NAME _____ DATE _____

To revise the following sentences, begin by changing the underlined word or words in the manner described in parentheses. Then rewrite, being careful to make all the revisions for subject-verb and pronoun-antecedent agreement required by the initial change.

> EXAMPLE: The doctors (change to singular) encourage their patients to eat a balanced diet.
> *The doctor encourages her patients to eat a balanced diet.*

1. The well-known advocate (change to plural) for vitamins and minerals supplements her meals with assorted tablets and capsules, varying in size from pinhead to impossible-to-swallow.

2. The office workers (change to singular) are on the verge of collapse. They suffer from chronic fatigue because of flourescent lights and inadequate exercise. They are nervous and irritable from too much coffee. And their hunger alarms, tripped by the lack of a satisfying breakfast, tempt them to consume doughnut after doughnut, adding pounds to their already ample hips and another anxiety to their already overloaded subconsciouses.

3. Either the office manager or the assistant manager (change to plural) has been bringing his own homemade snacks of oatmeal cookies and granola bars and leaving his leftovers by the coffee urn for us all to try.

4. You (change to *she*) just don't handle white flour well, so it is not for you. It generally makes you stomach-conscious, being very apt to produce gas in your stomach, often heartburn after eating, and constipation. The effect on you will be to upset the timetable of your digestive tract. Generally you handle corn and rye foods well, so your breads should be corn or rye. On the whole, as you study yourself, you will note that you do not digest cereals any too well. (From D. C. Jarvis, M.D., *Folk Medicine*)

Score ___

Review 23

Find and correct any errors in agreement in the following sentences.

1. Soaking rusty iron shavings in vinegar water and then drinking the water is an old (and possibly dangerous) remedy for anemia.

2. Six teaspoonfuls of honey, given at twenty-five-minute intervals, supposedly cure the alcoholic of their craving for liquor.

3. In the early voyages of exploration, there were usually a loss of half the crew to scurvy.

4. Captain Cook is one of the first of those who shows that long sea voyages are possible without deaths from scurvy.

5. The crew of the *Endeavor* takes its sweetwort in its breakfast cereal and every evening as a drink.

6. Neither the cattle nor the chicken tested use soybean foods as effectively as human beings do.

7. Each of the countries studied have their favorite remedies for warts, hair loss, and stomach cramps.

Score _____

Check your answers against those in the back of the book. Deduct 10 points for each error in correction. A score of 80 percent or higher shows you understand the principles of agreement.

The Writer's Casebook #23

Application: Agreeing Throughout an Essay

Agreement, as we have seen, may go beyond the grammatical relationships of a single sentence to link separate sentences or even to knit together an entire paragraph. Controlling these larger patterns of agreement contributes significantly to the coherence of an essay and at the same time helps maintain a consistent point of view. The following paragraph is neither consistent nor coherent.

> Some so-called folk medicine practiced in the Appalachians probably had its origins in the superstitions of Tudor England. To prevent hemorrhaging, mountain people drive an axe in the floor. To ward off disease you tie a string around the wrist or you wear a foul-smelling asafetida bag around your neck. Swallow a mixture of vinegar, honey, and moonshine for rheumatism. They use just as much quinine as you can put on the blade of a knife for curing the common cold.

The shift from the third person to the second person and back again confuses both the point of view and the logic of the paragraph. Revising the paragraph for agreement of person, starting with the antecedent *mountain people*, results in a clearer structure and perspective.

> Some so-called folk medicine practiced in the Appalachians probably had its origins in the superstitions of Tudor England. To prevent hemorrhaging, <u>mountain people</u> drive an axe in the floor. To ward off disease, <u>they</u> tie strings around <u>their</u> wrists or wear foul-smelling asafetida bags around <u>their</u> necks. <u>They</u> swallow a mixture of vinegar, honey, and moonshine for rheumatism, and <u>they</u> use just as much quinine as <u>they</u> can put on the blade of a knife for curing the common cold.

Cases for Writing: Writing About Nutrition

Case #1

Be your own nutritional analyst. Inventory your eating habits, listing the foods you eat daily, the foods you like, the foods you don't like, the food you eat at regular meals, the food you eat for snacks. Then write a paper evaluating your habits and making recommendations (if needed) for improvement. Write from the first-person point of view.

Case #2

Prepare a factual report on good nutrition. Use the formal, third-person pronoun *one* throughout your paper. Divide nutrition into its major parts or requirements and examine each part.

24

Adjectives and Adverbs

Preview 24

Cross out inappropriately used adjectives and adverbs in the following sentences. Write the corrections directly above the errors.

1. Jack jumped nimble and quick over the candlestick.

2. Michael Jackson's glittering glove is more famous than any other glove in entertainment history.

3. The ruby slippers worn by Judy Garland in *The Wizard of Oz* were less unique than the Wicked Witch thought; Dorothy had several pair.

4. Beautiful people are often beautifuler in photographs than in person.

5. To be great, an entertainer must perform great but a statesman must do great deeds.

6. Most queenliest of all the First Ladies were Jacqueline Kennedy and Nancy Reagan.

7. The comic strip character, John Darling, sure wants to be on the cover of *People* magazine.

8. We are real hesitant to believe most of what the movie magazines say about the stars.

> 9. Wealth, stardom, and public office are surer ways to fame and a place in the encyclopedia.
>
> 10. Of the two actors, Robert Taylor and Jimmy Stewart, the latter was probably the most famous.
>
> **Score** _____
>
> Check your answers against those in the back of the book. Deduct 5 points for each error in identification and for each error in correction. A score of 80 percent or better demonstrates understanding of the materials in this chapter.

Adjectives and adverbs are modifiers. They enrich sentences by describing, limiting, or qualifying other words, phrases, or clauses.

BARE: The politician spoke from a box of causes.
ENRICHED: The <u>angry</u> politician spoke <u>vehemently</u> from <u>atop</u> a <u>soapbox</u> of <u>lost</u> causes.

The first sentence is skeletal; the basic ideas are there, but they lack life. In the second sentence modifiers add both a tone and the descriptive details needed to flesh out the skeleton and create a picture.

Adjectives modify nouns or pronouns. Most are descriptive. Some—such as articles, possessive pronouns, and demonstrative pronouns—limit or qualify nouns, pointing out "which one" or "whose." Still others may be compound, consisting of two words or more. Usually adjectives are placed before or after the words they modify or after a linking verb when they function as subjective complements.

FUNCTION: <u>The</u> <u>fat</u> clown squirted <u>the</u> <u>unfriendly</u> audience with <u>red</u> paint. (Adjectives modify the nouns *clown, audience,* and *paint.*)
He will paint you <u>blue</u>. (Adjective modifies the pronoun *you.*)

FORM: <u>Ragged</u>, <u>muddy</u> players limped onto the <u>soggy</u> field. (descriptive adjectives)
<u>These</u> players had fought bravely, losing <u>the</u> game but winning <u>our</u> hearts. (demonstrative pronoun *these,* article *the,* and possessive pronoun *our,* telling which *players* and *game* and whose *hearts*)
The <u>hard-hearted</u> referee threw her out of the game. (compound adjective)

POSITION: The <u>imperturbable</u> station manager, <u>smiling</u> and <u>confident</u> in spite of <u>the</u> <u>surprise</u> inspection, invited <u>the</u> FCC team to visit <u>the</u> <u>busy</u> broadcast studio. (adjectives, before and after the noun *manager* and before the nouns *FCC team, inspection,* and *studio*)
The investigators appeared <u>nervous</u> and <u>irritable</u>. (adjective subjective complements describing the subject *investigators* but following the linking verb *appeared*)

Adjectives and Adverbs

Adverbs modify verbs, adjectives, or other adverbs. They may be formed from adjectives, or they may take several special forms—interrogative, relative, or conjunctive. Usually they will be located close to the words they modify, but frequently they can be located in more than one position in the sentence. Adverbs answer the questions: How? When? Where?

FUNCTION: The talk-show host ran his tongue nervously over his teeth. (adverb modifying verb *ran*, describing "how")

The guest has come extremely late. (Adverb *extremely* modifies adverb *late*, which modifies verb *had come*. *Extremely* describes "how late"; *late* describes "when.")

"Here I am," said the completely relaxed guest. (Adverb *here* modifies verb *am*, describing "where"; adverb *completely* modifies adjective *relaxed*, describing "how.")

FORM: The officer stood up and advanced purposefully toward the suspect. (adverb *up* derived from a preposition and adverb *purposefully* formed by adding *-ly* to adjective *purposeful*)

Where have you been? Why are you here? When did you get home last night? (interrogative adverbs, introducing questions)

I know the time when the drop will be made. (relative adverb, introducing relative clause)

Very soon we will know whether the drop will be made now, then, or never. (familiar adverbs not derived from other parts of speech)

POSITION: Grandmother lurched noisily into the driveway on her Harley-Davidson. (adverb positioned close to *lurched*, the verb it modifies)

She dismounted quickly.
Quickly she dismounted. } (adverb occupying variety of positions)
She quickly dismounted.

24a Using Adjectives

Use adjectives appropriately as subject complements or object complements.

INAPPROPRIATE: Ichabod, our overly aggressive setter, smelled foully after his encounter with the skunk. (*Smelled* is a linking verb and, therefore, should be followed by a subjective complement, in this case an adjective.)

REVISED: Ichabod, our overly aggressive setter, smelled foul after his encounter with the skunk.

INAPPROPRIATE: We called Ichabod stupidly for attacking a skunk. (The direct object, *Ichabod*, is described, rather than the verb *called*; therefore, the word is an objective complement and in this case should be an adjective.)

REVISED: We called Ichabod stupid for attacking a skunk.

24b Using Adverbs

Use adverbs appropriately to modify a verb, an adjective, or another adverb.

INAPPROPRIATE: People in this town sure performed great on *Home Town Magazine*'s friendliness test. (adjectives used to modify verb)

REVISED: People in this town <u>surely</u> performed <u>well</u> on *Home Town Magazine*'s friendliness test.

NOTE: Both *real* and *really* have been so often misused and overused as modifiers that they have become "empty" words with only vague meanings: Apples are a *real* treat. (As opposed to an "unreal" treat?) Usually we can eliminate *real* or *really* from the sentence without subtracting much meaning, or we can replace them with stronger words to sharpen meaning: Drive *carefully* and *slowly*. Apples are a treat. We want to be *cautiously* (or *financially* or *spiritually* or *politically*) helpful.

24c Distinguishing Between Comparative and Superlative Forms

Distinguish between comparative and superlative forms of adjectives and adverbs by understanding degree and comparison. *Degree* indicates the extent to which a modified word possesses the quality or characteristic ascribed to it by the modifying adjective or adverb—that is, whether it is *more* or *less lovely* than something else, the *loveliest* or *least lovely* of its kind, or simply *lovely*. The base form of the word is the *positive degree*. It describes one quality with no comparisons. The *comparative degree* compares two persons or things; the *superlative degree* compares one person or thing with all others of its kind. The comparisons may be either positive or negative.

(−) superlative degree	comparative degree	positive degree	comparative degree	superlative (+) degree
least loud	less loud	loud	louder	loudest
least bright	less bright	bright	brighter	brightest
least slowly	less slowly	slowly	more slowly	most slowly
least early	less early	early	earlier	earliest

(1) The comparative degree

Form the comparative degree to show a *greater* extent by adding *-er* to all one-syllable and many two-syllable adjectives and to some adverbs (small + *-er* = smaller, grouchy + *-er* = grouchier, soon + *-er* = sooner) or by placing *more* in front of other two-syllable adjectives, all long adjectives, and adverbs that end in *-ly* (more awkward, more intelligent, more timidly). Form the comparative degree to show a *lesser* extent by placing *less* before both adjectives and adverbs (less awkward, less timidly).

Use the comparative degree when you are comparing two persons or things.

A politician must be <u>more charismatic</u> than a brain surgeon.

Cudlow is a <u>funnier</u> name than *Garfield*.

Dr. Martinez speaks <u>less hoarsely</u> than Dr. Lee.

(2) The superlative degree

Form the superlative degree to show *greatest* extent by adding *-est* to all adjectives and adverbs that form the comparative by adding *-er* (smallest, grouchiest, soonest) and by placing *most* in front of all adjectives and adverbs that form the comparative with *more* (most awkward, most intelligent, most timidly). Form the superlative degree to show the *least* extent by placing *least* before both adjectives and adverbs (least grouchy, least intelligently).

Use the superlative degree when you are comparing three or more persons or things or one person or thing with all others of its kind.

> Of the three salespeople Maureen is the most aggressive and the least erratic.

> Only the hardiest people can survive a Yukon winter.

NOTE: A common error in comparison results when the uses of the comparative and the superlative are confused.

INCORRECT:	Georgina and Frederico are both avid skiers, but Frederico is the most avid. (incorrect because the comparison is of two people, not three or more)
REVISED:	Georgina and Frederico are both avid skiers, but Frederico is the more avid.

Another common error occurs when both methods of forming a comparative, *more* and *-er*, or superlative, *most* and *-est*, are used. Although some words use either form (happier/more happy, healthiest/most healthy), they do not use both at the same time.

INCORRECT:	Roseta prefers yogurt; it is more healthier than ice cream.
REVISED:	Roseta prefers yogurt; it is more healthy than ice cream.
REVISED:	Roseta prefers yogurt; it is healthier than ice cream.
INCORRECT:	Royce is the most craftiest chess player I know.
REVISED:	Royce is the most crafty chess player I know.
REVISED:	Royce is the craftiest chess player I know.

(3) Irregular comparatives and superlatives

Irregular comparatives and superlatives are formed by changing the base word. You should learn some of the common, irregular adjectives and adverbs, but check your dictionary when in doubt.

Positive	*Comparative*	*Superlative*
good, well	better	best
bad, badly	worse	worst

(4) Illogical comparisons

Avoid illogical comparisons of words such as *perfect, unique,* and *impossible,* which make sense only in the positive degree. (Once something has attained perfection, it cannot improve. Something unique is one of a kind; no comparison is possible.)

INCORRECT: The vector problems are the <u>most impossible</u> part of the assignment for me to do.
REVISED: The vector problems in the assignment are <u>impossible</u> for me to do.

24d Using Nouns as Adjectives

Although nouns may modify other nouns, using more than two or three may confuse the reader.

CONFUSED: The Four Hills Joggers and Tennis Bums Club summer fitness workshop begins on June 5.
REVISED: The summer fitness workshop of the Four Hills Joggers and Tennis Bums Club begins on June 5.
REVISED: The Joggers and Tennis Bums Club has scheduled its annual fitness workshop. This summer it begins on June 5 in Four Hills.

Adjectives and Adverbs

Identifying Adjectives and Adverbs   Exercise 24–1

NAME _____ DATE _____

Underline the adjectives and the adverbs in the following passage. Label adjectives *adj* and adverbs *adv*.

> EXAMPLE: The *adj* tall woman with the *adj* curly, *adj* brown hair sprinted *adv* breathlessly across the *adj* line.

Grandfather was like a gnarled oak—bent by the winds but still strong enough for his family to lean on. Like the oak he was firmly rooted; he rarely left the old-fashioned surroundings of his hill-top farm. But also like the oak his branches reached far—to the youngest daughter who was stationed in Germany, to the granddaughter who taught school in Alaska and to me, struggling to carry on the family tradition of "scribbling," as Grandfather called our excursions into print.

All of us, whether we followed in his sturdy yet cautious footsteps or not, felt the unspoken influence. We remembered on Sundays that he would be in his church pew, after arriving unfashionably early. On voting days we knew he would be faithfully on time, ready to vote his convictions rather than his party or his personal interests. And when we needed advice, we knew he would be there—on the other end of his three-party line.

Score _____

© 1986 by CBS College Publishing. All rights reserved.

Enriching with Adjectives and Adverbs   Exercise 24–2

NAME _____ DATE _____

Enrich the following sentences by adding appropriate adjectives and adverbs. Rewrite the sentences in the space provided.

    EXAMPLE: Our gallery boasts pictures in frames.
    Our family portrait gallery boasts old-fashioned pictures in heavy, gilt frames.

1. The pose of a picture makes the people look like dolls.

2. A cousin had a picture painted of himself in a costume.

3. In a watercolor, my grandmother smiles.

4. Great-uncle Frank leads a cavalry charge in a Civil War painting.

5. Families can remember each other in the poses of our daily lives.

6. The camera takes portraiture out of the studio and peeks into the worlds of life.

7. Instead of a mother in her gown and hairdo, the camera captures her in curlers and housecoat.

8. The photographer pursues the moment of truth.

9. We are surprised in poses and clothes.

Adjectives and Adverbs

10. I would prefer to be remembered, not as I was—a slob—but as I would have liked to have been—a figure in a portrait.

Score _____

Using Adjectives and Adverbs Appropriately   Exercise 24–3

NAME _____ DATE _____

Choose the appropriate adjective or adverb from the words in parentheses. Circle your choice, and draw an arrow to the word modified.

    EXAMPLE: Of all the comedians we saw, Rich Little was (funnier, *funniest*).

1. Geraldine Ferraro looked (calm, calmly) and (intelligent, intelligently) during the 1984 vice presidential debates.
2. The candidates spoke (calm, calmly) and (intelligent, intelligently).
3. Politics (sure, surely) needs (real, really) dedicated people.
4. Go (slow, slowly) on a (slow, slowly) turn.
5. Both Richard Rodriquez and N. Scott Momaday write movingly of minority concerns, but Momaday is probably the (better, best) writer.
6. Of the three Oscar-winning performances, Henry Fonda's performance in *On Golden Pond* was (perfect, most perfect).
7. The loser of the Senate race felt (bad, badly), but the winner, a reluctant candidate, felt (worse, worst).
8. Senate candidate Pratt came out (loud, loudly) and (strong, strongly) for ERA.
9. Iacocca did (real, really) (good, well) in his efforts to save Chrysler.
10. Margaret Thatcher is one of the (brighter, brightest) prime ministers to serve Great Britain.
11. Howard Hughes built the *Spruce Goose*, a (unique, more unique, most unique) aircraft.
12. Look (sharp, sharply) and be (sharp, sharply).
13. Phyllis Diller performed (good, well) on the first night but (better, best) on the second and last night of her engagement.
14. Media personalities like Barbara Walters must have (excellent, more excellent, most excellent) communication skills.
15. Jimmy Stewart appeared (heroic, heroically) in films but also acted (heroic, heroically) as a combat pilot.

Score _____

Adjectives and Adverbs 419

Revising for Appropriate Modifiers   Exercise 24-4

NAME _____ DATE _____

In the following sentences, find and revise any inappropriate use of adjectives, adverbs, or noun modifiers and any errors in comparison or degree. Change, add, or delete words as necessary.

    EXAMPLE: The more meaner the coach became, the more oftener we skipped practice.
The meaner the coach became, the more often we skipped practice.

1. To me Tom Landry is a greater gridiron hero than Roger Staubach and Danny White.

2. Howard Cosell is the most unique sportscaster of them all.

3. The clown in the baggy pants and the red wig seemed more sad than funnier, but the crowds applauded long and loud.

4. Those guests who come earlier than the others will be given better seats.

5. The ABC evening newscast New York anchor Peter Jennings called the Reagan campaign officials' banquet "a news event without news."

6. Actors feel badly if their audiences are small, but they feel worst if there are none at all.

7. Of all the tasks given me by my boss, xeroxing and collating a hundred reports an hour is the less impossible.

8. The traffic controller at our station logged a Big-O Tire commercial next to a competing Firestone commercial, then forgot the "promo" spots for a nationally syndicated show. He was least unhappiest when he discovered his mistakes but most unhappiest when the station manager found them.

9. The Nob Hill Bookstore afternoon Fairy Tales Club will host a marathon of Mother Goose and Brothers Grimm readings.

© 1986 by CBS College Publishing. All rights reserved.

10. Some history books have labeled Andrew Johnson cowardly and weakly, but he acted heroic and decisive when President Lincoln was assassinated.

11. Coretta Scott King has carried on brave and uncompromising with the civil rights efforts of her assassinated husband.

12. In Hollywood Greta Garbo and Marilyn Monroe often appeared glamorously in films more memorable for the stars than the scripts.

13. In the mega-bucks big business entertainment world today, glitter has replaced glamour.

14. "Get there firstest with the mostest" was the general's battle strategy.

15. Michael Jackson did great on his latest video.

16. People-watchers claim that the biggest stars are less jealous of their privacy than the smaller.

17. For many public figures fame comes quick and brings with it quicker and more expensive divorces.

18. The world may not need more people, but it needs better people.

19. Feeling badly, she sure needed help, but the system moves slow and easy, not quick and sudden.

20. The most perfectly wretched day of his life began with a speeding ticket and ended with his girlfriend's calling him stupidly because he had left the most invaluable concert tickets in a rolled-up newspaper on the bus.

Score _____

Adjectives and Adverbs

Review 24

Cross out inappropriately used adjectives and adverbs in the following sentences. Write the corrections directly above the errors.

1. When the fog is thick, drive slow and be careful.

2. If we drive real careful, we can avoid causing as well as having accidents.

3. Senator Hatfield felt badly when his wife's real estate deal was questioned.

4. Getting an interview with Jacqueline Kennedy is the most impossible task an editor can give a reporter.

5. Many famous people seem much less happier than they were before they became famous.

6. Of the two senators, Domenici and Hatfield, Hatfield is probably the best educated but Domenici is the more powerful.

7. The voting records of Mondale and McGovern are most similar while the voting records of Mondale and Goldwater are least similar.

8. Sometimes it seems that scandals just make the scandalous richer and famouser.

9. Mamie Eisenhower was the more grandmotherly of all the First Ladies.

Score _____

Check your answers against those in the back of the book. Deduct 5 points for each error in identification and 5 points for each error in correction. A score of 80 percent or better demonstrates understanding of the materials in this chapter.

The Writer's Casebook #24

Application: Writing the Descriptive Essay

Adjectives and adverbs as well as vivid nouns and verbs are important tools of descriptive writing. They are content words, adding substance to the bare outlines of actions, people, and objects. The principles of showing rather than telling are fundamental to description since the writer's objective is to write, as the artist's objective is to paint pictures. (See Writer's Casebooks #6 and #31 for more about "showing rather than telling.") As you write descriptively, search for words, including adjectives and adverbs, that will convey clear images without being overblown and that will supply details without being tedious.

OVERBLOWN: Her eyelashes fluttered provocatively, sweeping and dipping like the lucious, jeweled wings of a gorgeous Monarch butterfly.
CLEAR: Her eyelashes fluttered provocatively.
TEDIOUS: Scowling eyebrows bunched together over the bridge of the nose; corners of the mouth curved down; lips set in a thin line; thick, gold-rimmed glasses slipping towards the tip of his nose—my father silenced my giggling sisters—their heads together as they whispered their silly secrets—with a single look over the top of his Thursday evening, November 10, 1986, copy of the *Seattle Sun*.
CLEAR: Father silenced my giggling sisters with a single scowl over the top of his evening paper.

Description is a method of developing ideas rather than a "mode" of discourse or a rhetorical pattern; however, when an essay consists primarily of description, we sometimes refer to it as a "descriptive" essay.

Like organizing any description, organizing the descriptive essay requires a systematic plan and liberal use of transitional expressions. For example, in describing a room, you might begin at the right and move to the left, making ample use of transitions such as *to the left, next to, beside, behind, in back of*. Or if you were describing a person, you might begin with the head and move down to the toes, adopting a "first I see," "second I see" approach that signals your progress.

One type of descriptive essay is the character sketch. A sample working outline follows.

Introduction
    Identity of character (name, relationship, or jobs)
    Suggestion of character's importance to or interest for you or for the world
    Thesis that expresses a judgment or opinion or summary comment about the character

Body
    Description of character physically   Three or more paragraphs, each beginning with a topic sentence and adding supporting descriptive details and examples
    Description of character's personality
    Description of character's actions

Conclusion
    Reiteration of opinion or comment stated in the thesis
    Final image, or idea, or personal note

Cases for Writing: Describing People

Case #1

Become a painter in words. Write a portrait gallery of family members (real or imaginary). Introduce the family in your first paragraph and then take a walking tour through your gallery. The portraits might span a long period of the family's history; in that case, you will probably want to organize them chronologically. If the portraits are all contemporary, you might organize according to likenesses or differences, such as brown eyes versus green eyes or forceful versus weak personalities.

Case #2

Rewrite the following skeletal paper, fleshing out the bare bones of ideas with descriptive details and actions that show rather than tell.

>It's hard for me to get going in the morning. I hate the alarm clock. It's hard to get out of bed. I'm hardly awake when I shower. I'm so sleepy when I put on make-up (or shave) and comb my hair that I make mistakes. I also make mistakes when I put on my clothes. I get a cup of coffee and once in a while a quick breakfast. A lot of times the car will not start. I'm usually late getting to work (or school).

SECTION VI
Understanding Punctuation and Mechanics

25
The Period, the Question Mark, and the Exclamation Point (.; ?; !)

Preview 25

Find and correct any errors in end punctuation in the following sentences.

1. E.N.I.A.C. was an early electronic "brain."
2. I asked the salesman if the daisy wheel printer was worth the extra cost?
3. Will you please stop pirating software?
4. The terminal user in Dallas sent a "handshake" message. To see if the user in New York would be ready to receive information.
5. Help!! An industrial saboteur is trying to bomb our computer system!
6. The operator began working at 8 A.M.; she was still working at 8 P.M..
7. Send your questions about computers to InfoWorld, 375 Cochituate Rd, Box 880, Framingham, MA.
8. "Can computers improve your writing," they asked?
9. Dr. Joyce R Mason wrote the article on pp 11–20.
10. To play the game, use the joystick to move the cursor, or blip, on the screen, try to keep the ghost from grabbing your blip.

Score _____

Check your answers against those in the back of the text. Deduct 10 points for any sentence in which errors remain.

25a Using Periods

A period is a mark of end punctuation. It marks the end of most sentences and the end of abbreviations or of the parts of some literary references.

(1) Marking an end point

Use periods to mark the end of most complete sentences: a statement; a mild command or polite request; and an indirect question (a statement that a question has been asked).

STATEMENT: Charles Babbage, a nineteenth-century inventor, is known as the father of the modern computer.
MILD COMMAND: Use a personal computer to balance your checkbook.
POLITE REQUEST: When you finish writing the program, please store it on a floppy disk.
INDIRECT QUESTION: She asked whether I were computer literate.

(2) Marking an abbreviation

Use periods to end abbreviations.

TITLES OR DEGREES: Ms., Mr., Mrs., Dr., M.D., Ph.D., Prof., R.N.
NAMES AND INITIALS: J. F. Kennedy, Booker T. Washington, Margaret H. R. Thatcher, Susan B. Anthony.
PARTS OF ADDRESSES: 383 Madison Ave., N.Y., N.Y., U.S.A.
COMMON WORDS, LABELS, AND EXPRESSIONS: abbrev., etc. (et cetera), a.m. (ante meridiem), adj. (adjective), p. (page), pp. (pages), oz. (ounce), m.p.h. (miles per hour), A.D. (Anno Domini), B.C. (before Christ)

Periods are not used in *acronyms*, new words formed from the first letters of a name or phrase, or in most capital-letter abbreviations.

BASIC (Beginner's All-purpose Symbolic Instruction Code)
GIGO (Garbage In, Garbage Out)
kips (kilo instructions per second
flak (fliegerabwehrkanone)
MSU (Michigan State University)
CIA (Central Intelligence Agency)
ETA (estimated time of arrival)
DNA (deoxyribonucleic acid)
RAM (random-access memory)
IBM (intercontinental ballistic missile)
NBC (National Broadcasting Company)
OK (Oklahoma), UT (Utah), VT (Vermont)

Check the glossary of abbreviations in your dictionary for current usage. Do *not* use periods to end dependent clauses, verbal phrases, or prepositional phrases or to separate subjects from verbs. (See Chapter 11 for more about correcting fragments.)

When I bought my home computer, I planned to upgrade it. Within a year, But upgrading is extremely expensive and overloads the machine.

Do use periods between sentences to avoid run-ons—fused sentences or comma splices. (See Chapter 12 for more about correcting run-ons.)

I wrote the letter on my word processer. Then I sent it by Telemail. I hope I corrected all of the errors.

(3) Marking citations

Use periods to separate parts of some literary references—for example, act, scene, and line numbers in plays (*Hamlet* IV.i.55–87) or book and line numbers in epics (*Paradise Lost* II.994).

25b Using Question Marks

A question mark, used to end sentences or phrases that ask direct questions, is also primarily end punctuation, but it may be used within a sentence to indicate doubt about the accuracy of dates or numbers.

(1) Marking the end of a direct question

Use the question mark to end a direct question. A direct question repeats the exact words of the speaker in the order in which he or she spoke them and often begins with an interrogative word such as *who, what, why,* or *when* or with a verb.

> <u>What</u> is the difference between a bit and a byte? (question beginning with interrogative word)
> <u>Should</u> we buy a mainframe, a minicomputer, or a microcomputer? (question beginning with verb)

When a sentence contains a direct question in quotations, parentheses, or dashes, the question mark will directly follow the exact words of the question.

> "Is your company's computer user-friendly?" the buyer asked. (declarative sentence opening with a question)
> The buyer asked, "Is your company's computer user-friendly?" (declarative sentence closing with a question)

But

> Did the salesman state, "The Apple IIc is user-friendly"? (question containing declarative sentence)
> Someone—an anxious student?—is accessing midterm grades on the registrar's computer.
> In a very short time (one or two nanoseconds?) the mainframe can make a decision.

(2) Marking questionable dates or numbers

Use the question mark in parentheses to note a doubtful date or number.

> A minicomputer may cost from $20,000 to $200,000 (?), but experts estimate that by 1990 (?) every home will have its own microcomputer.

(3) Editing to eliminate misuse or overuse of question marks

Do not use question marks after indirect questions, after words used ironically, or after an exclamation phrased as a question.

MISUSED: The computer-wise student asked whether the terminal was "smart," able to do some data processing on its own, or "dumb," able only to communicate with the computer?

REVISED: The computer-wise student asked whether the terminal was "smart," able to do some data processing on its own, or "dumb," able only to communicate with the computer. (The sentence states rather than asks; it is, therefore, an indirect question.)

REVISED: The computer-wise student asked, "Is the terminal 'smart,' able to do some data processing on its own, or 'dumb,' able only to communicate with the computer?" (The sentence has been rewritten, placing the student's exact words—a direct question—within a declarative sentence. Notice that the direct question begins with the verb *is*.)

MISUSED: A personal computer is available at the exorbitant (?) price of $500.

REVISED: A personal computer is available at the reasonable price of $500. (The question mark is inadequate to show the writer means the opposite of *exorbitant*.)

MISUSED: Will you please debug this computer immediately?

REVISED: Will you please debug this computer immediately! (phrased as a question but actually an emphatic command)

25c Using Exclamation Points

The exclamation point is the third mark of end punctuation. It shows surprise or strong emotion.

(1) Marking emphasis

Use the exclamation point to end an emphatic statement, interjection, or command.

STATEMENT: We must become computer literate!
INTERJECTION: Oh! You have the new Trivia video game.
COMMAND: Give me the joystick! It is my turn to play.

(2) Editing to eliminate misuse or overuse of exclamation points

Do not overuse the exclamation point by making it a substitute for forceful words.

MISUSED: Computers make students want to learn!
REVISED: Computers motivate students to learn. (*Motivate* is a stronger word than the combination of *make* and *want*.)

Generally avoid exclamation points in academic writing, and in informal writing use them sparingly: in fact, a good rule of thumb is to use them no more often than you would shout in a speech.

NOTE: Avoid doubling up on end punctuation. Do not use double periods, question marks, or exclamation points.

INCORRECT: The computer has revolutionized merchandise pricing, game playing, communicating, etc..
Did you really buy IBM's PC jr??
Upgrading the Apple Macintosh is too expensive!!!
CORRECT: The computer has revolutionized merchandise pricing, game playing, communicating, etc.
Did you really buy IBM's PC jr?
Upgrading the Apple Macintosh is too expensive!

Do not use periods, question marks, and exclamation points together, unless the period marks the end of an abbreviation.

INCORRECT: She asked, "Is it true that many traffic lights are controlled by computers?".
The computers in some cars actually talk!?
CORRECT: She asked, "Is it true that many traffic lights are controlled by computers?"
The computers in some cars actually talk!
Will Jonathan Rotenberg of the Boston Computer Society speak at 7:30 P.M.?

Using Periods, Question Marks, and Exclamation Points

Exercise 25–1

NAME _____ DATE _____

Delete any unnecessary end punctuation, circle and correct errors in end punctuation, or add needed end punctuation.

    EXAMPLE: In Japan housewives can use home computers to vote!

1. Dr Griego asked the students if they could explain the difference between analog and digital computers?
2. A department store computer in Washington DC sends birthday cards to regular customers, to employees, to sales representatives, etc..
3. L.O.G.O. is a computer language for children.
4. Will you please remember that taping copyrighted programs is illegal?
5. "Have you finished using the keypunch," the operator asked?
6. The abacus, developed in China around the (?) sixth century, is the oldest mechanical calculator.
7. Ms Morrison, head of our data processing department, is training Mr Alvarez to run E.L.F., the Electronic Letter Follow-up program.
8. I wonder if storing information on cassettes is too burdensome?
9. In the middle of my recording of *Much Ado* (II,iii,92–97)) five lines have been erased.
10. "Have you never heard of Colossus I?" she cried!
11. Colossus used 2,000 vacuum tubes! Filled a room! And read tape at 5,000 characters per second!
12. "Is it true that during World War II Colossus deciphered German secret codes?" she asked?

                                                                                        Score _____

© 1986 by CBS College Publishing. All rights reserved.

Adding End Punctuation   Exercise 25-2

NAME _____ DATE _____

Add periods, question marks, and exclamation points to the following paragraphs. You will also need to add capital letters to indicate the beginning of each sentence.

> EXAMPLE: We are living in the fifth decade AC (After Computer), and many feel that BIBROC (Big Brother the Computer) is watching.

are our lives becoming too computerized are computers taking over could computers soon be using humans instead of humans using them the questions concern members of HUMOC (Humans Over Computers), a nonprofit organization with offices in Washington, DC, New York, and the Silicon Vally of Calif "computer relations are replacing human relations" says HUMOC President Jason Elder "interpersonal communication is fast becoming computer-person or intercomputer communications" by the year 1990, according to organization analysts, an average worker could wake up on the command of his or her computer alarm, spend the day at a computer terminal installed to save company space in the employee's own home, eat a computer-cooked meal, and retire at night without having had any human contact outside the immediate family

already computers telephone us to conduct surveys, send us bills, and correspond with us about our accounts when we travel, computers plot our air-routes, fly the plane, and reserve a room and charge our credit card for it before we have even reached our destinations when we work, computers process information, analyze problems, and suggest solutions as well as write our paycheck and deposit it directly in the bank in some experimental situations people have even shopped by computer and voted by computer humans at best are treated as an equal part of the system—liveware to complement the software and the hardware "do we want this kind of computerized future" asks techno-skeptic Elder.

"no," say those who feel their humanity threatened by a sterile computer perfection, but others who dream of increased freedom and leisure as computers take over life's most mundane chores shout, "yes"

Score _____

Review 25

Find and correct any errors in end punctuation in the following sentences.

1. The first mechanical calculators were built during the seventeenth century A.D..
2. James T Brown, MD, can access the hospital computer from his home terminal at 63 Gresham St, Ashland, Ore
3. In the morning before we get up, the computer turns on the coffee maker, then it starts the dishwasher and cooks our breakfast in the microwave.
4. They wondered if the price of the Apple IIc would decrease after Christmas?
5. Oh no!?! I forgot to store the program before I turned off the machine!!
6. F.B.I. agents gained access to the C.I.A. computer data banks.
7. Is it true that all computers are very smart? and can answer any question?
8. The beginner asked? "How many nibbles make a byte"?
9. Will you please do a leap frog test to check out the information in the computer memory?
10. C.O.B.O.L. is a useful computer language for business.

Score _____

Check your answers against those in the back of the text. Deduct 10 points for any sentence in which an error remains.

The Writer's Casebook #25

Application: Using Professional Language

In this chapter you may have encountered some unfamiliar terms in the examples about computers. These terms illustrate the special language—called "computerese" by some—that computer experts have developed to communicate easily with one another. Most of us have at some time experienced the bewilderment of trying to understand a message written for somebody else. Lacking the key to the special language used or the special events mentioned, we are as lost as though the message were written in a foreign language. "St MA at 8, Lib" could mean "study math at eight o'clock in the library" or "start machine at eight, (signed) Libby." "We need more RAM power" could mean we need more male goats in our herd or our truck does not push as well as we would like or we need to expand the random-access memory of our personal computer.

Each profession, including those in the humanities, has a special language of technical terms as well as special conventions for using the words and symbols, such as numbers, of the general language. Professional language enables specialists to save time and deal with complex subjects. When you are writing for fellow specialists, you may use technical terms without explanation because you know your audience will understand them. However, when you write for a general audience, you must either explain such terms or write in more generally understood language. Some experts feel that even in professional writing, technical language should be kept to a minimum.

In the sentence pairs that follow, the first was written for an audience of specialists, the second for general readers. As you read, look for the characteristics that distinguish the different methods of writing.

ENGLISH:
1. The use of anaphora contributes to an effect of rhetorical amplification.
2. The repetition of key words or phrases makes the ideas seem more important.

PSYCHOLOGY:
1. In order for classical conditioning to take place, one must identify a neutral stimulus and an unconditioned stimulus that elicit an unconditioned response (under specified conditions, of course).
2. Classical conditioning involves the training of emotions and/or reflexes.

GEOMETRY:
1. $A = \frac{1}{2}h(a + b)$
2. The area of a trapezoid is equal to one half the product of the height and the sum of the lengths of the two bases.

COMPUTERS:
1. The portable PC boasts 32k of ROM, but the LCD scrolls slowly.
2. The portable personal computer has a read-only memory power capable of handling 262,144 units of information, but its liquid crystal display registers characters slowly.

Notice that professional language may involve using symbols or abbreviations instead of words, using unfamiliar words, and using familiar words in unfamiliar ways. At times, as in the first two examples, the multisyllabic words and involved syntax may result in the "inkhorn" style. (See Writer's Casebook #18.) When you are deciding whether to use professional language, first consider your audience. Are they specialists or general readers? Then, whatever your audience, ask yourself, "Does professional language add significantly to either the clarity or the efficiency of my message?" If you cannot answer "yes," use general language.

Finally, as you have seen in this chapter, professional language creates special demands for end punctuation—particularly periods. Pay special attention to the use of periods, question marks, and exclamation points as you write the papers discussed below.

Cases for Writing: Using a Special Language

Case #1

Use the specialized language of some academic, recreational, or special-interest area that you know well to explain an idea to other experts in the field. Then rewrite your explanation for the general reader.

Case #2

Do you see computers as the saviors of mankind, as potential Big Brothers, or as important but perhaps hazardous tools? Write a paper about your reactions to the computerization of life in the 1980's. Follow standard practices in the humanities for numbers. (See Chapter 35.)

The Comma (,) 26

Preview 26

Add commas, as necessary, in the following paragraph. In the space at the right, indicate the reason for the use of each comma or set of commas: compound sentence, series, introductory element, interrupter, convention, or misreading. If the sentence does not need commas, write C.

¹To start a small business you need determination and ability. ²Most beginning entrepreneurs cannot afford much help and that means they must be masters-of-all-trades. ³The boss must also be salesperson buyer accountant and even custodian. ⁴In addition the new business owner must be an expert in advertising and merchandising. ⁵Those who can get help with taxes. ⁶Many on the other hand must find their own way through the paper mazes of tax laws and tax forms. ⁷Surviving the first years of big dreams and small returns requires a watershed of capital. ⁸Business owners who can wait three or four years to make a profit have the best chance of succeeding. ⁹Often new owners will form partnerships and one or more of the partners will work at an outside job to meet living expenses. ¹⁰Write to Small Businesses 119 San Marcos Ave. Los Angeles California for guidelines to becoming an entrepreneur.

1. _____
2. _____
3. _____
4. _____
5. _____
6. _____
7. _____
8. _____
9. _____
10. _____

Score _____

Check your answers against those in the back of the book. Deduct 5 points for each sentence you have incorrectly punctuated and 5 points for each incorrect reason for comma use. A score of 80 percent or higher indicates understanding of comma usage.

Commas are marks of internal punctuation—that is, they help clarify the relationships of words and word groups within a sentence. The uses of the comma are related directly to the structure and sense of the sentence, rather than to its oral interpretation. Therefore, although a comma may occur where you would pause in reading a sentence out loud, the pause itself is not an adequate reason for using a comma. Pauses in reading may indicate emphasis, difficulty in pronunciation, or even shortness of breath; for example, Calvin Coolidge's famous statement about American business might be read: "The business [pause] of America [pause] is business!" However, the sentence structure is simple (subject + prepositional phrase + verb + subjective complement), requiring no clarification and no commas: "The business of America is business!"

If you do not have a logical reason for using a comma (that is, a reason related to the structure of the sentence), do not use one. In the remainder of this chapter, we will discuss the use of commas to clarify or underscore sentence structure.

26a Setting Off Independent Clauses

Use a comma before a coordinating conjunction or a correlative conjunction when it joins independent clauses in a compound sentence.

The coordinating conjunctions are *and, but, or, nor, for, yet,* and *so.* The correlative conjunctions (coordinating conjunctions used in pairs) include *not only/but also, neither/nor, either/or, both/and, just as/so.*

> The business of America may be business, but the business of business is jobs and money.
>
> Businesses may specialize in developing products, or they may specialize in marketing products, yet the goal in each case is the same—to find or create a demand and fill it.
>
> Not only do businesses invest capital, but they also invest people.

Note: Do *not* use commas before coordinating conjunctions that join two subjects, two verbs, two predicates, two phrases, or two dependent clauses.

MISUSED: Products, and services cost money, and make money.
REVISED: Products and services cost money and make money. (two subjects and two predicates)

(1) Comma plus coordinating conjunction

You may omit the comma before the coordinating conjunction if the independent clauses are very short.

> Sell AT&T and buy IBM.
> Iococca saved Chrysler and he revolutionized the auto industry.

(2) Omitting the comma

You may substitute a semicolon before the coordinating conjunction if one or more of the clauses already contains commas, if one clause is especially complex, or if the second clause contrasts sharply with the first.

> The Dow Jones average, up 5.63 on Monday, closed down 3.02 Tuesday with heavy trading; but brokers expect a rally on Wednesday.
>
> Late Tuesday the Federal Reserve Board announced a reduction from 9½ to 9 percent in the discount rate charged on loans to private financial institutions; and analysts predicted an increase in business expansion as a result.
>
> The stock market and Consumer Price Index point to a healthy economy; but jobless rates point in the opposite direction.

26b Setting Off Items in a Series

(1) Coordinate elements

Use commas to separate three or more coordinate elements—words, phrases, or clauses that serve the same function in a sentence.

SERIES OF WORDS:	E. F. Hutton predicts solid returns on investments in electric, gas, and telephone stocks.
SERIES OF PHRASES:	The market reacts to changes in government, to international crises, to fluctuating interest rates, to natural disasters.
SERIES OF CLAUSES:	If inflation remains under control, if interest rates go down, and if production stays up, 1986 should be a good year for business.

If the last two elements in the series are connected by a coordinating conjunction, always use a comma before the conjunction. However, if there are coordinating conjunctions between each of the series elements, no commas are needed.

> E. F. Hutton, Merrill Lynch, and Dean Witter Reynolds agree in the assessment of utility stocks.

But

> E. F. Hutton and Merrill Lynch and Dean Witter Reynolds agree in the assessment of utility stocks.

(2) Coordinate adjectives

Use commas to separate items in a series of two or more coordinate adjectives—adjectives that modify the same word or word group.

> The sophisticated, new toys called Gobots are selling faster than Tonka can make them. (Both *sophisticated* and *new* modify *toys*.)
>
> The chubby, cuddly Cabbage Patch dolls continue to be strong sellers. (Both *chubby* and *cuddly* modify *Cabbage Patch dolls*.)

Test adjectives for coordination by reversing their order. If they still make sense when reversed, they are coordinate and should be separated with a comma.

> The cuddly, chubby Cabbage Patch dolls . . .
>
> The new, sophisticated toys . . .

But

> One Japanese variety of toy robots was called Machine Men.
>
> Japanese one variety of toy robots . . . (The reversal does not make sense; *Japanese* and *one* are not coordinate adjectives.)

If the coordinate adjectives are all connected by coordinating conjunctions, no commas are needed.

> The absurd but endearing pet rock craze was a marketing triumph.

26c   Setting Off Introductory Elements

A comma after a clause, long phrase, or transitional expression that introduces a sentence clarifies the sentence structure and signals the reader to get ready for the main idea in the subject and verb that follow.

(1)   Introductory adverb clauses

Use a comma to set off introductory adverb clauses, including elliptical (or abbreviated) clauses.

> Although the prospects for business careers will continue to be good during the next decade, job qualifications will be shifting from semiskilled to highly skilled.

When an adverb clause concludes a sentence, no comma is needed.

> New England provides an ideal environment for high-technology industries because it combines excellent educational institutions with a well-developed industrial infrastructure.

(2)   Introductory phrases

Use a comma to set off introductory verbals or verbal phrases and long prepositional phrases.

> Self-assured, the business administration graduate applied for a job with Intel. (introductory participle)
>
> Carrying her résumé, the woman arrived for an interview with the personnel manager. (introductory participial phrase)
>
> To qualify, you need a college degree. (introductory infinitive)

> To qualify for the best jobs, you need both experience and a college degree. (introductory infinitive phrase)
>
> Because of increasingly sophisticated analytical requirements, some business careers require a master's rather than a bachelor's degree. (long introductory prepositional phrase)
>
> With the rapid growth in the size and complexity of hospitals, the need for managers with graduate degrees in health administration increases. (The prepositional phrases together make a long introductory element.)

NOTE: A short introductory prepositional phrase requires no comma.

> Because of computers job opportunities may decline in stenography and bookkeeping.

(3) Introductory transitional expressions

Use commas to set off introductory transitional words and phrases, including most conjunctive adverbs (such as *however, therefore, moreover, consequently*).

> Overall, the outlook for jobs in business is good. (introductory transitional word)
>
> On the other hand, fewer opportunities may exist for the semiskilled office worker. (introductory transitional phrase)

26d Setting Off Nonessential Elements from the Rest of the Sentence

Use commas to set off parenthetical elements, interrupters not essential to the structure or meaning of the sentence.

Parenthetical elements may add to the meaning of the sentence, but they interrupt the main idea; without them the sentence still makes sense. Commas contain or "set off" these interruptions to signal their subordination to the main idea.

> Managers, the backbone of modern corporate structure, are needed wherever there are organizations. (parenthetical element, not essential to sentence's sense)
> Those who can analyze the present and plan for the future are needed wherever there are organizations. (not a parenthetical element; essential to defining the main idea *those*)

(1) Nonrestrictive modifiers

Use commas to set off nonrestrictive (nonessential) modifiers.

Restrictive, or essential, modifiers are needed to complete the meaning of the word or word group they modify; therefore, they should not be separated from it by commas.

The secretary who has learned word processing has a more secure job future than the secretary who can only type and take dictation.

Two different secretaries are discussed; the adjective clauses are needed to define each one. Without them the sentence would not make sense.

The secretary has a more secure job future than the secretary.

Nonrestrictive, or nonessential, modifiers are not needed to complete the meaning of the word or word group they modify; therefore, they should be separated from what is modified by commas.

The July report, which was sent by Federal Express, was late.

The nonrestrictive modifiers tell how the reports were sent, but they do not define which report was sent.

Both phrases and clauses may be restrictive or nonrestrictive. Wherever you place them in a sentence, nonrestrictive phrases or clauses should be set off from the words they modify—with two commas if a modifier comes in the middle of the sentence or with a single comma if it comes at the beginning or at the end of the sentence.

The MBA offered by our small school is as rigorous as that of many larger schools. (Restrictive phrase tells which MBA.)

The MBA, offered by our school since 1963, is required for many high-level positions. (nonrestrictive phrase—The required MBA is not restricted to one earned at *our school*.)

or

Offered by our school since 1963, the MBA is required for many high-level positions.

or

Many high-level positions require the MBA, offered by our school since 1963.

(2) Nonrestrictive appositives

Use commas to set off nonrestrictive (nonessential) appositives. An appositive is a noun or noun phrase that identifies, renames, or describes a noun, pronoun, or noun phrase (see pp. 111–112). When the appositive provides essential information, do not use commas; when the appositive provides nonessential information, use commas.

The magazine *Monthly Labor Review* published projections for the economy through 1995. (restrictive—The appositive *Monthly Labor Review* defines which magazine we are talking about.)

Monthly Labor Review, a magazine for economists, published projections for the economy through 1995. (nonrestrictive—The appositive *a magazine for economists* describes the magazine but is not needed to tell us which magazine we are discussing.)

(3) Conjunctive adverbs and other transitional expressions

Use commas to set off conjunctive adverbs and other transitional expressions when they interrupt or conclude a sentence as well as when they introduce a sentence.

> Opportunities for stenographers and typists, <u>unfortunately</u>, will decrease during the next decade.
>
> Opportunities for bank officers will increase rapidly, <u>however</u>.

(4) Contradictory phrases

Use commas to set off parenthetical expressions that contradict or show contrast.

> Choose a career based on talent and job satisfaction, <u>not salary alone</u>.
>
> Business careers, <u>not teaching</u>, offer high salaries and upward mobility.

(5) Absolute phrases

Use commas to set off absolute phrases consisting of nouns plus participles.

> <u>Her workload doubling</u>, Suzanne accepted the promotion.
>
> The secretary, <u>his dictation skills rusty from disuse</u>, took a refresher course.

(6) Miscellaneous nonessential elements

Use commas to set off miscellaneous nonessential elements—tag questions, names in direct address, mild interjections, and *yes* and *no*.

> Business administration is one of the most popular majors, <u>isn't it</u>?
>
> Are you taking the exam this semester, <u>Yvonne</u>?
>
> <u>Oh</u>, I hope not. <u>Well</u>, take it next semester then.
>
> <u>Yes</u>, the personnel office is down the hall, but, <u>no</u>, the personnel manager is not in.

26e Using Commas in Other Conventional Contexts

1. **Indirect quotations.** Commas set off a direct quotation from the phrase that identifies the speaker unless the quotation is an exclamation or question that begins the sentence.

> "Many business fields are still dominated by men," she said.
>
> She said, "Many business fields are still dominated by men."

But

"Are many business fields still dominated by men?" she asked.

When the phrase that identifies the speaker interrupts a quotation, the first part of the quotation determines the punctuation. If the first part constitutes a complete sentence, use a period after the tag identifying the speaker; if the first part is not a complete sentence, use a comma.

"Hispanic working women are the fastest growing economic group in the country," the speaker told us. "They also own more small businesses than any other ethnic group."

"Hispanic working women," the speaker told us, "are the fastest growing economic group in the country."

2. With titles and degrees. Commas set off titles and degrees when they follow but not when they precede names.

Dr. Marshall, president, will preside at the meeting of the board.
Patricia Sands, Ph.D., spoke on choosing an office computer.

3. In dates and addresses. Use commas to separate items and to set off final items from the rest of the sentence.

On December 12, 1984, First Interstate will open a new branch at 116 Paradise Road, Paradise Hills, California, a posh bedroom community.

Do *not* use commas to separate the state name from the zip code (383 Madison Avenue, New York, New York 10017) or the items of a date when the day precedes the month (12 December 1984).

4. In correspondence. Use commas after the complimentary close and after the salutation in informal letters.

Dear Cousin Maria,

Sincerely,

5. In numbers. Counting from right to left, use commas to separate large numbers into groups of three digits.

3,333   (comma optional with four digits)
33,333

When large numbers are written out in words, use commas in the same places as when the number is written in digits: three million, three hundred thirty-three thousand, three hundred thirty-three.

6. For left-out words. Occasionally, in a balanced construction you may leave out a word or words that complete a phrase or clause if the meaning is clear. A comma takes the place of the left-out word or words.

Mohsen earned a BBA with a concentration in finance; Jin, a BBA with a concentration in data management.

7. Between consecutively repeated words or phrases.

What is done, is done.

26f Using Commas to Prevent Misreading

A comma may be used to separate words if running them together might confuse readers or alter the meaning of the sentence.

MISLEADING: For those who attend the workshop may mark the beginning of a new career.
REVISED: For those who attend, the workshop may mark the beginning of a new career. (The comma prevents misreading *the workshop* as the object of the verb *attend*.)
MISLEADING: Executives who can use a word processor.
REVISED: Executives who can, use a word processor. (The comma prevents misreading can and use as a verb phrase and misunderstanding the sentence as a fragment, requiring a predicate.)

26g Editing to Eliminate Misuse or Overuse of Commas

Do not use commas to separate subjects from verbs or verbs from objects or complements; to separate independent clauses when there is no conjunction; to set off indirect quotations; or to indicate pauses taken for breath or emphasis in a sentence.

MISUSED: Earnings for the second quarter were up, earnings for the third quarter promise to exceed all expectations. (The comma separates two independent clauses, creating a comma splice.)
REVISED: Earnings for the second quarter were up; earnings for the third quarter promise to exceed all expectations.
MISUSED: Management and labor, negotiated, a new contract. (The commas separating subject and verb and verb and direct object serve no useful purpose.)
REVISED: Management and labor negotiated a new contract.
MISUSED: The union leader said, that the contract undermined workers' job security. (The union leader's words are paraphrased rather than quoted directly.)
REVISED: The union leader said that the contract undermined workers' job security.

Adding Commas for Series and Compound Sentences

Exercise 26–1

NAME _____ DATE _____

Add commas and semicolons in the series and compound sentences in the following paragraphs. You should have a total of *sixteen* commas and *four* semicolons.

EXAMPLE: Today young children must learn about business,‌for they are the targets of hard-sell advertising.

The energetic pursuit of children as a major consumer market has led some educators to begin teaching children about business and finance as early as elementary school. The husband-and-wife illustrator-author team of Roger and Marilyn Bollen has borrowed a page from the advertisers' book of tricks and used a story line and fantasy characters to motivate children to learn about production labor and investment.

They call their basic economics booklet *Ump's Fwat*. Ump is a cave dweller and he builds a better fwat (or bat) to be used in the game of fwap (or baseball). Ump realizes that his fwat will make better fwappers of Eorg Uggle Comah and Ignam. He can make and sell fwats to other cave dwellers to tree dwellers and to cliff dwellers who play fwap and in return he will receive many flinks (or money).

Ump has a marketable product but no flinks. He needs an investor to help him get into production. Ump's frugal rich friend Bunt invests his flinks to buy tools and materials and hire workers. Soon the demand for fwats exceeds Ump's ability to supply them. Ump must expand but he also must reward his investor so he pays Bunt a dividend and uses the rest of his profits to start a night shift to hire more fwat-makers and to hire fire-tenders to keep the cave lit.

Not only does the Bollens' innovative motivational approach to instruction remove the dryness and abstractness from economics but it also places economics in a child's world of games and make-believe. Children are amused by the cave dwellers yet they can identify with the basic situations and values—with the canceled fwap practice with the need to be a better fwapper with the concern to make better playing equipment. Teachers use *Ump's Fwat* as a beginning point for classroom activities by having the students set up mock corporations or engage in marketing studies. Teachers also hope Ump and his fwat business will help more children understand their role as consumers and the attempts to persuade them to part with their "flinks."

Score _____

Using Commas with Introductory and Nonessential Elements
Exercise 26–2

NAME _____ DATE _____

Add or delete commas, as needed, in the following sentences. If the sentence is correct, write C beside it.

> EXAMPLE: When they decide upon a career, students in the United States have more than 25,000 jobs to choose from.

1. The career field, chosen by more than 20 million Americans, is business.
2. Combining a broad background in business with a concentration in a specific field the business administration major offers flexibility and practicality.
3. The far-sighted student who understands that most professionals will change fields three or four times during their careers plans a course of study, that will prepare him or her for successful changes.
4. One of the largest professions a field anticipating rapid growth through 1995 is accounting.
5. To become an accountant you now need a college degree.
6. In the past on-the-job training sometimes qualified a worker for an accounting job.
7. However computers and the demand for increasingly complex financial records have made college-level training a necessity the demand for specialized knowledge exceeding the demand for experience.
8. Becoming a CPA requires both earning a college degree and passing a state examination.
9. Market research analysis another business career involves collecting and interpreting data, about the need for a particular product or service.
10. Although a degree in economics is good preparation for a career in market research analysts should also have a solid background in statistics and computers since they will need to use the latest methods and tools for analyzing data.
11. Competition is stiff for positions in merchandising isn't it?
12. Managers, who enjoy meeting and working with people, sometimes specialize in personnel but not data management.
13. A background in psychology and testing helps in personnel work since managers must evaluate workers' abilities.
14. In addition to administering tests and measuring the results personnel managers often set wage scales and develop morale and safety programs.
15. At the top of the wage and responsibility scales are the executives, the managers, who run the managers.
16. In 1982 nearly a half-million people were employed as bank officers or managers.
17. The number, of jobs in banking, a fast growing field will increase faster than the average, as banks expand increasing their services.
18. Business majors, who wish to specialize in hotel or hospital administration, should pursue graduate training in those areas.
19. Yes there will be more jobs in computer operations but fewer in keypunch because methods of data entry are improving.
20. Increasing from nearly two and a half million the number of secretaries will continue to increase not because of automation but in spite of it.

Score _____

Using Commas to Conform to Conventions and to Prevent Misreading   Exercise 26–3

NAME _____ DATE _____

Add or delete commas as necessary in the following sentences. If the sentence is correctly punctuated, write a C beside it.

EXAMPLE: On the whole‚ women earn less than two-thirds of what men earn.

1. In 1982 the median weekly wage for men was $371; the median weekly wage for women $241.
2. The mid-point in men's salaries is $19292 compared with $12532 for women.
3. "The disparity," says analyst Dawn Addington, "goes beyond differences in productivity or training."
4. "The disparity goes beyond differences in productivity or training," says analyst Charlene Addington, "It seems rooted in the distribution of men and women in different jobs."
5. "Do you," asked a student. "believe companies should pay equal wages for comparable work?"
6. Since January 1 1979 the Bureau of Labor Statistics has been collecting data on earning patterns.
7. In general jobs in the low-to-middle-paying categories have attracted more women than jobs in the high-paying categories.
8. Send your data to Jennifer Gonzales Ph.D. Office of Employment and Unemployment Statistics Bureau of Labor Statistics Washington D.C.
9. Some complacent people believe that whatever is is right.
10. Dear Juan;

Score _____

Sentence Combining with Commas and Conjunctions

Exercise 26–4

NAME _____ DATE _____

Combine short sentences below to make a single sentence that fits the description or includes the element or elements listed in parentheses. Add commas and conjunctions as necessary.

> EXAMPLE: The number of self-employed minorities has increased. The increase has been 43 percent. It has not been 31 percent. The increase has taken place in the last decade. (contradiction)
>
> *The number of self-employed minorities has increased 43 percent, not 31 percent, in the last decade.*

1. Minorities are becoming successful in small businesses. Their successes are the result of several factors. One factor is better formal education. Another factor is occupational training. Another factor is access to capital and credit. (series)

2. More minority entrepreneurs are investing in enterprises. These enterprises show high growth. These enterprises show high earnings. (coordinate adjectives)

3. Westinghouse Electric Corporation has openings for engineers. The corporation wants more of its engineers to be Hispanic. (compound sentence)

4. Westinghouse wants to encourage young Hispanics. Young Hispanics are encouraged to major in engineering. Westinghouse distributes an information and incentive kit. Westinghouse distributes this kit to high school students. (introductory infinitive phrase)

5. Mexican frozen-food lines enjoy a booming market. The lines include Rosita-brand products. (nonrestrictive clause).

6. Americans' appetite for Mexican food is increasing. Americans spent $51,000,000 on Mexican frozen food in 1976. They spent $147,000,000 on Mexican frozen food in 1982. (absolute phrase)

The Comma (,) **447**

7. The magazine is called *Hispanic Business*. It surveys business topics of interest to Hispanic entrepreneurs and workers. (restrictive appositive)

8. More women are enrolling in business administration programs. Women are still underrepresented in managerial positions. (introductory dependent clause)

9. "Equal pay for comparable work is next on the women's rights agenda." This was said by a famous women's rights activist. (direct quotation)

10. Are truck drivers more skilled than secretaries? If not, the salaries of truck drivers and secretaries should be the same. The activist also said this. (indirect quotation)

Score _____

© 1986 by CBS College Publishing. All rights reserved.

Review 26

Add commas as necessary in the following paragraph. In the space at the right indicate the reason for the use of each comma or set of commas: compound sentence, series, introductory element, interrupter, convention, or misreading. If there is no need for commas, write C.

[1]Which comes first—the luxury or the demand for the luxury? [2]With necessities the demand is there to begin with but with luxuries the demand is often created. [3]Take for example designer-brand clothes. [4]Although clothes are a necessity Calvin Klein's or R&K's or Leslie Fay's clothes are luxuries. [5]Producers must create a need by appealing to buyers' dreams desire for status or love of novelty. [6]Advertising agencies the shills or barkers of modern marketing respond with sophisticated fantasies and story lines. [7]Wearing the designer's clothes is made to seem the through-the-looking-glass entrée to the designer's fantasy. [8]Often the fantasy-makers are so successful that buyers do feel an emotional boost from wearing their product; they feel more attractive more exciting or more special. [9]Overall demand has been created by moving past physical necessities to appeal to people's psychological needs. [10]The buyer's ego is fed while the company feeds its bank account with $40000000 in profits.

1. _____
2. _____
3. _____
4. _____
5. _____
6. _____
7. _____
8. _____
9. _____
10. _____

Score _____

Check your answers against those in the back of the book. Deduct 5 points for each sentence incorrectly punctuated and 5 points for each incorrect reason for comma use. A score of 80 percent or higher indicates understanding of comma usage.

The Writer's Casebook #26

Throughout this chapter you have been reading examples and writing exercises that focus on the theme of business. In this casebook you will study some general principles that are fundamental to writing in the business world. As you study these principles and apply them to the cases at the end of the section, continue to work on comma usage—on using commas to underscore and clarify sentence structure and on observing the conventions of comma punctuation.

Application: Writing at Work—KIS and TEL

In a required writing course in the early 1970's, a utilities company executive complained, "I don't need to write well. I tell my secretary what to say and she writes for me." Even then the argument was no stronger than a cobweb: How could the executive evaluate the secretary's product if he or she were not a competent writer? But the executive did have a secretary, and that secretary was expected to specialize in communications—composing as well as producing letters, memos, and reports.

In the 1980's, however, the situation has changed. More and more companies are replacing personal secretaries with personal computers. The word-processing capacity of the computer allows executives to draft letters in as little time as their 1970's counterparts dictated letters. A push of a button sends the drafted letter to the word-processing pool, where a completed letter is produced without editing.

The modern businessperson needs to write well—not to compose elegant literary prose but to communicate clearly and effectively in writing. Good business writing is both simple and lean. The frills associated with some writing—elaborate descriptive details, figurative language, and elegant sentences—are usually out of place in business communications. Two general principles to follow are Keep It Simple and Trim Excess Language—or KIS and TEL.

1. KIS: The advice "keep it simple" applies to both the structuring of ideas and the structuring of sentences. Generally, business writers avoid surprise tactics. Because they are busy people writing for busy people, they design communications that can be grasped at a glance. Reports, memos, proposals, and many letters begin with a direct statement of main ideas, then elaborate in subsequent paragraphs. If the body of the communication is long or complex, the writer highlights major points and subdivisions with underlined headings.

Business writing style emphasizes short, active sentences. Leisurely periodic constructions are fine for fiction or essays, but in a report or memo, the message should be direct and to the point.

FICTION: At nine o'clock, waiting only for the precision instrument behind her chair to finish chiming, Jennifer Hartmore rose from the president's chair, glanced coldly around the table at the stony-faced board members, and announced the merger.

The Comma (,) 451

BUSINESS: Company President Jennifer Hartmore announced the merger to board members at a nine o'clock meeting.

Not only is the second version of Hartmore's announcement simpler and more direct, but it also lacks the emotional content of *glanced coldly* or *stony-faced* in the first sentence.

2. TEL: Trimming excess language—words that add nothing to the content or style—is good advice for any kind of writing. However, in this regard business writing has some special traps that can cause embarrassment. Some businesspeople who would not think of mailing a letter with typing errors or smudges regularly sign their names to poor prose. Clichés litter the pages, and incisive language is mixed with penny-a-dozen phrases. Compare the two versions of the following short letter.

January 30, 1986

Jonathan Wittier
President, XLQ Corporation
XLQ Building
Seattle, Washington 97720

My dear Mr. Wittier:

I am in receipt of your letter of recent date, and it is my heartfelt wish that you allow me to express my deepest appreciation for the message therein and my most profound concern about its potential ramifications.

Rest assured that every effort is being made to effect a mutually satisfactory solution to the dysfunction factor experienced with our PC-116, model 91 unit.

A specialist in terms of eradicating PC-116, model 91 operational inconsistencies is being dispatched by this office. If optimum satisfaction is not rendered, the dysfunctional unit will be replaced or the monies expended will be refunded.

Sincerely,

Carole T. Gallegos
Customer Relations

January 30, 1986

Jonathan Wittier
President, XLQ Corporation
XLQ Building
Seattle, Washington, 97720

Dear Mr. Wittier:

Thanks for your recent letter. I am concerned about the problem you are experiencing with our new model 91 personal computer.

I am sending a computer repair person immediately. If repairs are not possible, we will replace the unit or refund your money.

Sincerely,

Carole T. Gallegos
Customer Relations

The letter on the left combines convoluted sentences with clichés and jargon for a difficult-to-read and confusing message. The letter on the right is simple, economical, and clear.

Cases for Writing: Writing for Business

Case #1

Imagine you are the personnel manager for a large corporation that designs and manufactures electronic parts. Your company is interested in hiring large numbers of workers in all areas—engineering, assembly line, management, office work. The kind of people who have the best chance of being hired are well-trained, flexible, and willing to work long hours to complete projects. Write a letter to the career placement offices at local technical schools and colleges, explain your company's needs, and give some advice to potential applicants. Use the plain, business style.

Case #2

The gas company has sent you two gas bills for the month of July—one for $102.60 and one for $89.63. Both are much higher than what your records show for past Julys. Write a letter to the gas company asking for a correction of the bill. Keep your letter direct and to the point, avoiding emotional accusations.

The Semicolon (;) 27

Preview 27

Correct the use of semicolons in the following sentences. Then in the space at the end of the sentence, identify the reason for using the semicolon: compound sentence without coordinating conjunction, compound sentence with complex or punctuated clauses, clause with conjunctive adverb, or series with internal commas. If you have deleted a semicolon, explain why.

1. Recreation is big business in the United States, moreover, university professors are now specializing in recreation and leisure studies. _____

2. The need for supervised recreational activities in urban areas was recognized first by the nineteenth-century social workers; who built playgrounds and gamerooms in their settlement houses. _____

3. National parks, recreation and conservation areas to be held in trust for future generations, originated in the United States, now countries around the world have established such parks. _____

4. At first, the parks were nearly inaccessible, preserved from misuse or overuse by their remoteness, but by the mid-twentieth century the idea of the park resort, a highly developed tourist mecca, took hold. _____

5. Considered to be more important now are the wilderness aspects of the parks, the need to preserve natural treasures untouched by development, and the need of visitors to experience nature directly, unhampered by tourist traps and money-making gimmickry. _____

Score _____

Check your answers against those in the back of the book. Deduct 10 points for each error in semicolon use and 10 points for each error in identifying the reason for using the semicolon. If your score is 80 percent or higher, you have demonstrated an understanding of the materials in this chapter.

A semicolon is stronger than a comma but weaker than a period. Unlike the colon (:), which points forward to emphasize the remaining part of the sentence, the semicolon separates phrases or clauses within a sentence to clarify their relationship. It is used when a comma or a period would confuse or weaken sentence structure.

27a   Separating Independent Clauses

Use a semicolon between closely related independent clauses not joined by a comma and a coordinating conjunction. The semicolon shows that the meanings of the clauses tie them together logically but that the structures are grammatically complete and independent. The resulting construction is a compound sentence.

> *Recreation* means literally "to create again"; recreational activities recreate or restore emotional balance and sense of well being.

> Both the greater stress and greater leisure time of our society demand more play activity; play diffuses the stress and gives purpose to our leisure.

> Play more often but less intensely; rest frequently; laugh and smile all the time.

27b   Separating Complex, Internally Punctuated Clauses

Use a semicolon between complex, punctuated clauses. If one or more of the clauses in a compound sentence already contain commas, using another comma before the coordinating conjunction could be confusing. Using a semicolon clarifies the structure of the sentence and strengthens the separation of the clauses.

> To many, gardening is the perfect recreational activity; for growing vegetables, fruit, and flowers contributes to the re-creation of our environment.

> Campers find their recreation amid mountains, trees, and streams; but many bring the comforts of home with them in elaborate recreational vehicles.

27c   Separating Clauses Containing Conjunctive Adverbs

Use a semicolon between independent clauses when the second clause begins with or contains a conjunctive adverb, such as *therefore, moreover, consequently,* and *however*. (See 7a.2 for more about conjunctive adverbs.)

> Playgrounds began to appear in schoolyards and urban areas at the end of the last century; moreover, churches and charities began to build recreational centers to provide supervised activities for children and young adults.

The YMCA was one of the earliest recreational clubs; Hall House in Chicago, however, offered recreational programs as early as 1889.

NOTE: Set off the conjunctive adverb from the rest of the clause in which it appears with a comma or commas—one if the adverb follows the semicolon or ends the sentence, two if it is placed within the clause.

27d Separating Items in a Series

Use semicolons to clarify items in a series when one or more items contain commas or an item is long or complex.

> Commercial recreation is a billion-dollar business in the United States with millions of people spending their leisure time and money in bowling alleys, which offer food and drink as well as the game; in motion picture theaters; and in amusement parks like Disneyland or Knotts' Berry Farm.
>
> Public parks and gardens are noncommercial ventures that provide something for everyone—playgrounds with swings and other play equipment for the children; rambling walks and soothing prospects of trees and grass and flowers for those who prefer a sedate pace for their recreation; and tennis courts for the more active and competitive.

27e Editing to Eliminate Misuse of Semicolons

Avoid overusing or misusing semicolons. Do *not* use semicolons to separate dependent from independent clauses or phrases from clauses or to introduce a direct quotation.

MISUSED: When school is out in the summer; many community centers, clubs, and churches fill the gap with summer camps or vacation Bible schools. (Semicolon separates dependent and independent clause. The series commas in the independent clause do not affect the punctuation.)

REVISED: When school is out in the summer, many community centers, clubs, and churches fill the gap with summer camp or vacation Bible schools.

MISUSED: Attendance at summer camps is great; perhaps as many as 5,000,000. (The semicolon separates an independent clause and a phrase. Commas in the number do not affect the punctuation.)

REVISED: Attendance at summer camps is great, perhaps as many as 5,000,000.

MISUSED: The camp director said; "Welcome to Camp Winnemucca." (The semicolon introduces a direct quotation.)

REVISED: The camp director said, "Welcome to Camp Winnemucca."

Do not use semicolons to string together clauses that should be separated by periods. To be effective, semicolons should be used sparingly and only when the logical connection between ideas calls for a compound sentence.

OVERUSED: Every summer many college students work as counselors in summer camps; they direct activities, such as hiking and swimming; they watch over the physical well-being of the campers; and, when the inevitable homesickness strikes, they offer emotional support; for many campers these athletic, caring young men and women are excellent role models.

REVISED: Every summer many college students work as counselors in summer camps. They direct activities, such as hiking and swimming. They watch over the physical well-being of the campers; and, when the inevitable homesickness strikes, they offer emotional support. For many campers these athletic, caring young men and women are excellent role models.

The Semicolon (;)

Using Semicolons   Exercise 27-1

NAME _____ DATE _____

Correct the punctuation in the following sentences, adding or deleting semicolons and exchanging them for other punctuation as necessary. If a sentence is correct, write C beside it.

   EXAMPLE: Two of the most elaborate recreation centers in the world are Disneyland and Disney World(,)the brain children of the entertainment genius of Walt Disney.

1. When Disneyland opened in 1955; it brought film fantasies to life.
2. Disney organized his parks around favorite film themes, consequently, in Disneyland we find Frontierland, Adventureland, and Fantasyland, among other make-believe worlds.
3. An early Disney film hit was *Peter Pan*, the Peter Pan ride at Disneyland lets visitors experience the magic of flying to Never-Never land.
4. For some park goers it is enough to walk around and look, but others prefer the excitement of participating.
5. One exciting ride, the Mattahorn, resembles a kind of sophisticated, vertical roller coaster, but some people consider the ride too dangerous.
6. Disney amusements faithfully represent the fantasies of Disney films; rather than the realities of history; for example, Sleeping Beauty's Castle is a dream structure with fanciful turrets and towers beckoning from the clouds; not a replica of a squat and solid medieval fortress; it would be difficult to defend Disneyland against an invasion; from the delicate walls of Sleeping Beauty's Castle.
7. Knott of Knott's Berry Farm in California reconstructed a ghost town on the site of his jam-and-jelly factory, built a narrow-gauge railroad to carry passengers around the farm, and opened a home-style restaurant where visitors can enjoy fried chicken and some of his delicious berry pies.
8. Young passengers on the Farm railroad experience a special thrill; when the James gang holds up the train.
9. Other amusement parks include Six Flags Over Georgia in Atlanta, Astroworld in Houston, Texas, Kings Island in Cincinnati, Ohio, and Great Adventure in Jackson, New Jersey.
10. These parks provide exciting rides with enticing, thrill-promising names like Greezed Lightnin'; Kamikaze Slide, Sky Whirl, and the Beast.

Score _____

© 1986 by CBS College Publishing. All rights reserved.

Sentence Combining with Semicolons   Exercise 27-2

NAME _____ DATE _____

Combine the following groups of sentences to make a single sentence that uses one or more semicolons.

> EXAMPLE: The national parks were established by acts of Congress. They are our largest recreational centers. They offer some of the most fascinating activities.

The national parks, established by acts of Congress, are our largest recreational centers; moreover, they offer some of the most fascinating activities.

1. At one time visitors to Crater Lake National Park enjoyed feeding the squirrels. The squirrels were very tame. They would take peanuts directly from one's hand.

2. Recreational activities in the parks feature camping, admiring the scenery, and hiking. Often rangers conduct tours. These rangers are trained in botany or geology.

3. You could go to Carlsbad Caverns in the winter. Then you will miss the spectacular flight of the bats. The bats are only in residence during the summer.

4. At the Grand Canyon tourists can ride mules. The mules go to the bottom of the canyon. Under no circumstances may the tourists drop rocks from the canyon trail.

5. Yellowstone was the first national park. It is located in Wyoming and Montana. The park was established in 1872. It was established by an act of Congress.

Score _____

Using Semicolons and Commas Exercise 27–3

NAME _____ DATE _____

Add semicolons and commas wherever needed in the following paragraphs. In the space at the right explain your choice of punctuation. If no punctuation is needed, write C in the blank space.

EXAMPLE: ᵉSome people, incomprehensibly to me, spend their leisure time flirting with danger; however, others—like me—take their fun slowly and sedately.

e *(,) interrupter, (;) conjunctive adverb*

¹Some of the wildest rides worthy of the most inveterate thrill-seeker occur outside the amusement parks. ²The Cumbres-Toltec Railroad a narrow-gauge line in northern New Mexico offers the thrills of breathtaking heights. ³When the passengers board the train in Chama New Mexico they have little idea of what is ahead of them. ⁴They do not know that there are two engines pulling the train for a reason that the rules about not climbing on the cars are important safety precautions or that narrow-gauge railroads were built because of the rugged terrain not because the builders were partial to miniature steam engines.

⁵The first hint of the thrills ahead comes when the train reaches a trestle that towers above the Rio Grande River. ⁶The trestle is made of wood and looks like a matchstick construction its spindly legs dwindling to mere lines where they span the river far below. ⁷Not only must the train creep across this bridge but also one of the engines must be unhooked and sent ahead so as not to overtax the supports.

⁸The greatest excitement however comes in the Rio Grande Gorge itself. ⁹Creeping across the face of a sheer rock precipice the train is inches from a several-thousand-foot plunge.

1. _____
2. _____
3. _____
4. _____
5. _____
6. _____
7. _____
8. _____
9. _____

© 1986 by CBS College Publishing. All rights reserved.

¹⁰To sharpen the thrill passengers rush to the cliff side of the train moreover they lean out the window to get a better view of the tiny white ribbon of water nearly out of sight at the bottom of the gorge.

10. _____
    _____
    _____
    _____
    _____

Score _____

The Semicolon (;) **461**

> **Review 27**
>
> Correct the following sentences for semicolon use. Then in the space at the end of the sentence, identify the reason for using the semicolon: compound sentence without coordinating conjunction, compound sentence with complex or punctuated clauses, clause with conjunctive adverb, or series with internal commas. If you have deleted a semicolon, explain why.
>
> 1. Community centers and schools can play an important role in providing recreational activities to densely populated urban neighborhoods; areas where money is scarce and time is abundant. _____
>
> _____
>
> 2. Not only do supervised, constructive activities in these centers keep young people off the streets, but meaningful occupation and association with trained, caring counselors and teachers can also help youngsters set goals and give their lives direction. _____
>
> 3. Today photography or dancing may be pursued as a hobby, a skill to enrich the quality of life, however, tomorrow the hobby may become the foundation of a satisfying career. _____
>
> 4. Sharing, the ability to take turns and give as well as take, team playing, essential for the increasingly corporate life-style of our society, and discipline, that imposed by oneself as well as that imposed by authorities—all can be learned through recreational activities. _____
>
> 5. Equally important, recreation can teach us to stop our daily battle, it allows us to slow down, regroup, and rejuvenate—the best insurance against high-pressure burnout. _____
>
> **Score** _____
>
> Check your answers against those in the back of the book. Deduct 10 points for each error in semicolon use and 10 points for each error in identifying the reason for using the semicolon. If your score is 80 percent or higher, you have demonstrated an understanding of the materials in this chapter.

The Writer's Casebook #27

Using semicolons allows you to make some subtle distinctions about sentence elements and their relationships. You must see the little things—such as the presence of a comma in a series item to be punctuated—and then select the semicolon as an organizational device to show that elements are grammatically equal and logically related but structurally separate.

In this casebook you will be sharpening other, more general skills of observation, selection, and organization. But as you write, continue to sharpen your punctuation skills, paying special attention to your use of semicolons.

Application: Sharpening Your Reporting Skills

Reporting has two important dimensions: observing and telling what you observe.

1. To be a good observer, you must see the little things—the orange paper clip holding the paper, the mismatched socks worn by a professor—without missing the larger patterns—the use of colored, plastic paper clips by all students, except one who stapled her paper, or the tendency of some professors to be casual about dress.

If you look at an empty classroom and see nothing, your observation skills are dull—blunted, perhaps, by the habit of not seeing, since too often we dismiss the details of familiar objects and see them only in outline. No classroom is truly empty. If there are no students, there will be chairs and walls smudged with the fingerprints or graffiti of past occupants. The floor may be worn around certain desks, suggesting hours spent digging into difficult subjects. The chalkboard will be smooth or scratched, clean or dirty.

Your journal can help you sharpen your observing skills. Detailed descriptions of people, places, or events; inventories of minute-by-minute perceptions; sensory charts listing sensations associated with each of the five senses—each of these techniques will help you develop habits of awareness.

2. To tell what you observed, begin by organizing your materials and selecting significant details. The journalistic questions—who, what, when, where, why, and how—provide an effective guide.

Who did you see?
    What did you see?
        When did you see it?
            Where did you see it?
                Why did it happen?
                    How did it happen?

These questions may also be used to organize your materials into a thorough and effective report. In the first paragraph, give an overview that answers briefly as many of the questions as are pertinent to your subject. Then in subsequent paragraphs explore each question in greater depth, perhaps taking one question per paragraph.

Cases for Writing: Reporting Your World

Case #1

Visit a park, either in person or in your imagination. Use your journal or a notebook to record your observations. Then write a report that focuses on some person, place, or event that you observed.

Case #2

Assume that you are a member of the Neighborhood Improvement League, an organization that is very concerned about recreational opportunities for young people in your area. As a member of the league you have been asked to study the neighborhood, and to determine the available and needed recreational facilities. Write a report presenting your findings.

The Apostrophe (')   28

Preview 28

Correct apostrophe usage in the following sentences.

1. Human being's artistic impulse seems as integral to they're nature as the social impulse.

2. Abundant examples of the artwork of prehistoric people's have been found in the cave's of France and Spain.

3. Our' Stone Age ancestor's decorated the wall's and ceiling's with relief sculpture and painting's, perhaps as long ago as 20,000 to 100,000 years.

4. In 1833 an engraved bone was found near Geneva, and in 79 cave paintings were discovered in Spain.

5. Who's paintings were they? At first the Celts, whose homes had been in the cave areas fairly recently, were given credit; it was'nt until the twentieth century that they're great age was fully understood.

6. Its amusing to imagine Og and Mog, the cave artists, working on a mural and perhaps fighting over whether to call it Og's and Mog's or Mog's and Og's *Bison in Flight*.

7. The editor's in chief's selection of photographs for the book of cave art called *Underground Painting* illustrates the range and power of the cave artist's.

8. The public has reacted to the book with *oohs* and *ahs*.

Score _____

Check your answers against those in the back of the text. Deduct 5 points for each error. A score of 80 percent or better indicates a good grasp of the conventions of apostrophe usage.

28a Forming the Possessive Case

Use the apostrophe to show possession.

In English, possession is shown in two ways: (1) with a prepositional phrase and (2) with an apostrophe (') or an apostrophe and *-s* ('s).

prepositional phrase	*' or 's*
the versatility of Michelangelo	Michelangelo's versatility
Old Friends by Beatian Yazz	Beatian Yazz's *Old Friends*
the art collection of Gonzalo Martinez	Gonzalo Martinez's art collection
the genius of the sculptor	the sculptor's genius
the works of the artists	the artists' works

The apostrophe is used to form the possessive case of nouns *(Hossein's string art, the art student's garret)* or indefinite pronouns *(anyone's guess, one's creativity)*. But it is not used to form the possessive case of personal pronouns (see Chapter 21).

NOTE: Some writers use the apostrophe to show possession primarily when dealing with something animate, or alive. They use a prepositional phrase when dealing with inanimate objects, ideas, or things—except for certain measurements. Therefore, they write *the texture of the painting* instead of *the painting's texture; the message in the stone* instead of the *stone's message;* but *an hour's labor, a minute's rest, five cents' worth.*

1. Form the possessive case of singular nouns and indefinite pronouns by adding *-'s*.

    Cézanne's *Basket of Apples* added an element of action to the traditional still life.

    Appreciating the painter's work depends upon one's taste and background.

Most singular nouns that end in *-s* or *-z* also form the possessive case by adding *-'s;* however, if pronunciation of the added *-s* is awkward, only the apostrophe is used.

Doris's class project is to copy one of Rubens' paintings.

Yazz's contribution to Navajo art includes stylized turquoise deer, typified by paintings in Norman Velardes' gallery in Gallup, New Mexico.

Adding an extra syllable to *Doris* and *Yazz* does not sound awkward, but adding a syllable to *Rubens* and *Velardes* does.

2. Form the possessive case of plural nouns that end in -*s* by adding only an apostrophe.

   Critics' attacks hurt Cézanne, but his friends' scorn was even more devastating.

   Critics' attacking him hurt Cézanne, but his friends' mocking his work was even more devastating.

   The Joneses' art work is sold at every garage sale in town.

Form the possessive case of plural nouns that do not end in -*s* by adding -*'s*.

   The children's favorite artist is Dr. Seuss.

   The cave people's paintings found at Lascaux, France, focused on game animals.

3. Form the possessive of compound nouns by adding -*'s* to the last word.

   Suzanne guest-lectured in her sister-in-law's ceramics class.

   The matron of honor's gift to the couple was an original Manet.

   The matron of honor's giving the couple an original Manet astounded them.

4. Form the possessive case by adding -*'s* to each item in a compound when ownership is individual.

   Manet's and van Gogh's revolutionary styles were both greeted unfavorably by the public.

5. Form the possessive case by adding -*'s* to the last item in a compound when ownership is joint.

   Antonio and Monica's export/import shop specializes in art work from around the world.

28b   Omitting the Apostrophe

Do not use an apostrophe to form the plurals of nouns or the possessive case of personal pronouns.

MISUSED: The paintings' must be restored by an expert.
REVISED: The paintings must be restored by an expert.
MISUSED: The photograph by Julia Margaret Cameron is their's but the photograph by Ansel Adams is our's.
REVISED: The photograph by Julia Margaret Cameron is theirs but the photograph by Ansel Adams is ours.

The Apostrophe (') 467

28c Indicating Omissions in Contractions

Use the apostrophe to replace omitted letters or numbers in contractions.

> It's a wonder many art treasures survived the bombings in Europe during '44 and '45. (The apostrophe indicates the omission of the *i* in *is* and the *19* in *1944* and *1945*.)

(1) Omitted letters

Apostrophes replace omitted letters in the contraction of pronouns and verbs (*she + is = she's*) or of verbs and *not* (*would + not = wouldn't*).

Generally contractions should be avoided in academic or other formal writing.

INCORRECT:	Isnt that sculpture of St. Francis by Ed Vega? Hes known for his work with bronze.
REVISED INFORMAL:	Isn't that sculpture of St. Francis by Ed Vega? He's known for his work with bronze.
REVISED FORMAL:	That sculpture of St. Francis is by Ed Vega, is it not? He is known for his work with bronze.

NOTE: Be careful not to confuse contractions with possessive personal pronouns. Test a sentence for the appropriate form by substituting a possessive noun or the uncontracted form of the pronoun and verb.

	You're/your style is neoimpressionistic.
TEST 1:	You are style is neoimpressionistic.
TEST 2:	Jennifer's style is neoimpressionistic.

The uncontracted form of the pronoun and verb does not fit sensibly, but the possessive noun does, indicating that the appropriate choice is the possessive pronoun.

> Your style is neoimpressionistic.

Contractions such as *o'clock* and *will-o'-the-wisp* are acceptable in both formal and informal writing because they are the only forms of the words.

(2) Omitted numbers

In informal writing an apostrophe replaces the omitted century in dates, but the dates should be written out in college writing.

INCORRECT:	Le Corbusier's work matured during the 50's and 60's.
REVISED INFORMAL:	Le Corbusier's work matured during the '50's and '60's.
REVISED FORMAL:	Le Corbusier's work matured during the 1950's and 1960's.

28d Forming Plurals

Use the apostrophe plus -*s* to form the plurals of letters, numbers, symbols, abbreviations followed by periods, and words discussed as objects or entities; all except the abbreviations are also underlined.

Yazz is spelled with two *z*'s.

The sculpture was an elaborate intertwining of figure *8*'s.

The *$*'s in the surrealistic portrait of the tycoon denote his obsession with money.

Four Ph.D.'s worked for two years developing an interpretation of Picasso's last sculptures.

Nevertheless, the interpretation was sprinkled with *maybe*'s, *possibly*'s and *if*'s.

The Apostrophe (')

Using and Not Using Apostrophes to Show Possession Exercise 28–1

NAME _____ DATE _____

Form the possessive case of the word in parentheses; write it in the space provided.

EXAMPLE: (Michelangelo) _Michelangelo's_ Creation of Adam adorns the ceiling of the Sistine Chapel in the Vatican.

1. Greek (artist) _____ idealization of the human form influenced the humanists of the Renaissance.
2. The conscious effort of Renaissance artists to create a new style is apparent in (Ghiberti and Donatello) _____ sculpture, (Brunelleschi) _____ architecture, and (Masaccio) _____ painting.
3. (They) ____ work laid the foundations for the Italian Renaissance.
4. (Leonardo da Vinci) _____ Mona Lisa is (everyone) _____ favorite.
5. (He) ___ approach to art was thoroughly modern, blending art with science to explore (men) ____ and (women) _____ identity and understand (we) ___ relationship as human beings to the world we live in.
6. Raphael, on the other hand, blended art and philosophy, applying the (Neoplatonist) _____ logical spirit to solve (painters) _____ visual problems.
7. The fourth (Pope Pius) _____ patronage of the arts and particularly of Michelangelo were instrumental in enriching Italy and humanity with some of (it) __ greatest artistic treasures.
8. Michelangelo, (who) _____ genius still astounds, created masterpieces of sculpture, painting, and architecture.
9. "(You) ____ influence defies description," said the awestruck critic to Michelangelo.
10. (Rubens) _____ plump, female figures are among (he) __ best-remembered works.
11. A new art book reflects the (editor-in-chief) _____ partiality for the French rococo style.
12. Modern artists like Rodin gain inspiration rather than models for (they) _____ work from Michelangelo.
13. (Picasso) _____ and (Rodin) _____ cubism owes something to Einstein's theory of relativity.

© 1986 by CBS College Publishing. All rights reserved.

14. Subjects are fragmented to increase (one) _____ understanding of the shifting relationships of objects in space and time.
15. In the mid-twentieth century (action painters) _____ colorful, subjectless canvasses caused a sensation.

Score _____

The Apostrophe (') **471**

Distinguishing Possessives from Contractions and Plurals Exercise 28-2

NAME _____ DATE _____

Revise and rewrite any of the following sentences that reveal problems with apostrophe use related to possessives, contractions, and plurals.

    EXAMPLE: The art dealers collection includes two genuine Picasso's as well as you're usual works by unknown's or almost-unknowns.
The art dealer's collection includes two genuine Picassos as well as your usual works by unknowns or almost-unknowns.

1. Georgia O'Keeffes style seems almost Oriental in it's simplicity and clarity.

2. Do'nt expect beauty only from this womans' painting's; bleached skull's and bone's found in the desert are often motif's.

3. But its the close-ups of flowers' that most frequently have earned the publics admiration.

4. Photographer's like Julia Cameron helped raise photography from it's original status as a craft to it's current status as an accepted artistic medium.

5. These black pot's of Maria Martinez' soon became the San Ildefonso potters' trademark.

6. Even the smallest prayer pots' sell for enormous sum's in art gallery's around the world.

7. One of artist Peggy Bacons best-known childrens story's is *The Lion-Hearted Kitten*.

8. This art work of Fay Greenawaye's sets the tone and the standard for many illustrator's that followed.

Score _____

© 1986 by CBS College Publishing. All rights reserved.

Using Possessive Personal Pronouns and Contractions Exercise 28–3

NAME _____ DATE _____

Each of the following passages provides practice in distinguishing between problem pairs of contractions and possessive personal pronouns. In each passage fill in the blanks with the appropriate pronoun or contraction.

    EXAMPLE: (your/you're) *You're* fortunate to have had *your* work shown at the Brandywine Galleries.

(Your/You're)

_____ painting has improved dramatically this semester. _____ using more color; _____ proportions are better; _____ adding perspective to _____ landscapes and depth to _____ shadows. _____ next step is to find _____ own subject matter and break away from the purely representational style of _____ current work. But _____ on _____ way to developing _____ skills and beginning _____ studies as an art major.

(Its/It's)

_____ an unusual rug. _____ motif is the tree of life; _____ colors are a vivid combination of greens, yellows, reds, and blues. _____ like a haphazard bouquet of garden flowers, _____ mismatched colors adding to _____ careless, natural charm. To describe _____ pattern, _____ necessary to begin at the center. The tree of life, erect in a white field, is actually a stalk of corn. _____ light, golden-green color matches the border of the rug and _____ stylized shape, the stalks of corns with exaggerated golden ears at the four corners. _____ an effective addition to the usual tree-of-life symbolism since corn is a kind of staff of life. Moreover, the birdlike creatures sitting on the corn-stalk are more convincing since we can imagine they are there to eat _____ ears of corn.

(Whose/Who's)

_____ name comes first to mind when you are asked, "_____ the greatest painter of all time?" One artist _____ accomplishments still astound is, of course, Michelangelo, the "man for all seasons." But also there's Leonardo da Vinci, _____ been called "the true Renaissance man," or Rembrandt, _____ name is known to everyone, or Cézanne, _____ influence on twentieth century art is unrivaled. _____ most remembered, most loved, most imitated? _____ works are most coveted and most shown? There are too many _____ claims to greatness are undeniable for anyone to choose one _____ the greatest of all.

The Apostrophe (') **473**

(Their/They're)

_____ arriving for the art class, _____ canvasses under _____ arms and _____ paints in _____ hands. _____ a mixed group—youngsters, with _____ first watercolors fresh on _____ fingertips; dabblers with _____ new sets of paints and unstained pallets; and the art majors, _____ splotched smocks and dirty, scraped pallets contrasting oddly with _____ well-kept brushes.

_____ work like themselves will be mixed—some practiced, some fresh, some timid. But whatever _____ product may be, _____ delight in it will share a common foundation—the knowledge that _____ the creators of works of art.

Score _____

© 1986 by CBS College Publishing. All rights reserved.

Review 28

Correct apostrophe usage in the following sentences.

1. At the childrens Art Awards Banquet the master's of ceremonies' speech was filled with anecdote's about art classe's she had taken.

2. In 71 she was asked to build a box sculpture overnight at the entrance to Mitchell Hall and to be on hand to observe the surprise of the students' when they saw the sculpture.

3. Five minutes worth of throwing globs of paint at a canvas produced an "action" painting, praised by an instructor who's reaction to her' earlier, more careful work had been several *interestings* and even a couple of contemptuous *cutes*.

4. "Its important to believe in yourself, no matter what your told by anyone, even by people whose opinion you respect," she told the audience.

5. "Artists gifts are as many and varied as there are artist's. No ones going to like Chris work unless Chris likes and believes in it's worth first."

6. The top award was given to Orona's and Curran's joint effort, *Climbing the Mountain*, while second place was split between Kim Liu and Al Bronski's paintings.

Score _____

Check your answers against those in the back of the text. Deduct 5 points for each error. A score of 80 percent or better indicates a good grasp of the conventions of apostrophe usage.

The Writer's Casebook #28

A major problem in apostrophe use arises because the apostrophe creates a difference in meaning but no difference in pronunciation or even in spelling. For example, *artists*, *artists'*, and *artist's* are pronounced the same, and the letters are the same; but the first word is a plural noun, which may be used as a subject, an object, or a complement, whereas the second and third words are possessive forms and may only be used to modify nouns or their substitutes.

The artists built an artists' gallery to show the struggling artist's paintings.

Using analogy (the subject of this casebook) also requires writers to recognize similarities among differences. But as you make connections among distinct ideas, remember to discriminate also between plural and possessive forms.

Application: Explaining with Analogy

You have already worked with comparison as a way to develop your ideas in an essay and a paragraph (see 4e.6 and Writer's Casebook #7). Analogy is also a kind of comparison; however, it differs from the standard method of comparison in two major ways. First, with analogy one subject is subordinate to the other, whereas with standard comparison both subjects are equal. Secondly, analogy is more imaginative than comparison, relying primarily upon a figurative rather than a literal use of language.

Analogy	Comparison
Oriental painting is like a ballet. Each movement of the artist is tightly controlled art in motion. The brush touches and skips across the page, pointing and pirouetting. A single stroke like the dancer's *glissade* creates a tree or a bird on a branch. A set of flying touches, the *pas de bourrée* of the painter, dots the sky with birds in flight.	Oriental and Occidental watercolors differ dramatically, both in the method of their creation and in the effect of the final product. Oriental painting is itself a ritual, and the Oriental watercolor is mystical and ritualistically simplified. The Occidental painter is freer. He or she washes or layers color with an artistic spontaneity that is reflected in the often fluid quality of the finished painting.

In the comparison paragraph on the right the two styles of painting discussed are equally important; however, in the analogy paragraph on the left, ballet is introduced only to explain an important quality of the main subject, Oriental painting. The language and details of the comparison are meant to be taken literally, but those of the analogy are not. Oriental painting is not really a ballet, nor are the strokes of the painter actually called a *glissade* or a *pas de bourrée*. The terms are literally those of the dance, and only figuratively, or metaphorically, applied to painting.

To use analogy as a method of explanation, begin with a metaphor or simile—a comparison between two unlike but somehow related things. Then extend the comparison from part to part of the subjects. For example, you might begin by presenting a metaphor: Writing a description is like painting a picture. Then you can develop the analogy by comparing the writer's pen to the painter's brush, paints to words, perspective to viewpoint, the tonal qualities of paints to the moods and connotations of words, and so forth.

Cases for Writing: Writing About Art

Case #1

Beginning with the explanation above, write an analogy comparing descriptive writing to painting.

Case #2

Use one of the following or a subject of your own choice as the main topic of an analogy: punk-rocker fashions, the school library at exam or term paper time, an office party, a football game, yuppies, books, bees, thunderstorms, party crashers. You may continue our discussion of art by drawing an analogy between your main topic and a particular art work or school of art. Or you may choose another appropriate comparison.

Quotation Marks
(" "; ' ')

29

Preview 29

Add, delete, or change as necessary the position of single or double quotation marks in the following sentences. You may also need to revise other punctuation that functions in relation to the quotation marks.

1. Folktales and legends says my American literature professor often glorify the picturesque and daring elements of our society.
2. "Some of those glorified in this way may have been scoundrels," she continued. "It doesn't matter, as long as their deeds capture our imagination".
3. Perhaps the best-known and best-loved heroic scoundrel of all time is Odysseus, immortalized in Homer's great epic poem <u>The Odyssey</u> the professor told us.
4. She asked, "if any of us knew the story of Odysseus and the Trojan Horse."
5. Yvonne replied That has to do with a hollow horse filled with soldiers, which the Trojans are tricked into dragging inside their gates
6. "The trickery is planned by Odysseus, whom the goddess Athena calls 'a bottomless bag of tricks."
7. Odysseus is also one of the greatest "liars" and "tall-tale" spinners of all time.
8. In an article entitled Odysseus, the Chameleon, admirer Jean Conrad calls the last twelve books of *The Odyssey* "the saga of lies;" for in the space of a few epic pages Odysseus tells elaborate lies about himself to his servants, to his son Telemachus, to his wife Penelope, and even to Athena herself.

Score _____

Check your answers against those in the back of the book. Deduct 4 points for each misused or missing punctuation mark. A score of 80 percent or better indicates you have mastered the conventions for using quotation marks.

29a Setting Off Direct Quotations

Use double quotations marks (" ") to set off directly quoted words, phrases, or sentences.

"Central to the purpose of fairy tales is wish-fulfillment," said the lecturer.

She described the tales as "a window of social values."

NOTE: Indirect quotations, reporting what someone said or wrote without using the speaker's or writer's exact words, do not use quotation marks. (See 26e for more about indirect quotations.)

The lecturer said that wish fulfillment is a central purpose of fairy tales.

Use single quotation marks (' ') to set off a quotation within a quotation.

Tomás wrote, "The White Rabbit told Alice, 'I'm late, for a very important date.'"

In an article about the Brothers Grimm version of *Cinderella*, the critic notes, "Even Martinez, who finds the tale humorous, admits that the blinding of the stepsisters in the wedding episode 'fulfills a revenge motif that seriously undermines the innocence of the tale and its heroine.'"

29b   Setting Off Titles

Use double quotation marks to set off the titles of short works (articles in periodicals, essays, short stories, short poems, songs, speeches, episodes of broadcast series) and chapters or sections of books.

In "The Dark Side of the Urn," an article in the Spring 1983 issue of *Essays in Literature*, Deborah Pope reevaluates the speaker in Keats's poem "Ode on a Grecian Urn."

Cooper's short story "Rip Van Winkle" had its origin in German legend.

The song "Puff the Magic Dragon" was recorded by Peter, Paul, and Mary.

Use single quotation marks to punctuate a title when it appears in material already set off with double quotation marks.

"In 'The Two Mousequiteers' the mice speak French," Ramoncita told herself to justify watching *Tom and Jerry* cartoons instead of studying French verbs.

29c   Setting Off Words Used in a Special Sense

Use double quotation marks to set off invented or made-up words and words used in a special sense.

The "witch" growled the supposedly magic word, yet no "frog princes" were created.

The "fairy tale" had no fairies; therefore, it is a "fairyless tale."

In each example the first term is used in a special sense (skeptically or ironically); the second is invented.

29d Editing to Eliminate Misuse or Overuse of Quotation Marks

Avoid overusing or misusing quotation marks. Do *not* use quotation marks to set off titles of long works, titles on a title page, technical terms or words being defined. Also remember that using quotation marks will not make slang, trite expressions, or nicknames acceptable in formal writing nor add strength to diction; to correct those problems, you must rewrite the sentence using standard vocabulary and more emphatic words.

MISUSED: Legends about the Greek hero Odysseus are brought together in "The Odyssey," an epic by the blind poet Homer.
REVISED: Legends about the Greek hero Odysseus are brought together in *The Odyssey*, an epic by the blind poet Homer.
MISUSED: "Odysseus the Deceiver"
by
Stephanie Gallegos
REVISED: Odysseus the Deceiver
by
Stephanie Gallegos
MISUSED: Homer often uses "epithets" instead of names—for example, "gray-eyed goddess" for Athena and "Achaians with the flowing hair" for the Greeks.
REVISED: Homer often uses epithets instead of names—for example, "gray-eyed goddess" for Athena and "Achaians with the flowing hair" for the Greeks.
MISUSED: The word "epithet"means a descriptive phrase that highlights an outstanding characteristic of someone or something.
REVISED: The word epithet means a descriptive phrase that highlights an outstanding characteristic of someone or something.

(See 32c for use of underlining or italics for words being discussed as words.)

MISUSED: Odysseus's "honesty" earns him the admiration of the equally wily Athena; but the less admiring Dante "rewards" Odysseus with a liar's place in *The Inferno*, or hell.
REVISED: Odysseus's deceptiveness earns him the admiration of the equally wily Athena; but the less admiring Dante punishes Odysseus with a liar's place in *The Inferno*, or hell.
MISUSED: Odysseus was one "slippery dude."
REVISED: Odysseus was a chameleon.

29e Setting Off Dialogue, Long Prose Passages, and Poetry

Follow standard practice when using quotation marks with dialogue, long prose passages, and poetry.

(1) Dialogue

Start a new paragraph with each new speaker when you record dialogue, and enclose the exact words of the speaker in quotation marks.

> It happened one day that Cinderella's father was going to mass, and he asked his stepdaughters what they would like him to bring them.
> "Beautiful clothes," said one.
> "Pearls and precious stones," said the other.
> "But you, Cinderella," he said, "what will you have?"
> "Father, break off the first twig that jabs your hat on your way home and bring it to me." (Translated from the Brothers Grimm, *Aeschenputtel*)

When you record several paragraphs of a single speaker's words, begin each new paragraph with quotation marks, but place closing quotation marks only at the end of the entire passage.

> "Love is a trick played on us by the forces of evolution," continued the monster monotonously. "Pleasure is the bait laid down by the same. There is only power. Power is of the individual mind, but the mind's power alone is not enough. The power of strength decides everything in the end, and only Might is right.
> "Now I think it is time that you should go away, young master, for I find this conversation excessively exhausting. I think you ought to go away really almost at once, in case my great disillusioned mouth should suddenly determine to introduce you to my great gills, which have teeth in them also. Yes, I really think you ought to go away this moment. Indeed I think you ought to put your very back into it. And so, a long farewell to all my greatness." (T. H. White, *The Sword in the Stone*)

(2) Long prose passages

Set off prose quotations of more than four lines from the body of the paper, indenting ten spaces from the left-hand margin, triple-spacing above and below the quotation, and double-spacing within it. Omit quotation marks. If there is a tag identifying the speaker, it is followed by a colon.

> When Hans Christian Anderson wrote "The Emperor's New Clothes," he began the story like an old folk tale:
>
> > In ages long past there lived an emperor who was excessively fond of new clothes. He spent at least half of his time in his wardrobe, looking at his costly robes, and trying on one after another to see which best pleased his fancy.
> > One day there came to his capital two clever rogues who declared that they were weavers. . . .
>
> Adopting the manner and tone of the traditional tale, Anderson created a tale as imperishable as any of the traditional märchen.

Within long quotations set off in this manner, retain double quotation marks for quoted material.

(3) Poetry

Enclose three or fewer lines of poetry in quotation marks and place in the text; separate lines with slashes; leave space around the slashes.

> In J. R. R. Tolkien's *The Hobbit* the dwarves tease Bilbo Baggins by singing violently while they carefully clean his kitchen: "Chip the glasses and crack the plates! / Blunt the knives and bend the forks!"

Four or more lines or fewer lines requiring special emphasis may be set off from the text in the same manner as a long quotation.

> In J. R. R. Tolkien's *The Hobbit* the dwarves tease Biblo Baggins by singing violently while they carefully clean his kitchen:
>
>> Chip the glass and crack the plates!
>> Blunt the knives and bend the forks!
>> That's what Bilbo Baggins hates—
>> Smash the bottles and burn the corks!

29f Using Quotation Marks with Other Punctuation

Place quotation marks carefully in relation to other punctuation marks. Some guidelines follow.

1. Place commas and periods before final quotation marks.

   > "The time has come," the walrus said, "to talk of many things—of shoes and ships and sealing wax and why the sea is boiling hot and whether pigs have wings."

2. Use commas to set off tag phrases (like *she said*) that identify the source of the quotation.

   > Little Red Riding Hood said, "Grandmamma, what big teeth you have!"
   >
   > "The better to eat you with, my dear," said the wolf dressed in Grandmamma's nightcap.

When the tag phrase interrupts a single sentence, set it off completely. When it comes between two complete sentences, follow it with a period.

> "In Thurber's version of *Little Red Riding Hood*," said Jacquine, "the little girl shoots the wolf."
>
> "Thurber's Red Riding Hood shoots the wolf," said Jacquine. "Thurber says that it isn't 'so easy to fool little girls nowadays.'"

No comma is needed when a concluding tag follows a quoted question or exclamation.

> "Have you read Tolkien's fantasy tale, *The Hobbit*?" she asked.

No comma is needed when you quote a word or short phrase.

> Tolkien said hobbits call us "big folk" and hide when we come by.

Quotation Marks (" "; ' ')

3. Place question marks and exclamation points inside or outside final quotation marks, depending upon the meaning of the sentence.

When the quotation itself is an exclamation or a question, put the exclamation point or question mark inside quotation marks.

"Seven at a blow!" exclaimed the tailor.

"Did I kill seven at a blow?" asked the tailor.

When the sentence of which the quotation is a part rather than the quotation itself is an exclamation or question, put the exclamation point or question mark outside the quotation marks.

Did he say "seven at a blow"?

He did say "seven at a blow"!

4. Place semicolons and colons outside final quotation marks.

Cinderella told her father that she loved him "like salt"; yet she meant that without him life would be "like food without salt": flavorless.

5. Use a colon instead of a comma after the introductory tag to a long or formal quotation (see 30a).

The King sent forth a proclamation: "He who slays the dragon and saves the kingdom will win the hand of my daughter, the peerless Princess Alena, as his bride."

Using Quotation Marks   Exercise 29–1

NAME _____ DATE _____

Rewrite the following items, adding, deleting, or altering the position of quotation marks and changing other punctuation, such as commas, as necessary.

EXAMPLE: Did you say that "you know of 345 versions of 'Cinderella'?"
Did you say that you know of 345 versions of Cinderella?

1. "Some people consider fairy tales to be infantile", said the professor, "and unworthy of serious study."

2. 'But fairy tales are much more than so-called "escape" literature" she continued, reading from an article entitled *The Power of Tale-Telling*, Tales are a powerful force for teaching the young about the values of our society.

3. Some of these 'values,' however, do not seem to be too 'valuable.'

4. In *Cinderella*, for example, the power of beauty and money are "socially validated," or reinforced as major criteria of social worth.

5. "Aeschenputtel", the Grimm Brothers' version of *Cinderella*, also fulfills some of our negative wishes!" claims one folklorist "with an orgy of violence and revenge".

6. "Cinderella's Revenge"
by
Peter Ponowski

7. Peter writes: "Aeschenputtel's stepsisters are, as Dr. Strauss puts it, "mutilated and ostracized" for their sins."

8. It is not enough that the stepsisters lose the prince; they must be crippled and blinded besides. Dr. Strauss makes Aeschenputtel directly responsible and calls her a witch: "Whoever offends the bewitching heroine is destined for trouble. As soon as

© 1986 by CBS College Publishing. All rights reserved.

Aeschenputtel calls her familiars, the birds who sit in the magic hazel tree, anything is possible. It is the birds who call the prince's attention to the stepsisters' not being the right brides for him. And it is the birds who peck out the stepsisters' eyes at Aeschenputtel's wedding."

9. According to Dr. Strauss, the rhymes in the story are much like incantations. When Aeschenputtel needs a dress for the ball, she tells the hazel tree, Dear tree, rustle yourself and shake yourself, / Dress me in silver and gold. After the stepsisters hack off toes or heels to make their feet fit into Aeschenputtel's tiny slipper, the birds point out the women's deceit by chanting to the prince, Rucke diguck, rucke diguck, / There's blood in the shoe; / The shoe is too small, / She's not the right bride after all."

Score _____

Quotation Marks (" "; ' ') 487

Using Quotation Marks in Dialogue Exercise 29–2

NAME _____ DATE _____

Add quotation marks and other appropriate punctuation to the following story. Indicate the beginning of a new paragraph with the symbol ¶.

The Golden Slipper

An old man and his old wife had two daughters. Once the old man went to town and bought a fish for the elder sister and a fish for the younger sister. The elder sister ate her fish, but the younger one went to the well and said Little mother fish, what shall I do with you? Do not eat me said the fish but put me into the water; I will be useful to you The maiden dropped the fish into the well and went home. Now the old woman had a great dislike for her younger daughter. . . . She dressed her elder daughter in her best clothes, went with her to mass, and left three measures of barley for the younger one, saying While I pray to God, you husk the barley. So she went to mass and her younger daughter went to fetch water at the well. She sat down at the edge and wept. The fish swam to the surface and asked Why do you weep, lovely maiden How can I help weeping the maiden answered My mother has dressed my sister in her best clothes and taken her to mass, but she left me at home and ordered me to husk three measures of barley before she returns from church. The fish said Weep not. Dress and go to church after her. The barley will be husked. The maiden dressed, went to church, and began to pray to God. That day the king's son was attending mass; our beautiful maiden pleased him tremendously and he wanted to know whose daughter she was. So he took some pitch and threw it under her golden slipper. The slipper remained when the girl went home. I will marry her whose slipper this is, said the young prince. Soon the old woman too came home. What a beauty was there! she said And just look at you, what a tatterdemalion you are! In the meantime the prince was traveling from one district to another, seeking the maiden who had lost her slipper, but he could not find anyone whom it fitted. He came to the old woman and said Call your young daughter hither; I want to see whether the slipper fits her. My daughter will dirty the slipper answered the old woman. The maiden came and the king's son tried the slipper on her; it fitted. He married her and they lived happily and prospered. (Condensed from Aleksandr Nikalaevich Afanas'ev, ed., *Russian Fairy Tales*)

Score _____

© 1986 by CBS College Publishing. All rights reserved.

Review 29

Add, delete, or change as necessary the position of single or double quotation marks in the following sentences. You may also need to revise other punctuation that functions in relation to the quotation marks.

1. American as well as Greek folklore celebrates the "bottomless bag of tricks:" the Odysseus-style braggart and trickster.
2. Old Coyote is the trickster-hero of many Native American folktales said Yvonne.
3. "In an unusual variation on the Promethean myth", she continued "Old Coyote steals fire from the heavens to give to the human tribes".
4. Antonio asked. "if it was Old Coyote who turned the animal-people of Bryce Canyon into stone"?
5. "Yes said Yvonne, "the people were fighting and stealing and Coyote became 'very' angry with them."
6. "The Utes call the Bryce Canyon stone people red-painted faces and say the animals streaked their faces with paint."
7. Dr. E. Philip Jones in his book "*The Wiley Coyote*" notes; "Like many legends the exploits of Old Coyote have their basis in fact—in this case in the remarkable intelligence of the animal.
8. Is it true that coyotes will cure themselves when they have been poisoned by eating juniper berries asked the city-dweller.
9. "Believe it or not, the expert said, "Yes!"

Score _____

Check your answers against those in the back of the book. Deduct 4 points for each misused or missing punctuation mark. A score of 80 percent or better indicates you have mastered the conventions for using quotation marks.

The Writer's Casebook #29

Application: Using Quotations in Expository Writing

Handled properly, quotations can add to the interest and the credibility of your writing; handled improperly, they can mar a paper by making it seem fragmented or derived. Some guidelines for using quotations in expository writing follow.

1. Use quotations sparingly.

Avoid making the mistake of writing "quote-sandwiches": layers of quotations that are held together by nothing more substantial than the writer's penmanship and an occasional identifying tag. When quoting sources, more is definitely not better; in fact, it is usually worse. In general, one or at most two short quotations in a paragraph are all you can effectively use.

2. Avoid dangling quotations.

Rarely can you assume that a quotation explains itself or that it fits without explanation into your discussion. You must show how it fits in or is related to your purpose—that is, does the quotation illustrate, substantiate, or contradict your point?

3. Avoid opening with a quotation.

Although an apt quotation may fit effectively into your introduction and serve to heighten the reader's interest, the quotation should not begin the paragraph. When not properly introduced, a quotation may send the readers' thoughts in the wrong direction. Remember that quoted material was originally part of another writer's text and another writer's purpose. To fit the quotation to your different needs, you must adapt it by adding a sentence or two that ties it into the rest of your paragraph.

4. Avoid overlong quotations.

If you find yourself feeling that another writer has said what you want to say better than you can say it, you might be tempted to use long passages from that writer, introducing them with short tags such as *according to* or *as the eminent authority so-and-so says.* This practice is another variation on the "quote-sandwich" and suggests the need to dig deeper to find something of your own to say about the subject.

5. Be careful not to rely too much on the appeal-to-authority to make your point.

Quotations from written sources may help substantiate your arguments or clarify your explanation, but the weight of the discussion should nonetheless rest upon your own reasoning and analysis. If you find you are using an authority as your sole support ("This is so because so-and-so says it is so"), you may be guilty of the appeal-to-authority fallacy in reasoning.

Cases for Writing: Writing Dialogue and Tales

Case #1

Listen to a conversation that you are not participating in. Then later try to reconstruct what was said in dialogue form. Try to reproduce the special characteristics—sound, vocabulary, sentence structure—of the different speakers. Rely totally upon the words of the speakers rather than upon identifying tags (*she said happily*) to convey mood and tone.

Case #2

Write your own version of a favorite tale or fable. You may either embellish the story (add more details and incidents) or fracture it (reverse the ending or write a mock version). For example, you might rewrite *The Emperor's New Clothes* by adding descriptions of the emperor and the palace and further developing the dialogue of the characters. Or you could reverse the roles in *Sleeping Beauty* and write *Sleeping Hunk* about a handsome prince who has been awakened by the kiss of a beautiful princess.

Other Punctuation Marks 30

Preview 30

Add punctuation as needed to the following sentences.

1. "Use your microscope to examine the structure of the flars *sic*," said the professor.
2. Flowers those brightly colored, delightfully scented messengers of love and comfort are actually the reproductive mechanism of the plant.
3. Everyone knows and loves the poem that begins "I wandered lonely as a cloud."
4. "Roses are red, violets are blue."
5. The air is filled with the aroma, scent of blossoms.
6. We planted an old-fashioned garden of old-fashioned flowers hollyhocks, sweet peas, marigolds, nasturtiums, zinnias, and sunflowers.
7. In his quotation Eric omitted the scientific names that followed the common names for plants in the original: "The yucca grows well in high desert while the saguaro must have the year-round warmth of a low-desert climate."
8. Joseph's Coat, Starfire, Condessa, First Edition these are some of my favorite roses.
9. Cornflowers bachelor buttons in the Northwest can be dried for attractive flower arrangements.
10. To raise healthy houseplants, the right amount of sunshine and light is as important as no, more important than the right amount of water and food.

Score _____

Check your answers against those in the back of the book. Deduct 10 points for each incorrectly punctuated sentence. A score of 80 percent or better indicates mastery of the materials in this chapter.

The Colon

30a Using a Colon to Introduce Material

Use the colon to introduce lists or series, explanatory material, and long or formal quotations or to follow the salutation of a business letter.

> The house was a jungle of plants: rubber trees in the living room, asparagus ferns and spider plants at every window, and African violets in the showers and over the dishwasher to catch the steam. (series in apposition to *plants*)
>
> Kitten-ear is the common name for a tuliplike wildflower: small, white, and soft, with just a touch of pink inside. (description of the flower including explanation of its name)
>
> In *Hamlet* Ophelia explains the language of flowers: "There's rosemary, that's for remembrance; pray, love, remember; and there is pansies, that's for thoughts." (IV.v.) (formal quotation)
>
> Dear Ms. Appleby: (salutation)

30b Using a Colon Where Convention Requires It

Use a colon, as convention requires, to separate titles from subtitles (*Orchids: Hardy and Delicate*); chapter from verse in Biblical citations (I Corinthians 13:6); minutes from hours (12:15 A.M.); and place of publication from the name of the publisher in a reference list or bibliography (New York: Holt, Rinehart and Winston).

30c Editing to Eliminate Misuse or Overuse of the Colon

Do *not* use the colon after expressions like *such as, namely, for example,* or *that is,* which take the place of a colon. Also do *not* use the colon between verbs and their objects or complements and between prepositions and their objects.

Except when it introduces a quotation, a colon should always follow a complete independent clause.

> MISUSED: Brighten your office with flowering plants, such as: begonias, chrysanthemums, African violets, and geraniums. (The colon and *such as* mean the same thing; using both is repetitious.)
>
> REVISED: Brighten your office with flowering plants, such as begonias, chrysanthemums, African violets, and geraniums.
>
> MISUSED: Varieties of African violet include: *confusa*, which has deep violet flowers; *diplotrich*, which has small leaves and pale lilac flowers; and *pusilla*, which has blue and white flowers. (The colon comes between verb and a series of direct objects.)

REVISED: Varieties of African violet include *confusa*, which has deep violet flowers; *diplotrich*, which has small leaves and pale lilac flowers; and *pusilla*, which has blue and white flowers.

The Dash

30d Setting Off Parenthetical Material

Use dashes to set off nonessential material for emphasis or clarity.

> Our office landscaping—designed and maintained by Pretty Plants, a plant rental firm—has changed a sterile atmosphere into a living and livable environment. (Because the modifier already contains a comma, using dashes instead of additional commas to set it off clarifies the structure of the modifier and its relationship to the rest of the sentence.)
>
> The rubber tree in the foyer—a huge green monster—is too large to move to our new location. (Dashes emphasize the appositive phrase.)
>
> I sometimes talk to myself—but never to plants. (The single dash sets off and emphasizes an afterthought.)

NOTE: Form the dash in handwriting with a solid line about a fourth of an inch long. In typing indicate a dash with two unspaced hyphens. Leave no space before or after dashes.

30e Introducing a Summary

Use the dash after a series or list and before a word or phrase that sums up the list.

> Classical music, Sousa-style marching tunes, and rock beats—all have been found to promote plant growth.
>
> "Water once a week," "feed every other week," "talk soothingly"—we have heard plant authorities say these things hundreds of times.

30f Indicating an Interruption

Use the dash to indicate an abrupt interruption or shift in thought.

> Not overwatering is as important as—no, more important than—not overfeeding.
>
> Stephen told the salesperson, "Give me six—make that eight Easter cactuses."

30g Editing to Eliminate Misuse and Overuse of the Dash

Avoid misusing or overusing dashes. Using dashes is like shouting, "See this!" Used sparingly, they focus attention and add emphasis or clarity. Used carelessly, they will distract the reader and make your writing seem awkward and fragmented.

OVERUSED: The meadow was a wildflower heaven—paved with blooms rather than gold—colored paths and stepping stones—of red bells, buttercups, and paintbrush—trailed from the edge of the forest—through the grass—over the stream—its white tumbling water flecked with rose and cream-colored petals—hung azalea bushes—heavy with blossoms.

MODERATE USE: The meadow was a wildflower heaven, paved with blooms rather than gold. Colored paths and stepping stones of red bells, buttercups, and paintbrush trailed from the edge of the forest through the grass. Over the stream—its white, tumbling water flecked with rose and cream-colored petals—hung azalea bushes, heavy with blossoms.

Parentheses

30h Setting Off Nonessential Material

Use parentheses to set off and hence deemphasize nonessential elements.

> The habitat of the Mariposa (butterfly) Lily is the forests of Oregon and California. (nonessential, explanatory word)
>
> Kitten-ear (another variety of the Mariposa) gets its name from the soft hairs on its petals. (nonessential explanatory phrase)
>
> Mariposa Lily bulbs (they're delicious!) were roasted and eaten by Native Americans and pioneers. (nonessential supplementary idea)

NOTE: When material set off in parentheses is a complete sentence within a sentence, do not capitalize the first letter of the parenthetical sentence or end it with a period. You may, however, use question marks and exclamation points as in the example above. When a parenthetical sentence stands alone, use standard punctuation within the parentheses.

> Mash the berries of manzanita (they look like little apples) to make a delicious drink.
>
> Fireweed shoots, sautéed in butter, make a tasty vegetable dish. (French Canadians call the shoots Wild Asparagus.) Or you can mix fireweed with beaten eggs and serve over toast.

30i In Other Conventional Situations

Use parentheses to set off letters and numbers when they signal items in a list. Also use parentheses around dates, cross-references, numerals that repeat a written number for clarity, and a question mark indicating uncertainty about a date or fact.

> For year-round blooms try these flowering house plants: (1) the begonia, (2) the African violet, and (3) miniature gardenias.

> The horticulturist worked for fifteen years (1962–1985) on the new species explained in Chapter 2 (pp. 93–105).

> By 1982 (?) club enthusiasts had successfully raised nearly a hundred (100) varieties of iris.

Brackets

30j Setting Off Comments Within Quotations

Use brackets when you place editorial comments within quotations.

> "The price of dragon trees has gone up $3.00 [to $19.95]," said the salesperson at Rowland's Nursery.

> "The use of the miraculous flower kingsfoil in [J. R. R.] Tolkien's *The Return of the King* is reminiscent of Homer's use of *molü* [in *The Odyssey*]."

> "Even handled by experts, they [orchids] can be temperamental."

Some writers use the Latin word *sic*, meaning "thus," after an error in a quotation to tell readers the mistake was made by the original, not the present, authors. Others prefer to correct the error without comment.

> "The hydrangia [sic] has large pom-poms of flowers."

Or

> "The hydrangea has large pom-poms of flowers."

30k In Place of Parentheses Within Parentheses

Use brackets when one set of parentheses falls within another.

> In their survey of wildflowers from the Rocky Mountains to the Pacific Coast (*Wildflowers in Western America* [New York: Alfred A. Knopf, 1974]), Orr and Orr group species by color and habitat.

The Slash

30l Separating One Option from Another

Use the slash to separate alternatives or options.

> Valerie registered for Botany 223 as a credit/no credit course.
>
> The botanist/horticulturist has written both scientific and popular books about plants.

30m Separating Lines of Poetry Run into the Text

Use the slash to separate three lines or fewer of poetry, not set off from the text.

> The poet Emily Dickinson writes: "In the name of the Bee / And of the Butterfly— / And of the Breeze—Amen!"

30n Separating the Numerator from the Denominator in Fractions

Use the slash to separate the numerator from the denominator in fractions.

> $1/3$ $2/10$ $6/8$

NOTE: No spaces set off the slash when it is used to separate parts of a fraction or alternatives, but add a space before and after a slash when it separates lines of poetry.

The Ellipsis Mark

The ellipsis mark consists of three spaced periods (. . .) that take the place of an omitted word or words.

30o Indicating an Omission in a Quotation

Use the ellipsis to indicate omitted words in quotations.

> The ellipsis mark alone indicates something has been left out within a sentence.
>
> In *Nature*, the first major work of American transcendentalism, Emerson writes: "In the tranquil landscape . . . man beholds somewhat as beautiful as his own nature." (omitted: "and especially in the distant line of the horizon")

A period followed by an ellipsis mark indicates that the omission comes after a complete sentence.

> "The greatest delight which the fields and woods minister," Emerson writes in *Nature*, "is the suggestion of an occult relation between man and vegetable. . . . They nod to me and I to them." (omitted: "I am not alone and unacknowledged.")

An ellipsis mark followed immediately (without a space) by a period indicates that the omission has been made from the end of the quoted sentence.

> In *Nature* Emerson writes: "The flowers, the animals, the mountains, reflected all the wisdom of his best hour . . .." (omitted: "as much as they had delighted the simplicity of his childhood.")

30p Indicating an Omission Within Verse

Use a complete line of spaced periods to indicate that one or more lines of poetry have been omitted.

> When "Landlords" turn the drunken Bee
> Out of the Foxglove's door—
> . . . .
> I shall but drink more!
>
> *(Emily Dickinson, "I taste a liquor never brewed")*
> (omitted: "When Butterflies—renounce their 'drams'—")

30q Indicating Unfinished Statements

Use the ellipsis in informal writing to indicate unfinished statements.

> "Do you mean . . . ?" she gasped.

Other Punctuation Marks   **499**

Using Colons, Dashes, and Parentheses   Exercise 30–1

NAME _____ DATE _____

Add or delete colons, dashes, and parentheses wherever appropriate. You may need to change some existing punctuation.

> EXAMPLE: *Castilleja miniata, Gilia aggregata, Ranunculus*— these are the scientific names for Indian paintbrush, skunkflower, and buttercups.

The Colon

1. Biblical flowers include: the "lilies of the field" in Matthew 6.28 and the desert-blooming rose of Isaiah 3.51.
2. "The African Violet, A Star Is Born" is a chapter in *How to Grow African Violets* (Menlo Park, California, Lane Publishing).
3. Literature is filled with symbolic flowers, the poison purple blossoms of "Rapacinni's Daughter," Ophelia's pansies or heart's ease in *Hamlet*, and the magic *molü* of *The Odyssey*.
4. Foxglove, which gives us the heart medicine digitalis, also produces beautiful blossoms, four-foot-tall stalks of large white-, blue-, purple-, or rose-colored bells.
5. Oberon, the Fairy King, describes his queen's sleeping place in *A Midsummer Night's Dream*,

    > I know a bank where the wild thyme blows,
    > Where oxlips and the nodding violet grows,
    > Quite over-canopied with luscious woodbine,
    > With sweet musk-roses and with eglantine. (II:i:249–252)

6. Many flowers are edible, such as: squash blossoms, which are delicious fried in batter; violets, which can be eaten in soup; and yellow pond lillies, whose seed pods can be popped like popcorn.

The Dash

7. Foxglove, catnip, male fern, and mullien, these are plants with medicinal properties.
8. The root bark of burning bush an attractive hedge shrub with pink berries, ripening to flaming-red seed pods makes a good fever remedy.
9. Poultices of roasted chia seeds were used by California mission padres to cure gunshot wounds—while the seeds themselves made a delicious garnish for cooked cereal—and a good meal.
10. The flowers of hound's tongue look like violets, no, more like forget-me-nots.
11. The roots of blue columbine—the state flower of Colorado—can be boiled to make a diarrhea medicine—or mashed to put on arthritic joints.
12. Cattle, but not sheep, die from eating large amounts of larkspur in the spring.

© 1986 by CBS College Publishing. All rights reserved.

13. Teas, jams, jellies, candies, salads, all are uses for rose hips—the fruit of the rose, or rose petals.

Parentheses

14. Scarlet locoweed *Astragalus coccineus*, delphinium *Delphinium polycladon*, and blue monkshood *Aconitum columbianum* are all poisonous.
15. The nightshade family, or *Solanaceae*, the name comes from the Latin word *solamen*, "quieting," consists of a variety of poisonous, acrid, or narcotic plants.
16. The tomato (It was once called a "love apple" and used only as an ornamental plant.) is a member of the nightshade family.
17. The potato another nightshade is made safe by cooking.
18. In the nineteenth century? young girls took drops of poison made from the nightshade belladonna on sugar cubes to make their cheeks flush and their eyes sparkle.
19. Digitalis the important heart stimulant derived from foxglove must be taken in small, prescribed doses because it accumulates in the body.
20. Locoweed may kill or derange. (Its common name comes from the Spanish word *loco*, or "insane".) Unfortunately, many of the species are very difficult to identify.

Score _____

Other Punctuation Marks   **501**

Using Brackets, Slashes, and Ellipsis Marks   Exercise 30–2

NAME _____ DATE _____

Rewrite exercise items following the directions in parentheses.

> EXAMPLE: "Christmas trees are $10 a foot at Treeland," the Seattle newspaper reported. (Add editorial comment: double last year's price!)
> *"Christmas trees are $10 a foot [double last year's price!] at Treeland," the Seattle newspaper reported.*

1. "They are particularly dangerous to children and to pets," the article warned. (Add editorial comment: poinsettas.)

2.   The Pedigree of Honey
         Does not concern the Bee—
         A Clover, any time, to him,
         Is Aristocracy—
             (Emily Dickinson)
   (Quote two lines in a sentence.)

3. Mix one and a half bags of potting soil with one-half bag of peat moss; add three-fourths a cup of fertilizer crystals and a third of a cup of bone meal; and you're ready to repot your bulbs. (Change written numbers to numerals.)

4. Look at your thumb. It isn't green. The desirable green thumb comes from knowledge of good gardening principles and the putting of these principles into practice. The person with a so-called green thumb is the one who loves flowers with the same sort of love one feels for his family, dog, riding horse, or any other thing that lives. (Rosalie Doolittle, *Southwest Gardening*) (Delete a phrase from the middle of a sentence.)

5. (In the passage above delete a phrase from the end of a sentence.)

6. (Delete one complete sentence.)

© 1986 by CBS College Publishing. All rights reserved.

7. "The hyasinth is valued for its scent as well as its colorful blooms," writes the horticulturist. (Indicate that the spelling error is in the original.)

8. He bent down glittering for the magic plant
    and pulled it up, black root and milky flower—
    a *molü* in the language of the gods—
    fatigue and pain for mortals to uproot;
    but gods do this, and everything, with ease.
    (Homer, *The Odyssey*)

    (Leave out line 2.)

9. The author has written six books on orchids. (Add the options: teacher researcher.)

10. Rosalie Doolittle has written the definitive book on high-desert gardening. Her book is called *Southwest Gardening* and was first published in Albuquerque, New Mexico, by the University of New Mexico Press in 1953. (Include the information from the second sentence as a parenthetical reference in the first sentence.)

Score _____

Review 30

Add punctuation as needed to the following sentences.

1. Dandelions weeds to me are delicious salad greens to some people.
2. The carelessly cultivated garden was a jungle of weeds wild morning glories, milkweeds, dandelions, tumbleweeds, and sand burrs.
3. The famed horticulturist began his speech formally, "Ladies and gentlemen, we are here today to talk about the science and the pastime of raising plants!"
4. The editor amended the writer's mistaken reference to the red leaves of the poinsettia as red flowers: "The red flowers actually leaves of the poinsettia make the plant a fitting Christmas decoration."
5. The novelist, horticulturist E. P. Roe raised and wrote about strawberries.
6. The student omitted the second sentence of the quotation: "Orchids are tropical plants. Most need a moist, warm atmosphere to bloom and thrive."
7. Jade plants I have three in a south window lose their leaves when kept too long in the dark.
8. Decorate the Easter Lilies with foil no make that baskets and ribbons.
9. "There is a garden in her face, Where roses and white lilies grow." (Thomas Campion)
10. Jerusalem artichokes, dandelions, blackberries one person's weeds are another person's food.

Score _____

Check your answers against those in the back of the book. Deduct 10 points for each incorrectly punctuated sentence. A score of 80 percent or better indicates mastery of the materials in this chapter.

The Writer's Casebook #30

Three of the punctuation marks discussed in this chapter—the colon, brackets, and the ellipsis mark—are used in punctuating quotations. The colon introduces a formal quotation—for example, lines from *Hamlet*. The brackets and ellipsis are useful when we must alter the quotation in some way.

Application: Altering Quotations

The *MLA Handbook for Writers of Research Papers* (2d edition, 1984) presents two major principles to follow in altering quotations or in omitting words, phrases, or sentences from quoted passages.

1. Be fair to the quoted author or speaker. Avoid lifting quotations out of context or using omissions to alter meaning to fit your own purposes.

ORIGINAL: Rather than theorize about explaining the presently unexplainable, it is perhaps easier to say that the Bermuda Triangle exists only in the imagination of mystics, cultists, the superstitious and the sensational-minded. (From Charles Berlitz, *The Bermuda Triangle* [New York: Doubleday, 1974], pp. 241–242)

INCORRECT USE: According to author Charles Berlitz, "The Bermuda Triangle exists only in the imagination of mystics, cultists, the superstitious and the sensational-minded."

CORRECT USE: According to author Charles Berlitz, some people choose to ignore or try to explain away the unexplainable catastrophes in this area because "it is perhaps easier to say the Bermuda Triangle exists only in the imagination of mystics, cultists, the superstitious and the sensational-minded."

ORIGINAL: If planes, ships, and people are being kidnapped, especially from the Bermuda Triangle, and from other areas of the world, by UFOs or other means, an important factor of any investigation should be the consideration of a possible reason or reasons. (Berlitz, p. 231)

INCORRECT USE: According to Charles Berlitz, "[P]lanes, ships, and people are kidnapped, especially from the Bermuda Triangle, and from other areas of the world by UFOs. . . . "

CORRECT USE: According to Charles Berlitz, "If planes, ships, and people are being kidnapped . . . by UFOs or other means, an important factor of any investigation should be the consideration of a possible reason or reasons."

Similarly, avoid adding editorial emendations, with or without identifying brackets, that alter meaning.

ORIGINAL: His little speech is a perfect gem; deep in feeling, compact in thought and expression, and tasteful and elegant in every word and comma. (The Springfield *Republican* on Lincoln's *Gettysburg Address*, quoted in Carl Sandburg, *Abraham Lincoln*, Vol. 2 [New York: Harcourt, Brace, 1926])

INCORRECT USE: The reporter wrote, "His little speech is a perfect gem [of rhetorical and learned brilliance]; deep in feeling, compact in thought and expression [rivaling the Bible], and tasteful and elegant in every word and comma."

CORRECT USE: The reporter wrote: "His little speech [the *Gettysburg Address*] is a perfect gem; deep in feeling, compact in thought and expression, and tasteful and elegant in every word and comma."

2. Be faithful to the grammatical integrity of your own writing. Avoid using quoted phrases or clauses that confuse the structure or sense of your own sentence.

ORIGINAL: The cheek of every American must tingle with shame as he reads the silly, flat, and dish-watery utterance of the man who has to be pointed out to intelligent foreigners as The President of the United States. (The *Chicago Times* on Lincoln's *Gettysburg Address*, quoted in Carl Sandburg, *Abraham Lincoln*, Vol. 2)

INCORRECT USE: The reporter wrote that Americans "must tingle with shame as he reads the silly, flat, and dish-watery utterances. . . . " (Pronoun *he* does not agree with antecedent *Americans*.)

CORRECT USE: The reporter wrote that Americans would be embarrassed as they read the President's "silly, flat, and dish-watery utterances."

Cases for Writing: Using Quotations

Case #1

The solitary places do not seem quite lonely. At the gates of the forest, the surprised man of the world is forced to leave his city estimates of great and small, wise and foolish. The knapsack of custom falls off his back with the first step he takes into these precincts. Here is sanctity which shames our religions, and reality which discredits our heroes. Here we find Nature to be the circumstance which dwarfs every other circumstance, and judges like a god all men that come to her. We have crept out of our close and crowded houses into the night and morning, and we see what majestic beauties daily wrap us in their bosom. (Ralph Waldo Emerson, *Nature*)

Write a paragraph about the romantic view that nature is noble and contact with it ennobling. Draw upon the preceding passage from Emerson's *Nature* to support your comments.

Case #2

Write three brief paragraphs in which you practice altering quotations by (a) omitting words, (b) quoting only part of a sentence, and (c) adding an editorial comment. Refer to earlier pages of this or another text for materials to quote.

Capitalization 31

Preview 31

Add capitals as necessary in these sentences. Delete lowercase letters, and write the capitals directly above them. If the sentence is correct without any additions, write C beside it.

1. the sea is calm tonight,
   the tide is full, the moon lies fair.
   (Matthew Arnold, "Dover Beach")
2. It was on monday, april 1—april fool's day—when the spring rains started.
3. Who painted *basket of apples*, and who wrote *seize the day?*
4. Please finish the first half of the *rig veda* by monday, and be ready to discuss buddhism, sikhism, and mysticism.
5. When jacqueline completed her m.s. degree in agriculture, she joined the peace corps.
6. The eighteenth century is sometimes called the age of enlightenment.
7. A typical course load for a beginning college student includes english, math, western civilization or american government, and biology.
8. billy the kid was a major figure in the lincoln county range war.
9. The president called the senate majority leader to the white house for a conference.
10. Finish your rice krispies; then you can play with your gobot.

Score _____

Check your answers against those in the back of the book. Deduct 10 points for any sentence in which an error remains. A score of 80 percent or better indicates that you understand capitalization.

The use of upper- and lowercase, or capital and small, letters is part of our means in English of indicating major divisions between ideas and of differ-

Capitalization   **507**

entiating words that refer generally to things, people, or ideas from those that refer to specific things, people, or ideas. Capitalization is governed by convention or general practice, and that practice may change. An up-to-date dictionary will reflect the most current conventions.

31a   Capitalizing the First Word of a Sentence or of a Line of Poetry

Capitalize the first word of a sentence, including one directly quoted.

> The French peasants were angry when Marie Antoinette said that they should eat cake.
>
> She said, "Let them eat cake."

Do not capitalize after a semicolon in a compound sentence.

> The French peasants had no bread; therefore, according to Marie Antoinette, they should eat cake instead.

Do not capitalize a sentence set off within another sentence by dashes or parentheses.

> The French peasants—they were starving—asked for bread. Marie Antoinette (the Queen was noted for her lack of financial sense) suggested a diet of cake.

Capitalize the first word of a line of poetry unless the poet uses a lowercase letter.

> Something there is that doesn't love a wall,
> That sends the frozen ground-swell under it,
> And spills the upper boulders in the sun;
> And makes gaps even two can pass abreast.
>
> (Robert Frost, *"Mending Wall"*)

But

> anyone lived in a pretty how town
> (with up so floating many bells down)
> spring summer autumn winter
> he sang his didn't he danced his did.
>
> (e.e. cummings, *"anyone lived in a pretty how town"*)

31b   Capitalizing Proper Nouns, Titles Accompanying Them, and Adjectives Formed from Them

Capitalize proper nouns (names of specific persons, places, things), adjectives made from proper nouns, and titles.

PROPER NOUNS: Caesar Chavez, Attila the Hun, Jennifer Jones, Mark G. Ross, Sylvia Plath (names of specific people)

Juneau, Glacier National Park, Maine, Cape Cod Bay, the Hesperides, Iceland, Pike's Peak, the Rocky Mountains (names of specific places or geographical formations)

the Space Needle, Golden Gate Bridge, Interstate 40 (names of specific things)

Monday, July, Pan-American Day (names of specific days of the week, months of the year, holidays)

the Korean Conflict, the Battle of the Bulge, the Magna Carta, the Renaissance, the Nobel Peace Prize, *Marbury v. Madison* (names of specific historical events and periods, documents, legal cases, awards)

Native American, Greek, Iranian, Vietnamese, Hispanic, Black (names of specific races, ethnic groups, nationalities and their languages)

Christianity, Presbyterians, Catholics, Buddhists, Bahai, Judaism, Sikhism, God, the Great Spirit, the Blessed Virgin, Saint John, the Bible, the Rig Veda, the Apocrypha (names of specific religions and their followers, dieties, religious figures, and sacred books)

Modern Language Association, the Bolshoi Ballet, Chicago Cubs, Greenpeace, Republican Party, People's Party, Populists, Democrats (names of specific groups and their members)

Moncor, the Senate, the Bureau of Indian Affairs, Rutgers, University of Texas at El Paso, Job Corps, AT&T, IBM, Albuquerque Academy, UCLA (names of specific business, educational, and political institutions and their acronyms)

Chevrolet, Tylenol, Crest, Rice Krispies (names of specific brands of products)

NOTE: The points of the compass are considered to be proper nouns when they name a specific area but common nouns when they point in a direction.

The storm blasted the West, covering states from the Rocky Mountains to the Pacific with up to six inches of new snow.

But

The storm began in the west and moved east, drowning Texas.

The names of academic subjects are capitalized only when they name specific, numbered courses or are derived from a proper noun.

This semester I am taking English 111, Math 162, and Sociology 235.

But

This semester I am taking English, math, and sociology.

PROPER ADJECTIVES: Skinnerian behaviorism (from B. F. Skinner)
Joycean memorabilia (from James Joyce)
English language (from England)
Hobbesian theory (from Thomas Hobbes)
Judaic doctrine (from Judaism)
Victorian poetry (from Queen Victoria)

TITLES: Ambassador Gavin, Lieutenant Colonel Crowley, King Richard, Count Dracula, Uncle Sam, Chairperson Glenda Gray, Professor Warren Lee (preceding a name)

the Senator, the Ambassador, the Colonel (referring to a particular senator, ambassador, or colonel)

Dr. Georgina McGuire; Rosalie Otero, Ph.D.; Gerald Brennan, R.N.; Randy Glover, Attorney at Law; Sr. Joella Revers, Joella Revers, O.S.N.D. (academic degrees and religious orders preceding or following a name)

the Vice President of the United States, the Secretary of Education, the Attorney General (titles referring to a high-ranking position)

NOTE: Except for academic degrees, religious orders, and extremely high positions, titles that *follow* names are usually not capitalized.

Peter Crowley, a colonel in the USAF; Dracula, a count from Transylvania; Warren Lee, a professor at Princeton

Also, titles that refer to a general position rather than a specific person are not capitalized.

We have invited a professor, two generals, and a priest to the seminar.

Words denoting family relationships are not capitalized after possessive nouns or pronouns and after articles.

When my aunt married his uncle, we became cousins of a sort.

When Susan's aunt married Ruben's uncle, they became cousins of a sort.

31c   Capitalizing Important Words in Titles

Capitalize the first and last word and all words in a title except articles and prepositions and conjunctions of fewer than five letters.

"Mending Wall"
The Rape of the Lock
Boot Hill Rosaries
"The Lottery"
The Spirit of St. Louis
The Last Supper
"Amazing Grace"

31d   Capitalizing the Pronoun *I* and the Interjection *O*

Capitalize the pronoun *I*, the interjection *O*, and other letters used alone, as indicated by your dictionary.

I left campus at noon, but I'll return for my evening class.
"O sages standing in God's holy fire" (W. B. Yeats, "Sailing to Byzantium")
After I played D flat instead of D major, my grades in music dropped from a B to a C.

31e Capitalizing Salutations and Closings of Letters

Capitalize the first word in the salutation and complimentary close of a letter.

Dear Ms. Sanchez:
Dear Hossein,
Sincerely yours,
Cordially,

31f Editing to Eliminate Misuse and Overuse of Capitals

Do not misuse capitals to get attention, to begin the names of seasons, or to set off the names of centuries, general historical periods, or medical tests and diseases (unless a proper noun is part of the name).

MISUSED: I KNOW that this Winter will be like those people experienced in the Nineteenth Century.
REVISED: I know that this winter will be like those people experienced in the nineteenth century.
MISUSED: Down's Syndrome refers to Congenital Mental Deficiency, once commonly called Mongolism.
REVISED: Down's syndrome refers to congenital mental deficiency, once commonly called Mongolism.

Adding Capitals Exercise 31–1

NAME _____ DATE _____

Add capitals wherever necessary in these sentences.

EXAMPLE: *I*n 1972 *M*arlon *B*rando won an *A*cademy *A*ward for best actor for his part in *T*he *G*odfather.

1. alexander pope, a major poet of eighteenth-century neoclassicism, wrote *the rape of the lock, the dunciad,* and *an essay on criticism*.
2. it was a cloudy day in winter—it was monday, december 24—and my aunt was hurrying to finish her christmas shopping in time to attend the *messiah* at st. john's episcopal church.
3. traveling west on i40 they crossed the continental divide near grants, new mexico, and knew they had finally arrived in the fabulous west of jesse james and billy the kid.
4. the professor is teaching a new english course in popular literature, which will feature popular novels like h. beam piper's *little fuzzy,* a science fiction classic, and professor tony hillerman's mystery, *the blessing way*.
5. in 1984 geraldine ferraro was chosen by the democratic party as nominee for vice president of the united states.
6. ibm's new personal computer, the pc jr, competes well with the apple and the macintosh.
7. in high school we studied english for four years, math for three years, american history for one year, and economics for one semester.
8. dr. kim, who holds both m.d. and ph.d. degrees, has done research on leukemia as well as on klinefelter's syndrome.
9. in *the grapes of wrath,* steinbeck writes: "the spring is beautiful in california."
10. "i entered congress in 1946," said the congressman, "and i made the house ways and means committee a household word."
11.
    cock-a-doodle-doo the brass-lined rooster says,
    brekekekex intones the fat greek frog—
    these fantasies do not terrify me as
    the bow-wow-wow of dog.
    (John Crowe Ransom, "Dog")
12. columbus day is still celebrated nationally; however, many native americans as well as americans of scandinavian descent have protested that the famous italian did not "discover" the new world.

Score _____

512 Understanding Punctuation and Mechanics

Adding and Deleting Capitals Exercise 31–2

NAME _____ DATE _____

Add or delete capitals wherever necessary in the following paragraphs.

> EXAMPLE: In the Spring an ~~A~~merican's thoughts turn anxiously to ~~I~~ncome ~~T~~ax ~~D~~ay and the i̶r̶s̶ IRS.

1. the Southwest wind picked up turbulence around the San Francisco peaks, howled across the emptiness of the moenkopi plateau, and made a thousand strange sounds in windows of the old hopi villages at Shongopovi and Second Mesa. Two hundred vacant miles to the North and East, it sandblasted the stone sculptures of monument valley navajo tribal park and whirled eastward across the maze of canyons on the Utah-Arizona Border. (Adapted from Tony Hillerman, *Listening Woman*)

2. Wilhelm suspected the Truth, but he could Lie and one of the things he lied often about was his education. He said he was an Alumnus of Penn state; In fact he had left school before his Sophomore year finished. His Sister Catherine had a b.s. degree. Wilhelm's late Mother was a Graduate of Bryn Mawr. He was the only member of the family who had no education. This was another sore point. His Father was ashamed of him. (Adapted from Saul Bellow, *Seize the Day*)

3. Marie Montoya entered the capitol building at a fast walk that broke into a run as she crossed the Rotunda and hurried toward the Newsroom. It was her first major assignment for the *Seattle Herald*, and she was excited. The News Conference had been a melodrama of accusations and counter-accusations. The Press had exploded angrily as the Governor accused Reporters of libeling him and manipulating the News. Marie could see the headline now: "Governor scorches media."

4. Spring had really come at last. There were leaves on the Ailanthus-Tree that evelina could see from her bed, gentle clouds floated over it in the Blue, and now and then the cry of a Flower-seller sounded from the Street.

One day there was a shy knock on the back-room door, and Johnny Hawkins come in with two yellow Jonquils in his fist. He was getting bigger and squarer, and his round freckled face was growing into a smaller copy of his Father's. He walked up to Evelina and held out the flowers.

"They blew off the cart and the fellow said i could keep'em. But you can have'em," He announced.

Capitalization

Ann eliza rose from her seat at the sewing-machine and tried to take the flowers from him.

"They ain't for you; They're for her," he sturdily objected; and Evelina held out her hand for the Jonquils. (Adapted from Edith Wharton, *Bunner Sisters*)

Score _____

Review 31

Add capitals as necessary in these sentences. Delete lowercase letters, and write the capitals directly above. If the sentence is correct without any additions, write C beside it.

1. The republican party held onto its majority in the senate but failed to win a majority in the house during the 1984 elections.
2. They fled from the winter snow, traveling south to the sun belt states of texas and new mexico.
3. During the renaissance in sixteenth-century england, dramas were written in unrhymed ten-syllable lines called blank verse!
4.   the falling flower
   i saw drift back to the branch
   was a butterfly
   (Maritake, a Japanese haiku)
5. The lecture hall—it was an old room with a leaky roof—creaked and dripped during the storm.
6. Hans earned a b in sociology 230 and a c in american literature.
7. The reading list for his western civilization course included machiavelli's *the prince*, more's *utopia*, and milton's *the doctrine and discipline of divorce*.
8. On the fourth of july the veterans of foreign wars marched in parade down central avenue.
9. The professor stepped to the lectern and announced, "there will be no questions this semester."
10. Admittedly, I was given the job because president bowers is my uncle and john knots, chairman of the board, is my grandfather.

Score _____

Check your answers against those in the back of the book. Deduct 10 points for any sentence in which an error remains. A score of 80 percent or better indicates that you understand capitalization.

The Writer's Casebook #31

Application to Writing: Using Specific Nouns to Improve Your Writing

Capitalization is one way to distinguish a general from a specific noun. Notice that as we move from left to right in the following chart, most capitalized words appear at the right hand side of the chart.

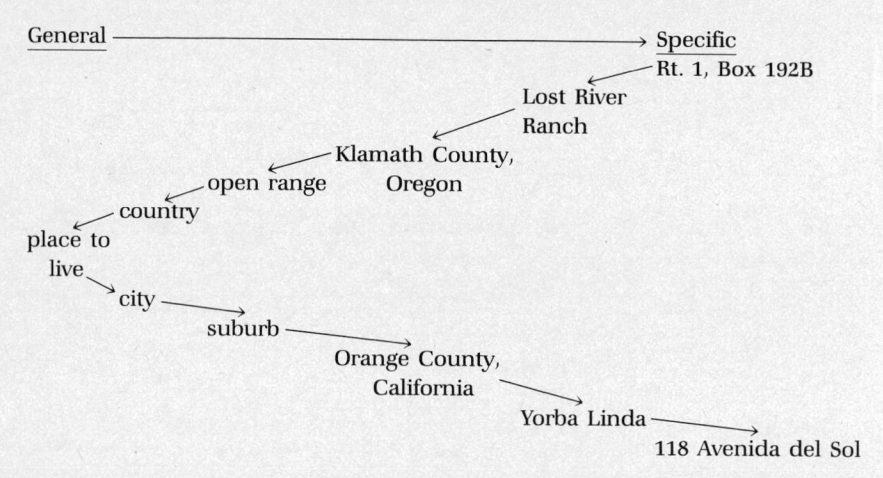

General ──────────────────────→ Specific
- Rt. 1, Box 192B
- Lost River Ranch
- Klamath County, Oregon
- open range
- country
- place to live
- city
- suburb
- Orange County, California
- Yorba Linda
- 118 Avenida del Sol

Overgeneralizing—that is, using vague or nonspecific words—is sometimes a problem for the beginning writer. Consider, for example, the following paragraph from a student paper.

> I started hunting very young in my home state. My initial pleasure came from being able to provide us with a dinner. As I grew older, my job took me everywhere, and I developed a taste for many kinds of game. I believe it would be easy for me to spend every day hunting with my dog.

The content of the paragraph is general rather than specific. The reader is left without a definite idea of what kind of hunting the writer is doing, where he or she is doing it, and what kind of game he or she has developed a taste for. No clear picture or mental images are created by the paragraph, and very little concrete information is conveyed.

The depth of the paragraph can be improved considerably by changing common to proper nouns and by adding more specific nouns wherever appropriate.

> I started hunting <u>birds</u> as a very <u>young boy</u> in <u>Texas</u>. My initial pleasure came from being able to provide <u>my family</u> with a <u>quail dinner</u>. <u>Some people like steak; some like chicken; I love southern-fried quail</u>. As I grew older my job with the <u>U.S. Air Force</u> took me to the <u>Pacific Northwest and to Alaska</u>, and I developed a taste for <u>grouse and pheasant</u>. I believe it would be easy

for me to spend everyday <u>from September until the end of January</u> hunting with <u>my Irish setter, Samantha</u>.

If your writing seems vague, or its content thin, try the following.

1. Underline all nouns and pronouns in your paper.
2. Replace vague references with more specific nouns, either common or proper.
3. Add nouns wherever a gap in information appears—that is, wherever the reader is left with a question: Who? What? When? Where? Why? How?

Cases for Writing: Writing with Specific Nouns

Case #1

Write a brief autobiography, using only general nouns and pronouns (i.e., I am a woman; I was born in a Midwestern state; and so forth). Then rewrite your essay, replacing the vague references with more specific nouns and adding proper nouns wherever possible.

Case #2

Analyze a prose passage from one of your favorite novels. Underline all the specific nouns, either common or proper. Then rewrite the passage, replacing specific words with vague ones. Compare the two versions. What is the effect of the changes you made?

Italics

32

Preview 32

Italicize (by underlining) as necessary in the following sentences. You may also need to add some quotation marks.

1. The Bing Crosby/Danny Kaye musical White Christmas features Irving Berlin's song White Christmas.
2. Louis XIV, le Dieudonné, endowed the throne of France with la gloire.
3. The Spruce Goose is an enormous flying boat built by Howard Hughes.
4. In Walden, Thoreau sketches a blueprint for the contemplative life in tune with nature and the seasons; in Walden II, B. F. Skinner envisions a society based upon his behavioristic philosophy.
5. Michelangelo's David vies with his Creation of Adam as artistic statements of the near-divinity of man.
6. The word eminent should not be confused with imminent.
7. The Enterprise warped out of orbit without its shuttlecraft Galileo.
8. I said maybe, not yes.
9. The painting depicted the yei spirit, Abalone Girl.
10. The x's and y's of the equation are its variables.

Score _____

Check your answers against those in the back of the book. Deduct 10 points for each sentence in which an error remains. A score of 80 percent or higher indicates that you understand the use of italics.

Named for the typeface designed for an Italian edition of Virgil's *Aeneid* in 1501, Italic typeface features characters that slant upward to the right. In printed matter, titles of books, magazines, and newspapers as well as some names and words are set off by a change in typeface to Italic. As a result, *to italicize* has come to designate our method of punctuating these items. In written or typed text, we indicate italics by underlining: The Aeneid.

32a Setting Off Titles and Names

Use italics or underlining to set off titles of books, newspapers, magazines, journals, pamphlets, films, television and radio programs, long poems, musical works, plays, published speeches, legal cases, and works of art such as paintings and sculptures; also italicize or underline the names of specific ships, trains, aircraft, balloons, and spacecraft.

Death Comes for the Archbishop, The Awakening, Utopia (books)
The Richmond Examiner, The Chicago Tribune (newspapers)
Newsweek, Playboy, Space World (magazines)
Huntington Library Quarterly, Journal of Reading (journals)
A Modest Proposal, The Shortest Way with Dissenters (pamphlets)
Purple Rain, Ghost Busters, High Noon (films)
Amos 'n' Andy, Stop the Music!, Dallas, Meet the Press (radio and television programs)
The Odyssey, Orlando Furioso, La Traviata, The Sorcerer's Apprentice, Eroica (long poems and musical works)
Hamlet, Playboy of the Western World, Boot Hill Rosaries (plays)
I Have a Dream, On Accepting the Nobel Prize for Literature (published speeches)
Schenck v. United States, Miranda v. Arizona (legal cases)
Creation of Adam, Bird in Flight, Mona Lisa (works of art)
Terre Nova, Rainbow Warrior, Titanic, Bismarck (names of ships)
City of Portland, Zephyr, Stourbridge Lion (names of trains)
Winnie Mae, Spirit of St. Louis, Graf Zeppelin (names of aircraft)
Eagle, Soyuz 26, Millennium Falcon (names of spacecraft)

Do not italicize or underline titles of your own papers (A Day in My Life), names of sacred books (the Bible) and well-known documents (the Emancipation Proclamation, the Constitution), articles and punctuation that are not part of a title (Have you read the *Journal*?), and types of aircraft (Douglas DC-8, Concorde).

NOTE: Remember that titles of short written or musical works are punctuated with quotation marks (see 29b)—for example, chapters in books ("Escape and Interpretation" in *Literature: Structure, Sound, and Sense*); articles in periodicals ("Utopian and Anti-Utopian Logic" in *Science Fiction Studies*); short poems ("Bees Are Black with Gilt Surcingles"); and songs ("I'll Be Home for Christmas").

32b Setting Off Foreign Words and Phrases

Use italics or underlining for foreign words or phrases (except proper nouns) that have not been adopted as part of the English language.

My favorite heroine of the German *märchen* is Aeschenputtel.

In the Southwest we live *la vida buena*, the good life.

The Navajo *yataalii* Hosteen Tso sang the Blessing Way.

"Victor was the younger son and brother—a *tête montée*, with a temper which invited violence and a will which no ax could break." (Kate Chopin, *The Awakening*)

In Italy one must speak *la belle langue* to be accepted.

Use your dictionary when you are not certain if a word has become part of the English language.

32c Setting Off Elements Spoken of as Themselves and Terms Being Defined

Use italics or underlining to set off words, phrases, numbers, and symbols that you are defining or discussing.

> There are two *e*'s and two *a*'s in *separate*, but many people misspell it with three *e*'s: *sepearate*.

> The phrase *it goes without saying that* adds padding rather than meaning to a sentence.

> In the equation $E = mc^2$, E refers to energy, m to mass, and c^2 to the speed of light squared.

32d Using Italics for Emphasis

Use italics or underlining in moderation to add emphasis to a word or phrase.

> Drama "normally presents its action (1) *through* actors, (2) *on* a stage, and (3) *before* an audience." (Lawrence Perrine, *Literature: Structure, Sound, and Sense*)

> "And who—*who!*—had done the leaving?" (Saul Bellow, *Seize the Day*)

32e Using Italics for Clarity

Use italics or underlining when necessary to clarify.

> This time I *passed* the test. (Last time I failed it.)

Italics

Using Italics or Underlining   Exercise 32–1

NAME _____ DATE _____

Underline to indicate italics where necessary. If a sentence is correct, mark it with a C.

   EXAMPLE: <u>Deor</u>, the Old English version of our word <u>deer</u>, referred to all wild animals.

1. "I can hear them cry de profundis and wring their hands. . . . poor human beasts." (Saul Bellow, *Seize the Day*)
2. In his Inaugural Address, President Kennedy emphasized the citizens' duty to their country, rather than a country's duty to its citizens.
3. In Star Wars the Millennium Falcon is a spaceship piloted by Han Solo and his awesome friend, Chewie.
4. In Spenser's allegorical epic, The Faerie Queene, Red Cross Knight champions the fair Una.
5. Tragedy is a genre in which hubris plays an important role.
6. When the chindi, or spirit, leaves the body, it may do harm to the living.
7. The schwa sound, represented by the symbol ə, may be spelled a, e, i, o, u, or y.
8. On June 3, 1965, astronaut Edward White stepped outside his Gemini 4 spacecraft to become the first American to walk in space.
9. "Steamin' and rollin'" Casey Jones was an engineer on the Cannonball Express.
10. Milton's Paradise Lost alludes frequently to passages in the Bible, The Odyssey, and The Aeneid.
11. Tell me, muchachos, what the viejo said to you.
12. The sinking of the Lusitania on May 7, 1915, helped create a climate of war in the United States.
13. Because I misspelled the word hierarchy, I received a B rather than an A on the spelling quiz.

                                                                Score _____

© 1986 by CBS College Publishing. All rights reserved.

Punctuating Titles Exercise 32–2

NAME _____ DATE _____

Either underline to indicate italics or place in quotation marks each title in the following sentences. (You may need to do some research if you are not familiar with some of the works listed.)

EXAMPLE: My favorite song from <u>The Sound of Music</u> is "Edelweiss."

1. Emily Dickinson's short poem   I Am Nobody   provides an interesting contrast to Walt Whitman's much longer Song of Myself.
2. In Fitzgerald's translation of The Odyssey, the second chapter or book is called   A Hero's Son Awakens.
3. Beethoven's Eroica, his Third Symphony, was originally inscribed to Napoleon.
4. In the episode of King Edward called   King at Last,   Queen Victoria dies.
5. Jack Anderson's column   Hostility Doesn't Stop Investigator   chronicles the trials of citizens' rights advocate Tom Dunn.
6. A hit song from the musical Singing in the Rain is   Singing in the Rain.
7. In Shakespeare's As You Like It, the melancholy Jacques speaks the cynical lines, sometimes entitled   All the World's a Stage,   and Amiens sings the song   Under the Greenwood Tree.
8. Hawthorne's works include The Scarlet Letter and Young Goodman Brown.
9. Jonathan Swift wrote Gulliver's Travels and A Modest Proposal as well as   A Description of the Morning.
10. Goat-songs in Hamlet

by

Nancy Jean Conrad

Eng. 430

May 1981
11. Starry Night was one of van Gogh's last paintings.

Score _____

Italics   523

Review 32

Italicize (by underlining) as necessary in the following sentences. You may also need to add some quotation marks. If a sentence is correct, mark it with a C.

1. The second episode of The Adventures of The Lone Ranger is called He Finds Silver.
2. At 8:10 A.M. on August 28, 1985, the Yukon Chief was flying toward Fairbanks, Alaska.
3. Brown v. Board of Education reversed the decision of the Supreme Court in Plessy v. Ferguson by ruling that separate educational facilities are by nature unequal.
4. John F. Kennedy won a Pulitzer Prize for his book Profiles in Courage.
5. Van Cliburn's performance of Rachmaninoff's Concerto No. 2 was a tour de force.
6. The word for can be used both as a preposition and as a conjunction.
7. Cole Porter's Kiss Me, Kate is based in part on Shakespeare's Taming of the Shrew.
8. Return the enclosed form by December 24, por favor.
9. Melville draws important thematic materials for Billy Budd from the Bible.
10. Do not use the ampersand, or &, in place of and in your writing.

Score _____

Check your answers against those in the back of the book. Deduct 10 points for each sentence in which any error remains. A score of less that 80 percent indicates that you should review this chapter.

The Writer's Casebook #32

Application to Writing: Writing Titles

As you have learned, a function of italics as well as of quotation marks (see 29b) is to set off titles. Italics identify long or complete works—epic poems, books, magazines, newspapers, and so forth, while quotation marks indicate short works or parts of longer works—short poems, chapters of books, articles in magazines, columns in newspapers, and so forth.

    A title, like a thesis statement, may be difficult to write because, to attract the attention of your readers, it should capture the essence of your paper. Professional writers use a number of techniques that may be helpful to you as you select a title for your paper.

1. <u>Use a phrase or key idea from your text</u>. Tony Hillerman, for example, names his 1982 mystery *The Dark Wind* because the murderer is "out of

control," ruled by the "dark wind" of insanity, as the Navajo say. Jane Austen calls her best-known novel *Pride and Prejudice* to indicate the conflicting attitudes of her characters.

2. <u>Use a question that you will answer in the paper.</u> Some examples include *Is Paris Burning?* by Larry Collins and Dominique Lapierre; "The Writing What?" by Theresa Petosa, an article in *The Beaver News* about a college writing center; and "Can Computers Improve Writing?" by David Sanger, in the *New York Times.*

3. <u>Use a quotation from a literary work.</u> Hemingway takes the title of his novel *For Whom the Bell Tolls* from a seventeenth-century sermon by John Donne and the title of *The Sun Also Rises* from Ecclesiastes. Kipling's *Captains Courageous* is from the anonymous work *Mary Ambree*. James Herriot takes the titles of his series of books about a Scottish veterinarian from a nineteenth-century poem by Cecil Francis Alexander. Each line of the poem becomes a title: *All Things Bright and Beautiful, All Creatures Great and Small, All Things Wise and Wonderful, The Lord God Made Them All.*

4. <u>Use the name of a featured person, place, action, or item.</u> Charlotte Brontë's major novel is named for her heroine *Jane Eyre;* Emily Brontë's, for the setting *Wuthering Heights*. The title of Milton's epic *Paradise Lost* describes the major action: Adam and Eve's fall and loss of Eden. And Terry Brooks names his fantasy novels for fabulous weapons: *The Sword of Shannara, The Elfstones of Shannara.*

Some student essays with titles that follow these techniques include "Mock-Epic of the Cosmic Fool," a paper about Satan's debasement in *Paradise Lost;* "Did the Grinch Steal Christmas?" a paper about a lack of the true Christmas spirit; "To Read or Not to Read," a paper about censorship; and "Another Star Is Born," the paper printed earlier in this text about Maellen's becoming an actress.

NOTE: A title is important but it does not replace your thesis. Do not make the mistake of giving your key idea in the title but not in the paper itself. If you have captured the essence of your paper in the title, repeating it in the first paragraph will reinforce rather than detract from your purpose.

Cases for Writing: Composing and Reading Titles

Case #1

Choose several literary or popular works (such as *Southwest Gardening* or *How to Play Golf*) whose titles you feel lack impact. Compose new titles; then explain how your titles fit the works and why your titles might attract readers.

Italics   **525**

Case #2

Write titles for the following untitled poems. Explain how and why you made your choices and also whether you feel your title improves or detracts from the poem.

> To make a prairie it takes a clover and one bee,
> One clover, and a bee,
> And revery.
> The revery alone will do,
> If bees are few.
>
> (Emily Dickinson)

> Not marble, nor the gilded monuments
> Of princes, shall outlive this powerful rhyme;
> But you shall shine more bright in these contents
> Than unswept stone, besmeared with sluttish time.
> When wasteful war shall statues overturn,
> And broils root out the work of masonry,
> Nor Mars his sword nor war's quick fire shall burn
> The living record of your memory.
> 'Gainst death and all-oblivious enmity
> Shall you pace forth; your praise shall still find room
> Even in the eyes of all posterity
> That wear this world out to the ending doom.
> So, till the judgment that yourself arise.
> You live in this, and dwell in lovers' eyes.
>
> (Shakespeare, Sonnet 55)

Hyphens 33

Preview 33

Correct errors in word division and hyphenation in the following sentences. Cross out incorrectly divided words and rewrite the correct division above the line. Cross out or insert hyphens as needed.

1. We depend upon oil and natural gas for seventy five percent of our energy.

2. The United States, self centered and shockingly wasteful, uses twice as much energy as any other country.

3. Ex President Jimmy Carter launched in 1977 a campaign against too fast con-sumption.

4. He proposed far reaching sacrifices to solve the by then critical energy crisis.

5. Oil consumption increases of 5 percent per year necess-itated the purchase in 1977 of about $45,000-000,000 worth of imported oil.

6. Americans must understand that to avoid future e-nergy crises, we must develop new sources of ener-gy now.

Score _____

Check your answers against those in the back of the book. Deduct 10 points for each error. A score of 80 percent or higher indicates that you understand the conventions of hyphenation and may turn to another chapter.

33a Breaking Words at the End of a Line

Divide words, when you must, by placing a hyphen between syllables at the end of the line.

A *syllable* is a unit of pronunciation—letters pronounced together with a single sound and a single movement of the mouth. Dictionaries use dots and accent marks to indicate syllabication.

   syl·lab·i·ca′tion

Try to avoid breaking a word at the end of a line; but if you must do so, hyphenate between prefix and root (sur·pass), between root and suffix (good-·ness), or between doubled letters (scrab·ble). Avoid ending consecutive lines with hyphens, and never end a page with a hyphen.

(1) One-syllable words

Do not hyphenate one-syllable words (wrench, placed) or proper names (Molly, Jennifer).

MISUSED:	The energy crisis in the late 1970's ma-de us aware of our energy gluttony.
REVISED:	The energy crisis in the late 1970's made us aware of our energy gluttony.
MISUSED:	In his *Energy Address to the Nation* President Jim-my Carter urged Americans not to be selfish.
REVISED:	In his *Energy Address to the Nation* President Jimmy Carter urged Americans not to be selfish.

(2) Short syllables

Avoid leaving a single letter at the end of a line or one or two letters at the beginning of a line.

MISUSED:	We must not believe, Carter said, that a-bundant, cheap energy will always be available.
REVISED:	We must not believe, Carter said, that abundant, cheap energy will always be available.
MISUSED:	The crisis, he continued, will continue through this centur-y, becoming progressively worse.
REVISED:	The crisis, he continued, will continue through this century, becoming progressively worse.

(3) Compounds

Divide compounds between elements or, if a compound contains a hyphen, after the hyphen.

MISUSED:	"We have always wanted to give our children and grandchil-dren a world rich in possibilities . . . ," Carter said.

REVISED: "We have always wanted to give our children and grand-
children a world rich in possibilities . . . ," Carter said.

(4) Illogical or confusing hyphenation

Avoid leaving a fragment that looks like another word.

MISUSED: The alternative to conservation is national catastrophe.
REVISED: The alternative to conservation is national
catastrophe.

(5) Numbers, contractions, and abbreviations

Avoid hyphenating numbers, contractions, and abbreviations. Also avoid dividing numbers from abbreviations or symbols.

MISUSED: The growth rate of consumption should not exceed 2
% a year.
REVISED: The growth rate of consumption should not exceed 2%
a year.
MISUSED: We should not consume more than 6,000-
000 barrels of oil per day.
REVISED: We should not consume more than 6,000,000
barrels of oil per day.

33b Dividing Compound Words

Hyphenate compound words when a hyphen is used in the dictionary (*self-centered, make-believe*); when a compound adjective precedes a noun (*well-written paper, hard-working professor*); when a prefix is attached to a proper noun (*pro-Yankee, mid-December*); when the prefixes *all-, ex-, half-, quasi-,* and *self-* or the suffixes *-elect* and *-odd* are added to a noun (*quasi-stellar, President-elect*); when clarity or pronunciation requires it (to distinguish *re-solve* from *resolve,* to show the syllables of *pre-empt*); when fractions and numbers between twenty and a hundred (*one-fourth, thirty-five*) are written out; when a compound (*a glad-to-be-alive smile, a welcome-to-my-house handshake*) is coined.

Do not hyphenate compound adjectives that contain words ending in *-ly* or compound adjectives that follow a noun.

MISUSED: Many highly-conscientious citizens have installed storm windows.
REVISED: Many highly conscientious citizens have installed storm windows.
MISUSED: Carter's energy speech was well-received.
REVISED: Carter's energy speech was well received.
REVISED: Carter's well-received speech was about conserving energy.

Hyphens

Dividing Words Exercise 33–1

NAME _____ DATE _____

Use your dictionary to divide each word into syllables. Then use the word in a sentence so that you must divide it at the end of a line.

    EXAMPLE: knowledge
                     knowl-edge
                     Many Americans lack knowl-
                     edge about the sources and limitations of our energy resources.

1. negotiations

2. conservation

3. luxury

4. inconvenience

5. realize

6. environment

7. challenge

8. cornerstone

9. petroleum

© 1986 by CBS College Publishing. All rights reserved.

10. vulnerability

Score _____

Review 33

Correct errors in word division and hyphenation in the following sentences. Cross out incorrectly divided words and rewrite the word with the correct division above the line. Cross out or insert hyphens as needed. If a sentence is correct, mark it with a C.

1. The internal combustion engine is a major cause of increases in petroleum-use since the nineteenth-century.

2. In the 1970's the Soviet Union supplanted the United States as the leading oil producing nation.

3. The widely-held belief that energy supplies were lim-itless gave way in the 1970's to awareness of ap-proaching doom.

4. Many Americans responded to this unwelcome know-ledge by buying small cars.

5. Owning the car with the highest miles to the gallon record became a status symbol.

6. This highly-admirable attitude began to diminish in the 1980's, and cars once again are big and gas-hungry.

Score _____

Check your answers against those in the back of the book. Deduct 10 points for each error. A score of 80 percent or higher indicates you understand the conventions of hyphenation and may go on to the next chapter.

The Writer's Casebook #33

Applications to Writing: Avoiding the Overuse of Hyphens

Using too many hyphenated words—both in word division and in compounds—may make your writing awkward or hard to read. It is better to have an irregular right-hand margin than to break words frequently.

AWKWARD: In order to save energy, we first weather-
stripped each window and door in the house. We insulated the attic, the walls, the water heater, the basement, and the porch. We installed new storm windows and put in solar-heating panels and a greenhouse.

IMPROVED: In order to save energy, we first
weatherstripped each window and door in the house. We insulated the attic, the walls, the water heater, the basement, and the porch. We installed new storm windows and put in solar-heating panels and a greenhouse.

Using too many compound words can also be awkward.

AWKWARD: The oil-rich, energy-hungry nations with their I-don't-care and what's-mine-is-mine attitudes are self-servingly and self-righteously consuming the all-too-precious, all-too-rare energy reserves that are by-right-of-birth legacies of all Earth-born creatures.

IMPROVED: Nations with great reserves of oil have traditionally justified their equally great appetites for energy with the selfish, isolationist view: "What's mine is mine." But they are rapidly consuming a rare and precious legacy of energy that belongs by right of birth to all of Earth's creatures.

Cases for Writing: Writing About Energy

Case #1

Imagine that you are a future citizen of the world who will be born in the year 2090. Write a letter to the present inhabitants of the Earth, expressing your concerns about their use of energy and about your fears for the future you must live in.

Case #2

Some people feel that the best source of energy for the future is nuclear power, while others feel its dangers far outweigh its advantages. Go to your library and read some recent articles about nuclear power; be sure to include articles on both the positive and the negative aspects of this energy source. From your reading and other information you know, form an opinion about this issue and write a paper in support of that opinion. (See Chapter 5 for a review of argumentation.)

Abbreviations 34

Preview 34

Correct misused or overused abbreviations, or abbreviate a written-out term when required by convention.

1. Antoinette is studying to be a bilingual ed. teacher.

2. Frankie & Johnny were lovers.

3. Have a merry Xmas and a happy New Yr.

4. Sr. Winifred Moerson and Fr. Thomas Hogan staff the Campus Ministry Offices.

5. In Tucson, Ariz., even in Oct. temperatures may climb as high as ninety-five degrees Fahrenheit.

6. Mister and Mistress Martinez are having an open house at 116 Morningside Dr.

7. My 10:00 ante meridiem call to N.Y. cost $5 and sixty-two ¢.

8. The BYU Cougars are No. one in football and in basketball.

9. Pfc. Gomer Pyle, United States Marine Corps., terrorized Camp Pendleton.

10. We drove around Mount Hood at a slow 20 m.p.h.

Score _____

Check your answers against those in the back of the book. Deduct 5 points for each error. A score of 80 percent or higher indicates mastery of this topic.

Abbreviations, shortened forms of words followed by a period, are used primarily in informal writing. Only a few are appropriate in academic writing.

34a Abbreviating Titles

Abbreviate certain titles before and after proper names.

> Dr. Joseph Sanchez   Mr. Julius Gassner
> Hugh Currin, D.D.S.   Ms. Rose Pesata
> Clare Sun, Ph.D.   Mrs. Roberta Serafin
> St. Augustine   W. V. Grant, Jr.

Do not abbreviate these titles: military (Colonel Sanders), religious (the Reverend Peter Marshall), academic (Professor Linus Pauling), or governmental (Vice President George Bush, Representative Geraldine Ferraro).

34b Abbreviating Technical Terms and Agency Names

Use familiar initials and acronyms for technical terms (DNA, EKG), names of agencies (FBI, CIA), businesses (IBM, CBS), and organizations (NOW).

If you believe your reader may not understand the abbreviation, you should first cite the term in full with the abbreviation following in parentheses.

> The Food and Drug Administration (FDA) and the Federal Communications Commission (FCC) have both suffered drastic budget cuts. Sources at the FDA and at the FCC indicate that morale is low and tempers high.

34c Abbreviating Designations of Specific Dates, Times of Day, Temperatures, and Numbers

Abbreviate designations of specific dates (500 B.C., A.D. 1066), times of the day (11:06 A.M., 7 P.M.), and temperatures (30°C, 98°F). In nontechnical writing use the abbreviation *no.* (number) only in endnotes and bibliographic entries: *The Journal of Anthropology, Vol. 3, No. 4, Winter 1986.*

34d Editing to Eliminate Misuse or Overuse of Abbreviations

Do not misuse or overuse abbreviations.

You may abbreviate *D.C.* for District of Columbia in the phrase *Washington, D.C.* and *Mt.* for Mountain and *St.* for Saint in the names *Mt. Shasta* and *St.*

Louis; and you may use *U.S.A.* or *USA* and *U.S.S.R.* or *USSR.* But *write out* the following.

The names of most places, streets, states, countries, and geographic regions: Rocky Mountains, Germany, New York, Central Avenue—*not* Rocky Mts., Ger., N.Y., Central Ave.
The names of days, months, and holidays: Tuesday, December 25, Christmas Day—*not* Tues., Dec. 25, Xmas Day.
Units of measurement: miles per hour, gallon, feet—*not* m.p.h., gal., ft.
The names of academic subjects: English, chemistry, education—*not* Eng., chem., ed.
The names of business organizations, unless the firm itself uses an abbreviation: Thompson and Sons, Component Building Corporation—*but* G. K. Hall and El Encanto, Inc.

You may use some Latin abbreviations in parenthetical notes (*e.g.*, this note), but generally you should use *that is* instead of *i.e., and so forth* instead of *etc.,* and *for example* instead of *e.g.*

You may use the symbol *$;* however, write out *and, percent, equals, plus, number,* and *cents* rather than using the symbols &, %, =, +, #, or ¢.

NOTE: Technical writing and documentation allow you to use more abbreviations. In technical writing you may use symbols, such as %, =, >, <, and #. You may abbreviate units of measurement, such as *m.p.g.* for *miles per gallon* and *km* for *kilometer,* if the abbreviation is preceded by a number: 200 km, 20 m.p.g. And you may use the abbreviation *no.* or *No.* for number when it precedes a number: no. 39.

In documentation you may abbreviate publication information and references to parts of a written work: John Dewey, *Psychology,* Vol. 2 of *John Dewey: The Early Works,* 1882–1898, ed. Jo Ann Boydston (Carbondale: Southern Illinois UP, 1967), 85–87.

Abbreviations

Using Abbreviations Exercise 34–1

NAME _____ DATE _____

Rewrite the following sentences to eliminate any misused abbreviations or to change written-out terms to abbreviations when required by convention.

EXAMPLE: Gen. Walker feuded with Att. Gen. Kennedy during the sixties.
General Walker feuded with Attorney General Kennedy during the sixties.

1. We go to work at 8 ante meridiem and return home at 8 post meridiem.

2. Sen. John Glenn campaigned in 1984 to be the Dem. Party cand. for Pres. of the U.S.

3. Doctor Edith Buchanan met with Mister John Velarde to discuss a scholarship for John Velarde, Junior.

4. Both International Business Machines and American Telephone and Telegraph announced a large profit in the fourth quarter.

5. On Sat., Dec. 21, the temperature in Duluth, Minn., was −8 degrees Fahrenheit.

6. Mount Saint Helens is an active volcano near Seattle, Wash.

7. VP George Bush and Rep. Geraldine Ferraro debated on national tv during the 1984 pres. campaign.

8. This sem. soph. Lindell Chavez is studying Eng., bus. comm., econ., bio., and Spanish lit.

9. The bill for two typewriter ribbons + a gal. of spirit fluid for the mimeo. machine = twenty dollars and sixty-two cents, but 50% of that bill will be paid by the admin.

© 1986 by CBS College Publishing. All rights reserved.

10. The univ. has invited several large corps. to the campus to study the possibility of contributions—e.g., financing research, endowing chairs, sponsoring building projects, etc.

Score _____

Review 34

Correct misused or overused abbreviations, or change a written-out term to an abbreviation when required by convention.

1. According to Prof. Gassner, my poli. sci. instructor, State Sen. Maureen Newcomb may make a good showing in the next congressional race.

2. The Trojan War may have occurred around 1200 Before Christ, but we are still reading Homer's epics about that war and its aftermath in Anno Domini 1986.

3. In the U.S.A. the 4th of July is Independence Day.

4. Suzanne Montoya lives at 913 Girard Blvd. Albuq., N.M.

5. Because I had only 63¢ in my pocket, I could not buy a gal. of gas.

6. The main lecture hall at the U. is named for Abraham Lincoln.

7. When Mister Desaulniers had a heart attack, the M.D. on duty at Bernalillo Gen. Hospital took an EKG.

8. In my soc class we study people in groups, & in my psych class we study them as individuals.

9. Some readings indicate Mount Shasta and Mount Hood are hotter than Mt. St. Helens was before it erupted in 1980.

Score _____

Check your answers against those in the back of the book. Deduct 5 points for errors. A score of 80 percent or higher indicates mastery of this topic.

The Writer's Casebook #34

Application: Using Abbreviations Effectively

To be effective, your use of abbreviations should be consistent and unobtrusive. Although either abbreviating or writing out terms may be acceptable in many cases, you should generally use one option consistently throughout a paper. For example, in the following sentences the writer's shifting from acronyms to written-out names is awkward and confusing, giving the impression that the paragraph concerns two schools rather than one.

AWKWARD: In the UNM General College, students with academic deficiencies take a holistic course in skills development. However, the University of New Mexico faculty question whether developmental education is a proper function of a state university like UNM. State officials, on the other hand, argue that it is precisely because the University of New Mexico is a state university that it should serve the state by admitting and teaching New Mexican students, regardless of their needs.

IMPROVED: In the UNM General College, students with academic deficiencies take a holistic course in skills development. However, UNM faculty question whether developmental education is a proper function of a state university. State officials, on the other hand, argue that it is precisely because UNM is a state university that it should serve the state by admitting and teaching New Mexican students, regardless of their needs.

Whenever you choose the option to abbreviate, do not overuse abbreviations. Because of the popularity of acronyms, it is possible to produce prose that looks like a complex code or chemical formula.

> When FDA officials found traces of PCB in the water supply of BIA-run AIS, the EPA called in UNM scientists and WWS technicians to find the source of the contamination.

Translation: When Food and Drug Administration officials found traces of polychlorinated biphenal in the water supply of Bureau of Indian Affairs–run Albuquerque Indian School, the Environmental Protection Agency called in University of New Mexico scientists and Well-Water Service technicians to find the source of the contamination.

Cases for Writing: Writing with Abbreviations

Case #1

Use a published list of abbreviations and acronyms (many dictionaries have them) to survey the practice of abbreviating in English. Then write a paper about the advantages and disadvantages of this practice. Can you think of times when abbreviating is useful and times when it could be confusing? Write a paper about your findings, illustrating each point with specific examples.

Case #2

Abbreviations form a key part of campus slang. It is not at all uncommon to hear: "What stats. did you come up with in chem. lab? Take the SAT or ACT; then get your ap. in right away. This semester I'm taking soc., French comp. and con., psych., anthro., and D.P. I'll meet you in the SUB to talk about grad. school. The frat. house was raided. Take your papers to the admin. building. Ed. majors will take more lit. and comp. courses because of the new regs. passed by SATE. Sig. Ep. members will be tutoring in the bio. lounge." Examine the abbreviations in popular use on your own campus. Then write a paper about the purposes and effects of this special language. How did it make you feel as a new student? How does it make you feel now? Has it had any effect on your use of standard English?

Numbers 35

Preview 35

Revise the use of numbers in the following sentences according to humanities conventions. If a sentence is correct, mark it with a C.

1. 630 people attended the performance.

2. Hamlet's famous soliloquy that begins "O, what a rogue and peasant slave am I!" comes in Act Two, Scene Two (lines five hundred and fifty–six hundred and five).

3. The performance was attended by 630 people.

4. The stage of the Fortune Theatre measured fifty-five' and extended twenty-seven' into the yard.

5. Of the 38 plays now accepted as Shakespeare's, thirty-six were published in the First Folio.

6. A replica of the Fortune Theatre will be built at 22 2nd Street.

7. Be sure to watch the BBC production of *The Tempest* at eight o'clock on Channel Five.

Score _____

Check your answers against those in the back of the book. Deduct 10 points for each error. A score of 80 percent indicates mastery.

Whether you use numerals (36) or spell out numbers (thirty-six) may vary with your audience and purpose. Generally, you use numerals when you write for scientific and business audiences about technical subjects, and you spell out numbers when you write for humanities audiences. The guidelines that follow cover the humanities conventions for writing numbers. For a discussion of the conventions of technical writing, see the Writer's Casebook at the end of the chapter.

35a   Spelling Out Numbers That Begin Sentences

Spell out numbers that begin a sentence or reword the sentence.

M<small>ISUSED</small>: 400 years after Shakespeare's birth, his plays are still acted and enjoyed throughout the world.
R<small>EVISED</small>: Four hundred years after Shakespeare's birth, his plays are still acted and enjoyed throughout the world.
R<small>EVISED</small>: Shakespeare's plays are still acted and enjoyed throughout the world 400 years after his birth.

35b   Spelling Out Numbers That Can Be Expressed in One or Two Words

Spell out numbers if they can be written in one or two words.

M<small>ISUSED</small>: Shakespeare wrote 2 long narrative poems in addition to his 38 plays.
R<small>EVISED</small>: Shakespeare wrote two long narrative poems in addition to his thirty-eight plays.

35c   Using Numerals for Numbers That Cannot Be Expressed in One or Two Words

M<small>ISUSED</small>: Shakespeare also wrote one hundred and fifty-four sonnets.
R<small>EVISED</small>: Shakespeare also wrote 154 sonnets.

However, if there are several numbers in a passage, avoid awkwardness by spelling them all out or using only numerals, regardless of convention.

A<small>WKWARD</small>: Shakespeare wrote two long narrative poems, thirty-eight plays, and 154 sonnets.
R<small>EVISED</small>: Shakespeare wrote two long narrative poems, thirty-eight plays, and one hundred and fifty-four sonnets.

35d Using Numbers Where Convention Requires Their Use

Use numerals as directed by convention for addresses (91 Hatheway Drive); dates (April 26, 1564); exact times (8:13); exact sums of money ($4.54); pages and divisions of written works (Act 3, Scene 2 of 1 Henry IV, lines 4–11, page 867); measurements (62°, 6″); numbers containing percentages, decimals, or fractions (99 percent, 3.1416, 66⅔); ratios, scores, and statistics (ratio of 4 to 1; final score: Lobos 61, Georgetown 69; a median of 28 but a mean of 22); identification numbers (Interstate 40, Channel 4, SS# 585–41–2536).

NOTE: Both sums of money and times of day may be written out if they can be expressed in round numbers of fewer than three words: two dollars; up at four. You should also write out times of day when they are used with *o'clock*: six o'clock.

35e Using Numerals with Spelled-out Numbers

Use numerals if spelling out numbers would be confusing.

CONFUSING: The Little Theatre is at 444 4th Street.
CLEARER: The Little Theatre is at 444 Fourth Street.
CONFUSING: The large class was divided into thirty three-person research teams.
CLEARER: The large class was divided into thirty 3-person research teams.

Using Numbers Exercise 35–1

NAME _____ DATE _____

Rewrite the following sentences, revising use of numbers according to the humanities conventions.

> EXAMPLE: The title page of the Shakespeare First Folio, published in sixteen twenty-three, is reproduced on page fifty-nine.
> *The title page of the Shakespeare First Folio, published in 1623, is reproduced on page 59.*

1. In Act two, Scene one of *A Midsummer Night's Dream,* Puck describes his mischief-making (lines forty-three–fifty-four).

2. When we attended the Ashland Shakespearean Festival, we stayed 4 days and saw 4 plays.

3. We stayed at 222 2nd Street.

4. On opening night 562 people attended the production of *Much Ado About Nothing;* during the next few nights crowds increased to 630, seven hundred, 896, and one thousand.

5. The book contains 300 allusions to Shakespeare.

6. Shakespeare died on the twenty-fifth day of April in the year sixteen hundred and sixteen.

7. Although the temperature was only forty-six° F, we stayed through the outdoor production of *As You Like It.*

8. The actor had played 20 different Shakespearean roles during his career, including 36 performances as Shylock in *The Merchant of Venice.*

9. Tickets for opening night Row fifteen cost ten dollars and fifty cents each.

© 1986 by CBS College Publishing. All rights reserved.

10. *12th Night* is a comedy with a carnival atmosphere while *Henry Five* is an historical drama that emphasizes 16th-century English nationalism.

Score _____

Review 35

Revise the use of numbers in the following sentences according to humanities conventions. If a sentence is correct, mark it with a C.

1. The demanding role of Hamlet calls for the actor to speak two hundred and seventy-six lines in Act One alone.

2. Ninety-nine percent of the audience enjoyed the play.

3. Beatrice and Benedick's coordinated costumes in *Much Ado* cost eight hundred and seventy-five dollars each.

4. Fire destroyed the Globe Theatre in the year sixteen hundred and twenty-one.

5. Of Shakespeare's 38 plays, 19 were published in quarto form.

6. The play begins at 8 o'clock at the Barn Theatre, sixteen Forty-second street.

7. A capacity crowd of 993 gave the 16 actors a standing ovation.

Score _____

Check your answers against those in the back of the book. Deduct 10 points for each error. A score of 80 percent or better indicates mastery.

The Writer's Casebook #35

Application: Numbers and Conventions in Technical Writing

Generally, the technical style of writing numbers uses more numerals than the humanities style. Compare, for example, the following sentences.

HUMANITIES STYLE: The twenty-six data-processing students will write ten programs in each of three required computer languages.

TECHNICAL STYLE: 1. The 26 data-processing students will write 10 programs in each of the three required computer languages.

2. The twenty-six (26) data-processing students will write ten (10) programs in each of the three (3) required computer languages.

The first example of technical style illustrates a convention common to usage in the sciences or in business: single-digit numbers are written in words; all others, in numerals.

one		100
five	*but*	19
nine		32

The second example of technical style illustrates a convention common in some social science or legal writing: both words and numbers are used to ensure accuracy and clarity. Usually the numbers follow the words and are placed in parentheses.

seventy-two (72)
three (3)

In technical style as in humanities style you use words when numbers begin a sentence.

One hundred and two consultants submitted entries for the science fair.

Also in technical style you use numbers for technical units, measurements, sums of money, dates, street addresses, decimals, and mixed numbers.

My personal computer has 32k of ROM (read-only memory)

Tuition this year has gone up to $150 per credit hour.

Write to the Right-to-Write Foundation at 114 Eleventh Street.

The mixed number 1¼ can be written as the decimal 1.25.

Numerals may be used throughout when shifting from verbal to numerical symbols becomes awkward.

AWKWARD: Personnel records show three employees who play rugby, 16 who play tennis, 23 who are joggers, and eight who swim.
REVISED: Personnel records show 3 employees who play rugby, 16 who play tennis, 23 who are joggers, and 8 who swim.

Occasionally the amount or complexity of information may make a prose presentation ineffective. In those cases technical writers organize the information in a table or graph to make the data easier to read.

For example, a record of rainfall contrasting the months of March, August, and November over a period of several years would be difficult to understand in prose, and the relationships would be unclear.

In March of 1983 1.5 inches of rain fell; in August of that same year .3 of an inch fell, followed by 2.0 inches in November. In 1984 2.1 inches fell in March, .6 of an inch in August, and 3.2 inches in November. In 1985 there were .9 of an inch of rainfall in March, only .1 of an inch in August, and 1.6 inches in November.

However, written in table form, the information is clear and easy to understand, and a pattern of relationships emerges.

TABLE OF RAINFALL (measured in inches)

Month	1983	1984	1985
March	1.5	2.1	.9
August	.3	.6	.1
November	2.0	3.2	1.6

As you write the following assignments, consider your audience carefully; then choose the conventions for writing numbers appropriate for your audience.

Cases for Writing: Writing with Numbers

Case #1

You are the fund-raising chairperson for a newly created community theater. Your nonprofit group is hoping to raise enough money to build a new theater. The public schools, which will also use the facility, will provide half the funds for the project. Write two different letters requesting contributions: one to be sent to Jo Ann E. Richards, the vice president in charge of contributions at International Electronic, Inc. and one to Norman Manns, director of the state's Council on the Arts, a state-funded organization. In each letter describe the proposed theater in detail, including information about size, costs, seating capacity, and so forth. Observe the appropriate conventions for writing numbers.

Case #2

Thanks to the generous support of two major contributors—International Electronics and the Council on the Arts—your fund-raising efforts have been successful. The new community theater opened on March 10 with a capacity audience. Write letters of thanks to both Norman Manns at the Council on the Arts and Jo Ann E. Richards of International Electronics, Inc. Include in the letter a report on opening night, using details and data that the boards of these contributing organizations would consider significant, and choose the appropriate number-writing conventions for each letter.

Answers to Previews and Reviews

(References to text are given in parentheses.)

1 / Planning an Essay
A. 1. F(1b) 2. F(1a) 3. F(1a) 4. F(1b.1) 5. F(1b.2) 6. F(1b.2)
    7. F(1a) 8. F(1b.4) 9. F(1a) 10. F(1b.3)
B. 1. T(1a) 2. T(1b) 3. T(1b.1) 4. T(1a) 5. T(1b.2)
    6. T(1b.2) 7. T(1a) 8. T(1b.3) 9. T(1a) 10. T(1b.4)

2 / Shaping Your Material
A. 1. b(2a) 2. b(2b) 3. b(2b) 4. b(2c,d) 5. b(2d) 6. b(2b)
    7. b(2b) 8. b(2b) 9. b(2b) 10. b(2b)
B. 1. a(2a) 2. b(2b) 3. b(2d) 4. b(2c) 5. b(2d) 6. a(2b)
    7. a(2b) 8. a(2b) 9. a(2b) 10. a(2b)

3 / Writing and Revising
A. 1. F(3a) 2. T(3a) 3. F(3b) 4. F(3a) 5. F(3b) 6. T(3c)
    7. F(3c) 8. T(3c) 9. F(3a) 10. F(3a)
B. 1. F(3a) 2. F(3b) 3. T(3b) 4. T(3c) 5. F(3c) 6. T(3a)
    7. F(3b) 8. F(3c) 9. F(3c) 10. T(3a)

4 / Writing Paragraphs
A. 1. a subtopic sentence (4a) 2. parallelism (4c.2) 3. narrative (4e.1)
    4. how (4e.4) 5. why (4e.5) 6. classification (4e.7)
    7. define (4e.8) 8. introduction (4f.1) 9. topic sentence (4a)
    10. coherence (4c)
B. 1. unity (4b) 2. coherent (4c) 3. transitions (4c.4)
    4. exemplification (4e.3) 5. division (4e.7) 6. concluding paragraph (4f.2) 7. essays (4a) 8. pronoun (4c.1)
    9. repeating (4c.3) 10. a basis (4e.6)

5 / Constructing an Argument
A. 1. b(5a) 2. b(5a) 3. b(5a) 4. a(5a) 5. b(5a) 6. a(5c)
    7. b(5c) 8. b(5c) 9. b(5c) 10. a(5c)
B. 1. b(5a) 2. a(5a) 3. a(5a) 4. b(5a) 5. b(5a) 6. b(5c)
    7. b(5c) 8. b(5c) 9. b(5c) 10. b(5c)

Answers to Previews and Reviews 551

6 / Building Simple Sentences

A. 1. <u>spacecraft</u>(s), <u>carried</u>(v), <u>astronauts</u>(do) (6a,b)   2. <u>Neil Armstrong</u>(s), <u>was</u>(v), <u>human being</u>(sc) (6a,b)   3. <u>astronauts</u>(s), <u>considered</u>(v), <u>moon</u>(do), <u>desolate</u>(oc) (6a,b)   4. <u>They</u>(s), <u>showed</u>(v), <u>viewers</u>(io), <u>pictures</u>(do) (6a,b)   5. <u>moon</u>(s), <u>orbits</u>(v) (6a,b)
6. <u>of the surface</u>(prep phrase) <u>of Venus</u>(prep phrase), <u>the bleak landscape ending many romantic dreams about the love goddess's special planet</u>(absolute phrase, with prep phrase underlined). (6f.1,3)
7. <u>Blending heroic fantasy and science fiction</u>(verbal phrase, compound) (6f.2,5) <u>to dream great dreams and attempt great deeds</u>(verbal phrase, compound).
8. <u>the citizens</u>(appositive) <u>of earth</u>(prep phrase), <u>of the stars and space</u>(prep phrase, compound) (6f.4,1,5)

B. 1. <u>Hollywood</u>(s), <u>rewrote</u>(v), <u>history</u>(do) (6a,b)   2. <u>Roy Rogers</u>(s), <u>became</u>(v), <u>cowboy</u>(sc) (6a,b)   3. <u>audience</u>(s), <u>makes</u>(v), <u>performer</u>(do), <u>star</u>(oc) (6a,b)   4. <u>Disney</u>(s), <u>gave</u>(v), <u>world</u>(io), <u>features</u>(do) (6a,b)   5. <u>Hollywood</u>(s), <u>beckons</u>(v) (6a,b)
6. <u>of the movie colony</u>(prep phrase), <u>the luxury and extravagance setting trends and creating insatiable consumer appetites</u>(compound absolute phrase, compound). (6f.1,3,5)
7. <u>star of Magnum P.I.</u>(appositive, prep phrase), <u>as well as a variety</u>(prep phrase) <u>of adventure movies</u>(prep phrase) (6f.4,1)
8. <u>In addition to creating</u>(prep phrase) <u>a bigger-than-life spectacle</u>(verbal phrase), <u>making movies</u>(verbal phrase), <u>financing a multimillion-dollar budget</u>(verbal phrase) (6f.1,2)

7 / Building Compound and Complex Sentences

A. 1. cx, Seeking a western route to India, Columbus did not "discover" America when he landed in the West Indies. (7b)
2. cx, Leif Ericson, who was called "Leif the Lucky," probably explored some part of North America around A.D. 1000. (7b)
3. cd, The Incas, Mayans, Aztecs, and many other native peoples were already here, and they were the true discoverers of America. (7a)
4. cx, The Viking explorers called what they discovered "Vinland." (7b)
5. cx, Columbus, who thought he was in the Orient, actually landed in the West Indies. (7b)
6. cd, Columbus's voyage led to the exploration and colonization of the Americas by European countries, but Columbus never fully understood the magnitude of his accomplishment. (7a)
7. cd, Englishmen on a fishing voyage may have sailed almost as far as North America in the late sixteenth century, but they did not land. (7a)
8. cx, Spanish explorers named the isthmus of Central America "Golden Castile" because the inhabitants wore gold ornaments. (7b)
9. cx, The peoples who are now called Native Americans may have discovered the New World as long ago as 40,000 or 50,000 B.C. (7b)
10. cx, Columbus incorrectly identified what he found as islands of the Orient and who he found as Indians (7b)

B. 1. cd, The explorers mapped the world, and many wrote fanciful accounts of their adventures. (7a)
2. cx, Ptolemy, who was an armchair Greek geographer, underestimated the size of the world. (7b)
3. cx, When he met a ship that had sailed north from San Francisco, Amundsen had successfully negotiated the Northwest Passage. (7b)
4. cd, Today's explorers are scientists, exploring space, the oceans, and time, and their exploration vessels are their laboratories. (7a)
5. cd, Many hope the Space Age will be another Age of Discovery, and they dream of being a Space-Age Columbus or Magellan. (7a)
6. cx, Whoever wrote *Space Vikings* dreamed of a universe filled with people and treasure. (7b)
7. cx, In some science fiction, when space captains discover a new world, they conquer it, colonize it, and rule it. (7b)
8. cd, Like Sir Francis Drake, they are out for adventure and plunder; scientific discoveries and communication among races are incidental at best, destroyed or forgotten at worst. (7a)
9. cx, So far, however, the space that we dream of finding alive and exciting is a lonely place. (7b)
10. cx, Whoever conquers the red planet, no matter which country, must look to earth for praise, not to little green Martians. (7b)

8 / Writing Emphatic Sentences
A. 1. b(8a)   2. a(8b)   3. a(8c,d)   4. b(8e)   5. b(8a)   6. a(8b)
7. b(8a)   8. a(8c)   9. a(8c,d)   10. b(8a)
B. 1. b(8a)   2. b(8a)   3. b(8b)   4. a(8e)   5. b(8c,d)   6. b(8a)
7. a(8c,d)   8. b(8b)   9. b(8c)   10. b(8e,b)

9 / Writing Concise Sentences
A. Hobbies are as much mental-health as leisure activities. In fact, many busy people have made time for hobbies to relieve stress. Churchill, for example, painted. J. Edgar Hoover built pipe organs. Peter Marshall, the noted Presbyterian clergyman, raised roses, while Cardinal Spellman collected stamps.
B. Five to 10 million Americans are numismatists, or coin collectors. Numismatists may collect coins by topic, by metal, by design, or by historical period. A collection of historic U.S. coins might include a Washington-Lafayette silver dollar, issued in 1900; the peace dollar of 1921; and all or many of the forty-eight commemorative half-dollars issued, beginning with the 1892 half-dollar commemorating the world's Columbian Exposition.

10 / Writing Varied Sentences
A. 1. Transition opener—2, 10(10e)   2. Subject separated from verb—3, 6(10f)   3. Modifiers at beginning—3, 4(10e)   4. Coordination—4, 5, 6, 8 (10b)   5. Verbal phrase as subject—5 (10e)   6. Complex sentences—2, 5 (10d)   7. Short, alternating with long—1–2, 7–8 (10a)   8. Conjunction opener—9 (10e)   9. Question—9 (10d)   10. Dependent clause as subject—2 (10d,e)
B. 1. Clause opener—1(10e)   2. Subject separated from verb—2, 9(10f)
3. Coordination—2, 3, 5, 6, 7, 9, 10(10b)   4. Question—3(10d)

Answers to Previews and Reviews 553

5. Command—4(10d)   6. Phrase opener—5, 9(10e)   7. Subject at end—7(10f)   8. Transition opener—8(10e)   9. Verbal phrase opener—6(10e)   10. Compound sentences—7, 10(10d)

11 / Correcting Sentence Fragments
A. 2. everyone—from the . . . (11b)   3. pollution, to the . . . (11b)   4. scow, carrying . . . (11c)   5. granted, clean . . . (11c)   7. it, our . . . (11e)   9. to be limited and in . . . (11f)   10. up, laws to . . . (11a)   12. enacted and enforced! (11f)   13. faucets, we are . . . (11d)   15. responsibilities—to ourselves . . . (11b)

B. 1. destruction, the . . . (11a)   3. catastrophes, such as . . . (11b)   5. destructive, far exceeding . . . (11c)   7. volcanoes, which have . . . (11a)   8. Island destroyed . . . (11d)   9. 1902 with 38,000 . . . (11b)   10. Tambora killed . . . (11d)   11. eruption and released . . . (11f)   13. Helens erupted in 1980 and El Chichon, in 1982. (11g)   15. steam and rumble . . . (11f)   19. power with the . . . (11b)   21. China, which lost . . . (11c,a)   23. quake; in 1976 23,000, in Guatemala. (11b)   26. tornadoes with 700 . . . (11b)   28. period—hence the . . . (11e)   30. thunderclouds, then hits . . . (11f)   31. automobiles—whatever is . . . (11a)   34. States, killing . . . (11c)   36. property, while . . . (11c)   38. We cope by learning . . . (11b,c)

12 / Comma Splices and Fused Sentences
A. 1. men; it . . . (12b)   2. *sophia*. Put . . . (12f)   4. philosophy; moreover, . . . (12g)   6. fragmented; it . . . (12b)   9. meaning. Philosophers . . . (12f)

B. 2. philosophy. At . . . (12f)   3. said. "What . . . (12a)   6. life. One . . . (12a)   8. wrote. He . . . (12a)   10. job. It is . . . (12f)

13 / Misplaced and Dangling Modifiers
A. 1. The public idolizes glittering and glamorous stars. (13b)   2. Fans make their stage or screen favorites the subject of dreams and myths. (13b)   4. Fans admire, love, and imitate their heroes; they endow the stars with every virtue. (13a,b,c)   6. The play or movie creates an emotional atmosphere that is infectious; it seems to grow more intense as the audience increases in numbers. (13e)   7. However, since an actor has become one of the most popular presidents in history, one cannot help wondering if the spell of drama has supplanted reality. (13f)

B. 1. Taking place in a small cemetery, James Galloway's play *Boot Hill Rosaries* is set in New Mexico in the late 1800's and early 1900's. (13b)   2. The characters are people who, over a period of years and for a variety of reasons, have died and been buried in the cemetery. (13d)   5. Angry and insecure, Belle tells her story of hard times. (13a)   6. While a beginning actress, Belle found it impossible to get parts in London, so . . . (13g)   9. While not accepted by society, Belle spent the rest of her life making money and being contented. (13g)

14 / Faulty Parallelism
A. 1. a(14a.2)   2. b(14a.1)   3. a(14a.2)   4. b(14a.2)   5. a(14b.1)   6. a(14a.2)   7. b(14b.2)   8. b(14a.2,b.1)   9. a(14b.2)   10. a(14a.2,b.1)

B. 1. a(14a.2) 2. a(14b.2) 3. a(14a.1) 4. a(14a.2) 5. b(14b.2)
6. a(14a.2) 7. b(14b.1) 8. a(14a.1) 9. b(14b.1) 10. a(14b.1)

15 / Shifts and Mixed Constructions
A. 2. For many, play is a time to . . . (15b)   3. When people are infants, they play . . . (15a)   4. As toddlers, they play hide and seek. (15a)   5. Ten-year-olds learn to deal with competition by . . . (15b)   6. Teenagers learn more complex social interactions in team play. (15a)
B. 3. For some species, such as cats, play hunting is important behavior. (15a)   4. Puppies play at chasing and fighting. (15a)   5. Dolphins play off the prow of a ship. (15a)   6. Their antics develop maneuverability. (15a)   8. Symbolic play begins at age two . . . (15b)

16 / Choosing Words
A. 1. continuously/continually; continual/continuous (16b)   2. an interesting/a gripping; good/weak; nice/greedy (16b)   3. dude/man; fox/beautiful woman (16a)   4. aroma/stench (16b)   5. man/a human; mankind/humankind (16b)   6. complementary/complimentary; complimenting/complementing (16b)   7. It goes without saying that Monica/Monica; fleet as a deer/fast as a Nike missile (16c)   8. investmentwise/of investments (16c)
9. he/a public official; his/the (16b)   10. C   11. Cogitating on/Thinking about; the tribulations/the trials; of my state of incarceration/of being in prison; I determined/I decided; to effect/to; an unauthorized egress/escape (16c)
12. Dark clouds, like giant, smudged desk pads/Dark clouds; rumbled across the sky, blotting up the rain/rumbled across the sky (16d)
B. 1. pulled/earned; chem/chemistry; psych/psychology (16a)   2. smirked/smiled; scrawled/drew (16b)   3. he/the doctor; her/the nurse (16b)
4. Mankind/Humankind (16b)   5. intervening/interfering; interfered/interceded; intercede/intervene (16b)   6. It is interesting to note that the/The; tall, dark, and handsome/six feet six inches tall, black, and attractive (16c)   7. penultimate/best; inculcates/teaches (16c)   8. was interesting/posed worthwhile questions; less-than-satisfactory grade/D (16b)
9. started swimming with the wrong school of fish/made the wrong friends (16d)   10. extinct/dormant (16b)   11. C   12. The chief perpetrator of nefarious activities/The crime boss; in our fair city/in Las Vegas; resolved to/decided to; decimate competition/reduce competition; by liquidating his competitor's warehoused assets/by blowing up his competitor's warehouse of stolen goods (16c)

17 / Using the Dictionary
A. 1. three, ju · di · cial (17d)   2. intransitive verb, transitive verb (17d)
3. Latin, *depressus*, pp. of *deprimere*, to press down, sink (17d)   4. Robert Devereaux (17d)   5. June 18, 1815 (17d)   6. 17,410 square miles (17d)
7. No, it is colloquial. (17d)   8. educible (Ex. 17-1.6)   9. eisteddfodau (Ex. 17-1.6)   10. dript (Ex. 17-1.6)
B. 1. No, it is colloquial. (17d)   2. two, in' trist (17d)   3. 2,193,000 (17d)
4. effluvia (Ex. 17-1.6)   5. 1953–1961 (17d)   6. the condition of being like the boisterous, jovial, drunkard son of Rabelais' Gargantua (17d)   7. six *a* in *ago*, *e* in *agent*, *i* in *insanity*, *o* in *comely*, *u* in *focus*, *y* in *idyll* (17d)

Answers to Previews and Reviews   555

8. prefix *inter* + Latin *montanus* (17d)   9. lay an egg, meaning "to fail" (17d)   10. drunken (17d)

18 / Vocabulary
A. 1. valetudinarian/valedictorian, matriculation/graduation   2. Irregardless/Regardless   3. autobiography/biography   4. high places/water   5. fission/fissure, vault/fault   6. prospective/perspective, magniloquent/magnificent   7. chaldron, cauldron   8. C
B. 1. too much gluten in the diet/eating too much.   2. C   3. notorious/famous   4. disputatious/debatable   5. large/small, small/large   6. contingent/contingency   7. focalize/vocalize   8. end/beginning   9. dissimilate/disseminate   10. communicative/communicable

19 / Spelling
A. 1. site/sight, cite/site, sighted/cited, exchange/change   2. criteria/criterion, committment/commitment   3. conscious/conscience   4. greivance/grievance, noticably/noticeably   5. valevictorian/valedictorian, congradulated/congratulated   6. C   7. beautyfy/beautify, nieghborhood/neighborhood, rectyfy/rectify, commision/commission   8. Nancies/Nancys, Maria's/Marias   9. they're/their, Oxes/Oxen   10. sister-in-laws/sisters-in-law
B. 1. echos/echoes, heros/heroes   2. canvaser/canvasser, canvass/canvas   3. of/have   4. shiek's/sheik's, foriegn/foreign   5. C   6. Nomes/Gnomes, gaurd/guard, thier/their   7. liesure/leisure, knowlledge/knowledge   8. cupsful/cupfuls   9. aisle/isle, I'le/I'll, wonder/wander, isles/aisles, cocanut/coconut   10. alga/algae, acquarium/aquarium

20 / Identifying the Parts of Speech
A. adj, adj (20d), n (20a), v, v (20c), prep (20f), n (20a), adj (20d), n (20a), adv (20e), adj, adj, adj (20d), adv, adv (20e), adj (20d), n (20a), adv (20e), conj (20g), prep (20f), pro (20b), prep (20f), v (20c), n (20a), adj (20d), n (20a), pro (20b), adv, adv (20e), n (20a), pro (20b), v (20c), prep (20f), conj (20g), adv (20e), v (20c), adj, adj, adj (20d), conj (20g), pro (20b), n (20a), int (20h), n (20a), adj (20d), n (20a), v (20c), adv (20e), v, v (20c)
B. prep (20f), n (20a), v (20c), adj, adj (20d), n (20a), conj (20g), pro (20b), prep (20f), adj (20d), conj (20g), adv (20e), v (20c), adj (20d), n, n (20a), adj (20d), prep (20f), adj (20d), v (20c), n (20a), prep (20f), pro (20b), conj (20g), int (20h), n (20a), adv (20e), adj (20d), prep (20f), adj (20d), n (20a), conj (20g), n (20a), adv (20e), v (20c), n (20a), adj, adj (20d), n (20a), prep (20f), pro (20b), adv (20e), adj (20d), prep (20f), adj (20d), n (20a), pro (20b), v (20c), n (20a), adj (20d)

21 / Nouns and Pronouns Case
A. 2. They/Americans (21f), theirselves/themselves (21d)   3. This/This acculturation (21f)   5. they/Americans (21g)   7. Its/It's (21d,e)   8. Him/His (21c)   10. He/Warren (21f), their/his (21f)   11. them/the Germans (21f)
B. 1. who's/whose (21c,d)   2. Them/Their (21c)   3. It/This greeting (21f)   4. it's/its (21c)   5. they/students (21f)   6. which/who (21f), you/them (21f)   7. their/her Chinese (21f)   9. that/the time off (21f)   11. who/whom (21b)

22 / Verbs

A. 1. has often been marked/Violence has often marked (22k)   2. was precipitated/slur precipitated (22k)   3. would be dead/died, goes/went, to have led/to lead (22f)   4. laying/lying (22b)   5. had been caned and . . . crippled/Brooks had caned and . . . crippled the Senator. (22k)   6. Consider also/A history of violence also surrounds . . . (22g,h)   7. was/were (22i)   8. Having won/Winning (22f), had dealt/dealt (22d,c)   9. will be/have been (22d), attempt will be made/Hinkley made (22k)   10. occur/occurred (22c)   11. is accompanied/violence accompanies (22k)   13. having precipitated/precipitating (22f)   14. knew/had known (22i), had taken/took (22f)   15. comes/come (22i)

B. 1. is being questioned/is questioned (22e)   2. was described/president described (22k), was/were (22i)   3. will cite/cite (22c)   4. were/are (22c)   5. to be developed/sports are supposed to develop (22k), are boosted by/teams boost (22k)   6. are, are advanced, having supported/Other reasons for supporting college athletics are the alumni's demands that their schools' teams be winners, and the schools' needs for the alumni's money. (22i,k,f)   7. lamented/lament (22c)   8. might have costed/might cost (22b,d), would of cost/could cost (22b)   9. are disturbed by/distortion disturbs (22k)   10. having passed/passing (22f), is raised/coaches raise (22k), who would have placed/who place (22d)   11. exploitation is protested/opponents also protest (22k), will have graduated/will graduate (22d)   12. is remaining/remains (22e)

23 / Agreement

A. 1. Stress . . . poses . . . (23a)   2. How well . . . depends . . . (23a)   3. A fight . . . drains . . . (23a)   4. There are . . . their toll . . . (23a)   5. Probably the majority . . . are . . . (23a)   6. Every one . . . needs to assess his or her . . . (23a, b)   7. The amount . . . varies . . . you lead. (23a, b)

B. 1. Soaking . . . and drinking . . . are . . . (23a)   2. . . . cure the alcoholic of his or her . . . (23b)   3. . . . there was . . . (23a)   4. . . . those who show . . . (23a, b)   5. The crew . . . take their . . . in their . . . (23a, b)   6. Neither the chicken nor the cattle . . . use . . . (23a)   7. Each . . . has its . . . (23a, b)

24 / Adjectives and Adverbs

A. 1. nimbly and quickly (24b)   2. the most famous glove (24c)   3. were not unique as (24c)   4. more beautiful (24c)   5. greatly (24b)   6. Queenliest (24c)   7. surely (24b)   8. very hesitant (24b)   9. the surest (24c)   10. more (24c)

B. 1. slowly (24b)   2. very carefully (24b)   3. bad (24a)   4. most difficult task (24c)   5. happy (24c)   6. better educated (24c)   7. more similar, less similar (24c)   8. more rich and famous (24c)   9. most grandmotherly (24c)

25 / The Period, the Question Mark, the Exclamation Point

A. 1. ENIAC (25a)   2. cost. (25a, b)   3. software. (25a, b)   4. message to see (25a)   5. Help! An . . . system. (25c)   6. P.M. (25a,c)   7. Rd., (25a)   8. writing?" they asked. (25b,a)   9. Joyce R. Mason . . . pp. (25a)   10. screen. Try (25a)

Answers to Previews and Reviews

B. 1. A.D. (25a,c) 2. James T. Brown . . . M.D. . . . St. . . . Ore. (25a)
3. maker. Then (25a) 4. Christmas. (25b,a) 5. Oh no! I forgot . . . machine. (25c, a) 6. FBI . . . CIA (25a) 7. smart and can (25a,b)
8. asked, "How . . . byte?" (25b) 9. memory. (25a, b) 10. COBOL (25a)

26 / The Comma

A. 1. business, you . . . introductory element (26c) 2. help, and that . . . compound sentence (26a) 3. salesperson, buyer, accountant, and . . . series (26b) 4. In addition, the . . . introductory element (26c) 5. Those who can, get . . . misreading (26f) 6. Many, on the other hand, must . . . interrupter (26d) 7. C 8. C 9. partnerships, and . . . compound sentence (26a) 10. Businesses, 119 San Marcos Ave., Los Angeles, California, for . . . convention (26e)

B. 1. C 2. with, but . . . compound sentence (26a) 3. Take, for example, . . . interrupter (26d) 4. necessity, Calvin . . . introductory element (26c)
5. dreams, desire for status, or love . . . series (26b) 6. agencies, the shills . . . marketing, respond . . . interrupter (26d) 7. C 8. attractive, more exciting, or . . . series (26b) 9. Overall, demand . . . misreading (26f)
10. $40,000,000 . . . convention (26e)

27 / The Semicolon

A. 1. States; moreover . . . clause with conjunctive adverb (27c) 2. workers who built . . . restrictive dependent clause (27e) 3. States; now . . . compound sentence without coordinating conjunction (27a) 4. remoteness; but . . . compound sentence with complex or punctuated clauses (27b) 5. parks; . . . development; and the need . . . series with internal commas (27d)

B. 1. neighborhoods, areas . . . appositive, not independent clause (27e)
2. streets; but . . . compound sentence with punctuated clauses (27b) 3. life; however, tomorrow . . . clause with conjunctive adverb (27c) 4. take; . . . society; and . . . series with internal commas (27d) 5. battle; it . . . compound sentence without coordinating conjunction (27a)

28 / The Apostrophe

A. 1. beings' (28a), their (28b) 2. peoples, caves (28b) 3. Our (28b), ancestors, walls, ceilings, paintings (28b) 4. '79 (28c) 5. Whose (28b), wasn't (28c), their (28b) 6. It's (28c), Og and Mog's, Mog and Og's (28a) 7. editor-in-chief's (28a), artists (28b) 8. ooh's, ah's (28d)

B. 1. children's, master of ceremony's (28a), anecdotes, classes (28b) 2. '71 (28c), students (28b) 3. minutes' (28a), whose, her (28b), interesting's, cute's (28d) 4. It's, you're (28c) 5. Artists' (28a), artists (28b), one's (28c), Chris's (28a), its (28b) 6. Orona and Curran's, Liu's (28a)

29 / Quotation Marks

A. 1. "Folktales, and legends," says . . . professor, "often . . . society." (29a)
2. "imagination." (29f) 3. "Perhaps . . . The Odyssey," the (29a,b,f)
4. asked if any . . . Horse. (29a) 5. replied, "That . . . gates." (29a,f) 6. calls 'a . . . tricks.'" (29a,f) 7. greatest liars and tall-tale spinners (29c)
8. "Odysseus, the Chameleon," . . . lies"; (29b,f)

B. 1. tricks": the (29f)   2. "Old . . . folktales," said (28a)   3. myth," she continued, "Old . . . tribes." (28a,f)   4. asked if . . . stone. (28a)   5. "Yes," said . . . very angry with . . . (28d,c)   6. 'red-painted faces' (28a)   7. *The Wiley Coyote* notes: "Like . . . animal." (28b,e,f)   8. "Is . . . berries?" (28a, f)   9. Believe (28a)

30 / Other Punctuation Marks
A. 1. [sic] (30k)   2. (those . . . comfort) (30h)   3. begins: (30a)   4. red, / violets (30m)   5. aroma/scent (30l)   6. flowers: (30a)   7. yucca . . . grows, saguaro . . . must (30o)   8. Edition—these (30e)   9. (bachelor . . . Northwest) (30h)   10. as important as—no, . . . than— (30f)
B. 1. (weeds to me) (30h)   2. weeds: (30a)   3. formally: (30a)   4. [actually leaves] (30j)   5. novelist/horticulturist (30l)   6. plants. . . . Most (30o)   7. (I . . . window) (30h)   8. foil—no, . . . (30f)   9. face / Where (30m)   10. blackberries—one (30e)

31 / Capitalization
A. 1. The sea . . . /The tide (31a)   2. Monday, April 1—April Fool's Day (31b)   3. Basket of Apples, Seize the Day (31c)   4. Rig Veda (31c), Buddhism, Sikhism (31b)   5. M.S., Peace Corps (31b)   6. Age of Enlightenment (31b)   7. English, Western, American (31b)   8. Billy the Kid, Lincoln County Range War (31b)   9. President, Senate Majority Leader, White House (31b)   10. Rice Krispies, Gobot (31b)
B. 1. Republican Party, Senate, House (31b)   2. Sun Belt, Texas, New Mexico (31b)   3. Renaissance, England (31b)   4. The, I, Was (31a)   5. C   6. B, Sociology, C, American (31b)   7. Western, Machiavelli's *The Prince*, More's *Utopia*, Milton's *The Doctrine and Discipline of Divorce* (31b,c)   8. Fourth of July, Veterans of Foreign Wars, Central Avenue (31b)   9. "There (31a)   10. President Bowers, John Knots (31b)

32 / Italics
A. 1. White Christmas, "White Christmas" (32a)   2. le Dieudonné, la gloire (32b)   3. *The Spruce Goose* (32a)   4. *Walden, Walden II* (32a)   5. *David, Creation of Adam* (32a)   6. eminent, imminent (32c)   7. *The Enterprise, Galileo* (32a)   8. maybe, yes (32d)   9. yei (32b)   10. x's, y's (32c)
B. 1. *The Adventures of the Lone Ranger*, "He Finds Silver" (32a)   2. *Yukon Chief* (32a)   3. *Brown v. Board of Education, Plessy v. Ferguson* (32a)   4. *Profiles in Courage* (32a)   5. C   6. for (32c)   7. *Kiss Me, Kate, Taming of the Shrew* (32a)   8. por favor (32b)   9. *Billy Budd* (32a)   10. &, and (32c)

33 / Hyphens
A. 1. seventy-five (33b)   2. self-centered (33b)   3. Ex-president, too-fast (33b)   4. far-reaching, by-then (33b)   5. Oil-consumption (33b), necessitated (33a) $45,000,000,000 (33a)   6. energy, energy (33a)
B. 1. internal-combustion, petroleum use, nineteenth century (33b)   2. oil-producing (33b)   3. widely held (33b), limit-less (33a)   4. knowledge (33a)   5. miles-to-the-gallon (33b)   6. highly admirable, gas hungry (33b)

Answers to Previews and Reviews

34 / Abbreviations
A. 1. bilingual education (34d)   2. Frankie and Johnny (34d)   3. Christmas, Year (34d)   4. Sister, Father (34a)   5. Arizona, October (34d), 95°F (34c)   6. Mr., Mrs. (34a), Drive (34d)   7. A.M. (34c), New York (34d), $5.62 (34c)   8. number (34d)   9. Private First Class (34a), Corps (34d)   10. Mt. Hood, miles per hour (34d)

B. 1. Professor (34a), political science (34d), Senator (34a)   2. B.C., A.D. (34c)   3. Fourth (34d)   4. Boulevard, Albuquerque, New Mexico (34d)   5. sixty-three cents, gallon (34d)   6. university (34d)   7. Mr. (34a), doctor (34d), General (34d)   8. sociology, and, psychology (34d)   9. Mt., Mt. (34d)

35 / Numbers
A. 1. Six hundred and thirty (35a)   2. Act 2, Scene 2 (lines 550–605) (35d)   3. C   4. 55 feet by 27 feet (35d)   5. thirty-eight plays (35b)   6. 22 Second Street (35e)   7. Channel 5 (35d)

B. 1. 276 (35c), Act 1 (35d)   2. C   3. $875 (35c,d)   4. 1621 (35d)   5. thirty-eight plays, nineteen (35b)   6. eight o'clock (35d), 16 Forty-second Street (35d,e)   7. sixteen (35b)

Acknowledgments

Pp. 53–54, from *Matter, Earth and Sky* by George Gamow. Copyright © 1958 by Prentice-Hall, Inc. Adapted by permission of Prentice-Hall, Inc.

Pp. 54–55, 73, from *'Subtle Is the Lord. . . .' The Science and Life of Albert Einstein* by Abraham Pais. Copyright © 1983 by Oxford University Press, Inc. Reprinted by permission of Oxford University Press, Inc.

Pp. 55–56, adapted from "University Days" by James Thurber. Copyright © 1933, 1961 by James Thurber. From *My Life and Hard Times*, published by Harper & Row. Reprinted by permission of Helen Thurber.

P. 60, from *Sociology: A Critical Approach to Power, Conflict and Change*, 2d ed., by J. Victor Baldridge. Copyright © 1980 by John Wiley & Sons. Reprinted by permission of John Wiley & Sons.

P. 61, from "That Lean and Hungry Look" by Suzanne Britt Jordan. Copyright © 1978 by *Newsweek*. From *Newsweek*, Oct. 9, 1978. Permission courtesy of *Newsweek*.

P. 61, from "The Double Standard of Aging" by Susan Sontag. Copyright © 1975 by *Saturday Review*. Reprinted by permission of *Saturday Review* (Sept. 23, 1975).

Pp. 62–63, from *The Outdoorsman's Emergency Manual* by Anthony J. Acerrano. Reprinted by permission of Stoeger Publishing Company, 55 Ruta Court, South Hackensack, NJ 07606.

P. 62, from *Psychology* by John Darley, Sam Glucksberg, Leon J. Kamin, and Ronald A. Kinchla. Copyright © 1981 by Prentice-Hall. Adapted by permission of Prentice-Hall, Inc.

Pp. 62–63, from "New Names for Old" by Edward Kasner and James R. Newman. In *The World of Mathematics*, Vol. 3, annotated by James R. Newman. Copyrighted © 1940 by Edward Kasner and James R. Newman; renewed © 1967 by Ruth G. Newman. Reprinted by permission of Simon & Schuster, Inc.

P. 62, from *Around the World with Chemistry* by Kurt Lanz. Copyright © 1978 by Econ Verlag GmbH. Copyright © 1980 by McGraw-Hill Book Company. Reprinted by permission of McGraw-Hill Book Company.

Pp. 64–65, from *Realm of Algebra* by Isaac Asimov. Copyright © 1961 by Isaac Asimov. Reprinted by permission of Houghton Mifflin Company.

P. 64, from *The Bermuda Triangle* by Charles Berlitz. Copyright © 1974 by Charles Berlitz. Reprinted by permission of Doubleday & Company, Inc.

P. 65, from "Strangers on a Continent: An American Indian's View of America" by Vine Deloria, Jr. Reprinted by permission of *Washington University Magazine* (Summer 1972, Vol. 42, No. 4).

P. 65, from "'What's Wrong with Me, Me, Me'" by Margaret Halsey. From *Newsweek*, April 17, 1978. Copyright © 1978 by Margaret Halsey. Reprinted by permission of International Creative Management, Inc.

P. 73, adapted from *Maria: The Potter of San Ildefonso* by Alice Marriott. Copyright © 1948 by the University of Oklahoma Press. Reprinted by permission of the University of Oklahoma Press.

P. 73, from *Errors and Expectations: A Guide for the Teacher of Basic Writing* by Mina B. Shaughnessy. Copyright © 1977 by Mina B. Shaughnessy. Reprinted by permission of Oxford University Press, Inc.

Pp. 74, 243, from "On Accepting the Nobel Prize for Literature" by William Faulkner. Copyright © 1954 by William Faulkner (Random House, Inc.). Reprinted by permission from *The Faulkner Reader*.

Pp. 187, 192, 331–332, 368–369, from the *Guinness Book of World Records*, published by Sterling Publishing Company, Inc. New York, NY. © 1984 by Guinness Superlatives, Ltd.

P. 220, adapted from *Theory Z: How American Business Can Meet the Japanese Challenge* by William Ouchi. Reprinted by permission of Addison-Wesley Publishing Company.

Pp. 243, 245, from *I Have a Dream* by Martin Luther King, Jr. Copyright © 1963 by Martin Luther King, Jr. Reprinted by permission of Joan Davies.

Pp. 274, 525, "Hope is a thing with feathers . . . ," "A word is dead," "When 'landlords' turn the drunken Bee," "To make a prairie it takes a clover and one bee," and "The Pedigree of Honey" by Emily Dickinson. Reprinted by permission of Harvard University Press and the Trustees of Amherst College from *The Poems of Emily Dickinson*, edited by Thomas H. Johnson. Cambridge, Mass.: The Belknap Press of Harvard University Press, Copyright 1951, © 1955, 1979, 1983 by the President and Fellows of Harvard College.

Pp. 284–286, from "The Woolen Serape" by Robert Ramirez. Copyright © 1972 by Dr. Edward Simmen. Reprinted by permission of Edward Simmen.

P. 333, from *Return of the Jedi* by James Kahn. Copyright © 1983 by Lucasfilm Ltd. (LFL). Reprinted by permission of Random House, Inc.

P. 443, from *Ump's Fwat: An Annual Report for Young People* by Roger and Marilyn Bollen.

Copyright © 1980, 1984 by Figgie International Inc. Reprinted by permission of Figgie International Inc.

P. 482, from *The Hobbit* by J. R. R. Tolkien. Copyright © 1966 by J. R. R. Tolkien. Reprinted by permission of Houghton Mifflin Company.

P. 487, adaptation from *Russian Fairy Tales*, collected by Aleksandr Afanas'ev, translated by Norbert Guterman. Copyright 1945 by Pantheon Books, Inc.; renewed 1973 by Random House, Inc. Reprinted by permission of Pantheon Books, a division of the publisher.

P. 507, from "anyone lived in a pretty how town" by e. e. cummings. Copyright 1940 by e. e. cummings; renewed 1968 by Marion Morehouse Cummings. Reprinted from *Complete Poems 1913–1962* by e. e. cummings by permission of Harcourt Brace Jovanovich, Inc.

P. 507, from "Mending Wall" by Robert Frost. From *The Poetry of Robert Frost*, edited by Edward Connery Latham. Copyright 1930, 1939, © 1969 by Holt, Rinehart and Winston. Copyright © 1958 by Robert Frost. Copyright © 1967 by Lesley Frost Ballantine. Reprinted by permission of Holt, Rinehart and Winston, Publishers.

P. 511, from "Dog" by John Crowe Ransom. From *Selected Poems*, third edition, revised and enlarged, by John Crowe Ransom. Copyright by Alfred A. Knopf, Inc.; renewed 1955 by John Crowe Ransom. Reprinted by permission of Alfred A. Knopf, Inc.

P 515, "The Falling Flower," a Japanese haiku by Moritake. Reprinted from *Poetry Handbook; A Dictionary of Terms* by Babette Deutsch. By permission of the publishers, Funk & Wagnalls, New York.

Index

abbreviations, 268, 425, 428, 432, 468, 528, 534–536, 540
absolute phrases, 111, 179, 192, 440
abstracts, 175–176
abstract words, 271–272
acronyms, 425
active voice, 150–151, 368–369
addresses, 441
ad hominem argument, 93
adjective clauses, 134
adjectives, 106, 109, 110, 128, 229, 326–327, 410, 411, 414, 422
   comparative and superlative forms of, 412–414
   coordinate, 436–437
   proper, 326, 507, 508
adverb clauses, 134, 256, 437
adverbs, 109, 110, 128, 229, 327, 410, 411–412, 422
   comparative and superlative forms of, 412–414
   conjunctive, 132, 149, 438, 440, 454–455
agency names, 535
agreement, 388–396, 408
   pronoun-antecedent, 394–396
   subject-verb, 389–394
allusions, 274–275
analogies, 274, 476–477
antecedents, *see* pronoun antecedents
apostrophes, 464–468, 476
appositives, 111–112, 164, 179, 193, 339–340, 439
argument, logical, 89–93
   persuasion and, 102–103, 269, 288–289
articles, 241, 326, 410
audience, 2, 3, 63, 90–91, 102
   diction level and, 267–269
   revising for, 33–34
auxiliary verbs, 325, 326, 390

balance, 150
begging the question, 93
bodies, of essays, 31–32, 34, 102
brackets, 496
business writing, 449–452

capitalization, 133, 506–510
   of first word in sentence or line of poetry, 507
   of *I* and *O*, 509–510
   of personal titles, 507, 509
   of proper nouns and adjectives, 507–508
   of titles of works, 509
case, 339–341, 465–466
cause and effect, 60, 235–237
circumlocution, 163–164
classification, 61–62, 250–251
clauses, 108, 394, 439
   adverb, 134, 256, 437
   elliptical, 135, 229
   see also dependent clauses; independent clauses
clichés, 273
climactic word order, 149
coherence, 53–57, 87, 88, 408
collective nouns, 324, 391–392, 396
colloquialisms, 268
colons, 133, 148, 483, 493–494
commands, 107, 427
commas, 112, 239–240, 434–442, 454, 455, 482, 483
   between independent clauses, 132, 209–212, 214, 426, 435–436
   after introductory elements, 437–438
   nonessential elements set off with, 438–440
   in series, 436–437
comma splices, 209–212, 426
comparative degree, 412, 413
comparison and contrast, 60–61, 144–146, 250
compass points, 508

complements, 106, 134–135, 339, 393, 410, 411
complex sentences, 133–135
complimentary closes, 441, 510
compounds, 112, 193, 435, 466, 527–528
   agreement with, 390–391, 395–396
compound sentences, 131–133, 211
compound words, 528, 532
conciseness, 162–165
conclusions, 32, 34, 65, 103
concrete words, 271–272
conjunctions, 179, 241, 328
   coordinating, 112, 132, 212, 214, 239, 328, 435–436
   correlative, 112, 133, 239–240, 328, 435
   subordinating, 133, 134, 191, 212, 214, 328
conjunctive adverbs, 132, 149, 438, 440, 454–455
contemplative writing, 223–225
contractions, 268, 340–341, 467, 528
contradictory phrases, 440
coordinate adjectives, 436–437
coordinating conjunctions, 112, 132, 212, 214, 239, 328, 435–436
coordination, 131–132, 164
correlative conjunctions, 112, 133, 239–240, 328, 435
cumulative sentences, 149

dangling modifiers, 111, 228–229
dashes, 148, 426, 494–495
dates, 441, 467, 535
deduction, 91–92
definition, development by, 62–63, 301–302
demonstrative pronouns, 410
denotation, 270
dependent clauses, 108, 149, 191, 228, 435
   in complex sentences, 133–135
   sequence of tenses in, 365–366
description, 58–59, 128–129, 422–423
development, 57–63, 87, 88
   see also specific methods
dialogue, 481
diction, 162, 266–275
   see also language; words
dictionaries, 290–292, 362
direct discourse, 255
direct objects, 106, 107
division, development by, 61–62, 250

either/or fallacy, 93
ellipsis marks, 497–498
elliptical clauses, 135, 229
elliptical constructions, 164
emphasis, 147–151, 160–161, 427, 520
equivocation, 92
essays:
   argumentative, 89–93, 269, 288–289
   outlines of, 20–21, 29–30, 34
   planning, 1–5
   theses developed in, 18–19, 29–30
   titles of, 523–524
   unity, coherence, and development in, 87–88, 408
   writing and revising, 31–37, 321–322
euphemisms, 270
exclamation points, 427–428, 483, 495
exclamations, 427, 483
exemplification, 59, 206–207

fallacies, 92–93
false analogies, 93
figurative language, 273–275
first (rough) drafts, 32–33, 35
foreign words and phrases, 519–520
formal diction, 268, 269
fractions, 497
freewriting, 3

fused sentences, 209–210, 213–214, 426
future perfect progressive tense, 365
future perfect tense, 364
future progressive tense, 364
future tense, 363

gender, agreement in, 394
gerunds, 109–110, 325, 326

hyphens, 526–528, 532

I, 340, 509–510
imperative mood, 366, 367
indefinite pronouns, 324, 343, 389, 391, 396, 465
independent (main) clauses, 108, 109, 191, 210, 256
  commas between, 132, 209–212, 214, 426, 435–436
  in complex sentences, 133–135
  in compound sentences, 131–133
  semicolons between, 132, 133, 211–212, 213–214, 436, 454–455
  sequence of tenses in, 365–366
indicative mood, 366–367
indirect discourse, 255
indirect objects, 107
induction, 91, 92
infinitive phrases, 110, 111, 229
infinitives, 109, 325–326, 339–340, 366
informal diction, 268
informative writing, 269, 288
"inkhorn" style, 314
interjections, 328–329, 427
intransitive verbs, 105–106
introductions, 31, 32, 34, 63–65, 88, 102
introductory elements, 437–438
intrusive modifiers, 228
italics, 518–520

jargon, 272
journals, 4, 15–16

language:
  figurative, 273–275
  offensive, 270–271
  professional, 431–432
  see also words
letters (alphabet), 467, 468, 496
letters (correspondence), 441, 493, 510
linking verbs, 106, 325, 393
literature, writing about, 288–289, 386

main clauses, *see* independent clauses
metaphors, 274, 275, 477
misplaced modifiers, 111, 227–228
mixed constructions, 256
modifiers:
  dangling, 111, 228–229
  misplaced, 111, 227–228
  restrictive vs. nonrestrictive, 438–439
  see also adjectives; adverbs
mood, 253–255, 366–367

narration, 58, 335–336
neologisms, 273
nonessential (parenthetical) elements, 438–440, 494, 495
nonstandard usage, 268, 269
noun clauses, 134–135
noun phrases, 108, 111
nouns, 106, 109, 134, 324, 466
  case of, 339, 465–466
  collective, 324, 391–392, 396
  general vs. specific, 516–517
  proper, 128, 324, 507–508
  used as adjectives, 414
number:
  agreement in, 389, 394
  shifts in, 253–254, 255
numbers and numerals, 441, 467, 468, 496, 528, 535, 542–544, 547–549

O, 509–510
object complements, 106, 411
objective case, 339–340
objects, 106, 107, 134–135, 256, 339–340, 341
offensive language, 270–271
outlines, 20–21, 29–30, 34

paired items, 239–240
paragraphs, 34, 51–66
  concluding, 65
  introductory, 63–65
  transitional, 65–66
parallel structure, 54–55, 150, 238–241
paraphrases, 255
parentheses, 426, 495–496
participial phrases, 111, 229
participles, 109–110, 325, 326, 361–362, 364–366, 390
parts of speech, 323–329
passive voice, 151, 368–369
past participles, 109–110, 326, 361–362, 364, 366, 390
past perfect progressive tense, 365
past perfect subjunctive mood, 367
past perfect tense, 364, 365–366
past progressive tense, 364
past subjunctive mood, 367
past tense, 361–362, 363, 365–366, 386
perfect tenses, 362–364, 365–366, 390
periodic sentences, 149–150
periods, 211, 213, 425–426, 428, 454, 482
person:
  agreement in, 389, 394, 408
  shifts in, 253–254, 255
personal pronouns, 324, 465, 466, 467
personal writing, 269, 288
personification, 274
persuasive writing, 102–103, 269, 288–289
phrases, 110–112, 128–129, 149, 325, 435, 439
  absolute, 111, 179, 192, 440
  foreign, 519–520
  introductory, 437–438
  misplaced, 227–228
  verbal, 110–111, 192, 227, 229, 394, 437–438
  see also prepositional phrases
plurals, 389, 466, 468
poetry, 482, 497, 498
point of view, 160–161, 336
possessive case, 339, 340, 465–466
possessive pronouns, 340–341, 410
post hoc, ergo propter hoc fallacy, 93
predicate adjectives, 106
predicate nouns (nominatives), 106
predicates, 105–107, 108, 109, 193, 435
  see also verbs
predication, faulty, 257
prepositional phrases, 107, 108, 110, 192, 327, 390, 437–438
  misplaced or dangling, 227–228, 229
  possession shown by, 465–466
prepositions, 241, 327–328
present participles, 109–110, 326, 361–362, 364–365, 366, 390
present perfect progressive tense, 365
present perfect tense, 364
present progressive tense, 364
present subjunctive mood, 367
present tense, 363, 366, 386, 389–390
process analysis, 59–60, 188–189
professional language, 431–432
progressive tenses, 362–363, 364–365, 390
pronoun antecedents, 324
  agreement with, 394–396
  clarity of references to, 342–343
pronouns, 54, 134, 164, 324–325, 410
  agreement of verbs and, 389–390
  case of, 339–341

pronouns (cont.)
  indefinite, 324, 343, 389, 396, 465
  personal, 324, 465, 466, 467
  relative, 133, 134, 191, 212, 214, 241, 324, 393–394
pronunciation, 316, 322
proper adjectives, 326, 507, 508
proper nouns, 128, 324, 507–508
prose passages, 481
punctuation and mechanics:
  abbreviations, 534–536, 540
  apostrophes, 464–468, 476
  brackets, 496
  capitalization, 506–510
  colons, 493–494
  commas, 434–442
  dashes, 494–495
  ellipsis marks, 497–498
  exclamation points, 427–428
  hyphens, 526–528, 532
  italics, 518–520
  numbers vs. numerals, 542–544, 547–549
  parentheses, 495–496
  periods, 425–426
  question marks, 426–427
  quotation marks, 478–483
  semicolons, 453–456
  slashes, 497
purpose of writing, 1, 2, 102, 269

question marks, 426, 428, 483, 495, 496
questions, 107, 425, 426, 483
quotation marks, 426, 478–483
  for dialogue, long prose passages, and poetry, 480–482
  for direct quotations, 478–479
  other punctuation with, 482–483
  for titles, 479
  for words used in special sense, 479
quotations, 255, 489–490
  altering, 504–505
  comments within, 496
  omissions in, 497–498
  punctuation of, 440–441, 478–479, 493

red herring fallacy, 93
relative pronouns, 133, 134, 191, 212, 214, 241, 324, 393–394
repetition, 55–56, 150, 164, 441
reporting, 462
revision, 33–38, 321–322
rough (first) drafts, 32–33, 35

salutations, 441, 493, 510
semicolons, 239–240, 453–456, 483
  between clauses, 132, 133, 211–212, 213–214, 436, 454–455
  in series, 455
sentence fragments, 190–193
sentences, 34
  basic elements of, 105
  basic patterns of, 105–107
  capitalization of first word in, 507
  complex, 133–135
  compound, 131–133, 211
  conciseness of, 162–165
  cumulative, 149
  fused, 209–210, 213–214, 426
  numbers at beginning of, 543
  periodic, 149–150
  periods at ends of, 425
  simple, building, 109–112
  structure of, 149–150
series, 239, 436–437, 455
shifts, 253–256
showing vs. telling, 128–129, 358
similes, 274, 477

simple tenses, 362–363
slang, 268, 269
slashes, 497
spelling, 315–316, 321–322
style, 34
subject complements, 106, 339, 393, 410, 411
subjective case, 339, 340
subjects, 105–107, 108, 109, 134–135, 179, 191, 339–340, 341, 435
  agreement of verbs and, 389–394
subjunctive mood, 366, 367
subordinating conjunctions, 133, 134, 191, 212, 214, 328
subordination, 133, 164, 214
summaries, 175–176, 494
superlative degree, 412, 413
syllogisms, 91–92
symbols, 432, 468, 536

tag phrases, 482, 483
technical terms, 272, 431–432, 535
technical writing, 536, 547–549
temperatures, 535
tenses, 361, 362–366, 386, 389–390
  sequence of, 365–366
  shifts in, 253–254
theses, 18–19, 29–30, 32, 63, 87, 88, 90, 92
thesis-and-support pattern, 31–32, 224–225
titles (of persons), 441, 507, 509, 535
titles (of works), 392, 479, 509, 519, 523–524
tone, 2, 34, 91
topics, choosing, 2–3, 90
topic sentences, 31–32, 52, 53, 57, 58
topic trees, 18
transitional expressions, 56, 132, 149, 179, 422
  commas with, 438, 440
transitional paragraphs, 65–66
transitive verbs, 106, 107
tu quoque fallacy, 93

unfinished statements, 498
unity, 52–53, 87
utility words, 163, 272

variety, in sentence composition, 177–179
verbal phrases, 110–111, 192, 227, 229, 394, 437–438
verbals, 109–110, 325–326, 394, 437–438
verb phrases, 108, 325
verbs, 128, 191, 325–326, 360–369, 435
  agreement of subjects and, 389–394
  intransitive, 105–106
  linking, 106, 325, 393
  mood of, 253–255, 366–367
  principal parts of, 361–362
  tense of, 253–254, 361, 362–366, 386, 389–390
  transitive, 106, 107
  voice of, 150–151, 253–254, 368–369
vocabulary building, 304–306, 314
voice, 150–151, 253–254, 368–369

who, 341
whom, 341
word order, 148–149, 150–151, 179, 392–393
words, 34
  accuracy of, 270–272
  breaking at end of line, 527–528
  choosing, 266–275
  compound, 528, 532
  discussed as words, 468
  foreign, 519–520
  left-out, 441
  nonessential, eliminating, 163–164
  used in special sense, 479
  utility, 163, 272
  vocabulary building and, 304–306, 314
  see also language; spelling; diction
working plans, 19–20